The Nauvoo Legion in Illinois

FIGURE 1. *Lieutenant General Joseph Smith*, ca. 1842.
By Sutcliffe Maudsley (1809–81). Egg tempera and ink
on paper, 12 in. × 7 in. *Courtesy of Church History Museum,
The Church of Jesus Christ of Latter-day Saints, Salt Lake City, Utah.*

The Nauvoo Legion in Illinois

FIGURE 1. *Lieutenant General Joseph Smith*, ca. 1842.
By Sutcliffe Maudsley (1809–81). Egg tempera and ink
on paper, 12 in. × 7 in. *Courtesy of Church History Museum,
The Church of Jesus Christ of Latter-day Saints, Salt Lake City, Utah.*

The Nauvoo Legion in Illinois

A History of the Mormon Militia, 1841–1846

By

Richard E. Bennett,
Susan Easton Black, and
Donald Q. Cannon

THE ARTHUR H. CLARK COMPANY
An imprint of the University of Oklahoma Press
Norman, Oklahoma
2010

Library of Congress Cataloging-in-Publication Data

Bennett, Richard Edmond, 1946–

The Nauvoo Legion in Illinois : a history of the Mormon militia, 1841–1846 / by Richard E. Bennett, Susan Easton Black, and Donald Q. Cannon.

p. cm.

Includes bibliographical references and index.

ISBN 978-0-87062-382-0 (hardcover : alk. paper) 1. Illinois. Militia. Nauvoo Legion—History. 2. Illinois—Militia—History—19th century. 3. Mormons—Illinois—History—19th century. 4. Nauvoo (Ill.)—History—19th century. 5. Smith, Joseph, 1805–1844—Military leadership. I. Black, Susan Easton. II. Cannon, Donald Q., 1936– III. Title.

UA178.N38B46 2010

355.3'70977343—dc22

2009020965

The paper in this book meets the guidelines for permanence and durability of the Committee on Production Guidelines for Book Longevity of the Council on Library Resources, Inc. ∞

1 2 3 4 5 6 7 8 9 10

To the citizen soldiers of
the Nauvoo Legion

Contents

Illustrations

Tables

Acknowledgments

The Nauvoo Legion in Illinois would not have been possible without the able assistance of many individuals. Richard E. Turley, Jr., Assistant Church Historian and Recorder of The Church of Jesus Christ of Latter-day Saints, and the capable staff of the LDS Church History Department, including Ronald Barney, Ronald Esplin, Brent Reber, and the late Steven Sorenson have been helpful in making available source documents. Reviewers of the manuscript—Glen M. Leonard, Marvin Hill, Sherman Fleek, Ronald Barney, Alexander Baugh, and Roger Launius—have given invaluable suggestions along the way.

To Tom Swartz and his fine staff at the Illinois Preservation Society, the John Whitmer Historical Society, and the Mormon History Association, we express gratitude for opportunities to present our findings at their annual meetings. To the Religious Studies Center, the Department of Church History and Doctrine, and donors to Religious Education, we are indebted for funding, assistance, and encouragement. To document collectors, most notably Brent Ashworth, we are indebted for their sharing of relevant documents. To the staff members at the Church History Library of The Church of Jesus Christ of Latter-day Saints (hereinafter referred to as the Church History Library) and the Church History Museum of The Church of Jesus Christ of Latter-day Saints (hereinafter referred to as the Church History Museum); the L. Tom Perry Special Collection of the Harold B. Lee Library at Brigham Young University; the National Archives and Records Services of the United States; the Lands and Records Office of Nauvoo Restoration, Inc.; Utah State University; the University of Utah; Southern Utah University; Western Illinois University; Utah State Historical Society; and the Huntington Library, we express gratitude. Christina Smith and Tiffany Taylor, promising history majors at Brigham Young University, have provided valuable assistance with source checking. Emily Dart has been most helpful in organizing the charts and tables. Research assistants Zachary Largey, David Czech, Jeremy Leatham, and Nick Valetta have strengthened the text with library research. Heather Seferovich provided grammatical and editing changes where needed.

Last, but certainly not least, we wish to thank our publishers for their willingness to produce the volume. To all of those who have helped in any way, we express our sincere gratitude.

Introduction

In light of several recent studies on Nauvoo and the life of Joseph Smith, the Mormon prophet, it is timely and appropriate to present a new study on what is clearly one of the most colorful, legendary, and debatable chapters in the old city's history—the story of the Nauvoo Legion. Long since passed out of view, this once vibrant city militia garnered the support of thousands of Mormons as well as the fear and criticism of those intent on driving the Mormons out of Illinois.

While admirers regard it with a sense of proud nostalgia, the Nauvoo Legion has also garnered its fair share of critics and detractors. Some insist on viewing the Legion as a symbol of violence, a raw extension of Mormon political power, and of Joseph Smith's kingdom building—a lasting expression of Mormon militarism in a church increasingly at variance with the nation and its emerging democratic culture. Others see the Legion entirely differently—as a needed mode of defense and a barrier against a repeat of the Missouri persecutions that ended in the suffering and death of so many. Somewhere between an "Army of Israel" and a lesson learned from Missouri, between an extension of the Kingdom of God on one side and a legitimate arm of the state of Illinois on the other, the story of the Nauvoo Legion is indeed a complex affair and defies simple categorization and explanation. Some of those who served in its ranks were of the hothead variety, bent on seeing it as a repeat of the Mormon Danites. Others believed they were fulfilling the expectations of the law. Clearly perceptions from within and without Nauvoo were fluid and often times contradictory. The need to make sense of these persistent and contrasting points of view has existed since the demise of the Legion in Illinois.

We are persuaded that the Nauvoo Legion functioned fundamentally within the law, and that it was designed to defend the interests of the "City of the Saints," not to take an offensive posture against its enemies. It was in many ways a unique militia bound by religious convictions as well as a sense of national duty of those men who served in it. It was called into action by Lieutenant General Joseph Smith, functioning in his role as mayor of the city, to protect and safeguard himself and the citizens of Nauvoo. There can be little doubt that as tensions and emotions increased in 1843 and 1844, the actions of the Legion with respect to defending Smith, his church and the city of Nauvoo were viewed differently by friend and foe alike. These delicate and debatable issues are explored in this book.

In its inception, however, the Legion was not a worrisome imposition upon the state; rather, it was born out of the invitation of Illinois to shore up a state militia then in great disrepair. The Legion was essentially an American construct in design, appearance, and function. Because of this construct, we place the colorful story of the Legion within the broader American historical context and situate it squarely within the military history of the state of Illinois. We show how Smith came to be its leader and his exercise of that role. While Smith exerted tremendous influence over the men of the Legion, most of whom regarded him as a prophet of God, the Legion functioned fundamentally not at his sole command but at the behest of its commander in chief, the governor of the state of Illinois. The role of John C. Bennett, first in the chartering of the Legion, later in promoting its use against Mormon enemies, and finally in portraying it as a symbol of anti-American warfare is also examined. With these objectives accomplished, we present the Legion in light of the peculiar religious, social, and political debates that later came to characterize its history.

The focus of this study is the Nauvoo Legion as a regularly constituted arm of the Illinois State Militia; in other words, from its chartering in 1841 until its repeal by the state legislature in 1845. We show the daily operations, appearances, and general conduct of the Legion by mustering this force into action one last time by examining its parades, sham battles, uniforms, and military operations. Unique to this history will be a careful examination of the minutes and activities of the Legion, its courts-martial and what impact they had on the culture and character of the militia, and a presentation and analysis of approximately one thousand citizen soldiers, unknown before, who served in the Legion. We pay careful attention to the fears and changing perceptions of non-Mormons in outlying areas. These latter chapters provide an exciting new retelling of the many events and colorful personalities in the run-up to the killing of the Smith brothers in June 1844. After 1845, the members of the Nauvoo Legion acted under the direction of Mormon church leadership until reformulated under a civil statute authorized by the Provisional State of Deseret in 1849 and later as a militia in the Utah Territory in 1852. This later chapter of the Legion, although well deserving of a history of its own, is beyond the scope of the present work.

One of the motivations for this study was the recent discovery of unpublished, archival records of several hundred Nauvoo Legion privates found in the Newel K. Whitney Papers housed in the L. Tom Perry Special Collections, Harold B. Lee Library at Brigham Young University. Likewise, we gained access to militia records of the state of Illinois in the Illinois State Archives in Springfield, Illinois, which, if available before, were not utilized effectively by or well enough incorporated into previous studies. These long sought after materials allow us to portray a more complete, and certainly more accurate, description of the famed Mormon militia of Nauvoo. In addition, new works on the history of the American military, both at the state and federal levels, have enabled us to understand the place of the Nauvoo Legion within the broader panorama of American history.

The history of the Nauvoo Legion should have been written a long time ago. Willard Richards—apostle, scribe, and unofficial historian of early Mormonism—directed Hosea Stout as early as 1843 to compile the official records of the Legion; he intended to include Stout's study in the official history of The Church of Jesus Christ of Latter-day Saints. Persecution, oppression, and a forced exodus of the Mormons from Illinois to the Rocky Mountains prevented this from coming to fruition.

Although a complete history of the Legion has not been published, a few scholars have carefully studied it and have created significant preliminary works. The first was Hamilton Gardner's short but informative 1961 article "The Nauvoo Legion." John A. Sweeney's commendable 1974 master's thesis, "A History of the Nauvoo Legion in Illinois," brought together more statistics, accounts, and activities of the Legion than were ever before seen. James L. Kimball, Jr., published the very helpful article "A Wall to Defend Zion: The Nauvoo Charter" in 1975. For a complete listing of other works pertaining to the Legion and which were valuable to this work, see the bibliography and, particularly, the bibliographic essay.

A SINGLE WORK BY THREE AUTHORS RARELY SPEAKS WITH one voice. Our attempt is not to sing solo, but in three-part harmony. Richard E. Bennett has worked on placing the Legion within the broader context of state and national military history, reviewed its difficult Missouri antecedents, and examined the troubling events leading to Carthage as seen through the history of the Legion. Susan Easton Black, whose idea it was to write a book on the Legion, has concentrated her interests on the many new names of those who served in the Legion, finding and studying the original minutes and other extant records, and chronicling the order of events as spelled out in the courts-martial of the Legion. Donald Q. Cannon, having served in the United States military earlier in his career, has focused on Smith's role as lieutenant general and on what prepared him for such a leadership position, on the criticisms of the Legion, and the events that transpired in the history of the Legion after Smith's murder.

Although we admit to variety in our interpretations of Smith and the Nauvoo Legion, we do not see discord. We believe that our differences enrich this work without creating disharmony or dissonance, and have sought to complement each other's strengths and interests. We admit to our biases as Latter-day Saint scholars at Brigham Young University; however, we believe in independent thought and freedom of inquiry. We alone are responsible for the contents and interpretations which follow. We trust that our readers, thousands of whom are descendants of those who served within the Nauvoo Legion ranks, will find the story we present a truthful effort to understand the Nauvoo Legion in Illinois.

The Nauvoo Legion in Illinois

I

The Nauvoo Legion in Its American Context

Of late years the military spirit has seemed to pass away.
D. P. WILBANKS, SEPTEMBER 29, 1842

ARTICLE I OF THE CONSTITUTION OF THE UNITED STATES states,

> Congress shall have Power . . . [t]o declare War . . . [t]o raise and support armies, but no appropriation of money to that use shall be for a longer term than two years; [t]o provide and maintain a Navy; . . . [t]o provide for calling forth the Militia to execute the Laws of the Union, suppress insurrections and repel invasions; [t]o provide for organizing, arming, and disciplining, the Militia, and for governing such part of them as may be employed in the service of the United States, the officers, and the authority of training the Militia according to the discipline prescribed by Congress.[1]

This chapter reviews the origins, rise, and key developments in American military history between the earliest years of colonial America and the founding of the Nauvoo Legion in 1841. As unique as the Legion was in the early history of Illinois and of the Church of Jesus Christ of Latter-day Saints, it must be understood within

[1] Constitution of the United States, Article I, Section 8.

the broader context of American military history. In many ways the Legion, at least in origin and design, was one of the most American constructs in Nauvoo. Had the Latter-day Saints not been mustered into service in their own city militia, it is likely that they would have served, as many of them once did, in other regiments or battalions of the Illinois State Militia. Otherwise, they would have faced severe fines and other penalties.

Militias and the associated concept of the citizen soldier had long predated the minutemen of Lexington and Concord. Defined as "one whose interest in, and dedication to, military affairs is secondary to the major business of his life," the citizen soldier, even of ancient Rome, was a farmer, a butcher or a fisherman by profession and a soldier only by avocation.[2] The Great Fyrd of Henry II's Anglo-Saxon England, the so-called untrained masses, was a recognition of the need and obligation of everyone in the community to bear arms for common defense.[3] William the Conqueror and the Norman kings tamed the Anglo-Saxon militia only to train it "to be ready for the King's call to service."[4] The Statute of Winchester (1285) and the Instructions for General Muster (1572) developed the militia further, yet it remained primarily a system based on mandatory male service (the Assize of Arms). As military historian Russell F. Weigley put it, "The popular militia became conspicuous in England's preparations for defense against the Spanish during the Elizabethan wars."[5]

The British fear of a standing army was as much a borrowed concept as it was a native suspicion. After Oliver Cromwell's rule in the 1650s, when England got a "real taste of military dictatorship" thanks to a standing army of between forty and seventy thousand soldiers, Parliament deeply worried about the power of an established military.[6] After Cromwell died, Charles II (r. 1660–85) rose to power, propped up with the help of a small army from Louis XIV of France. In 1689 William, Duke of Orange, overthrew James II, Charles's brother, and put Parliament and the Protestants back in control. Parliament allowed William III to retain an army to ward off Louis

---

[2] Whisker, "Citizen Soldier under Federal and State Law," 950.

[3] Moncure, "Who Is the Militia?" 3.

[4] Weigley, *History of the United States Army*, 3. See also Ansell, Courts-martial," 471–80.

[5] Weigley, *History of the United States Army*, 3. These early English militia became known as trained-bands or train bands, the fundamental militia unit that later evolved into the company.

[6] Ropp, *War in the Modern World*, 79.

XIV, but did so only as long as necessary. The new English Bill of Rights stipulated that "the raising or keeping of a standing army within the Kingdom in time of peace, unless it be with the consent of Parliament, is against law." In this and other provisions restricting the army, Parliament set precedents for what later became the military clauses of the Constitution of the United States.[7]

In the aftermath of William and Mary's Glorious Revolution of 1688, the new English Bill of Rights ruled against a standing army in favor of local militias—variously defined as "a body of soldiers for home use"; "the whole body of freemen"; or, as Adam Smith phrased it, "all the citizens of military age, or a certain number of them, to join in some measure the trade of a soldier to whatever other trade or profession they may happen to carry on."[8] Common to all these early definitions was the sense that the local militia, unlike the standing army, was generally to be used for defense—the last line of homeland protection.

Even during the long conflicts of the late eighteenth century and up to the Napoleonic Wars of the early nineteenth century, the British Parliament "looked on standing armies as necessary evils and the middle classes showed little interest in military life."[9] Although Wellington's 1815 victory at Waterloo did much to increase the reputation of Britain's land forces, well into the nineteenth century and the Crimean War (1854–56) the British army grew in relatively small increments, never keeping pace with the overall growth in population. To the British, the first line of defense—and of empire—was the Royal Navy, which was ever regarded with far more pride and approbation and much less suspicion than was the army.

"The Power of Defense in the Body of the People"

The British concept of military service perpetuated into the colonial era of American history;[10] the Puritans "considered the defense of his inheritance, by force of arms if necessary, as nothing less than a

[7] See Ropp, *War in the Modern World,* 79. Other restrictions included the prohibition of soldiers at voting places, courts, and parliament. Also, there was no provision for a standing commander in chief in times of peace; therefore, there was no central control over the military.

[8] Smith, *Wealth of Nations,* as quoted in Whisker, "Citizen Soldier under Federal and State Law," 950.

[9] Ropp, *War in the Modern World,* 145.

[10] Wright, *The Continental Army,* 6.

religious duty."[11] Not only did the American colonies accept the necessity of having a local militia, they likewise inherited the phobia of a standing army. Ever too poor to fund such an army, the earliest colonist looked to local militias for defense. As early as 1623 the Virginia settlement imposed a statute requiring all citizens to bear arms.[12] Northern colonies later followed suit. In Plymouth, initial rules governing militias called for six drills per year (on public grounds), roll call and prayer, presentation of arms, target practice, sham battles, close order drills, reviews, and inspection—all followed by the customary socializing and refreshments.

Over time, a differentiation between the so-called common militia and the volunteer militia developed, much like what had happened earlier in England. The latter formed the active military force for the masses who, although they were part of the common militia, were generally disinclined and often ill prepared for actual conflict. Such elite volunteer companies later formed the Minutemen of 1775 and adumbrated the independent volunteer companies of the mid-nineteenth century.[13] Never really effective in fighting Native Americans, the common colonial militias were essentially defense oriented and "not a reliable instrument of offensive war distant from their own firesides."[14] And, as James Martin and Mark Lender have said, "The function of the militiaman was to protect hearth and home, not to engage in regular warfare."[15] Yet even in these earliest expressions of militia- and defense-mindedness, there was an equally strong fear and suspicion of a permanent military presence or standing army. As early as the 1630s, the Puritan leader of Massachusetts, John Winthrop, said, "How dangerous it might be to erect a standing authority of military men, which might easily in time overthrow the civil power."[16] Certainly American opposition to a British standing army was a major contributing cause of the Revolutionary War.

American revolutionary leader Simeon Howard described the mili-

---

[11] Osgood, *American Colonies,* 1:497.

[12] Weigley, *History of the United States Army,* 5. "In all the colonies, as in England, the militia system was based on the principle of the assize of arms. This implied the general obligation of all adult male inhabitants to possess arms, and with certain exceptions, to cooperate in the work of defense." Osgood, *American Colonies,* 1:499.

[13] Weigley, *History of the United States Army,* 8.

[14] Weigley, *History of the United States Army,* 12.

[15] Martin and Lender, *A Respectable Army,* 18.

[16] Osgood, *American Colonies,* 1:497.

tia as "the power of defense in the body of the people."[17] The law required every able-bodied male citizen aged nineteen to sixty-five to obtain arms at his own expense, maintain and present them on militia training days, and learn military discipline. Indeed, the militia system existed "only to discipline and train the men, not to produce combat units."[18] Lacking little centralized command, the militia was a strictly local creature. Often each city, town, and district had its own organization and hierarchy; their local leadership and aristocracy assumed officer roles. Even in these early years, militia musters, parades, and marches were highly social gatherings, characterized more by drinking and "tumultuous behavior" than rigid discipline and artful decorum.[19] And although with revolution imminent, the Continental Congress of 1775 passed a resolution urging all men aged sixteen to fifty to enlist in the Continental Army, the "mainstay of the American revolutionary army remained the [local] militia."[20]

Although few colonists enlisted in the army, those of legal age were obligated to serve in the local colonial militias, although the periods of service were very short and many found ways of evading them. Even though citizen soldiering had declined in the American colonies before the outbreak of the Revolutionary War, it "still represented a living tradition."[21] Washington's immediate objective, as James Martin and Mark Lender have argued, "became that of turning the citizen soldier into a well-disciplined fighter—a functioning cog in the machinery of war rather than the strutting individualist of militia muster days."[22]

In the ensuing Revolutionary War, the American colonists defeated the British not so much because of their knowledge of local topography or superior organization but because of a passionate citizenry, excellent leadership, rejuvenated militias, the determined resolve of the Continental Army established on June 14, 1775, and the

[17] Howard, "A Sermon Preached to the Ancient and Honorable Artillery Company in Boston," 199, as quoted in Whisker, "Citizen Soldier under Federal and State Law," 951.

[18] Whisker, "Citizen Soldier under Federal and State Law," 955.

[19] Moncure, "Who Is the Militia?" 5.

[20] Whisker, "Citizen Soldier under Federal and State Law," 957. Although called an army, it is more correct to refer to it as the Continental Line. The army consisted of militia and volunteers, but the core was the fifteen to twenty thousand–man Continental Line that evolved into the Regular Army.

[21] Millis, *Arms and Men,* 23.

[22] Martin and Lender, *A Respectable Army,* 45.

experienced military leadership of George Washington who was given the rank of general and commander in chief. With too little time to form a large and truly national professional army, Washington relied initially on a standing provincial, or New England, army—24,000 troops that had been raised earlier by Massachusetts, Rhode Island, New Hampshire, and Connecticut—a forerunner of the Continental Army. Over time thousands more flocked to Washington's banner, many of whom were citizen soldiers or amateurs, more enthusiastic than well trained, whereas many of those in colonial militias were unprepared to re-enlist year after year. While scholars have long debated whether regulars or militia were more essential to winning the war, Washington knew well he could not do without the tenacity of citizen soldiers, even if they were less prepared for battle. The key was to employ militia "on the periphery while developing a core of trustworthy regulars, combining the best of both the amateur and regular traditions."

Although the Americans did not always fare well on open battlegrounds against the British regulars, Washington succeeded largely because of his dogged perseverance, his mastery of strategic retreat, brilliant use of sortie and surprise, superior land transport, and excellent command of artillery.[23] Washington also concentrated on maneuver, avoiding major European-style field battles except when the odds were highly favorable (for example, Yorktown). As Walter Millis has argued, "It was the militia which presented the greatest single impediment to Britain's only practicable weapon, that of counter-revolution."[24]

"A Well Regulated Militia, Being Necessary to the Security of a Free State"

With freedom won and United States independence obtained, Congress promptly reduced the size of the Regular Army, disbanding "all but eighty men and a few officers of the Continental Army."[25] After

[23] See Weigley, *History of the United States Army,* chapter 4. See also Wright, *The Continental Army,* 183. One of Washington's most daring acts was his crossing of the Delaware at night, on Christmas Day, 1776, when he captured over nine hundred Hessian troops in Trenton, New Jersey. See Chadwick, *The First American Army,* 136–51.

[24] Millis, *Arms and Men,* 34.

[25] Millett and Maslowski, *For the Common Defense,* 86.

all, the fear of a large standing army had been one of the very reasons the country had gone to war. However, one of the most vexing issues now facing the new republic was the matter of ultimate authority. Did the authority reside in the federal government or within the constituent states? This issue was a long and divisive one. In few other aspects was this more hotly debated than the role and place of the military, specifically regarding a standing army. The eventual Constitution of the United States represented a delicate compromise between those Federalists, like Alexander Hamilton, who believed a strong, standing federal army was indispensable to the safety and security of the expanding nation—especially in light of contemporary French military successes in Europe—and the anti-Federalists, or Republicans, like George Mason, Patrick Henry, and Thomas Jefferson, who feared such a force and wanted real power to remain with the states and local militias as reflected in the clause that no appropriation for an army "shall be for longer than two years." Before the states would ratify the Constitution, Patrick Henry and other states' rights advocates demanded and obtained an amendment that eventually read: "A well regulated Militia, being necessary to the security of a free State, the right of the people to keep and bear Arms, shall not be infringed."[26] This tension, if not distrust and veiled hostility, between those favoring a strong federal government and advocates of the pre-eminence of the states lasted for at least a century and eventually led to the U.S. Civil War.

Yet the country was expanding ever westward and the inevitable wars with American Indians and other European powers in the West made the necessity of an army a continued source of discussion and debate. A string of embarrassing military defeats at the hands of Indians in the Northwest Territory revealed the woeful training and panicky nature of ill-prepared militia and an insufficiently manned standing army. As President George Washington put it, "The mili-

[26] Second Amendment. As Elbridge Gerry said, "Standing armies in time of peace, are inconsistent with the principles of republican governments, dangerous to the liberties of a free people, and generally converted into destructive energies for establishing despotism" (as quoted in Prucha, *Sword of the Republic,* 5). Article I, Section 8 of the Constitution gave Congress the right to appoint "officers, and the authority of training the militia according to the discipline prescribed by Congress." Constitution of the United States, Article I, Sections 15 and 17. Article II of the Bill of Rights gave additional approval for organizing militias.

tia . . . will never answer [our] expectations, no dependence is to be placed upon them; they are obstinate and perverse."[27]

The first real compromise on this issue came with the Militia Act of 1792. President Washington favored a larger army; Congress initially balked but finally authorized five thousand federal troops, enough, or so it was thought, to defeat the Indians on the frontier. Serving as "more of a gesture than a directive," the Militia Act did preserve and legalize under the Constitution universal military obligation, every male aged eighteen to forty-five having to take up arms as militiamen.[28] The result was an army that, at least on paper, was as great as Napoléon's Grande Armée: 1,033 infantry regiments and 647,827 soldiers, though in reality "a scratch lot of boys, invalids, and substitutes."[29] Their organization and training were left "almost entirely" to the state governments.[30] The Militia Act was also so strewn with divisions of responsibilities between Washington, D.C., and the states that its administration was difficult. There were no federal standards of training or standardization of arms. The appointment of officers and discipline was left entirely to the individual states. Although each state was to have an adjutant general, there were no provisions to enforce this or any other provision within the act.[31] Its inconsistencies and faults notwithstanding, the Militia Act of 1792 enshrined the principle of universal military obligation and set the tone for the American military for the next century.

The new five-thousand-man army was soon reconstituted in 1792 into the grandiloquent-sounding Legion of the United States to facilitate campaigning in the wilderness. Led by a major general or legionary general, it was subdivided into four sub-legions, each commanded by a brigadier general. The plan was to enhance tactical flexibility by creating miniature armies or combined army units complete

---

[27] Weigley, *History of the United States Army,* 16. Washington earlier said, "To place any dependence upon Militia, is, assuredly, resting upon a broken staff. Men just dragged from the tender scenes of domestic life, unaccustomed to the den of arms, totally unacquainted with every kind of military skill when opposed by troops regularly trained . . . makes them timid and ready to fly from their own shadow." Millis, *American Military Thought,* 12.

[28] Palmer and Strykes, *Early American Wars,* 58.

[29] Millis, *Arms and Men,* 52.

[30] Stagg, *Mr. Madison's War,* 124.

[31] Wiener, "The Militia Clause of the Constitution," 187. Wiener argues that the act had "the heart cut out of it" when the clause calling for "a select contingent of young men, uniformly trained" was removed.

with artillery, cavalry, and infantry.[32] Such a structure, no doubt, played a positive role in Major General Anthony Wayne's defeat of the Indians and the British at the Battle of Fallen Timbers in 1794.[33]

In the years that witnessed the French Revolution and the ensuing rise of Napoleon, Congress was more prone to support funding for a small navy and for coastal fortifications than it was a large standing army, rejecting President John Adams's call for a ten-thousand-man provisional army in case of European invasion. Thomas Jefferson, elected president in 1800 on an anti-Federalist ticket, pursued a passive foreign policy and reduced the size of the army even further. Ironically, he established the country's first professional military academy in 1802 at West Point, New York, albeit to train and graduate army engineers. With one stroke of a pen, Jefferson obtained in 1803 from Napoleon through the Louisiana Purchase more land than he could have ever obtained through military power. This transaction more than doubled the land size of the United States, stretching its boundaries from the Mississippi River to the Rocky Mountains. Ironically, rather than shunning the army, Jefferson immediately used such well-trained army officers as Captain Meriwether Lewis and Lieutenant William Clark to make firm America's claim to the West. "There is no clearer indication of the enterprise of army officers," wrote Theodore Crackel, "than the triumphant passage of these two captains and their company throughout the tribes of the Trans-Mississippi west."[34]

---

[32] Each sub-legion consisted of dragoons (80), artillery (60), four companies of rifles (380), and eight companies of infantry (760) with a legionary general or major general in overall command. These sub-legions never fought as independent units.

[33] "The term 'legion' had come into renewed military use during the 18th century, especially in Eastern Europe, to denote small mixed bodies of cavalry and infantry. As such it appeared in the American Revolution on both sides, as in Tarleton's Legion or Pulaski's Legion. . . . A more sentimental purpose of the legionary organization resided in the young American Republic's delight in drawing parallels between itself and the ancient Roman Republic." Weigley, *History of the United States Army,* 92.

Secretary of War John Knox had proposed the legion concept, borrowed from the French army, as early as 1792. For more, see *American State Papers,* 1:40–41. See also Knopf, *Anthony Wayne,* 32; and Pratt, "Anthony Wayne, The Last of the Romans." One reason for the adoption of the term "legion" was its romantic sounding appeal, in contrast to the more pedantic title Regular Army. Prucha, *Sword of the Republic,* 321.

[34] Some recent scholars disagree, arguing that military training was the first priority and that "formal engineering training was neither the sole nor the primary goal" of West Point, at least not until after 1817. See Crackel, *Jefferson's Army,* 60.

Later army expeditions included those led by William Dunbar, Thomas Freeman, and Zebulon Pike—who in 1806 explored the vast regions of the headwaters of the Red River in and near Santa Fe; all of these were designed to assert American ownership of these far-flung areas. Nonetheless, between 1804 and 1812, the army "lacked integrations, responsibility, unity, and energy, and was utterly inadequate for even the most modest military operations."[35]

"An Interesting Cabinet of Antiquities"

More than any other conflict in the history of the young republic, the War of 1812 fought between the United States and Great Britain (and its Native American allies)—a conflict primarily waged over control of the Northwest Territory and British maritime policies—manifested the fundamental flaw of the Militia Act and the inadequacies of state militias to defend the national interest. In 1812, "the nation faced a new war with a central government of more ample powers than in the Revolution, but with little more existing military strength or military administrative machinery than in 1775."[36]

The victories of John Paul Jones and Andrew Jackson notwithstanding, 527,000 United States militiamen could not overpower a British army of 5,000.[37] The United States, at best, fought to a draw, a bloody stalemate, and gained "far less" than it had hoped to accomplish.[38] Had it not been for its ongoing war against Napoleon, Britain may well have inflicted far more damage than it did at Detroit, Queenstown Heights, and the burning of Washington, D.C. State militias refused to take the offensive and cross international, let alone state, borders when victory seemed most assured. Many men who completed their three-month term of service simply quit the battlefield rather than pursue the British Redcoats to victory.[39]

The War of 1812 put in stark relief the problem of "bankrupt strategic direction and doctrine," an arrogant sense of American imperviousness. More than anything else, it highlighted the "basic fallacy" of the Militia Act: that it was "unselective," and "imposed a duty on everyone, with the result that [it] was discharged by no one.

---

[35] Prucha, *Sword of the Republic*, 81.
[36] White, *Jeffersonians*, 82.
[37] Weigley, *History of the United States Army*, 115; Wiener, "The Militia Clause of the Constitution," 187–88.
[38] Stagg, *Mr. Madison's War*, 501.
[39] Palmer and Strykes, *Early American Wars*, 59–73.

. . . [T]hey were, in Maitland's phrase, no more than 'an interesting cabinet of antiquities.'"[40] As West Point scholars Dave Richard Palmer and James W. Stryker have argued, "Education in the principles of strategy was lacking still; and the problem of how to raise an Army as opposed to improvising one remained unresolved" and almost cost the new nation a great deal of territory.[41] The near calamity of the war, largely forgotten in the American euphoria over the Battle of New Orleans, could have triggered something of a sea change in thought—from blind reliance on a system of uncoordinated, underfunded, and often untrained state militias to a better-trained, better-equipped, and better-funded Regular Army. Although there were some changes, including the appointment of a central army staff (consisting of an adjutant general, inspector general, quartermaster general, and commanding officers over various military districts), the change was in reality only a rising tide, which ebbed with the memory of the war.[42]

In 1817 President James Monroe appointed the young and aspiring John C. Calhoun as his secretary of war, a post he would hold for eight years. Calhoun's tenure "marked a transition from the semi-amateur army of the pre–War of 1812 era with its genuine reliance on the militia, to a professionalization of the Army, with its verbal reliance on the militias."[43] Anxious to affirm the nation's claim to the West, he pushed for a string of forts to be built up and down the Missouri and Mississippi Rivers.

Despite Calhoun's best efforts to increase and modernize what he called an "expansible" army, Congress, confident in the country's abilities to put down Indian threats, repel naval invasions, and anticipating an Era of Good Feelings (1817–25) now that the Napoleonic Wars were at an end, cut the army's budget by 40 percent.[44] Besides, the popular perception was that serving in the army was an "evasion,"

---

[40] Wiener, "The Militia Clause of the Constitution," 187.

[41] Palmer and Strykes, *Early American Wars,* 73.

[42] Immediately after the signing of the Treaty of Ghent, which ended the War of 1812, Congress authorized $200,000 a year for arms and equipment for the army; $200,000 for the Navy, and $830,000 for coastal fortifications in case of a European invasion. See Palmer and Strykes, *Early American Wars,* 82.

[43] See Smith, *Military Affairs,* 30, as quoted in Palmer and Strykes, *Early American Wars,* 87.

[44] Millis, *Arms and Men,* 81. Despite such setbacks, Calhoun succeeded in maintaining and funding a bigger and better army than many of his congressional opponents desired.

a "confession of failure," a place where "men with something to hide" would go—that is, the place of last resort.[45] The country need only work from a defensive posture, dependent primarily on the militia. Arms must remain with the people, not in a standing army. "The national military strategy after 1821" as Palmer and Strykes recently argued, "was a defensive concept designed to protect against a maritime threat from Europe." Theoretically, the militia would be "a large manpower pool responsible for the initial defense and for providing partially trained recruits for the war-time Army. The Regular Army, spread thin in peace-time and thus not dangerous to liberty, would police the frontier; provide a skeleton garrison for a system of forts; and prepare for war, thus providing a nucleus for a large citizen army in wartime."[46]

"The Military Spirit Has Seemed to Pass Away"

The Congress of Vienna and Napoleon's subsequent defeat at Waterloo in June 1815 ushered in a period of "profound peace" in Europe that would last for decades. The signing of the Treaty of Ghent in December 1814, ending the War of 1812, marked the beginning of a period of relative stability in North America. Although there were ongoing tensions with the British and short periods of intensive conflict—such as the Seminole [or Florida] Wars, the Black Hawk War in Illinois in 1832, and the Texas Revolution of 1835–36—the United States would not mobilize for war again until its 1846 conflict with Mexico. During such a long period of peace, state militias fell into even steeper decline than before.[47]

So, too, did the Regular Army decline. It never attracted enough recruits, and desertion rates were high among those who did serve. The percentage of foreign-born immigrants within the enlisted ranks was disproportionately high and the army's reputation for drunkenness, notorious. As Francis Prucha has so aptly put it, "The Sword of the Republic, alas, was often made of inferior steel."[48]

The egalitarianism of the 1830s and 1840s was, as Weigley has

---

[45] Cunliffe, *Soldiers and Civilians*, 116–17.

[46] Palmer and Strykes, *Early American Wars*, 92.

[47] Ehrman and Henigan, "The Second Amendment in the Twentieth Century," 36.

[48] Prucha, *Sword of the Republic*, 320. Nevertheless, the U.S. Army in this period did successfully uphold the nation's dominion in the West by protecting as well as punishing American Indians and in insuring the safety of a nation intent on moving west.

observed, "a different phenomenon from Jeffersonianism, and its nationalist aspect did not include a high regard for the Regular Army in the manner of Calhoun."[49] It was an era impatient with any kind of aristocracy, most certainly that of the military. It chose to view the Battle of New Orleans as a triumph of the naturally superior American militiaman over the professional soldier. West Point's image as a producer of an educated class of military superiors fell into sharp disrepute; some in Congress called it a "monster" of aristocracy and pushed for its abolition. Even during Andrew Jackson's presidency, America was "an utterly unmilitary society."[50]

Popular disdain for militia service can be attributed to several factors.[51] First, many men viewed it as unfair, "an instrument of inequality." Legislators, judges, teachers, county officers, sea captains, government clerks, clergymen, and others were granted exemption from service.[52] Second, those not exempted were often heavily fined for absenteeism; many of the well-to-do simply bought their way out of service by paying the fines incurred. Although later laws reduced or eliminated such fines, resentment lingered. A third factor was the very real loss of time that accompanied militia service. Muster days generally were held only once a year, but that day usually fell in April or October, during planting or harvest seasons. Travel to and from the muster sites could take hours, if not days. Roll call could take all morning, postponing the actual drilling until well into the afternoon; the day ended with dancing, barbecues, drinking, and other festivities.[53] And perhaps more galling than the loss of time was the perceived waste of it. Although privates usually elected their commanding officers, too often leaders knew less about warfare than their underlings. Many read out of field manuals and far too often such outfits "spent more time drinking than drilling."[54] Little wonder this annual occasion became "a burlesque on all things military."[55]

---

[49] Weigley, *History of the United States Army*, 153.

[50] Weigley, *History of the United States Army*, 156. See also Millis, *American Military Thought*, 117.

[51] For an excellent review of these reasons, in the Mormon context of Missouri, see Baugh, "A Call to Arms," 24–25.

[52] Weigley, *History of the United States Army*, 156.

[53] Smith, "Militia of the United States," 22.

[54] McPherson, *Battle Cry of Freedom*, 317.

[55] Smith, "Militia of the United States," 31. As another military scholar argues, "Annual musters fell into such disrepute that they gradually were discontinued in most states, often without so much as formal repeal of the law requiring the muster." Hill, *Minute Man in Peace and War*, 19.

As of 1842, fifty years after the passage of the Militia Act, the system still required that each militiaman provide his own equipment and supplies (save for a musket, was theoretically provided by an act of 1810). This included "a bayonet and belt, two spare flints, a knapsack, a pouch with a box therein to contain not less than 24 cartridges . . . each to contain a proper quantity of powder and ball."[56] Commissioned officers were also to provide for themselves swords or pistol holders and other trappings of their command. Since many families could not afford the costs of duty, some men showed up at roll call with obsolete weapons, or— especially in the western states—with such makeshift weapons as corn stalks, sticks, umbrellas, and ramrods. This, compounded by the fact that the federal government failed to provide most states a sufficient number of muskets to equip their regiments—plus the fact that uniforms were scarce, expensive, and usually left to the individual unit to select—paints the picture of a sorry army, indeed, without proper attire, equipment, leadership, or purpose.[57]

To these reasons must be added yet another: the sheer tedium and boredom involved and "the unwillingness on the part of a restless population to endure discipline."[58] "There can scarcely be a restraint more vexatious and disgusting to a grown man than the military lessons of the military act," admitted J. R. Poinsett, secretary of war under Martin Van Buren, in 1839. "Military discipline consists in the observance of a number of minute particulars which, to the novitiate in arms, have no apparent object. . . . It is believed that to this cause is to be attributed the little progress which has been made in training the militia of the United States."[59]

Nothing evidences more graphically this decay in the militia than the haphazard, intermittent, careless, and incomplete submissions of state adjutant general reports mandated by the Militia Act of 1792. The 1831 Illinois report remained unaltered for almost a decade—as did those from New Jersey, Tennessee, and Rhode Island.[60] Delaware

[56] Militia Act of 1792, a legislative act of the United States government.

[57] Smith, "Militia of the United States," 39.

[58] White, *Jeffersonians*, 530.

[59] From the report by J. R. Poinsett, "A System of Reorganization," March 20, 1840.

[60] "Report from the Secretary of War." Senate Documents, 26th Congress, 1st Session, 1839. During the entire 1830s, the Illinois report stood stagnant at 2 divisions, 5 brigades, 28 regiments, 70 battalions, 204 companies, 856 commissioned officers, and an indeterminate number of noncommissioned soldiers.

FIGURE 2. "The Militia Muster," ca. 1828.
By David Claypool Johnston. Watercolor on paper, 10¾ in. × 15 in.
Courtesy of American Antiquarian Society, Worcester, Mass.

was conspicuously unmilitary, and led the other states in abolishing fines and imprisonment for lack of service.[61]

Governor Daniel Dunklin of Missouri voiced the sentiment of most state governors when he wrote: "The militia is so threadbare a subject, that great reluctance is felt in approaching it; and were it not that I deem it a duty incumbent on me to endeavor to reclaim it from the ridicule into which it is fast sinking, it would be unnoticed. If, as it has been esteemed, the Militia is the bulwark of the

[61] Cunliffe, *Soldiers and Civilians,* 211. This decline in allegiance to the military, however, was not the case in the South. More attached to military virtues and more fearful of slavery insurrection and Native American uprisings, the South placed a greater premium on citizen soldiering than did the North. Military schools—such as the Virginia Military Institute at Lexington and the Citadel at Charleston, South Carolina—prospered there, as did volunteer and independent companies. See Franklin, *Militant South,* chapters 8 and 9.

nation, the friends of liberty have a great cause to lament the decay into which it is failing."[62]

The tone of the age may have been rightly captured in the following 1842 letter from one Illinois militia leader:

> I delight in more than military pride and improvement as the safety [of] our country depends upon the bravery and discipline of our citizen soldiers. . . . [W]e must rely on them chiefly to protect our homes and firesides from aggression, our national honor from insult, and our liberty from destruction. Of late years the military spirit has seemed to pass away. Let the organization of volunteer companies be promoted, let them be furnished with arms and accoutrements, let them devote all the time they can spare to the acquisition of military discipline and they will speedily raise the spirit again and strengthen the arms of their country's defense.[63]

By 1840, things deteriorated to such an extent that J. R. Poinsett wrote in exasperation,

> The mass of the militia of the United States, as at present organized, does not fall short of 1,500,000 men; and every day that they are mustered in for inspection [costs] at least $1,000,000 . . . without adding anything whatever to the military efficiency of the country, and too often affecting injuriously the moral conditions of those who are assembled for the purpose led by the little instruction they receive on such occasions, without discipline, subordination, and a knowledge of the use of arms, and totally ignorant of the manner of taking care of themselves or of each other in the field. Such a militia, if called out in mass, would rather prove a burden than an assistance.[64]

Congress appointed a special committee, led by Poinsett, to study means of bettering the system. His report, among other things, called for a two-tiered system starting at its base with the total mass of militia but sharpening into a true fighting force of 100,000 young men between the ages of twenty and thirty-seven, to be called the Active [or Moveable] Force, all of whom would serve for four years—in essence, a ready corps of militiamen. Congress, however, balked

[62] Shoemaker et al. *Messages and Proclamations,* 1:248–50, as quoted in Westover, "Evolution of the Missouri Militia," 81.

[63] D. P. Wilbanks to H. S. Cooley, September 29, 1842; Governor's Correspondence, 1841.

[64] Poinsett, "A System of Reorganization."

at so large and expensive an undertaking in a time of peace, and nothing came of it. The basic difficulty remained what it had been for half a century: "a casually administered, voluntary militia was militarily useless, while a well-trained, obligatory system was politically unattainable."[65]

The "Golden Age" of Uniformed Companies

Yet if state militias were in a woeful condition, exactly the opposite may be said about volunteer militias, the best drilled of which were called "uniformed companies." As the common or enrolled militia declined after the War of 1812, these uniformed volunteer companies were experiencing what one military historian has called their "golden age":

> Thousands of [such] companies were formed, many only to last for a short time, while others lasted for many years. The uniformed company and its soldiers possessed many advantages and disadvantages as volunteer soldiers. They accepted discipline and training. They were willing to make a personal sacrifice of time and money . . . [and] the permanency of their organization made it possible to achieve the *esprit de corps*.[66]

Unlike the common militia, these volunteer companies *chose* to serve, and prescribed their own patterns of training, dress, and organization.

The term "volunteer" needs defining. Under the Military Act of 1792, militia service was in conception universal and obligatory. Often those who enrolled did so reluctantly, simply because it was the law; they were ill prepared or ill disposed for service. Not so the volunteer or "amateur," who elected to serve and often chose his own pattern of training, dress, drill, and organization. To volunteer meant to enter militia duty deliberately and in a special or unique way—such as joining an elite local regiment of like-minded volunteers that far exceeded the minimum requirements in terms of dress, conduct, length of service, military skill, and performance.

The volunteer militia can trace its roots to England, with the establishment of London's Honourable Artillery Company in 1537.

---

[65] Cunliffe, *Soldiers and Civilians,* 185.

[66] Westover, "Evolution of the Missouri Militia," 17.

FIGURE 3. "The National Lancers with the Reviewing Officers on the Boston Common, 1837." By B. C. Hubbard. Hand-colored lithograph, 17¾ in. × 21¼ in. *Courtesy of Museum of Fine Arts, Boston.*

Boston's Ancient and Honorable Artillery Company, begun in 1638 (and still in existence nearly four centuries later), was a direct imitation. Hundreds of such units organized in the years following, including the Philadelphia City Cavalry (1774), the Chatham Artillery Company (1786), the Richmond Light Infantry Blues (1789), the Pittsburgh Blues (1807), and the famous Seventh Regiment of New York Volunteer Militia.[67]

Often organized in response to local disasters, riots, or some other crisis that city authorities could not handle, these elite city units originally existed "independently of the state-wide system of militia . . . provided their own uniforms . . . of a dazzling and expensive splen-

[67] Cunliffe, *Soldiers and Civilians,* 217–18. Other famous companies included the Cleveland Grays (1836), the Charleston Ancient Artillery (1836), the Norfolk Light Artillery Blues (1829), the Wayne Artillery of Philadelphia (1844), and the Albany Burgesses Corps (1833). For the study of city and independent militias, see *Military Collector and Historian.*

dor . . . [and] followed the international military fashions of the day: rifleman, grenadiers, light artillery, light infantry and general cavalry."[68] As the common county militias floundered, these volunteer uniformed companies flourished, and were often authorized by their respective state governors as substitute militias and as such counted in the ranks of state militias in annual reports—a salve upon the political conscience. They drilled weekly, paraded on muster days, escorted distinguished visitors, and celebrated patriotic holidays. And as these volunteer companies became more numerous, they formed battalions and regiments of their own. For instance, in Missouri in 1825, "it was provided that when eight or more uniformed companies of different corps existed in a brigade, they could form a legion . . . a military organization made up of mixed arms, similar to a present-day division."[69] After 1825, such volunteer companies were allowed to bear arms even in times of peace and could form themselves into artillery and cavalry units. The governor issued their charters, commissioned their officers, and assigned the companies a "nominal place in the paper militia structure."[70] As Robert Reinders astutely put it, "In many communities they *were* the militia" and were usually filled with the most public-spirited citizens of their communities.[71]

Although they sometimes were called independent companies, they served ultimately at the state's command. Such companies were independent of or, better stated, separate from the regular militia as well as separate from other city militias dominated by the opposing political party, religion, or cultural group. In some communities, as in Worcester, Massachusetts, a city would boast of two such independent companies: one Whig and the other Democratic.[72]

---

[68] Cunliffe, *Soldiers and Civilians,* 221–22.

[69] Westover, "Evolution of the Missouri Militia," 92–93.

[70] Todd, "Our National Guard," 5:83. Often, as was the case with the Salem, Massachusetts, Light Infantry, their charters were very formal, extensive documents. For example, in its preamble the Salem document stated, "Arms are placed in our hands, and we are directed by the most evident principles of duty to acquire that skill in the use of them which shall render invincible the courage of freemen fighting in the cause of liberty." What followed were twenty-two articles addressing such topics as the numbers and election of officers, uniforms and how to wear them, musicians, white silk standards, guns and ammunition, fines and assessments, funerals of members, militia finances, and more. See Whipple, *History of the Salem Light Infantry,* 123–27.

[71] Reinders, "Militia and Public Order in Nineteenth-Century America," 86.

[72] Cunliffe, *Soldiers and Civilians,* 294.

Many of these uniformed independent companies were dominated by ethnic or religious groups. Some of the more famous included the Atlanta Irish Volunteers, the Irish Jasper Greens, the Caledonian Blues, and the Chicago Montgomery Guards. There were more German-American companies than of any other ethnic group; these were followed by the Irish companies, "which tended to emphasize, in both title and uniform, their Celtic origin."[73] Additionally, there were companies of French, Prussian, and Italian immigrants that often dressed in ethnic costume and uniform. Some were restricted to Christians; others were entirely Jewish in makeup. There were even companies consisting solely of children between the ages of ten and fifteen.[74] And in the West, they bore ferocious-sounding names such as Invincibles, Avengers, Patriots, and Snake Hunters.[75] Gradually, nativist sentiment forced most of these out of existence, but during the 1840s such ethnic and religious independent military companies were very much in vogue.

Usually well funded, such companies also took on a genteel quality, the habitat of the upper class. They enjoyed parading prominently in the finest uniforms—and even in great bearskins—and partaking of the most sumptuous dinners. One 1835 observer, in writing of two Springfield, Illinois, companies, "showered praise on their rich and showy uniforms, their arms bright as sunbeams, their gallant military-looking officers . . . and the usual finale of good wine, good toasts, and good feeling."[76] Although they were primarily social enterprises, such volunteer companies sometimes served as the local police as well as state guards and were an outlet for those with genuine military interests—most of whom could never attend West Point. "They ought not to be dismissed as clowns in fancy dress," as scholar Marcus Cunliffe has argued, for it was such volunteer companies, now acting as citizen soldiers, that fought along with the Regular Army in the Black Hawk War, the war against the Seminoles in Florida, and in the Mexican War.[77]

---

[73] Todd, "Our National Guard," 5:86.

[74] Cunliffe, *Soldiers and Civilians,* 223–26.

[75] Cunliffe, *Soldiers and Civilians,* 223.

[76] Cunliffe, *Soldiers and Civilians,* 231. "Every company delighted in displaying its uniforms at dinners and dances as well as on parade and in camp." Cunliffe, *Soldiers and Civilians,* 234.

[77] Cunliffe, *Soldiers and Civilians,* 250.

"The Militia of the State of Illinois Shall Consist of all Free Male Able-bodied Persons"

The situation in Illinois deserves our special scrutiny. Article V of the original Illinois Constitution begins as follows:

> 1. The Militia of the State of Illinois shall consist of all free male able-bodied persons (negroes, mulattoes, and Indians excepted), resident of the state, between the ages of 18 and 45 years except such persons as now are, or hereafter may be exempted by the laws of the United States, of this state, and shall be armed, equipped and trained as the general assembly may provide by law.
> 2. No person or persons, constitutionally scrupulous of bearing arms, shall be compelled to do military duty in times of peace, provided such person or persons shall pay an equivalent for such exemption.
> 3. Company, battalion and regimental officers, staff officers excepted, shall be elected by the persons composing their several companies, battalions, and regiments.
> 4. Brigadier and Major General shall be elected by the officers of their brigades and divisions respectively. . . .[78]

In addition to the militia requirements specified in both the United States and Illinois Constitutions and in the Militia Act of 1792, the state enacted its own Militia Act on March 26, 1819.[79] Among its several provisions this act, like those of most other states, mandated that "all free white male inhabitants . . . of the age of eighteen years, and under the age of forty-five years . . . shall severally and respectively be enrolled in the militia."[80] All of the state's original nineteen counties (in southern Illinois) were divided into two divisions of two to six regiments, each regiment consisting of "not less than three nor more than six companies" (Section 3) with each company, in turn, made up of thirty-two to ninety-six privates (Section 4). Each regiment could have at least one company of artillery, one of cavalry, and one of riflemen (Section 10). Each division served under the command of a major general. Officers were to be American citizens, but this requirement did not apply to privates (Section 6). In the absence of a standard uniform, each company was allowed to choose "such uni-

[78] Revised Statutes of the State of Illinois, 36.

[79] *Laws Passed by the First General Assembly*, 270–97.

[80] Section 1 of the Militia Act of the State of Illinois. In *Laws Passed by the First General Assembly*, 270.

forms as may be agreed upon by a majority of such company" (Section 12). Companies were to muster or drill together four times each year "at 10 A.M. on the first Saturday of April, June, August, and October" (Sections 14 and 19). Fines and other penalties were to be assessed those failing to show; a fine as high as fifty cents per day could be assessed a noncommissioned officer or private "for attending any muster without a sufficient rifle, musket or fuse [fusil or light musket]" (Section 25). Since this was equivalent to a day's wage for many laborers, such fines were no small matter, although fines one believed improper could be appealed (Section 28). All courts-martial were given "power to punish any officer or private" for "neglect of duty, by suspensions, fining, cashiering and disqualification" (Section 50).

Two years later, in 1821, the state reduced the annual number of company musters from four to three—April, June, and August—and an effort was made to make the uniforms of at least the officers correspond with those of the army of the United States.[81]

Despite such laws and constitutional provisions, there remained more sound and fury than real action among the ranks of the Illinois State Militia in the 1820s. Records were poorly kept; annual returns sent to Washington were intermittent at best; equipment and arms were badly lacking; and enrollment remained persistently low. Governor Edward Coles admitted as much in 1823 when he wrote, "I am persuaded that the Adjutant General's estimates of the [State] Militia are short of the actual number in the different years stated."[82]

By 1826 Coles's successor, Governor John Reynolds, believed that despite deficiencies in the militia returns, there were about twelve thousand rank-and-file citizen soldiers in the Illinois state militias. However, he was forced to admit that the uniformed volunteer companies, those described above and not mandated by law, were "by far the most efficient" and would, "in case of war," be preferred.[83]

The state depended on these volunteer companies in the Black Hawk War of 1832. This conflict was led by the Sauk and Fox tribes, who were wary of what they believed would be further negotiations

[81] *Laws Passed by the Second General Assembly,* 106–13.

[82] Edward Coles to Lieutenant Colonel G. Bomford, September 22, 1823, in Greene and Alvord, *Governors' Letter-Books,* 1:54.

[83] John Reynolds to James Barbour, secretary of war, September 8, 1826, in Greene and Alvord, *Governors' Letter-Books,* 1:109.

unfair to Indian needs.[84] The state militia—a paper, toothless tiger—was in such sad disarray that not one of its regiments or companies fought in that bloody conflict. Rather, it was companies of seven hundred–plus mounted volunteers, together with several companies of the United States Regular Army, that skillfully wore down the "British Bands" of Sauk and Fox, Winnebago, Pottawattamie, and Kickapoo near Rock Island. Eventually, Chief Black Hawk was captured and the various tribes were deposed and forced to find refuge and solace west of the Mississippi River. During this conflict, young Abraham Lincoln served as a captain in the Thirty-first Regiment of Sangamon County and later in the Fourth Regiment of Mounted Volunteers.[85] If nothing else, the Black Hawk War clearly demonstrated the need for better organization of the militia.[86]

Thus it should come as no surprise that during the rest of the decade the state considered one proposal after another to improve and modernize its much maligned militia and to encourage a citizen-soldier sentiment. In December 1834 and then again in 1836 and 1837, the Illinois state legislature tried to pass a law authorizing "the raising of any number of volunteer companies."[87] In hopes of establishing a system of county militias, legislation passed in March 1837 encouraged the organization of volunteer companies in cities across the state to take up the slack in declining enlistments. Among its provisions, this "Act Encouraging Volunteer Companies" provided for each company to adopt its own constitution and bylaws so long as such "shall not be inconsistent with the constitution of the United States or of this state" and provided for fines and punishments for those who violated its bylaws. Finally, in December 1838, in terms reminiscent of George Washington's earlier efforts to restore the country's military, serious discussion centered on a proposal from independent companies from all over the state to create a new kind of Illinois state militia—an elite body of enlisted volunteers formed into "a large body of mounted men."[88]

Whether or not this proposal developed into that presented just

---

[84] Jung, *The Black Hawk War of 1832*, 15–16. For a more scathing indictment of American land-grab policies toward these tribes of Indians, see Cecil Eby, *That Disgraceful Affair.*

[85] Temple, *Lincoln's Arms*, 5–6.

[86] *Journal of the House of Representatives of the Eighth General Assembly*, 119.

[87] *Journal of the House of Representatives of the Eighth General Assembly*, 88; *Journal of the Tenth Assembly*, 762.

[88] *Journal of the House of Representatives, Eleventh General Assembly*, 55.

four months later in "An Act to Incorporate the Illinois Legion,"[89] it fanned a temporary revival of military spirit and soon resulted in the organization of several independent militias throughout the state.[90] Citizens of Chicago responded with the organization of the Chicago City Guards (August 1839) along with the Washington Guards (before 1842), and the Montgomery Guards, a cavalry company (in summer 1842).[91] In Ottawa two similar independent companies soon formed, as well as one in Joliet (see table 1).

Section 8 of the 1837 act bears further study in light of the eventual size of the Nauvoo Legion:

> It shall be lawful for any two or more volunteer companies to organize themselves into an odd battalion, and elect their major and all other staff officers; provided, the parade grounds of said companies are in the same county and not more than twenty-five miles apart, and in case there shall be four or more volunteer companies in one county, they may organize themselves into a regiment and two battalions, and elect their colonel and staff officers in such manner as may be mutually agreed upon by their respective companies.[92]

Consequently, the chartering of the Nauvoo Legion as an independent military body—independent only in the sense it was not part of nearby company regiments like the Hancock Fifty-ninth—must be seen as fulfilling both the letter and the spirit of Illinois law, an attempt to deliver on the encouragement and invitation of the state, whose own militia was in disarray. Little wonder, then, that there would be no initial opposition to it.

But it was all to no avail. As in most other parts of the country the Illinois citizenry was averse to militia training and found ingen-

---

[89] *Journal of the House of Representatives, Eleventh General Assembly,* February 5, 18, 21, and 26, 1839; and March 1, 1839. See also *Journal of the Senate, 1839,* January 6 and 9, 1839. For reasons not yet determined, the measure never passed. "The Senate has refused to order to a second reading bills from the House of Representatives of the following titles: viz., An Act to Incorporate the Illinois Legion." *Journal of House of Representatives, Eleventh General Assembly,* March 1, 1839, 575. For more on the Illinois Legion and John C. Bennett's involvement with it, see chapter 3.

[90] Bateman and Selby, *Historical Encyclopedia of Illinois,* 376.

[91] Andreas, *History of Cook County,* 208–209. The Montgomery Guards, an Irish company, lasted until the Civil War when it was absorbed into the Illinois Sixtieth and Sixty-second regiments. See also Goodspeed and Healy, *History of Cook County,* 1:421.

[92] *Illinois Statutes.*

Table 1
Selective Listing of Militia Units of the State of Illinois, 1837–1846

Title	City/County	Type	Year
Rochester Light Infantry	Rochester	Part of the Fifty-ninth Regiment	1837
Chicago City Guards	Chicago	Independent Company Infantry; Sixtieth Regiment	1838
Nauvoo Legion	Nauvoo	Independent Company	1841
Monmouth Artillery	Monmouth	Part of the Seventy-fifth Regiment	1842
Montgomery Guards	Montgomery	Cavalry Company	1842
Chicago Guards	Chicago	Volunteer Company; Infantry	1842
Equality Invincibles	Equality	Independent Company Infantry; Fourth Regiment	1843
Green Plains Minute Men	Warsaw	Part of the Fifty-ninth Regiment	1843
Dewitt Guards	Waynesville	Volunteer Company	1843
Lafayette Cyrenes	Lafayette	Independent Company; Forty-fifth Regiment	1843
Calhoun Rifle Rangers	Calhoun County	Unknown	1843
Cavalry Corps of South Davis	South Davis	Independent Company	1846
Chicago Rifle Corps	Chicago	A Uniformed Company	1846
Perseyville Independent Greys	Perseyville	A Light Horse Company	1846
Galena City Guard	Galena	A Volunteer Independent Company	n.d.
Guard of Liberty	Chicago	Rifle Company Part of Washington Regiment	n.d.
Western Rangers	Cook County	Volunteer Rifle Company	n.d.
Walker Rangers	Cook County	Uniformed Independent Company	n.d.

SOURCES: Governor's Correspondence, 1837, Military Affairs; Executive Sub-series of Governors Correspondence, 1842; Executive Sub-series of Governor's Correspondence, 1843; Governor's Correspondence, 1844, Military Affairs; and Governor's Correspondence, 1846–1847, Military Affairs. All found in the Illinois State Archives, Springfield, Illinois.

ious ways not to participate. Struggling to make a new life in a new land, settlers were simply in no mood for arcane, if legally mandated, distractions. While Illinois more than tripled in size—from 157,000 people in 1830, to 476,000 in 1840, and 851,000 in 1850—militia numbers remained stagnant. Most new growth would occur in the northern half of the state, with the arrival of immigrants from New York and New England. Chicago grew from a small village in 1830 to a city of nearly 30,000 twenty years later. And in the process, Illinois was transformed from its southern roots and heritage to a very cosmopolitan, heterogeneous mix—which eventually included the Mormons.[93]

Conclusion

Such was the American and Illinoisan context at the time of the formation of the Nauvoo Legion. It was a time of decline for both the Regular Army and the state militias; Illinois' was no exception. Nonetheless, mandatory militia service was still the law and those failing to serve were subjected to fines and punishment. The state militias in the West were in such particular disarray that Illinois passed a law encouraging the establishment of local city militias and recognizing the existence and superiority of volunteer companies—which were far more colorful, better trained, and efficient than their counterpart state militia counterparts.

---

[93] Greene and Thompson, *Governors' Letter-Books,* 2:xv.

2

Missouri Precursors to the Nauvoo Legion

The Impropriety of the Organization of Bands or Companies by Covenants or Oaths by Penalties or Secrecies

JOSEPH SMITH

The foregoing chapter placed the Nauvoo Legion within the context of American and Illinoisan militia law and culture; there were, however, other reasons the Mormons flocked to its standards. If, indeed, the age was one of peace and a steep decline in interest in all things military, and if so many Americans, especially in the western states, were refusing to enlist and fulfill their military duties no matter what fines were imposed, what was it that compelled the Latter-day Saints to enlist in the Legion with such enthusiasm and avidity? What other factors were at play? And what prepared them for the kind of military commitment few other towns or counties in Illinois came even close to manifesting? A primary reason was their immediate past, for in truth the story of the Nauvoo Legion begins in Missouri.

What began in 1831 with eager anticipation among a people anxious to establish Zion, their "New Jerusalem," in Jackson County, Missouri, ended with a solemn proclamation of expulsion in 1838 by a governor convinced that the Mormons must either leave the state or face extermination. And what transpired in Missouri caused them to react in ways for which they were totally unprepared. Rather than establishing a Zion of peace and a safe refuge from the world, they were forced to take up arms to defend themselves. By the time they quit Missouri en masse for Illinois in the winter of 1838–39, they had learned many bitter lessons—politically, militarily, culturally, and religiously—in how to survive in an American frontier setting, lessons they would later put to good use in establishing the Nauvoo Legion. This chapter identifies some of these difficult lessons, especially those of a military nature.

"The Unpardonable Sin"

Early Mormon history in Missouri may be conveniently divided into three distinct periods: the Jackson County years (1831–34); the Clay County interlude (1834–36); and the Caldwell-Daviess county climax (1836–39). With each period, Mormon thought evolved with respect to the use of military force. In Jackson County the Latter-day Saints refused to organize themselves militarily. By 1834, however, Joseph Smith organized a citizens' army, called Zion's Camp, to bring attention to their plight and, if possible, restore the dispossessed to their Jackson County homes. By the time they established Far West and Adam-ondi-Ahman in northern Missouri, the Mormons had organized themselves into both a legitimate regiment of the Missouri militia as well as an extralegal secret band that caused more problems than it solved.

There were at least three reasons for the Mormon failure in Missouri. First, the place or culture of western Missouri was one of potential violence for which they were totally unprepared. Second, this was a time in American history of extreme violence and profound social unrest—unparalleled save for the Civil War. And finally, they as a people came to believe they were unprepared to fulfill their mission of establishing a new religious center on the frontier.

So what brought them to this sorry impasse? Several years before, in April 1830, Smith had organized what became the Church of Jesus Christ of Latter-day Saints in a small village in upstate New York. Preaching the message of a restored primitive Christianity, a new book of scripture in the Book of Mormon, and the expectation of an imminent, premillennial return of Christ, Smith and his rapidly growing number of followers preached with notable success first in New York and Ohio and later in New England, Upper Canada, and Great Britain. Central to the religion's theology was the belief that Zion, the prophesied New Jerusalem, must be established before Christ's expected return. Their prophet leader, Joseph Smith, identified "the center stake" of Zion as Independence, Missouri, which in 1831 was a jumping-off point on the Santa Fe Trail, just across the Missouri River from American Indian lands on the western frontier of America. Likewise convinced that the American Indian was a remnant of God's ancient chosen people and the primary audience of the Book of Mormon, the Latter-day Saints began to congregate in western Missouri in the summer of 1831.[1]

Jackson County may have been Zion in Mormon parlance but in the colorful vocabulary of the rapidly expanding local populations it represented an exciting new commercial opportunity. Although Liberty, in Clay County, had earlier made a bid for the expanding western and southwestern trade, the physical challenges of crossing over the Missouri River had "prevented the town from attaining the importance that otherwise might have been hers."[2] Instead, Independence, located more conveniently to the south and on the western banks of the river, soon became the favored transfer point between heavily laden steamboats plying upriver from Saint Louis and the pack animals and long-wagon trains destined for travel on the Santa Fe Trail. By 1832 Independence so dominated the southwest trade as an outfitting point that one visitor described it as a town "full of promise . . . consisting of nothing but ragged congeries of five or six rough log-huts, two or three clap-board houses, two or three so-called hotels (alias, grog shops), and a few stores . . . but nevertheless a thriving and aspiring place."[3] One would be hard pressed to find any other place in the United States where the divide between a religious dream and cultural reality was any wider than in Independence in 1830.

On the one hand, the Mormons were northerners—primarily from New York, Pennsylvania, Ohio, and New England—who were seeking to establish collectively a new religious order. Endeavoring to live a life of consecration and strict obedience, they tried to think in terms of the good of the whole; of combining their time, money,

[1] See Micah 5:8 in the Book of Mormon, 3 Nephi 21:12.

[2] Wells, "Growth of Independence, Missouri," 33.

[3] Wells, "Growth of Independence, Missouri," 36.

and energy to establish their Zion community; of sacrificing worldly intents for heavenly promises. Their religion was the center of their lives and focal point of commitment. And they eagerly hoped to see the imminent return of Christ.

On the other hand, most western Missourians hailed from the upper South and had brought with them much of their southern culture. As southerners they supported the "peculiar institution" of slavery and reflected other southern cultural characteristics in their way of life. Predominantly Protestant, they, too, believed in God and in such values as industry, integrity, and the common good. Fiercely individualistic they were committed to the ideals of Jacksonian Democracy, including free enterprise, trade, and a strong capitalist work ethic. They were deeply suspicious of religious zealotry, especially the kind that looked upon their own backyards as temple lots and hallowed ground.

That western Missouri at the time of the coming of the Mormons was predominantly Southern is irrefutable. According to geographer D. W. Meinig, Jackson County was settled predominantly by Scottish and Irish Protestants from the upper southern states of Kentucky, Tennessee, and Virginia—what he called the "greater Virginia migration stream"—and they brought their slaves with them.[4] Consequently this area, and counties downriver of Jackson County, soon took on the name "Little Dixie" or "Dixie Belt."[5] In 1830 there were 193 slaves divided among 62 slaveholders in Jackson County. Most importantly, slavery there and in many nearby coun-

---

[4] Meinig, *Shaping of America,* 229, 236, 273–79, 285, 294, 451–52.

[5] Rafferty, *Historical Atlas of Missouri,* map 33. "The name 'Little Dixie' is applied, usually in connection with Missouri politics, to a distinctive section of the state . . . the mid section of Missouri, where Southern sympathies, slavery and Democratic politics had been prevalent." Robert M. Crisler, in an attempt to delimit Little Dixie, found eight counties in east central Missouri that represent the core of the region. He also identified nine additional counties that had been at various times included in the 'Dixie Belt.'" Included in this area were Jackson, Clay, Ray, and Carroll Counties. As of 1860, two-thirds of Missouri's slaves lived within a few miles of the Missouri River. The following twelve counties contained 50,280 of the state's 115,000 slaves: Boone 5,034; Howard 5,889; Calloway 4,257; Jackson 3,944; Chariton 2,837; Lafayette 6,357; Clay 3,456; Pike 3,313; Cooper 2,800; St. Charles 2,181; and Salina 4,876. See Stevens, *Centennial History of Missouri,* 1:684–85. As for the origins of Missouri's population to 1860, the rank of states according to the origins of immigrants was as follows: Kentucky, 99,814; Tennessee, 73,954; Virginia, 53,957; Ohio, 35,389; Indiana, 30,463; and Illinois, 30, 138. Rafferty, *Historical Atlas of Missouri,* map 36.

ties of Little Dixie was on the increase and gained a great deal of momentum during the 1830s, peaking in popularity just prior to the Civil War.[6] Although only a minority of the population owned slaves (since the plantation system was the exception and not the rule), many families aspired to slaveholding status and owned at least one slave for domestic or hemp-producing purposes.[7]

More than just holding onto slavery, Missouri—as was true in almost all corners of the South in the early 1830s—harbored fears that slavery was under attack. Northern abolitionists were becoming increasingly bold and strident in their war of words against it. More urgently, the recent Nat Turner Rebellion in Southampton County, Virginia, had spread fear among Southerners that slaves would revolt. The South had paid a price for the famous Missouri Compromise of 1820, which allowed Missouri into the union as a slave state but forbade any territories north of the parallel 36°30' to enter the nation as slave states. Missouri's earliest settlers, predominantly southerners, were committed to protecting their culture and way of life at all costs.

With respect to abolitionism, "All over the South, mob action began to replace orderly judicial procedure, as the feelings against abolitionists mounted and as the southern views on race became crystallized."[8] As W. J. Cash has argued, "Let a Yankee abolitionist be caught spreading his propaganda in the land, let a Southerner speak out boldly his conviction that the North was essentially right . . . and he was not merely frowned on, cursed, hated; he was, in this country long inured to violence, dealt with more pointedly and personally; he was hanged or tarred or horse-whipped. . . . The critic [of slavery] stood an excellent chance of being mobbed."[9]

John Hope Franklin has shown that "the persistence of the rural environment, the Indian danger, the fear of slaves [and of slave uprisings], an old-world concept of honor, an increasing sensitivity, and

[6] Dorsett, "Slaveholding in Jackson County," 26.

[7] Hurt, "Planters and Slavery in Little Dixie," 397–415.

[8] Franklin, *Militant South*, vii–ix, 2. Lest the reader overlook the value of Franklin's enduring reputation as a scholar of the South, David Grimsted has more recently argued: "Clement Eaton, more than any historians before or since, emphasized the negatively repressive character of group violence in the ante-bellum South while [John Hope] Franklin's study remains the most inclusive and balanced survey." Grimsted, *American Mobbing*, 304.

[9] Cash, *Mind of the South*, 89.

an arrogant self-satisfaction with things as they were" contributed to the Southern "penchant for militancy," a "climate of militancy," and a "remarkable spirit and will to fight."[10] The English traveler J. S. Buckingham, writing in 1842, declared that "five times as large a proportion of these [violent] crimes to population as is witnessed in the North, and ten times as large a proportion as is seen in any of the free countries of Europe" occurred in the South. His statement, as Dickson D. Bruce, Jr., has argued, "may be open to question, but his impressions were widely shared. The society of the Old South was inextricably associated with violence in the minds of many people."[11] And this was just as true on such western frontiers of the expanding South as Missouri.

W. J. Cash has also argued that the southern character of individualism and independence likewise contributed to the "perpetuation and acceleration of the tendency to violence which had grown up in the Southern backwoods. . . . [C]onflict with them could only mean immediate physical clashing, could only mean fisticuffs, the gouging ring, and knife and gun play . . . the tradition of vigilante action."[12] Such individualism contrasted markedly with the group mentality of the newly arrived Latter-day Saints who, in 1831, were pooling all their resources and energies into living an economic law of community cooperation and unity. They traded among themselves, shunned so-called Gentile merchants, and looked to one another for support and confirmation. Their bonding together in matters of religion, trade, and community only made their outsideness all the more pronounced—and suspect.

To these points of potential rupture must be added yet another—the contrasting visions Mormons and Missourians shared concerning Native Americans. To the former, at least theologically, the American Indian stemmed from the ancient House of Israel and was a chosen people, worthy of immediate conversion and sustained support. To the latter, they were an enemy and a threat to the state's well-being; Missourians strongly supported President Andrew Jackson's policy of expulsion, if not eradication, of the various tribes.

By 1830 the state of Missouri was actively implementing the U.S.

---

[10] Franklin, *Militant South,* 89.

[11] As quoted in Bruce, *Violence and Culture,* 3.

[12] Cash, *Mind of the South,* 43.

policy of dispossessing and relocating the various Indian tribes.[13] Although several Indians had proven their worth and had served in regiments of the Missouri militia, they were not highly regarded. Shawnees, Delawares, and other Algonquin-speaking tribes from the Great Lakes region had little choice but to sell out and leave. As Thomas Hart Benton, one of the state's original senators, inelegantly phrased it, "To remove the Indians would make room for the spread of slaves."[14] Whatever the cost, the Indian had to go so that white settlers could come. "With impunity," John Mack Faragher has argued, "the state allowed squatters to steal Indian farms and appropriate their improvements."[15] This policy had become so ensconced by 1830 that no power or persuasion could change its course. Whenever detachments of the Missouri militia were called out in the 1820s, 1830s, and 1840s, more often than not it was to contend with Indian problems—that is, to ensure the ultimate expulsion of the tribes.

While it was the policy of the United States government to allow carefully selected and approved religious denominations to Christianize the Indian tribes west of the Missouri River, such permission did not extend to newer religions, such as Mormonism, whose adherents' motives for proselyting were unclear, if not unsettling. "Those 'yankees' with their queer speech," said one local citizen of the Mormons, "who brought not a single slave and who were deluded enough to believe that the Indians and white men could cultivate the earth together in peace, bore watching."[16] Certainly Missourians in Jackson County, well aware of the recent Black Hawk War, chose to see in Mormon theology—and particularly in the Book of Mormon—an emphasis on befriending, if not empowering, Indians and worried that such a view would lead to increased bloodshed.

It would, of course, be unfair and simplistic to blame all the violence the Mormons eventually encountered in Missouri on the local populations. Northerners, the Saints included, could be, on occasion, just as violent. As Thomas Ford argued about Illinoisan violence of the 1830s, "The old, peaceful staid, 'Puritan Yankee' walked into a

---

[13] See Spicer, *A Short History of the Indians of the United States.*

[14] Benton, *Thirty Years' War,* 1:28, 626.

[15] Faragher, "From Ethnic Mixing to Ethnic Cleansing on the Frontier," 321.

[16] March, *History of Missouri,* 545.

fight or defense of his claim, or that of his neighbor, just as if he had received a regular backwoods education in the olden times. . . . [T]he readiness with which our puritan population from the East adopted the mobocratic spirit is evidence that men are the same everywhere under the same circumstances."[17] Nevertheless one would be hard pressed to say that the early Mormon settlers in Jackson County were as military minded, at least initially, as were their southern Missouri neighbors and may well have been ignorant—to their obvious later discomfiture—of the climate of fear and suspicion then prevailing in Jackson and surrounding counties. The two peoples were of entirely different backgrounds, operated on vastly different social, religious, and cultural frequencies, and shared only a common geography.

Warren A. Jennings, one of the few who has written extensively on the expulsion of the Mormons from Jackson County in November 1833, has identified several other reasons for this inevitable clash of cultures. They include the Mormon penchant for purchasing lands and the resultant Missourian fear of a Mormon takeover; the rapid influx of new Mormon settlers and the Missourian fear of losing political control; and published articles in the Mormon-owned Independence newspaper, *The Evening and the Morning Star,* on importing "free people of color."

If differences of views on slavery were not the only, or even the most important, issue, they certainly did crystallize opposition. W. W. Phelps's 1833 article "Free People of Color" and the popular perceptions of Mormon antislavery sentiment lit the spark that led to open dissent. As Missouri scholar Walter Stevens put it, "The unpardonable sin of the Mormons in Jackson County was opposition to slavery."[18] Local citizens lost little time interpreting it as part of a scheme for "inviting free negroes and mulattoes from other states to become Mormons, and remove and settle among us. . . . This would corrupt our blacks, and instigate them to bloodshed."[19] It was immediately after this that Jackson County residents destroyed Phelps's printing press, tarred and feathered two Mormons, and demanded Mormon removal from the county.

---

[17] Ford, *History of Illinois,* 246.

[18] Stevens, *Centennial History of Missouri,* 2:95.

[19] Dorsett, "Slaveholding in Jackson County," 28. See Stevens, *Centennial History of Missouri,* 2:96.

Jennings adds yet another, perhaps more basic reason: the Mormons were as politically naïve as they were religiously motivated and unprepared militarily for as violent a society as western Missouri turned out to be. "If a quarrel developed between two men it was expected that they meet, fight it out, take a drink, and settle the difficulty for all time. This attitude of the fighting Missourian was not understood by the Mormons."[20]

Well before 1830 local settlers kept up their military organizations and clubs with each township having a militia company and each county a regiment of up to ten companies. When the local citizenry banded together to drive them out of Jackson County, the Mormons "were in a state of shock as a result of their treatment. They were perplexed as to why it had happened; they were dismayed by their prospects, and they were puzzled about their future."[21] Poorly armed and ill equipped for this or any other kind of warfare, they "had not embodied for defense, though it appears that a number of them had guns. None had joined the local militia regiment." They concluded belatedly "that each branch would organize into its own defenses and muster its own men."[22] In early November 1833 after killings on both sides, the Mormons—fearing a full-scale massacre—were forced to sign an agreement surrendering their arms and vacating their homes and farms in the county by January 1, 1834. Religious refugees, they began crossing the river and settling near Liberty, where local citizens welcomed them, at least temporarily.[23]

Meanwhile, two Mormon emissaries, W. W. Phelps and Orson Hyde, traveled to Jefferson City to ask Governor Daniel Dunklin for a sufficient number of state troops to maintain order, but the governor refused to intervene. The Mormons thereupon enlisted the legal services of two Missouri attorneys, David R. Atchison and Alexander Doniphan, to plead their cause in court. To their argument that they be allowed to arm under state authority and return to their homes, Attorney General Robert Wells wrote "that if they

---

[20] Jennings, "Zion Is Fled," 20. "The clashes between the two groups can be traced, in large part, to the Missourian propensity for violence." The local citizens were "a disputatious lot," "quarrelsome and given to wrangling." Jennings, "Zion Is Fled," 323.

[21] Jennings, "Zion Is Fled," 203.

[22] Jennings, "Zion Is Fled," 169.

[23] Of interest is the fact that the state did not trust local militia regiments to escort the Mormons out of the state but relied on the better disciplined, uniformed companies to carry out such tasks. Westover, "Evolution of the Missouri Militia," 88. See chapter 1.

organized themselves into regular militia companies, they would, he thought, be given public arms, which could be used to repossess their property in Jackson County."[24] This, however, they refused to do, knowing full well that it would precipitate further violence. Rather, "they looked to the state to put them into possession of their property in Jackson County and to return their arms, after which they would undertake to defend themselves."[25]

"Something of an Ill Omen amongst Us"

If the Mormons picked a very difficult *place* to establish Zion, they certainly could not have chosen a worse *time*. "It is impossible to read the newspapers, correspondence, travel accounts, and speeches of this era and not be struck by the fact that violence was increasing in the United States."[26] While rioting was nothing new in America's history in the nineteenth century, "rioters relied upon physical violence on persons with a vehemence almost unknown in the 18th century."[27] In particular the decade of the 1830s has gone down in American history as the "Turbulent Era"; there was more rioting between 1834 and 1836 than in any other corresponding period. Race and labor riots marred the landscape from New Orleans to Philadelphia, from New York to Missouri. William Ellery Channing, theologian and social critic, remembered 1834 as a time "society was shaken to its foundations." John Quincy Adams despairingly wrote in that same year, "My hopes of the long continuance of this Union are extinct. The people must go the way of all the world."[28] It was, in the words of Carl Prince, "politics-out-of-doors."[29] The year 1834 still stands as America's most violent year; more riots occurred in that year than any before or since.[30]

A number of factors came together in the mid-1830s in an explo-

[24] March, *History of Missouri*, 550.
[25] March, *History of Missouri*, 551.
[26] Werner, *Reaping the Bloody Harvest*, 17.
[27] Gilje, *Rioting in America*, 63.
[28] Prince, "Great 'Riot Year,'" 3.
[29] Prince, "Great 'Riot Year,'" 4.
[30] John M. Werner's list of causes of such riots may help explain the Mormon dilemma: "First, a tradition of violence toward the minority group exists in the community; second, the minority group is trying actively to improve its position within the community; third, the police are antagonistic toward the minority group; fourth, there are one or more groups of people who malign the minority group; fifth, the news media does not report fairly the activities of the minority group." Werner, *Reaping the Bloody Harvest*, 273.

sive way. These include the rapid passing of an agrarian society and way of life, and with it rapid urbanization; concerns over property; nativism and the fear of the numerous new Irish and Negro immigrants in northern cities; an exploitative labor system that denied the worker a living wage; lingering anti-Catholic sentiments; antagonism toward Native Americans; the collapse of the national bank and the ensuing economic downturn of 1834; the rise of vigilante movements; and southern fears of northern abolitionism. Hundreds died in small skirmishes during these turbulent years. In 1835 alone there were nearly one hundred and fifty riots nationwide.[31]

Abraham Lincoln, writing in 1837, likewise expressed his great concerns for the contagion of violence then gripping his beloved land:

> There is even now something of an ill omen amongst us. I mean the increasing disregard for law which pervades the country—the growing disposition to substitute the wild and furious passions in lieu of the sober judgment of the courts, and the worse than savage mobs for the executive ministers of justice. This disposition is awfully fearful in any community; and that it now exists in ours, though grating to our feelings to admit it, would be a violation of truth and an insult to our intelligence to deny. Accounts of outrages commanded by mobs form the every-day news of the times. They have pervaded the country from New England to Louisiana; they are neither peculiar to the eternal snows of the former nor the burning suns of the latter; they are not the creature of climate, neither are they confined to the slaveholding or the non-slaveholding states. Alike they spring up among the pleasure-hunting master of Southern slaves, and the order-loving citizens of the land of steady habits. Whatever their causes be, it is common to the whole country.[32]

Some riots turned so violent that President Andrew Jackson called out the Regular Army to reclaim order.[33] In several states uniformed militia companies broke up several riots. What further made the 1830s a time of such widespread violence, especially in the slaveholding states, was rising uneasiness over fears of another Nat Turner–style slave insurrection. The revolt led by Nat Turner and his fellow slaves in Virginia in 1831 killed fifty to sixty white men and

[31] Grimsted, *American Mobbing*, 4.

[32] Williams, *Abraham Lincoln*, 7. See Feldberg, *Turbulent Era*, 4–5.

[33] Grimsted, *American Mobbing*, 5–12.

FIGURE 4. "The Lord's Army Marching to the Delivery of Zion," first published, 1873. *Courtesy of Mrs. Pearl Wilcox and the Utah State Historical Society.*

women and, in turn, led to the deaths of over four hundred blacks, Turner included. In Mississippi in 1835, fears of such uprisings led to scores of slaves being tortured, whipped, and "killed as examples"—their decapitated heads displayed on poles to stress the point.[34]

As one leading authority on the subject has recently argued, the South feared "the imminence of bloody slave revolts" with the result that "the violence of 1835 inaugurated the South's full-fledged acceptance of slavery as a total good: economically profitable, socially decent and desirable, and divinely favored."[35] From this time on southern public violence drew little or no official response and provides "a stomach-churning catalog of butchery."[36] While riots in both the North and South were common, those in the South were particularly brutal and sadistic with accounts in the hundreds of lynchings, people being flayed or burned alive, excessive whippings, and tarring and feathering.[37] Many other riots broke out during election

[34] Grimsted, *American Mobbing,* 140–44.

[35] Grimsted, *American Mobbing,* 20, 164.

[36] Grimsted, *American Mobbing,* 91.

[37] Grimsted, *American Mobbing,* 102, 122.

times, at polling stations, or during political speeches, in part because of nativist resistance to allowing foreigners who were not yet citizens the right to vote. Often alcohol was a factor. At least eighty-nine lives were lost during the election year of 1838.[38]

The treatment of the Mormons in Missouri, therefore, must be viewed against this backdrop of contemporary violence across America. Beginning in April 1834, some twelve hundred Mormons starting over in Clay County decided for the first time to organize themselves into militia companies "according to law." They had delayed organizing for fear of causing further excitement, but now, by so doing, they hoped to regain their weapons and protect themselves from further violence and disrupture: "Our object is purely to defend ourselves and possessions against another unparalleled attack from the mob."[39]

On hearing of the events in Jackson County, Joseph Smith petitioned President Andrew Jackson as well as Missouri Governor Daniel Dunklin for redress, but without success. Frustrated, he soon organized a citizen army of some two hundred men, which he christened Zion's Camp. With Smith as commander in chief and Lyman Wight as "major-general," Zion's Camp marched from Kirtland, Ohio, on May 1, 1834, and reached the outskirts of Liberty, Clay County, Missouri, six weeks later. Its purpose was to deliver twenty wagons of supplies and—with the anticipated support of state militiamen—redeem Zion by reinstating the Latter-day Saints on their lands in Jackson County. Zion's Camp may well have focused public attention on the plight of the Mormons—and surely everyone in western Missouri knew it was coming—but it "left a legacy of ill will." Many Missourians, "who otherwise had been friendly to the Mormons, were antagonized by the intrusion of a large force of armed men from outside the state."[40] In the end, such an alignment never occurred because Governor Dunklin, for all his assurances otherwise, knew he would have a war on his hands if state militia and armed Mormons teamed up to regain lost properties in Jackson County. No state regiments were ever allowed to participate in Zion's Camp's intended pursuit.

---

[38] Grimsted, *American Mobbing*, 184–85.

[39] Jennings, "Zion Is Fled," 246–47.

[40] Jennings, "Zion Is Fled," 293.

The significance of Zion's Camp must neither be under- nor overemphasized. A rather clumsy military operation, its importance lies in what it signaled rather than what it accomplished—if nothing else, it was an expression of unity and support by fellow members in Kirtland for their Missouri brothers. Proclaiming heaven's blessings for arming and marching this band of leaders across several states, Smith telegraphed the message that his people would take only so much violent treatment and persecution. And in the process it developed sterling leadership qualities among the faithful. As historian Alex Baugh has noted, faced with rising opposition on one hand, and the refusal of state and national leaders to intervene on the other, "a growing spirit of militarism was kindled in the hearts and minds of those most loyal to the faith—a spirit that would generate the desire to defend with force the Church and Kingdom of God."[41]

Klaus Hansen has even gone so far as to argue that despite its failure, Zion's Camp had "long-range significance for the future development of the political kingdom because it set a precedent for the establishment of the military arm of the Kingdom." All future Mormon military organizations, he argues, "including the Nauvoo Legion, as well as the militia of that same name organized by Brigham Young in Utah, and the Army of Israel that directed the exodus to the Great Basin, were patterned after Zion's Camp."[42]

We tend to see it differently. Neither part of the United States Regular Army nor of any state militia, Zion's Camp was a hastily organized, paramilitary, if understandable reaction to the unjust actions of Jackson County mobs and the inaction of elected government officials to redress Mormon losses. Inadequately provisioned, poorly trained, and insufficiently armed, Zion's Camp never intended to fight on its own. Had it taken the field against Missouri forces, the outcome would have been sore indeed. Its primary military purpose seems to have been to align itself with state militia units, which the Mormons hoped would be called into action in Jackson County, to restore order and return lost lands and properties.[43] A quasi-military action with untrained leadership that never gained legal recognition in any state, Zion's Camp was more a model of how *not* to

[41] Baugh, "A Call to Arms," 5.

[42] Hansen, *Mormonism and the American Experience*, 136–37.

[43] Baugh, "A Call to Arms," 5.

run a militia than it was a precedent for the future Nauvoo Legion. Nevertheless, the Latter-day Saints learned valuable lessons from the Zion's Camp experience. It also provided a military training ground for Joseph Smith and the other leaders. (See chapter 5.)[44]

Unable to reinstate themselves in Jackson County, the Mormons tarried in Clay County until 1836, when the citizens there—having grown uneasy over continued migrations—asked them to leave for Wisconsin or some other place.[45] Thanks to legislative action by Alexander Doniphan that led to the creation of two new counties—Caldwell and Daviess—in the northern part of Ray County, they began moving north en masse in late 1837.[46] While it was tacitly understood that they would settle primarily in Caldwell County, the Mormons lost little time in organizing new communities in both counties. Far West became their new capital in Caldwell County, and Adam-ondi-Ahman their central gathering place in Daviess County. In January 1838, following a bank failure and an ensuing bitter apostasy in Kirtland, Ohio, Smith and several hundred of his loyal followers arrived at Far West, where plans to build a new temple had been tentatively announced. Soon the Mormon population in northern Missouri rose to over five thousand.

During this, their last period in Missouri, the Mormons responded militarily in ways much different than they did before. First of all, by taking full advantage of the militia laws of the state, and with the encouragement of state officials, they organized themselves into a bona fide county militia—in this case, the Fifty-third Regiment of Caldwell County. Eventually placed under the direction of Smith

---

[44] "Out of the seeming disaster of Zion's Camp and amongst those who followed him in military order to fight, if necessary, for the repossession of their Jackson County lands and who, plagued and scourged, dribbled back to their homes singly or in disorganized small groups, [Joseph Smith] rose to call forth from his people even greater trust and devotion, for, while some criticized, the people generally and the greater ones of the Camp, still held him to be . . . Revelator of the Lord towards his people. Few men in history have survived such a seeming disaster." Clark, *On the Way to Immortality and Eternal Life,* 220.

[45] A series of resolutions was drafted which charged the Latter-day Saints with no crimes but sought their removal on the following grounds: (1) "they are eastern men, whose manners, habits, customs, and even dialect are different from our own; (2) they are non-slave holders and opposed to slavery . . . (3) they are charged . . . with keeping up a constant communication with the Indian tribes." March, *History of Missouri,* 555.

[46] Launius, *Alexander William Doniphan,* 40.

as commander in chief, but essentially directed by Lyman Wight, this "Army of Israel" was a detachment of the state militia with full right to state arms and equipment.[47]

The Danite Band

This Fifty-third Regiment should not be confused with that highly debatable band of Mormon zealots—or extremists—that came to be called the Danites, or Daughters of Zion. This secret band of vigilantes caused more problems than it solved and has been a focal point of continuing debate ever since. Secretly organized by Jared Carter and others and later directed by Sampson Avard, the Danites had, as Baugh argues, three purposes: to intimidate apostates into leaving Mormon society; to enforce obedience to their economic order, the Law of Consecration; and to influence state and county elections in favor of the Latter-day Saints.[48]

There can be little doubt that these so-called Avenging Angels took secret oaths and returned in kind much of the frontier treatment the Latter-day Saints were receiving at the hands of some of their hostile Missouri neighbors. Fluctuating in size from two hundred to five hundred armed men, they burned farmhouses and barns, killed cattle and horses, and even set small villages afire. Formed in reaction to persecution, the Danites consisted of many prominent rank-and-file Mormons and was led by a militant-minded, egotistical British-born Virginian who would shoot first and ask questions later.[49]

---

[47] Baugh, "A Call to Arms," 9. As Lyman Wight stated: "The county having been settled, the governor issued an order for the organization of the county and of a regiment of militia; and an election being called for . . . I was elected unanimously, receiving 236 votes in August 1837." As cited in Baugh, "A Call to Arms," 14. For a dramatically different interpretation of these events, and one much more critical of Joseph Smith and the Latter-day Saints see LeSueur, *The 1838 Mormon War in Missouri*, especially chapters 7 and 8. LeSueur argues that Joseph Smith "assumed leadership of the Mormon military operations" (112) and was far more involved with, and responsible for, Mormon "retributions" than are other scholars prepared to admit.

[48] Baugh, "A Call to Arms," 37.

[49] Sampson Avard was born October 23, 1803, on the isle of Guernsey. Later he immigrated to America where he married and settled first in Virginia and later in Pennsylvania. A former Campbellite minister, he converted to Mormonism in 1835. After spending almost two years in Kirtland, Ohio, he moved to Far West in May 1838 during the height of persecutions there. In company with Jared Carter and Dimick Huntington, Avard began holding secret meetings of the "Bro- (*continued, next page*)

D. Michael Quinn has argued, "What the Danites did militarily during the summer and fall of 1838 was by the general oversight and command of Joseph Smith,"[50] and that by this time "The Church militant was a literal fact in Mormonism."[51] Other leading scholars do not agree. Richard Bushman, in his recent biography of Smith, agrees that there were "militant elements" in Mormon society, but sees it as an expression of a distinct minority.[52] And, as Baugh argues, Smith knew of the Danites, but lacked a full knowledge of their more violent aims: he never denied "his knowledge or participation in Mormon-Danite military activity; rather, he did not know the full extent of what was being taught by Avard."[53]

Whatever the case, if Joseph Smith knew of the Danites, he should have restrained them much earlier—and if he did not know of them, as leader, he should have. The Danites proved to be perpetrators of violence not in keeping with the stated purpose of the Church in coming to Missouri in the first place—or its doctrines—and an embarrassment to the Mormon people. As thousands of new Mormon settlers arrived in Missouri from the eastern states, Canada, and Great Britain, men and women with no firsthand knowledge of the depredations of Jackson County came intending to establish peaceful communities. Coming not as fighters but as followers, they soon were caught up in the spirit of violence as committed by all sides, and scarcely knew how to act. Meanwhile, a particularly bellicose speech given in July 1838 by Sidney Rigdon, counselor in the Church's

thers of Gideon" or "Danites" named after the Old Testament prophet Daniel's prophecy of a stone cut out of the mountain without hands and rolling forth to fill the earth. Secretly and defiantly militant, the Danites returned violence for violence. And as for Avard's character, especially among ex-Mormons driven out of Caldwell County, the picture is none too flattering. He was "as grand a villain as his wit and ability would admit of," said John Corrill (*A Brief History of the Church of Christ of Latter-day Saints*, 31). Elias Higbee, a fellow commander, said he was "a man whose character was the worst I ever knew in all my associations or intercourse with mankind." *History of the Church*, 4:82–83. Avard eventually lost all influence among the Saints as one not to be trusted and went on to become a bitter enemy. His attacks against the Church and its leadership during the trial of Joseph Smith and others in Richmond, Missouri in November 1838 were so filled with anger and vituperation that many recoiled from his extremism. Avard died in Edwardsville, Illinois, in 1869.

50 Quinn, *The Mormon Hierarchy*, 99.

51 Quinn, *The Mormon Hierarchy*, 85.

52 Bushman, *Rough Stone Rolling*, 355.

53 Baugh, "A Call to Arms," 42.

First Presidency, coupled with disturbing rhetoric and accusations by various disaffected Mormon leaders, set off a chain reaction of anti-Mormon sentiment that culminated in a brawl at Gallatin, seat of Daviess County, over block voting in the primary election. At about the same time hundreds of Mormons were forced from their homes in Dewitt, Carroll County. Outbreaks of guerrilla warfare followed on both sides. Spurred on to use more force than they ever had before, bands of armed Mormon raiders sacked the small towns of Millport and Gallatin, burning homes and farms to the ground.[54] As several later testified, "The store house of Jacob Stollings in Gallatin was robbed and burned by the Mormons; the post office kept there was also destroyed, and we believe that the houses of five or six of the inhabitants of Daviess have been destroyed by fire, the property taken away, and the women and children obliged to flee."[55] Tensions mounted to such a degree that Governor Lilburn W. Boggs called out units of the state militia to stave off open warfare.

On October 25, 1838, in a case of Missouri militiamen facing each other, some sixty Mormons led by David W. Patten (Captain "Fear Not") fought against other detachments of the Missouri militia at Crooked River in Ray County.[56] Although the Mormons carried the day, a few men were killed on both sides, including Patten. The clash of arms so terrified those in nearby communities that civil war appeared imminent.

Historian Stephen C. LeSueur has argued that Mormon soldiers committed several "desperate crimes" against Daviess County citizens. Certainly the Fifty-third Regiment of Caldwell County had no authority to cross over county lines, nor did the Danites have any legal right to plunder and destroy. Such depredations likely resulted from the belligerent speeches of their leaders, "pent-up hostility and

[54] Robertson, "Mormon Experience in Missouri," 288–89. For a significantly different, more conciliatory view of the Danites, see Jessee and Whittaker, "The Last Months of Mormonism in Missouri," 5–41.

[55] Affidavit of the Citizens of Ray County to the Governor, Richmond, October 23, 23, 1838. As found in *Document Containing the Correspondence, Orders, etc.*, 49.

[56] Westover, "Evolution of the Missouri Militia," 75. The core of Mormon resistance was the Fifty-third Regiment, commanded by Colonel George W. Hinkle. All of its officers had been commissioned by Governor Boggs. However, like every other regiment in the state of Missouri, it was inadequately provisioned. Although the Fifty-third made great efforts to arm itself, it had "only 630 guns for its 700 to 1000 men when it was sanctioned." Westover, "Evolution of the Missouri Militia," 79.

frustration fostered by years of persecution," their certainty that they were "God's chosen people" who had been unjustly served, and their conviction that "their victims deserved their fate."[57] Fearing all-out war, Governor Boggs "ordered out the First, Fourth, Fifth, Sixth and Twelfth divisions of the Missouri militia on 26 October and the next day issued his infamous 'extermination order.'"[58] Three days later, on 30 October a militia-mob of two hundred men attacked the small Mormon settlement of Haun's Mill, where they shot and killed seventeen poorly armed men and boys, blowing the brains out of some unarmed children. A day of infamy in American history, the horror of Haun's Mill would never be forgotten, and it cast a pall of gloom all over western Missouri. That same day two thousand militiamen arrived in the vicinity of Far West and would surely have executed the surrendered Mormon leaders had it not been for the courageous remonstrances of their lawyer and Missouri militia leader, Alexander Doniphan.[59] On November 6, General John B. Clark, who had assumed command of the Missouri militia regiments and who was a political enemy of Boggs, ordered the Mormons to leave the state as soon as possible. Smith and his fellow leaders were dispatched to Richmond and later to Liberty Jail to await trial on a charge of treason while Brigham Young hastily organized and conducted the exodus of thousands of men, women, and children in the teeth of an unforgiving winter to Quincy, Illinois.[60]

---

[57] LeSueur, *The 1838 Mormon War in Missouri,* 197.

[58] Robertson, "Mormon Experience in Missouri," 289.

[59] Refusing the order of his commanding officer, Brigadier General Samuel D. Lucas, from Jackson County, to execute Joseph Smith and other Mormon leaders on the morning of November 2, 1838, Alexander Doniphan replied, "It is cold blooded murder. I will not obey your order. My brigade shall march for Liberty tomorrow morning at 8 o'clock; and if you execute these men, I will hold you responsible before an earthly tribunal, so help me God." *History of the Church,* 3:446. Doniphan purportedly also said to Lucas, "You hurt one of these men if you dare and I will hold you personally responsible for it, and at some other time you and I will meet again when in mortal combat and we will see who is the better man." Launius, *Alexander William Doniphan,* 64.

[60] There is some disagreement over the nature of these Missouri militias. Alexander L. Baugh argues that they were almost certainly local regiments, nearly mobs, with a strong degree of anti-Mormon feelings. See Baugh, "A Call to Arms," 28. "The county militia that came against the Mormons in Jackson County in 1833, and the units called out by Boggs in the 1838 conflict, were comprised almost exclusively of local and county irregulars, not volunteers. . . . It was not until the 1840s (*continued, next page*)

"There Were Jarrings and Contentions"

In addition to the place, time, and misunderstandings that provided context for their difficulties in Missouri, the Latter-day Saints confess to yet another problem—one they came to accept as a divine reprimand. Although they were convinced they were on God's errand to redeem Zion and prepare the way for Christ's millennial reign, as a people they came to realize that they were unprepared and simply not up to the task.

"I, the Lord, have suffered the affliction to come upon them," recorded their own prophet in December 1833, contemporaneous with their expulsion from Jackson County,

> wherewith they have been afflicted, in consequence of their own transgressions;
>
> Yet I will own them, and they shall be mine in that day when I shall come to make up my jewels.
>
> Therefore, they must needs be chastened and tried, even as Abraham, who was commanded to offer up his only son.
>
> For all those who will not endure chastening, but deny me, cannot be sanctified.
>
> Behold, I say unto you, there were jarrings, and contentions, and envyings, and strifes, and lustful and covetous desires among them; therefore by these things they polluted their inheritances.[61]

Later, after the march of Zion's Camp, this message was repeated and they were counseled to "wait for a little season . . . [i]n consequence of the transgressions of my people."[62] Thus Smith's own revelations placed much of the blame for their discomfitures squarely

---

and 50s that independent companies came into vogue in Missouri." Baugh, "A Call to Arms," 28.

Missouri militia historian John G. Westover, on the other hand, seems to think otherwise. Uniformed companies were better trained and better equipped than local regiments would have been. If so, many of them may have been uniformed companies. As late as 1825, such Missouri volunteers had been allowed to form battalions and regiments of their own. When eight or more such uniformed companies of different corps existed in a brigade, they could form a legion made up of foot regiments, cavalry, and artillery. Such "Legionary battalions" may have participated in the forces that faced the Mormons in October 1838. See Westover, "Evolution of the Missouri Militia," 92–93. The forces that were called out to fight the so-called Mormon War were likely a mixture of local militiamen who were stridently opposed to the Mormons and units of better-trained volunteers.

[61] *Doctrine and Covenants,* 101:2–6.

[62] *Doctrine and Covenants,* 105:9.

on their own shoulders and indicated that their timetable was indefinitely postponed because of it.

While there remains provision for military action and self-defense, both individually and collectively in Mormon scripture, actual warfare is the last resort: "I do not require at their hands to fight the battles of Zion."[63] The message of the post–Jackson County and Zion's Camp revelations is, in essence, "to renounce war and proclaim peace." They were not to go to war unless specifically commanded, and then only in a defensive posture. They were to be agents of peace: "Establish peace," "sue for peace," and "proclaim peace" were their instructions.[64] Not even the so-called Zion's Camp revelations condoned overt military action.[65] That some went against their own counsel and worked vengeance and violence was detrimental to their own cause and contributed to their difficulties. The overwhelming emphasis of the Missouri era, at least in Mormon scripture, is one of forgiveness, repentance, and proclaiming the gospel.

After the debacles in Missouri their revelations speak much "concerning the laws of the land" and that they "should observe to do all things whatsoever I command them" and to "befriend the law which is the constitutional law of the land" of seeking political redress for injustices, of continuously purchasing properties in the future, of seeking honorable men for public office—in short, of utilizing existing political systems at all levels of government to accomplish honorable aims.[66] Contrary to the argument that the tone of Mormonism became theocratic and extra-American, there developed a sense of working within the system. Whereas prior to the Jackson County confrontations, Mormon theology spoke of leaving Babylon and establishing Zion and a new kingdom of God in western Missouri independent of surrounding social and political realities, there developed afterward a tone not of surrender or abandonment of these aims but one closer to reconciliation, of gradual assimilation, of partnering with the United States and its representatives.[67] And as for fighting, "I do not require at their hands to fight the battles of Zion; for . . . I will fight your battles."[68] If Mormonism entered Missouri primarily as a religious ideal, it left it more mature politically. And from

[63] *Doctrine and Covenants,* 98:28–33; *Doctrine and Covenants,* 105:14.

[64] *Doctrine and Covenants,* 98:33; *Doctrine and Covenants,* 105:38–40.

[65] *Doctrine and Covenants,* 103 and 105.

[66] *Doctrine and Covenants,* 98:4–5.

[67] *Doctrine and Covenants,* 98 and 134.

[68] *Doctrine and Covenants,* 105:14.

this school of hard knocks would come efforts to establish a Nauvoo Legion within the existing parameters of American law and justice.

"A Haven for Contemplation and Reflection"

With Smith and several other Church leaders arrested and in jail awaiting trial for alleged treason against the state, the die was cast and their course now clear. Under the direction of Brigham Young,[69] the Latter-day Saints began to seek safety from the rising fury. Their trail of tears across Missouri to Quincy, Illinois, in the icy winter of 1839 is a tragedy in American history. Young summarized the scene as follows:

> We had entered into a covenant to see the poor Latter-day Saints all moved out of Missouri to Illinois, that they might be delivered out of the hands of such vile persecutors, and we spared no pains to accomplish this object until the Lord gave us the desires of our heart. We had the last company of the poor with us that could be removed. Bros. P. P. Pratt[70] and Morris Phelps[71] were in prison, and we had to leave them for a season. We sent a wagon after Bro. Yokum, who had been so dreadfully mutilated in the Haun's Mill massacre that he could not be moved. The covenant was fulfilled. And so was Gov. Boggs's extermination order.[72]

The forced confinement of Joseph Smith and several of his colleagues in Liberty Jail from December 1838 until their escape in April 1839 will forever rank as one of the most poignant, revealing interludes in early Mormon history. The prisoners spent almost five months enduring cold, filth, rotten food, solitude, and what Smith described as "grates and screeching iron doors, dirty straw couches, and nauseous smells."[73] Languishing in the dark and squalor of a

[69] Brigham Young (1801–77) served as a chaplain and lieutenant general in the Nauvoo Legion; President of the Church of Jesus Christ of Latter-day Saints, 1847–77.

[70] Parley P. Pratt (1807–57) was ordained an apostle in 1835; editor and publisher of the *Millennial Star;* assistant chaplain in the Nauvoo Legion.

[71] Morris Charles Phelps (1805–76) was imprisoned with Church leaders in Richmond, Missouri; escaped from Columbia Jail in Boone County, Missouri; captain and first lieutenant in the Nauvoo Legion.

[72] "Journal History of the Church," April 26, 1839, as cited in Hartley, "Missouri's 1838 Extermination Order," 23–24.

[73] See Jessee, "Walls, Grates, and Screeking Iron Doors," 19–25.

damp and sickening jailhouse, yet innocent of the crime he was charged with and awaiting trial for alleged treason against the state, Smith looked inward. As historian Leonard Arrington suggested, Smith, free as he was from the daily business of running the Church, "had uninterrupted time to think out the wider implication of the Latter-day movement. The Liberty Jail experience brought him to ponder his course, to synthesize ideas, to formulate goals, and to communicate in an unhurried manner with the Lord."[74] And as another scholar has written: "Liberty Jail was a spiritual watershed for Joseph Smith. He left jail a different man from the one who entered it. His own spiritual depths were plumbed, and a deeper understanding gained."[75]

Owing to the extent that Smith was the inspiration for the Nauvoo Legion, or at least partly responsible for it, an attempt to understand his feelings and sentiments is relevant to our study. Out of Liberty Jail came a new blueprint of action and a reshaping of attitude; a powerful combination of emotion, inspiration, and resolve; a careful reassessment of the state of his people; and a spirit of fiery indignation on the one hand, tempered with patience and forgiveness on the other. Smith penned,

> But oh! The unrelenting hand! The inhumanity and murderous disposition of this people! It shocks all nature; it beggars and defies all description; it is a tale of woe; a lamentable tale; yea a sorrowful tale; too much to tell; too much for contemplation; too much for human beings; it cannot be found among the heathens; it cannot be found among the nations where kings and tyrants are enthroned; it cannot be found among the savages of the wilderness; yea, and I think it cannot be found among the wild and ferocious beasts of the forest.[76]

Such attitudes would profoundly affect his views on the military and the future use of force. Touched by a grace that filled him with calmness and relative cheer, he reflected upon the injustices committed against his people while admitting to their own faults; saw room for his own improvement and the need to chasten his followers; and prayed for time and opportunity to reveal to his people more of the spiritual insights he had come to understand.

---

[74] Arrington, "Church Leaders in Liberty Jail," 23.

[75] Garrett, "Seven Letters from Liberty," 198.

[76] *History of the Church,* 3:290.

From start to finish his indignation against Missouri remained constant. Clearly he saw the conflict in Missouri in black and white, believing that they were an unjustly persecuted people, and he railed against his Missouri oppressors as "the most beastly set of men that the earth can boast of[, who] . . . steal to plunder to starve and to exterminate and burn the houses of the Mormons."[77] This attitude intensified as the weary winter wore on. The "conduct of the mob, the murders committed at hawns [Haun's] mill, and the exterminating order of the Governor, and the one-sided rascally proceedings of the Legislature [have] damned the state of Missouri to all eternity."[78]

And as incensed as Smith was with Missouri, he was only slightly less critical of the United States government and its supposed constitutional safeguards. "If these transactions had taken place among barbarians, under the authority of a despot, or in a nation, where certain religion is established according to law . . . than there might have been some shadow of defense offered," he wrote in November 1839. "But can we realize that in a land which is the cradle of liberty and equal rights . . . yea, in this land, a mob, regardless of those laws, for which so much blood has been spilled, dead to every feeling of virtue and patriotism . . . fell upon a people whose religious faith was different from their own . . . [It is] a tragedy, which has no parallel in modern, and hardly in ancient times."[79] And again, writing just before his escape, he asked, "But where is liberty? Where is humanity? Where is patriotism? Where has the genius of the pedestal of the laws and constitution of our boasted country fled? Are they not slain victims at the feet of prejudice, to gratify the malice of a certain class of men?"[80]

By March 1839, his sense of injustice had crystallized into a concrete plan of action. He now urged his people to seek reparations, to gather

> up a knowledge of all the facts and sufferings and abuses put upon them by the people of this state and also of all the property and amount of damages which they have sustained. . . . And perhaps a committee can be appointed to find out these things and to take statements and affidavits and also to gather up the libelous publications that are afloat . . . that we may not only publish to all the world

[77] *Personal Writings of Joseph Smith*, 418.
[78] *Personal Writings of Joseph Smith*, 433.
[79] *Personal Writings of Joseph Smith*, 481.
[80] *Personal Writings of Joseph Smith*, 457.

> but present them to the heads of government in all their dark and hellish hugh [hue]. . . . These should then be attended to with great earnestness.[81]

There is another side, however, to this hurtful equation, a painful recognition that his people were not without blame, and that as their leader he had more to learn. It is true that he attributed much of their distress to apostates: "Renegades, Mormon dissenters are running through the world and spreading various foul and libelous reports against us thinking thereby to gain the friendship of the world. . . . Such characters God hates we cannot love them the world hates them and we sometimes think the devil ought to be ashamed of them."[82] Specifically referring to the likes of George Hinkle, William W. Phelps, Sampson Avard, William E. McLellin, John and David Whitmer, and even Oliver Cowdery and Martin Harris "whose cloak of hypocrisy was not sufficient to shield them or to hold them up in the hour of trouble," he condemned such men as trucebreakers and despisers, traitors and tyrants, and the cause of so much affliction.[83]

Aside from his enemies, much of what Smith wrote while in jail seems pointed at the Latter-day Saints themselves. "Brethren, from henceforth let truth and righteousness prevail," he pleaded in yet another letter, this one written in December 1838,

> and abound in you and in all things be temperate, abstain from every appearance of evil, drunkenness, and profane language, and from every thing which is unrighteous and unholy; also from enmity and hatred, and covetousness and from unholy desires. Be honest one with another, for it seemeth that some have come short of these things and some have been uncharitable and have manifested greediness because of their debts. . . . Zion shall yet live though she seemeth to be dead. Remember that whatsoever measure you meet out to others it shall be measured to you again.[84]

And in unforgettable language, he reprimanded some of his fellow leaders in no uncertain terms:

> Behold, there are many called, but few are chosen. And why are they not chosen?
>
> Because their hearts are set so much upon the things of this world,

---

[81] *Personal Writings of Joseph Smith*, 443.
[82] *Personal Writings of Joseph Smith*, 419.
[83] *Personal Writings of Joseph Smith*, 421.
[84] *Personal Writings of Joseph Smith*, 422.

> and aspire to the honors of men, that they do not learn this one lesson—
>
> That the rights of the priesthood are inseparably connected with the powers of heaven, and that the powers of heaven cannot be controlled nor handled only upon the principles of righteousness.
>
> That they may be conferred upon us, it is true; but when we undertake to cover our sins, or to gratify our pride, our vain ambition, or to exercise control or dominion or compulsion upon the souls of the children of men, in any degree of unrighteousness, behold, the heavens withdraw themselves; the Spirit of the Lord is grieved; and when it is withdrawn, Amen to the priesthood or authority of that man. . . . No power or influence can or ought to be maintained by virtue of the priesthood, only by persuasion, by long-suffering, by gentleness and meekness, and by love unfeigned. . . . Let thy bowels also be full of charity towards all men.[85]

In short, he believed that as bad as their Missouri enemies had been, his followers were also at fault.

Liberty Jail showed him that he was not yet "like Job," that he had much to learn, including greater patience, and that "all these things shall give [him] experience, and shall be for [his] good."[86] He also had time to consider the excesses of his own people and the stark possibility that as their leader, he may not have given as strong and careful leadership at Far West as he should have. Certainly they would learn from their mistakes. "And again I would further suggest the impropriety of the organization of bands or companies by covenants or oaths by penalties or secrecies," he wrote just a fortnight before his escape, "but let the time past of our experience and sufferings by the wickedness of Doctor [Sampson] Avard suffice and let our covenant be that of the everlasting covenant as is contained in Holy Writ and the things that God hath revealed unto us. Pure friendship always becomes weakened the very moment you undertake to make it stronger by penal oaths and secrecy. . . . Our religion . . . gives scope to the mind which enables us to conduct ourselves with greater liberality towards one another."[87] Troubled by the excesses of the Danites, much of which he now repudiated, as prophet-leader he knew that he bore some of the responsibility for

---

85 *Doctrine and Covenants,* 121:34–37, 41, 45.

86 *Doctrine and Covenants,* 122:7.

87 *Personal Writings of Joseph Smith,* 405–406.

their doings and determined that in the future Mormon military and defense movements must abide by the law.[88]

Yet if he remained indignant, Smith was not vindictive. A spirit of vengeance, if ever in him, clashed with his native cheery temperament. He tried hard to instill such an attitude among others. "Do not have any feelings of enmity towards any son or daughter of Adam," he counseled in March 1839. "We must not take it in our hands to avenge our wrongs. 'Vengeance is mine,' saith the Lord, 'and I will have no fears.'"[89] He sought more than a mere change of heart—he sought a reformation among his people. "We would beseech you," he wrote, "to bear with the infirmities of the weak, and at the same time exhort one another to a reformation, both teachers and taught, male and female, so that honesty, sobriety, candor, solemnity, plainness, meekness, virtue may characterize us from henceforth, and that we be like children without malice, guile or hypocrisy."[90]

This sentiment only intensified as time wore on. Writing to his wife Emma on April 4, 1839, he penned, "Do not be self-willed, neither harbor a spirit of revenge: and again remember that he who is my enemy is yours also. . . . All feelings of dissatisfaction [are] far from my heart, I wish to act upon that principle of generosity, that will acquit itself in the presence of . . . God."[91] Little wonder that

---

[88] If Joseph Smith did not know the full extent of Danite excesses before he was incarcerated, he came to know them afterward. Six weeks after his arrest, he summarized the Danite situation as he understood it. "We have learned also since we have been in prison that many false and pernicious things which were calculated to lead the saints far astray and to do great injury have been taught by Dr. Avard as coming from the Presidency . . . which the presidency never knew of being taught in the church by any body until after they were made prisoners . . . the presidency were ignorant as well as innocent of these things." Smith, *Papers of Joseph Smith*, 420. See *History of the Church*, 3:321; and Baugh, "A Call to Arms," 42–43.

[89] *Personal Writings of Joseph Smith*, 428.

[90] Smith et al., "A History of the Persecution of the Church," *Times and Seasons* 1, no. 7 (May 1840): 103.

[91] *Personal Writings of Joseph Smith*, 465. No better example of this spirit of charity likely exists than in his free and open forgiveness of W. W. Phelps, one whose betrayal in part led to Smith's imprisonment: "Come on dear brother, since the war is past, For Friends at first are friends again at last." *Personal Writings of Joseph Smith*, 510. Likewise others, particularly the Twelve, taught similar principles: "Many of you brethren, with those whose souls are now beneath the alter, are crying for vengeance of heaven to rest upon the heads of their devoted murderers and saying 'how long O Lord . . . dost thou not judge and avenge our blood[?]' . . . Dear Brethren, (*continued, next page*)

some have noted "a moderating Christian influence in the Liberty Jail letters."[92] Likewise others, particularly the Twelve, taught similar principles: "Many of you brethren, with those whose souls are now beneath the altar, are crying for vengeance of heaven to rest upon the heads of their devoted murderers and saying 'how long O Lord . . . dost thou not judge and avenge our blood[?]'. . . . Dear Brethren, we should remind you of this thing, and although you have had indignities, insults and injuries heaped upon you . . . we would say, be patient. . . . Do not breathe vengeance upon your oppressors, but leave the case in the hands of the Lord."[93] Joseph Smith's brother Hyrum, a fellow prisoner, wrote "Look then at the things which are before, and not at those which are behind."[94]

Smith also sensed that while he had much to say, there might be little time in which to say it. "I want the blessing once more to lift my voice in the midst of the Saints," he wrote Presendia Buell in March 1839:

> I would pour out my soul to God for their instruction. It has been the plan of the Devil to hamper me and distress me from the beginning, to keep me from explaining myself to them and I never had the opportunity to give them the plan that God has revealed to me for many have run without being sent crying tidings my Lord and have done much injury to the Church . . . But trials will only give us that knowledge to understand the minds of the Ancients.[95]

Whether or not Lucy Mack Smith recalled accurately what her son told her in Ohio—that he had "a promise of life for five years and

we should remind you of this thing, and although you have had indignities, insults and injuries heaped upon you . . . we would say, be patient. . . . Do not breathe vengeance upon your oppressors, but leave the case in the hands of the Lord." Young et al., "To the Elders of the Church," *Times and Seasons* 1, no. 1 (November 1839): 575. See *History of the Church,* 3:393. And from his brother Hyrum, a fellow prisoner: "Look then at the things which are before, and not at those which are behind." Smith, "To the Saints Scattered Abroad," *Times and Seasons* 1, no. 2 (December 1839):24.

[92] Carmack, "Missouri Era," 4.

[93] Young et al., "To the Elders of the Church," *Times and Seasons* 1, no. 1 (November 1839): 575. See *History of the Church,* 3:393.

[94] Hyrum Smith, "To the Saints Scattered Abroad," *Times and Seasons* 1, no. 2 (December 1839): 24.

[95] *Personal Writings of Joseph Smith,* 427. Fawn Brodie takes another view of such writings, seeing plural marriage as part of the intent of this communication. See Brodie, *No Man Knows My History,* 253.

they cannot kill me until that time is expired,"—it seems apparent that upon leaving Missouri, Smith felt his time was limited. Historian Ronald K. Esplin is likely correct in his summation:

> Joseph Smith's Missouri imprisonment, from November 1838 into April 1839, had a profound impact on his sense of urgency about completing his life's work. . . . [He] did not emerge from Liberty Jail feeling invulnerable. Just as firmly as he believed he would be delivered, he apparently believed he would not live to see forty. . . . it is probable that Liberty Jail brought for the first time a conviction that his allotted time was both fixed and short.[96]

Conclusion

The Mormon losses in Missouri marked a turning point in their history. They had tried to establish a new Zion in a place most difficult and in a culture most unreceptive. They had tried to do so at a time in American history that teemed with riot and insurrection. And they had tried to do it as a people not fully prepared for so difficult a task. In the process they learned not to shun the legal recourses available to them but to take fuller advantage of them in ways they had never before considered.

Reluctant to respond in kind to the violence heaped upon them in Jackson County, the Mormons first reverted to seeking government assistance for their plight. Although Zion's Camp failed to persuade Missouri officials to call out the militia to help restore lost properties, it brought attention to their plight and unified and trained many of the Latter-day Saints. Later, in Daviess and Caldwell Counties, they took full advantage of the militia laws of Missouri and organized themselves into a county militia. Others, in a shameful spirit of vengeance, organized a force of Danites that came to be an embarrassment to the Church and its generally law-abiding membership. By the time of Joseph Smith's confinement in Liberty Jail, he was well aware of their legal recourse as well as their excesses and concluded to reestablish Zion temporarily, at least within the legal confines of America. From his experiences in Missouri, he learned lessons that would set a standard for future military and political activity in Illinois.

[96] Esplin, "The Significance of Nauvoo for Latter-day Saints," 26.

FIGURE 5. View of Nauvoo, 1848–50.
Artist unknown. Oil on canvas.
Courtesy of Church History Library.

3

Founding of the Nauvoo Legion

"It will enable us to show our attachment to the state and nation as a people."

JOSEPH SMITH, JANUARY 15, 1841

As to the military station I hold, and the cause of my holding it is as follows: when we came here, the state required us to bear arms, and do military duty according to the law, and as the church had just been driven from the state of Missouri, and robbed of all their property and arms, they were poor and destitute of arms, [and] they were liable to be fined for not doing duty, when they had not arms to do it with. They came to me for advice and I advised them to organize themselves into independent companies and demand arms of the state; this they did. . . . I then told the saints that though I was clear from military duty by law, in consequence of lameness in one of my legs, yet I would set the example, and would do duty myself, they said they were willing to do duty, if they would be formed into an independent company and I could be at their head; this is the origin of the Nauvoo Legion and of my holding office of lieutenant general . . . all the power that I desire or have sought to obtain has been the enjoyment of the constitutional privilege, for which my fathers shed their blood, of living in peace in the society of my wife and children, and enjoying the society of my friends, and that religious liberty, which is the right of every American citizen, of worshiping according to the dictates of his conscience and the revelations of God.[1]

JOSEPH SMITH, 1843

[1] Woodruff, *Wilford Woodruff's Journal,* July 4, 1843, 2:258.

NOW THAT THE MILITARY FOUNDATION IN THE UNITED STATES generally and Illinois particularly for the rise of the Nauvoo Legion has been laid, and the many factors that led to a variety of Mormon military responses in Missouri identified, this chapter will focus on the actual establishment of the Legion in Nauvoo by focusing on several key questions. Was Joseph Smith the founder of the Nauvoo Legion or was it the brainchild of that militant newcomer John C. Bennett? Or was it a combination of both? Who else may have contributed to its formation? Were there other military options besides the Legion or its precursors? What initial form did it take? And why were the efforts at establishing it so successful?

Smith's unexpected and unceremonious arrival in Quincy, Illinois, after escaping from Liberty Jail in Missouri makes for fascinating reading. Wrote Dimick Huntington on April 22, 1839,

> I saw Joseph land from the Quincy ferry boat about 8 oc. in the morning. He was drest in an old pair of boots full of holes, pants torn, tucked inside of boots, blue cloak with collar turned up, a wide brim black hat, rim soped down, not been shaved for some time, looked pale and haggard. I . . . rode down at the request of Emma to enquire the news, if any, from the west. When I got within about 16' of him he raised his head. I explained, My God is it you Bro. Joes? He raised his hand and stopped me saying Hush, Hush, He then asked where is my family. I told him they were 4 miles east at Judge Clevelands in a room I had provided for them. I asked him if he wished to see his father and mother as they were in Quincy. He said no, it would be too great a shock, they are old and cannot bear it. Take me to my family as quick as you can. In passing through the back streets of Quincy a number of men knew him. On arriving at the house where his family was Emma knew him as he was dismounting from his horse. She met him half way to the gate. Joseph not knowing the universal friendly feelings that existed in Quincy, was fearful he might be arrested again.[2]

After two weeks of recovery from his Missouri ordeal, Smith spoke for the first time in several months to his followers at an outdoor conference in Quincy's old Presbyterian campground. "He stood for an unusual length of time without uttering a word," Edward Stevenson remembered:

[2] Dimick B. Huntington statement, cited in Miller and Miller, *Nauvoo*, 26.

> His soul was full of emotion and it seemed as though relief could not be uttered only with a flood of tears. He looked calm, however. . . . He then said, "To look over this congregation of Latter-day Saints who have been driven from their homes and still in good faith as pilgrims in a strange land, and to realize that my life has been spared to behold your faces again seemed to me so great a pleasure."[3]

Smith's reunion with his family and friends brought more than tears and pent-up emotion; with it came a steely resolve that everything possible would now have to be done to prevent such a tragedy from ever happening again. The Mormons would learn from their Missouri mistakes. If it meant surrendering their dream of a Missouri Zion for a time, so be it. If it meant providing themselves with every protection under the law for a new city of Zion, why not? If it meant distancing themselves from the excesses of the Danites, so much the better. And if it meant defending themselves militarily against future attacks from their enemies, then that eventuality, too, would be explored. Security and protection were not a contrived option—they were a necessity.

The Mormon prophet brought to Quincy a desire to accomplish a great many things. He prevailed over the opinions of many of his followers who, mindful of their recent sufferings at Far West, had favored scattering the faithful in small communities in Pike, Adams, and other nearby counties. He believed that their future safety lay in numbers—a population concentrated in a single large community, a central gathering place for a religion which, for too long, had been on the run. After purchasing lands on long-term credit from Hugh White and Isaac Galland, he selected Commerce City, Hancock County, Illinois, some fifty miles north of Quincy, and in May 1839 began to settle his people on a great sweeping bend of the Mississippi River.

The following summer he spent much of his time dictating and preserving the long-neglected history of the Church, selecting hymns for a new hymnal, dealing with an appalling outbreak of malaria among his followers, draining swampland along the river banks, instructing the Twelve Apostles on their upcoming mission, and attending to various family matters.

[3] "Journal of Edward Stevenson," 139.

"Shall I See So Many Perish and Not Seek Redress?"

Among Smith's first priorities was to seek redress and compensation from the government of the United States for the loss of life, property, and liberties the Latter-day Saints had suffered in Missouri. Just when and where Smith decided that he should go to Washington, D.C., is not clear. While still in Liberty Jail, his counselor, Sidney Rigdon,[4] had determined to make the trip, sick or otherwise, and began collecting letters of introduction in preparation from such men as Robert Lucas, governor of the Iowa Territory. In late May, Joseph and Hyrum Smith wrote extensive letters to accompany Rigdon, explaining their perceived wrongs and sufferings in Missouri from as early as 1831.[5] No doubt Rigdon postponed leaving because of his enduring sickness. Consequently, the Church conference voted to have Joseph Smith and Elias Higbee[6] accompany Rigdon as soon as circumstances would permit.[7] Three weeks later, armed with sheaves of affidavits and petitions, Smith, Rigdon, and Higbee departed for Washington, along with Orrin Porter Rockwell.[8] "It will be a long and lonesome time during my absence from you," Smith wrote to his wife Emma, "but shall I see so many perish and not seek redress?"[9]

Weak and emaciated, Rigdon soon learned what Smith knew instinctively—that he was too sick to make the journey, at least while Congress was in session. Rigdon stayed behind at Springfield, Illinois, to recover—with Rockwell by his side—before continuing on. By the time Rigdon had recovered sufficiently to travel, his leader's work was all but done.[10]

[4] Sidney Rigdon (1793–1876) was a Campbellite preacher, tanner, fellow prisoner in Liberty Jail, and judge advocate of the Nauvoo Legion. See Van Wagoner, *Sidney Rigdon.*

[5] *History of the Church,* 3:368–74.

[6] Elias Higbee (1795–1843) lobbied in the nation's capital for redress of Missouri's wrongs against the Latter-day Saints; guard in the Nauvoo Legion; member of the Nauvoo Temple Committee.

[7] *History of the Church,* 4:13.

[8] Orrin Porter Rockwell (1815–78) cattle rancher; bodyguard for Joseph Smith; private in the cavalry of the Nauvoo Legion. See Schindler, *Orrin Porter Rockwell.*

[9] As quoted in Brodie, *No Man Knows My History,* 259.

[10] One wonders whether taking Sidney Rigdon along was a good idea anyway, considering his reputation as a firebrand in Missouri and his determination to disgrace and disenfranchise the state of Missouri. Left to his own devices, the combustible Rigdon likely would have alienated many in Congress and done more harm than good.

If Joseph Smith's six months in Missouri jails had been a time of forced reflection, his six months in the East appear to be a time of keen disappointment and utter frustration. Meeting with President Martin Van Buren on November 29, 1839—one day after his arrival in the nation's capital—and apparently again in February 1840, Smith ran square into party politics as well as the difficult issue of states' rights. Refusing to interfere with what he regarded as purely a Missouri matter, Van Buren dismissed Smith's petitions out of hand, to which the Mormon leader responded, "I became satisfied there was little use for me to tarry, to press the just claims of the Saints . . . and stayed but a few days."[11] Manifesting less than a benevolent attitude on the way home, Smith "did not fail to proclaim the iniquity and insolence of Martin Van Buren toward [himself] and an injured people," and declared, "[M]ay he never be elected again."[12] By the time he reached Nauvoo on March 4, 1840, almost a year since escaping from jail, he had had time to put events in perspective. As to his views on the political process, he said, "I discovered that popular clamor and personal aggrandizement were the ruling principles of those in authority, and my heart faints within me when I see, by the visions of the Almighty, the end of this nation, if she continues to disregard the cries and petitions of her virtuous citizens."[13]

Soon after his return, in a spirit of exasperation, Smith wrote the following "Memorial to the High Council of the Church," in which he signaled his desire to free himself as much as possible from temporal duties, though in truth he found it hard to delegate such matters:

> After the escape of your Memorialist from his enemies, he took such steps as has secured to the Church the present locations. . . . Under the then existing circumstances, your Memorialist had necessarily to engage in the temporalities of the Church, which he has had to attend to until the present time;—That your Memorialist feels it a duty to which he owes to God, as well as to the Church, to give his attention more particularly to those things connected with the spiritual welfare of the Saints . . . verily believes that the time has now come, when he should devote himself exclusively to those things which relate to the spiritualities of the Church, and commence the

[11] *History of the Church,* 4:80.
[12] *History of the Church,* 4:89.
[13] *History of the Church,* 4:89.

> work of translating the Egyptian records, the Bible, and wait upon the Lord for such revelation as may be suited to the conditions and circumstances of the Church.[14]

Although he would never disassociate himself from the many pressing political and financial matters of Nauvoo, on account of both general circumstance and his personal disposition, he knew that he had to make the effort to do so. The future doctrinal identity and survival of his Church were at stake.

Well before the formation of the Nauvoo Legion, the Latter-day Saints were enlisting in existing nearby militias, both to obey the laws of the state and to obtain needed arms. Many of them, pending further directions, had already joined the Illinois Fifty-ninth Regiment of Hancock County—a "light infantry" officially organized in 1835—almost as soon as they had taken up residence in the county.[15] By 1840 they constituted a significant percentage of the seventy-eight men belonging to it; Don Carlos Smith, Smith's younger brother, served as its lieutenant colonel.[16] Captain of the "Nauvoo Company of Light Infantry" of the Fifty-ninth was Albert P. Rockwood.[17] In September 1840, their formal request to Governor Thomas Carlin, commander in chief of the state militia, called for "88 muskets, bayonets and accouterments—the company being organized according to law."[18] Meanwhile over two hundred Mormons living across the river had also enlisted in the Iowa militia.[19] And as their numbers

[14] Memorial of Joseph Smith, Jr., to the High Council of the Church, June 18, 1840. *History of the Church,* 4:136–37.

[15] " 'Militia Regiments' Ledger."

[16] Among the many other Latter-day Saints serving in the Fifty-ninth Regiment of Hancock County were William and Wilson Law, Albert P. Rockwood, James Guyman, Amos Perry, Titus Billings, Charles C. Rich, Francis Higbee, Hiram Kimball, and Thomas Rich. See "Commission Records of the Illinois State Militia," 12:368–71.

[17] Certificate of election, July 4, 1840, in the "Papers of Albert Perry Rockwood, 1840–1845."

[18] Don Carlos Smith, lieutenant colonel Fifty-ninth, to Thomas Carlin, September 27, 1840, Executive Papers, "Governors Correspondence, 1840 Military Affairs,"480. There is some confusion as to the date of the organization of the Fifty-ninth (Hancock) Regiment. If organized in 1835, it was the Latter-day Saints who, needing arms and anxious to fulfill their legal duty, revitalized it.

[19] For example, Joseph B. Noble was commissioned a Second Lieutenant of the First Company of Mounted Dragoons in the Fourth Regiment of the First Brigade in the First Division of the Iowa Territory on July 29, 1841. Joseph B. Noble Collection.

continued to grow in Nauvoo, their representation far outpaced the Fifty-ninth's capacity. To accommodate the rapidly rising population and the demands of the law, either more county regiments or independent companies would have to be formed.

"Avenge Them Speedily"

Early in July 1840, Missouri raiders captured Benjamin Boyce, James Allred, and Noah Rogers and forcibly took them to Missouri, where they were whipped and beaten. This sent a chill throughout the Nauvoo community and prompted the Mormons to appeal to the governor for "protection from such unjust and before unheard of oppression."[20] At the same time, Missouri Governor Lilburn W. Boggs, infuriated less by Smith's escape from jail than by his recent charges in Washington against Missouri, began to step up his efforts to extradite the Mormon leader and bring him back to Missouri to stand trial.[21] Such difficulties underscored the pressing need to establish Nauvoo on a firm basis with clear legal protection, and to pursue and clarify the matter of a local police force and militia.

It was at this critical moment that John C. Bennett burst upon the scene. Destined to bring both short-term gain and long-term pain to the Saints, Bennett was initially greeted with open arms and thankful hearts. The first appearance of his name in the [Nauvoo] *Times and Seasons* in September 1840 was as secretary of a planning committee of medical personnel which had called for a "Medical Convention in Illinois" in Springfield later that year.[22] At the time Bennett was probably better known as quartermaster general of the Illinois State Militia—in charge of the disposition of arms, equipment, and payments to local county militias across the state. A physician who approved of the Mormon choice of a swampy riverbed

---

[20] Higbee, "Preamble," *Times and Seasons* 1, no. 9 (July 1840): 142–43. The Mormons were not, of course, entirely without blame. Some had tried to recoup some of their losses by raiding Missouri properties. Others were involved in counterfeiting rings and other forms of thievery not becoming members of the Church. Meanwhile, as Donna Hill argues, "the Missourians were blaming every incident of theft, however remote, upon the Mormons." Hill, *Joseph Smith,* 275.

[21] Hill, *Joseph Smith,* 274.

[22] Bennett et al., "Medical Convention of Illinois," *Times and Seasons* 1, no. 11 (September 1840): 174–75.

FIGURE 6. Gen. John C. Bennett, Doctor of Medicine. By A. Clark; engraving by O. Peltono. *From* The History of the Saints; or, An Exposé of Joe Smith and Mormonism, *by John C. Bennett (Boston: Leland and Whiting, 1842).*

settlement, a high-ranking officer in the state militia who opposed any efforts to extradite the Mormon leader, and a proven, professional lobbyist who knew state legislators and the intricacies of composing and passing difficult pieces of legislation, Bennett, whatever his faults, possessed that needed mix of talents and contacts to aid the Mormon cause. And Smith, absorbed with other pressing needs and priorities, cheerfully gave him the benefit of the doubt. "He has been one of the instruments in effecting our safety and deliverance from the unjust persecutions and demands of the authorities of Missouri," Smith would write of his new ally. "He is a man of enterprise, extensive acquirements, and of independent mind, and is calculated to be a great blessing to our community."[23]

Born in 1804 Bennett had forged a checkered career long before coming to Nauvoo. An ambitious wanderluster, he had a reputation of being a slick promoter of various community interests, which put his own name in lights. As Andrew C. Skinner has noted, "Many of his lofty positions really turned out to be manifestations of his marked interest in entrepreneurism, the promotion of new causes and self-

[23] *Times and Seasons,* January 1841, 2:273–74.

aggrandizement."[24] In one community after another, he was first welcomed and acclaimed, then soon disgraced and driven out of town. His interests in medicine (midwifery in particular) and in medical instruction had prompted him to petition state legislatures in Ohio, Virginia, and Indiana for the incorporation of medical schools and universities with himself as principal, but often without the support or knowledge of those with whom he worked. In December 1832, for example, while trying to incorporate Alexander and Thomas Campbell's Christian College in New Albany, Indiana, he had proceeded without their support or consent. Although the school was established and Bennett appointed as chancellor, Alexander Campbell had heard "nothing of this project until it was consummated"; consequently, the Christian Disciples renounced the entire initiative. The Campbellites more or less drove Bennett out of town, declaring him "a false brother, a person of no solid learning, and of very bad morals."[25]

Undaunted and unbowed, Bennett the following year lobbied the Ohio legislature for a university in Franklin County and later for Willoughby Medical University near Kirtland, Ohio. Between 1835 and 1838 he drifted in and out of six different localities establishing various schools and departments. Those who knew him well began to call him a "getter up of colleges," a "puff master general," a "diploma peddler," and a "bold bad man."[26]

When he was not pursuing his medical interests, Bennett immersed himself in his alternative passion—state militias and the uniforms and trappings of military life. In 1835 he joined the 104th Regiment of Pennsylvania as a surgeon. In Buffalo, New York, he tried to establish the Hocking Valley Dragoons in late 1837.[27] The following year he removed to White County, Illinois, where, in February 1839, he joined with others in successfully petitioning the legislature to create the Invincible Dragoons (and Flying Artillery), a company of the Second Division of the Illinois militia.[28] Two months

---

[24] Skinner, "John C. Bennett," 250.

[25] Smith, *Saintly Scoundrel,* 17, 25.

[26] Smith, *Saintly Scoundrel,* 32.

[27] Smith, *Saintly Scoundrel,* 46.

[28] Smith, *Saintly Scoundrel,* 47. See also *Journal of the Senate of the Eleventh General Assembly,* 143, 154, 169, 194, 198, 249, 285. The politics of the passage of the bill creating the dragoons is not known, but it is certain that it encountered opposition. One vote was twenty for and fourteen against. There may have been opposition from the existing county regiment. The dragoons lasted until at least 1841.

later he was "duly elected to the office of Brigadier General" of the same dragoons but held that command for only a very short time.[29]

He was also part of a failed effort to persuade the state legislature to establish yet another, more grandiose, military body called the Illinois Legion. It appears that this may have been what he had once envisioned for the dragoons—a very large, combined force of all the militias in White, Edwards, and Wabash Counties.[30]

Bennett's work on the failed Illinois Legion bill introduced him to members of the legislative Committee on Military Affairs and to the politics involved, and it may have contributed to his July 1840 appointment as quartermaster general. Dismissed from this post soon afterwards for "bad character," he managed to stay just far enough ahead of those wise to his unsavory reputation.

It was likely not a sudden change of heart or religious transformation that spurred his interest in the Mormons. The fact is he had first heard of them in Ohio in 1832 from William E. McLellin and had read about them in the writings of both Alexander Campbell and Eber D. Howe. In the words of Bennett's biographer, "He viewed the Mormons as a great personal opportunity . . . in using [them], as he had the Methodists and Christian Disciples, to promote his eminence and enhance his power."[31] He even wrote to Church leaders when they were undergoing fierce persecution in Missouri, offering to come with all the aid he could muster in Illinois. His proposal was, however, rejected.[32]

Whatever his true motivations, Bennett found a waiting and willing audience in Nauvoo. His series of summer 1840 letters smack of

---

[29] Signed statement by James N. Berry, adjutant general, Illinois Militia, April 25, 1839. "Governor's Correspondence, 1837–1839." For reasons not clear, Bennett held this commanding post only a very short time and was succeeded by William Pickering, who was commissioned brigadier general on October 19, 1839. See the foregoing Illinois Militia officer and rank listings, and "Governor's Correspondence, 1837–1839."

[30] See draft of House Bill #213, "A Bill for an Act to Incorporate the Illinois Legion." Executive Papers, Governor's Correspondence, 1837–1839. See *Journal of the House of Representatives, Eleventh General Assembly,* February 5 and March 1, 1839. See also *Journal of the Senate of the Eleventh General Assembly,* January 6 and 9, 1839. The Senate rejected the bill on March 1, 1839.

[31] Smith, *Saintly Scoundrel,* 55–56.

[32] Roberts, *Comprehensive History of the Church,* 2:49. In Bennett's defense, his interest in military affairs was not in itself a bad thing. Others were doing much the same thing. And if Joseph Smith did not "see through" him early on, he was not alone. John Taylor, who was well acquainted with Bennett, said that "at one time he was a good man." *History of the Church* 5:81, as quoted in Skinner, "John C. Bennett," 253.

overbearing, if not brazen, self-promotion, and manifest at least an initial sympathy for the Mormon wrongs—the kind of words a wounded people were too easily prone and perhaps too gullible to accept. "It would be my deliberate advice to you," he admonished Smith,

> to concentrate all of your Church at one point. If Hancock county, with Commerce for its commercial emporium, is to be that point, well; fix upon it, and let us co-operate with a general concerted action. You can rely upon me in any event . . . I desire to be happy, and am fully satisfied that I can enjoy myself better with your people with my present views and feelings, than with any other.[33]

Choosing not to reveal the fact that he was about to be dismissed from his post as quartermaster general, three days later he pressed even harder: "It is with difficulty that I can forego [*sic*] the felicity of an immediate immersion into the true faith of your beloved people. My anxiety to be with you is daily increasing."[34] In response, Joseph Smith offered him a hand of friendship: "Although I have not the pleasure of your acquaintance . . . I have no doubt you would be of great service to this community . . . and . . . I should be disposed to give you a special invitation to come as early as possible."[35] Bennett eagerly arrived in Nauvoo in September 1840. A boarder in the Smith home for the next thirty-nine weeks, Bennett was soon baptized and became a fast friend of Smith and of his entire family.

Bennett wasted little time in making his extremist militant views known, especially in regard to making war. Writing in the *Times and Seasons* in September, he urged an offensive military response to avenge the Mormon sufferings in Missouri. "Missouri has long bathed her hands in crimson gore, and drunk the blood of the innocent," he argued in September 1840, in the first of several articles using terms the most militant Danites would have relished:

> She must now be checked in her wild and mad career. . . . She must be met . . . not only by the Mormon people, but by the states—and all the friends of liberty and equal rights should gird on their armour

[33] John C. Bennett to Joseph Smith, Jr., July 27, 1840, as cited in *History of the Church*, 4:168–69.

[34] John C. Bennett to Joseph Smith, Jr., July 30, 1840, as cited in *History of the Church*, 4:172.

[35] Joseph Smith to John C. Bennett, August 8, 1840, as cited in *History of the Church*, 4:177.

> and sware by the everlasting God that the sword shall not depart from the thigh, nor the buckler from the arm until the contest is ended! And shall not God avenge his own elect? . . . I tell you He will avenge them speedily. . . . I tell you God will avenge the wrongs of his people. . . . Missouri has hewn down the innocent and defenseless, it is true, but she is entirely destitute of military knowledge or prowess . . . the day of righteous retribution and the avenging of blood will not be procrastinated.
>
> Respectfully, JOAB, General in Israel.[36]

This theme of vengeance and retaliation is one he returned to again and again:

> Missouri wages war on the entire Mormon church . . . violates their women; shoots down and scalps their innocent, defenseless children; confiscates their property, and throws it to the four winds . . . and orders them all exterminated, murdered, butchered, by an infuriated, savage, fiendish, diabolical, infernal, Missouri mob of ruthless brigades . . . Missouri has too long bathed her hands in crimson gore, and drank the blood of the innocent; she must now be checked in her wild and mad career.[37]

Several weeks later, again publishing his comments in the *Times and Seasons,* he returned to the same theme, this time seeking a leading role for himself in the coming battles against Missouri: "The grievances of this people must be redressed, and my hand shall help to do it—should they have to reach to the highest court in heaven, dig to the lowest bowels of hell, or encompass the broad expanse of the universe of God, to consummate so desirable a result."[38]

If Bennett had had his way he would have mobilized an army to wreak vengeance on Missouri—with himself leading the charge. It would ever rankle him that the Latter-day Saints chose not to go to war. Considering Bennett's future role in berating the Mormons and blaming them for a scheme far less militant than the one he was proposing in 1840 (see chapter 8), his threatening words are of more than passing significance. However, it must be conceded that no

---

[36] Bennett, "Burglary! Treason! Arson!!! Murder!!!!" *Times and Seasons* 1, no. 11 (September 1840): 165–67.

[37] Ibid.

[38] John C. Bennett, *Times and Seasons 1, no. 12* (October 1840): 189–90.

one in Nauvoo—Joseph Smith included—discouraged Bennett's militant viewpoints; in fact, several seemed to encourage them.

"Every Power We Asked Has Been Granted"

Still crusading, Bennett spoke at the general conference of the Church in October 1840 when, in reference to the recent Missouri kidnappings, he called on "the brethren to stand by each other and resist every unlawful attempt at persecution."[39] The conference also appointed him to a blue-ribbon committee to draft a bill to incorporate the city of Nauvoo "and other purposes" and that he in particular "be appointed delegate, to urge the passage of such bill through the legislature."[40]

Bennett soon joined Almon W. Babbitt, Esq., in Springfield in time for the December convening of the Illinois legislature. A more persuasive and colorful personality than the often intoxicated Babbitt, Bennett relished his role as chief lobbyist for the Mormon cause.[41] Renewing his acquaintance with legislators on both sides of the aisle, including Stephen A. Douglas and Abraham Lincoln, Bennett saw the bill to charter the city of Nauvoo sail through both houses. It was ultimately ratified and approved on December 15, 1840, despite Senator Sidney H. Little's reservations over the "extraordinary militia clause," which he nonetheless viewed as "harmless." Eager to encourage new immigration and settlement to strengthen a nondescript state militia, and to court votes among the rising Mormon population, both Whig and Democratic politicians passed the measure with scant discussion or debate. As Robert Flanders has rightfully argued, "Its routine enactment seems natural considering the high optimism that prevailed in the state."[42]

---

[39] Joseph Smith, Jr., "Minutes of the General Conference of the Church of Jesus Christ of Latter-day Saints held Nauvoo, Hancock, Illinois, October 3, 1840," *Times and Seasons* 1, no. 12 (October 1840): 186.

[40] *History of the Church,* 4:205. Joseph Smith Jr., "Minutes of the General Conference of the Church of Jesus Christ of Latter-day Saints held Nauvoo, Hancock, Illinois, October 3, 1840," *Times and Seasons* 1, no. 12 (October 1840): 186. Other members of the committee included Joseph Smith and R. B. Thompson. Flanders asserts that "Bennett had already been at work on the charter and probably had it completed before the conference met." Flanders, *Nauvoo,* 96.

[41] For the most complete study of Almon W. Babbitt, see the unpublished manuscript "Seeking Glory."

[42] Flanders, *Nauvoo,* 96.

Commissioned to secure one charter, Bennett returned in December with three: one for the city of Nauvoo, a second for the University of Nauvoo, and a third for the Nauvoo Legion.[43] The Nauvoo Legion Charter reads thus:

> The City Council may organize the inhabitants of said city subject to military duty, into a body of independent military men, to be called the "Nauvoo Legion," the Court Martial of which shall be composed of the commissioned officers of said legion, and constitute the law-making department, with full power and authority to make, ordain, establish, and execute all such laws and ordinances as may be considered necessary for the benefit, government, and regulation of said Legion; provided said Court Martial shall pass no law or act, repugnant to, or inconsistent with, the Constitution of the United States, or of this State; and provided also that the officers of the Legion shall be commissioned by the Governor of the State. The said Legion shall perform the same amount of military duty as is now or may be hereafter required of the regular militia of the State, and shall be at the disposal of the Mayor in executing the laws and ordinances of the city corporation, and the laws of the State, and at the disposal of the Governor for the public defense, and the execution of the laws of the State or of the United States, and shall be entitled to their proportion of the public arms; and provided also, that said Legion shall be exempt from all other military duty.[44]

Considering Bennett's close contacts with Smith before leaving for Springfield, it is reasonable to conclude that the two men had discussed the benefits of such a military force, although they may have differed on its intent.[45] While we may never know for certain who was the primary inspiration behind the Nauvoo Legion, Bennett likely was a driving force. Having established several other mili-

[43] See Bennett and Cope, "A City on a Hill," 17–40.

[44] The original handwritten charter is on file at the Illinois State Archives, Springfield, Illinois. See *History of the Church,* 4:239–48.

[45] James L. Kimball leaves open the possibility that Bennett was alone responsible for the chartering of the Nauvoo Legion: "Bennett might also have been instrumental in preparing the militia provision of the Nauvoo Charter. If one accepts Bennett as the source of the Nauvoo Legion, that section of the Charter was not Mormon at all but had its origin in an act passed before the Saints migrated to Illinois. It is ironic that Bennett, who became such a foe for the Mormons, might have been responsible for much of the criticism that the Mormons received on account of the Nauvoo Legion." See. Kimball, "The Nauvoo Charter," 44.

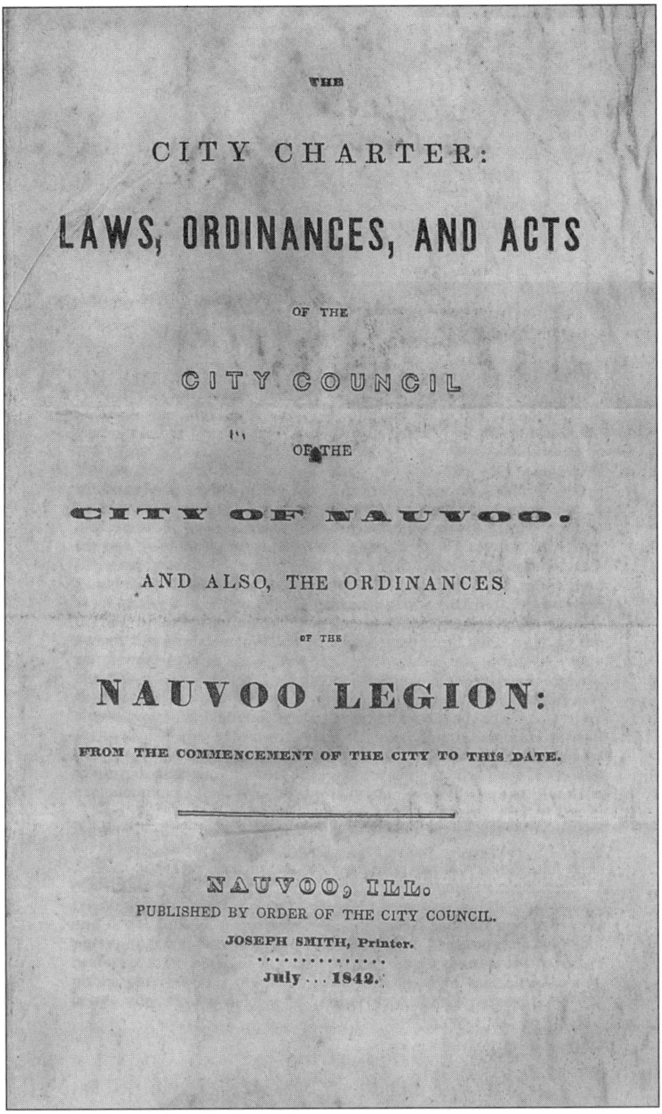

THE

CITY CHARTER:

LAWS, ORDINANCES, AND ACTS

OF THE

CITY COUNCIL

OF THE

CITY OF NAUVOO.

AND ALSO, THE ORDINANCES

OF THE

NAUVOO LEGION:

FROM THE COMMENCEMENT OF THE CITY TO THIS DATE.

NAUVOO, ILL.
PUBLISHED BY ORDER OF THE CITY COUNCIL.
JOSEPH SMITH, Printer.
July . . . 1842.

FIGURE 7. Title page of city charter, Nauvoo, Illinois. Published by order of the City Council, July 1842. Joseph Smith, printer. *Courtesy of Church History Library.*

tias in the past, and having very recently attempted to set up the Illinois Legion, he saw the Legion as yet another opportunity—not merely for the Mormons, but very possibly for himself. He was, after all, appointed the second ranking officer in the Legion.[46]

The Nauvoo City Charter, the Nauvoo Legion Charter, and the University of Nauvoo Charter—all three—were signed into law by Governor Thomas Carlin on December 16, 1840 to take effect February 1, 1841. "Every power we asked has been granted," Bennett cheerfully reported,

> every request gratified, every desire fulfilled. . . . Many members in the House . . . were warmly in our favor; and with only one or two dissenting voices, every representative appeared inclined to, and voted for the law . . . and I should not forget to mention, that [Abraham] Lincoln . . . had the magnanimity to vote for our act . . . And cordially congratulated me on its passage.[47]

As expected, Nauvoo did not merely embrace, but positively trumpeted, Bennett's political achievements. It was as if the black night of their Missouri persecutions was coming to an end. The city could go forward, and the Mormons could finally continue gathering. In the words of Joseph Smith, Sidney Rigdon, and Hyrum Smith,

> [T]he persecutions we suffered in Missouri were but the prelude to a far more glorious display of the powers of truth, and of the religion we have espoused. . . . We hope those days of darkness and gloom have gone by, and, from the liberal policy of our state government, we may expect a scene of peace and prosperity we have never before witnessed since the rise of our Church.[48]

Bennett even received qualified scriptural benediction: "And for his

---

[46] While it is true that Joseph Smith claimed authorship of the city charter, the matter of the Nauvoo Legion Charter is more dubious. "The City Charter of Nauvoo is of my own plan and device," he wrote. "I concocted it for the salvation of the Church, and on principles so broad, that every honest man might dwell secure under its protective influence without distinction of sect or party." *History of the Church,* 4:249. Bennett, on the other hand, was clearly the one who drafted the legislation (perhaps with Babbitt's assistance) and brought back to Nauvoo all three sub-charters of the Nauvoo Legion.

[47] *History of the Church,* 4:244. See also John C. Bennett, "Communications," *Times and Seasons* 2, no. 5 (December 1840): 266. It would be difficult to conceive that Abraham Lincoln, a former volunteer militiaman who had fought in the Black Hawk War, would have ever voted for a militia that saw itself as above the laws of the state.

[48] *History of the Church,* 4:271–72; *Times and Seasons* 2 (January 1841): 273–74.

love he shall be great, for he shall be mine if he do this, saith the Lord. I have seen the work which he hath done, which I accept if he continue, and will crown him with blessings and great glory."[49]

With reference to the charter and likely more particularly to the newly won powers of habeas corpus and a Nauvoo municipal court, Smith lavished praise on Bennett: "[Bennett] has been one of the principal instruments in effecting our safety and deliverance from unjust persecution and demands of the authorities of Missouri, and also in procuring the city charter. He is a man of enterprise, extensive acquirements, and of independent mind and is calculated to be a great blessing to our community."[50]

Upon his return to Nauvoo, Bennett accepted the welcome nomination by a grateful community to become the city's first mayor, which occurred on February 3, 1841. As mayor, one of his very first recommendations was to organize the Nauvoo Legion "with a provision allowing any citizen of Hancock County to unite by voluntary enrolment . . . to serve the state . . . and [it] should maintain the constitution, and the laws, and be ready at all times for the public defense."[51] The very next day, the new Nauvoo City Council passed a bill organizing, according to law, the Nauvoo Legion with two cohorts, "the horse troops [cavalry] to constitute the first cohort, and the foot troops [infantry] to constitute the second cohort"—all in six companies.[52] Smith was duly elected lieutenant general; John C. Bennett, major general; and Wilson Law, brigadier general. Several other former officers of the Hancock County Fifty-ninth Regiment were then elected to the various other commissions.

"Subject to the Military Laws of Illinois"

Several scholars have argued that the Nauvoo Legion was above and beyond the control of the state. William A. Linn states that the Legion's "independence of state control was provided for by a provision of law which allowed it to be governed by a court martial of its own officers." He accepts Governor Ford's face-saving, self-serv-

[49] *Doctrine and Covenants*, 124:17.

[50] Joseph Smith, Sidney Rigdon, and Hyrum Smith, "Ecclesiastical: A Proclamation to the Saints Scattered Abroad," *Times and Seasons* 2, no. 6 (January 15, 1841): 275.

[51] *History of the Church*, 4:290–91; *Times and Seasons* 2, no. 8 (February 3, 1841): 316.

[52] *History of the Church*, 4:293–94.

ing argument, written years after the fact, that Nauvoo was "a government within a government" and that the Mormons had "a military force at their own command."[53] And in his otherwise excellent and enduring study, Robert Flanders likewise argued that the Legion was "independent of and not subject to the military laws of Illinois."[54] Klaus Hansen likewise argued that the Legion was "separate from the state militia, subject only to the authority of the governor."[55]

The fact is, however, that the Nauvoo Legion could not function or pass laws "or act repugnant to" or be inconsistent with the military laws or constitutions of either the United States or the State of Illinois (see chapter 6). Furthermore, state adjutant general files clearly show that the Nauvoo Legion was, from its inception, a bona fide unit of the Illinois State Militia, serving its local presiding military authorities but ultimately at the beck and call of the Illinois governor, acting in his capacity as commander in chief.[56] The Mormons hoped that its very size and military prowess would serve as a deterrent against outside encroachment. Although it was predominantly a Mormon militia, since most of the men who enlisted were Latter-day Saints, it was not, as many others in the country were, a private or strictly a volunteer company, but rather a city militia, a kind of "odd battalion" of the state militia, independent only in the sense that it was not part of the local Fifty-ninth Hancock Regiment or any other. It was not a "Mormon army," even if some who enrolled perceived it as such. Its officers were selected by the rank and file, but reported to their lieutenant general, Joseph Smith, as their commanding officer. Although their loyalty was to him, they were ultimately responsible to the governor and, if ever called into service, subordinate to commanding officers of the standing Regular Army.[57]

Smith and other Church leaders clearly had other reasons in mind

---

[53] Linn, *The Story of the Mormons,* 237.

[54] Flanders, *Nauvoo,* 100.

[55] Hansen, *Quest for Empire,* 51.

[56] See "Commission Records of the Illinois State Militia," 39–44. See also "Governor Correspondence: Military."

[57] In Governor Carlin's communiqué of March 10, 1841, ratifying Joseph Smith's appointment as lieutenant general retrospective to February 5, he said: "I do strictly require all officers and soldiers under his command to be obedient to his orders; and he is to obey such orders and directions as he shall receive, from time to time, from the commander in chief or his superior officers." *History of the Church,* 4:309; Lieutenant General's Commission; in Joseph Smith Papers, box 6 fd. 5. Church History Library.

for establishing the Nauvoo Legion. As discussed in chapter 2, the excesses of the Danites had caused the Church no end of dissension, persecution, and apostasy. "And again I would further suggest the impropriety of the organization of bands or companies by covenants or oaths by penalties or secrecies," Smith had written in Liberty Jail. If they had learned anything from the Danite secret organization, they learned that secrecy breeds hate and suspicion.

Their Nauvoo military experience must be different. Smith would take a clear and very visible leadership role from the beginning. This time no Sampson Avards would be allowed to go lurking in the dark with some illegal force to embarrass the Church and discomfort its enemies. Everything about the Nauvoo Legion would be set in law, above board, and under the aegis of the state militia laws. It would be uniformed and drilled as becoming its place as a regularly commissioned company of the state's militia. And if it were so constituted—and drilled, trained, and equipped as a legal force—it could protect and defend their economic, political, and religious interests when and if absolutely necessary.[58] As the First Presidency of the Church argued right after the charter had been secured:

> [It] will enable us to perform our military duty by ourselves, and thus afford us the power, and privilege, of avoiding one of the most fruitful sources of strife, oppression, and collision with the world. It will enable us to show our attachment to the state and nation as a people . . . thus proving ourselves obedient to the paramount laws of the land.[59]

Conclusion

This chapter has attempted to show that the Nauvoo Legion originated in law, in the desires of the Latter-day Saints to protect themselves, and in the determination of their leaders to form a militia they could control. Even before the Legion was formed, early settlers in Nauvoo joined nearby local militia units. Frustrated by President Van Buren's rebuffs, concerned with renewed efforts by Missouri to seek his arrest, and anxious to address pressing spiritual and other

[58] Even William Linn argued that the Danites were not a presence in Nauvoo and that its City Council "made an affidavit that there was no such society there." Linn, *The Story of the Mormons,* 189, 192.

[59] Statement of the First Presidency. *Times and Seasons* 2, no. 6 (January 15, 1841): 274.

matters facing the Church in Nauvoo, Joseph Smith signaled an opportunity for others to rush in and help, in the process giving them the benefit of the doubt. Seeing an opportunity and pressing his agenda, one John C. Bennett, who had previous experience working with the state legislature on militia matters, burst upon the scene. Although he played an instrumental role in the creation of the Legion, Bennett viewed it as a tool for self-aggrandizement and took a very bellicose attitude from the beginning regarding it—a view that some Latter-day Saints, who had lived through the Missouri difficulties, clearly shared. Only time would tell how the Legion would play its perceived role. As the following chapter will show, the Legion was to develop into one of Illinois' finest militias.

4

Composition and Characteristics of the Nauvoo Legion

"A ragged, inefficient outfit" or "Illinois's finest."
M. C. FIELD, EDITOR OF THE *SAINT LOUIS REVEILLE*

With the Nauvoo Charter secured it was now time to organize the Legion and seek recruits for the newest militia in the state. Many of the original enlistees were "a ragged" group of men mustering in compliance with state law. But as enthusiasm for the Legion caught hold, hundreds soon joined. This chapter will discuss the "nuts and bolts" of the Legion, including the reasons for the Nauvoo Legion's growth from a few enlistees in 1841 to what was arguably the largest Illinois militia by 1845, the role of privates in the selection of Legion officers, and the six-tiered organizational structure that assured each officer and private of his station within the organization. The matter of how large the Legion actually became—which has long been debated—will also be addressed. Numbers tell only part of the story but they facilitate an understanding of the real workings and character of the Nauvoo Legion and why it had the potential to be the largest militia and one of the most efficient in the state.

"Enroll Every Man"

The Nauvoo Legion, unlike other militias in Illinois, began with enough enlistees to form more than one company. As Joseph Smith reported, "The Legion at its organization was composed of six companies."[1] New converts and immigrants arrived in Nauvoo daily, and because every male aged eighteen to forty-five was required to enlist, the Legion continued to grow. By Sunday, September 11, 1841, men in the first companies numbered 250. On that date, Hosea Stout reported, "The official returns of the Legion show the aggregate to be 1,490 men."[2] By late 1841, the Legion had grown to fourteen companies in Illinois and two in Iowa.[3] By May 7, 1842, twenty-six companies, or "about two thousand troops," were enrolled.[4] Before the year's end, Bennett claimed the Legion numbered between two and three thousand soldiers.[5] Editors of the *Sangamo Journal* concurred, reporting troop strength in May and June of 1842 at over two thousand men.[6] A few months later, the *Alton Telegraph* noted that the Legion count was nearing three thousand.[7] By 1843 the Legion had become the largest city militia in Illinois: 1,751 were enrolled in the infantry brigade alone (see table 2). A count of the cavalry cohort that year is not available.

---

[1] *History of the Church,* 4:296.

[2] "Minutes and Ordinances of Organization of the Nauvoo Legion"; *History of the Church,* 4:415; "Minutes of the Meeting which Organized the Nauvoo Legion," *Times and Seasons* January 1, 1842, 295.

[3] It is of interest that two companies were from Iowa, both largely composed of Mormons. This raises the question of why men who lived in Iowa Territory were legally granted the right to serve in an Illinois militia. Answers to this question are slow in coming. We can only assume that this was an example of Mormons wanting to muster with other Mormons. Of the fourteen companies of the Legion, eleven were infantry units and three cavalry. Joseph Holbrook recorded, "In February [1841], I received orders from Nauvoo to raise a company of mounted lancers for the Nauvoo Legion. I went immediately to work. I raised said company and I was nominated at Nauvoo for the office of captain, but someone wished to make a division in said company. I declined accepting the office and another was elected in my place, but in a short time I received orders from Nauvoo to raise a company of mounted riflemen and again [I was] nominated for a captain to which I was elected by unanimous vote." "Papers of Joseph Holbrook."

[4] *History of the Church,* 5:3; "Nauvoo Legion Papers," Fd. 10.

[5] Bennett, *History of the Saints,* 211.

[6] "Nauvoo Legion," *Sangamo Journal* 10, no. 37, May 6, 1842; "The Mormons," *Sangamo Journal* 10, no. 41, June 3, 1842.

[7] John C. Bennett, "Gen. Bennett's Third Letter," *Alton Telegraph and Democratic Review* 7, no. 30, July 23, 1842.

In June 1844, when the Saint Louis *Daily Evening Gazette* announced that the Legion had reached two thousand troops, Nauvoo citizens took issue—for commandants had been actively enrolling new recruits on a daily basis. It appears the number was closer to three thousand soldiers that June. In July the *Warsaw Signal* reported that the "Mormons say they have 4,000 well-drilled troops." A week later, the *Signal* editor confirmed the number.[8] An *Alton Telegraph and Democratic Review* reporter wrote of his confidence that Smith "by his mere nod, could command the attendance of 4000 armed men at a day's notice."[9]

Captain John Singleton of the Illinois State Militia and Governor Thomas Ford refuted the reported count. Captain Singleton, after inspecting the Legion on June 27, 1844—the day of Smith's murder—reported that he saw "something over 2,100."[10] Governor Ford, in speaking to those gathered in Carthage on that date, said, "What can your small force be against two thousand armed men entrenched in a city, and defending themselves, their wives and their children?"[11]

Was Governor Ford incorrect in his estimate of the number of men in the Legion on June 27, 1844? Written reports from various regiment officers on that day suggest there were many more than two thousand. Joseph W. Coolidge, adjutant, recorded the number of rank-and-file of the Second Regiment Second Cohort of the Nauvoo Legion, and penned that in the First Company there were "28 men rank and file, 22 guns and a sword." In the Second Company were "47 men rank and file, 20 guns, 1 sword." He concluded his report by indicating that there were 154 enlisted men in two battalions in the Second Regiment of the Second Cohort. If his report is representative of other companies, regiments, and battalions, the total number of men enrolled in the Nauvoo Legion by June 27, 1844, would have been 3,226.[12]

---

[8] Thomas Sharp, "Postscript," *Warsaw Signal* 136, no. 19, July 19, 1844.

[9] "Let Him that Is Without Sin Cast the First Stone," *Alton Telegraph and Democratic Review* 9, no. 28, July 13, 1844, as quoted in Thomas Sharp, "The Late Tragedy and the Alton Telegraph," *Warsaw Signal* 138, no. 20, June 20, 1844.

[10] Captain Singleton, as quoted in "Extra, Joe and Hyrum Smith are Dead," *Warsaw Signal*, July 24, 1844.

[11] Governor Thomas Ford, as quoted in Thomas Sharp, "The People of Warsaw in Hancock County," *Warsaw Signal* 141, no. 24, July 31, 1844.

[12] See "Return of J. W. Coolidge."

Table 2
General Return of the Second Cohort (Infantry Brigade) of the Nauvoo Legion, 1843

	General Staff	First Regiment Artillery	Second Regiment Rifle
Brigadier General	1	—	—
Colonels	—	1	1
Lieutenant Colonels	—	1	1
Majors	—	1	1
Brigadier Major	1	—	—
Quartermasters	1	—	—
Aides-de-camp to the Brigadier General	1	—	—
Commissary	1	—	—
Chaplains	5	—	—
Surgeons	1	—	—
Adjutants	—	1	1
Quartermaster Sergeants	—	1	1
Sergeant Majors	—	1	1
Captains	—	6	5
First Lieutenants	—	6	5
Second Lieutenants	—	6	5
Third Lieutenants	—	6	5
Sergeants	—	23	25
Corporals	—	16	20
Pioneers	—	—	—
Musicians	—	1	—
Privates	—	195	257
Total Commissioned	11	30	26
Total Noncommissioned Officers and Privates	—	235	302
Aggregate	11	265	328
Muskets	—	—	—
Rifles	—	6	59
Swords	—	63	2
Pairs of Pistols	—	—	—
Cannons and Equipage	—	2	—
Total Arms	—	71	61

Third Regiment Rifle	Fourth Regiment Rifle	Fifth Regiment Infantry	Aggregate
—	—	—	1
1	1	1	5
1	1	1	5
1	1	1	5
—	—	—	1
1	—	—	2
—	—	—	1
—	—	—	1
—	—	—	5
1	—	—	2
1	1	1	5
1	1	1	5
1	1	1	5
6	6	6	29
6	6	6	29
6	6	6	29
6	6	6	29
28	27	27	130
27	22	19	104
—	3	6	9
6	—	—	7
388	230	272	1342
32	30	30	159
449	282	324	1592
481	312	354	1751
—	21	42	63
40	28	—	133
20	13	—	98
1	3	—	4
—	—	—	2
61	65	42	300

Data as recorded by John Bills, Brigade Major.

Table 3
Return of the Fourth Regiment of Riflemen, 1844

	First Battalion	Second Battalion	Staff	Total
Colonels	—	—	—	1
Lieutenant Colonels	1	—	—	1
Majors	1	—	—	1
Captains	—	4	2	6
Adjutants	1	—	—	1
First Lieutenants	—	4	2	6
Second Lieutenants	—	2	1	3
Third Lieutenants	—	1	1	2
Ensigns	—	—	1	1
Sergeants	—	14	6	20
Corporals	—	12	3	15
Musicians	—	6	—	6
Pioneers	—	1	—	1
Privates	—	54	37	91
Total Commissioned	4	11	7	22
Total Noncommissioned Officers and Privates	—	97	46	133
Aggregate	4	98	53	158
Total Arms	—	—	—	101

NOTE: Signed by Jesse P. Harmon and L. N. Scovil.

Adjutant Coolidge's report may not be representative of the Legion, however. For example, the "Return of the Fourth Regiment of Riflemen" in 1844 shows a total of 133 men (see table 3). If this report is representative, then the Nauvoo Legion on June 27 would number 2,660 men. Furthermore, the "Return of the Third Regiment, Second Cohort, Nauvoo Legion, Illinois Militia, June 27, 1844," shows only 131 men, indicating that the Nauvoo Legion numbered 2,620 on June 27 (see table 4). If the "General Return of the Second Cohort, Nauvoo Legion, Illinois Militia, June 27, 1844" is used to determine the number of men enrolled (see table 5), the total would be 2,082—which validates Governor Ford's estimate. It is

Table 4
RETURN OF THE THIRD REGIMENT, SECOND COHORT, NAUVOO LEGION, JUNE 27, 1844

	COLONEL'S STAFF	FIRST BATTALION	SECOND BATTALION	AGGREGATE
Colonels	1	—	—	1
Lieutenant Colonels	1	—	—	1
Majors	1	—	—	1
Captains	—	3	2	5
Adjutants	1	—	—	1
Quartermasters	1	—	—	1
Paymasters	1	—	—	1
First Lieutenants	—	3	2	5
Second Lieutenants	—	2	1	3
Third Lieutenants	—	2	—	2
Surgeons	1	—	—	1
Ensigns	—	1	—	1
Sergeants	—	6	4	10
Corporals	—	5	3	8
Musicians	—	5	—	5
Pioneers	—	1	1	2
Privates	—	34	49	83
Total Commissioned	6	11	5	22
Total Noncommissioned Officers and Privates	1	51	57	109
Aggregates	7	62	62	131
Private Arms	3	—	—	—

obvious that the total number of soldiers on the June 27 Legion returns varied.[13]

It was not until years after the Legion was disbanded and most of its soldiers had trekked west to the Salt Lake Valley that the num-

[13] For example, on the morning of the 27th Hosea Stout, brigadier general, wrote of a "Morning Report of the 2nd Cohort." In his report he indicated that in attendance was the brigadier general, sergeant major, quarter master sergeant, cornet, herald and armor bearer. He wrote that as the brigadier general of the Second Cohort of the Nauvoo Legion, he was "armed, no rations, no water." He also wrote that John Bills, Alanson Ripley, and Joseph A. Kelting were also "armed, no rations, no water." "Morning Report of 2nd Cohort."

Table 5
General Return of the Second Cohort, Nauvoo Legion, June 27, 1844

	General Staff	First Regiment Artillery	Second Regiment Rifle
Brigadier Generals	1	—	—
Colonels	—	1	1
Lieutenant Colonels	—	1	1
Brigade Major	1	—	—
Quartermaster	1	—	—
Aides-de-camp	4	—	—
Majors	—	1	1
Captains	—	8	4
Adjutants	—	1	1
Quartermasters	—	1	—
Paymasters	—	1	—
First Lieutenants	—	8	4
Second Lieutenants	—	6	3
Third Lieutenants	—	5	3
Sergeants	1	—	—
Ensigns	—	1	—
Sergeants	—	26	12
Corporals	—	26	9
Musicians	—	8	7
Pioneers	—	32	2
Privates	—	160	116
Total Commissioned	8	34	18
Total Noncommissioned Officers and Privates	—	252	146
Aggregates	8	286	164
Muskets	—	—	91
Rifles	—	—	—
Pairs of Pistols	—	—	—
Swords	—	—	7
Total Arms	—	—	98

Third Regiment Rifle	Fourth Regiment Rifle	Fifth Regiment Infantry	Aggregate
—	—	—	1
1	1	1	5
1	1	1	5
—	—	—	1
—	—	—	1
—	—	—	4
1	1	1	5
5	6	7	30
1	1	1	5
1	—	1	3
1	—	1	3
5	6	7	30
3	3	8	23
2	2	6	18
1	—	—	2
1	1	1	4
10	20	24	92
8	15	22	80
5	6	8	34
2	1	6	43
83	91	202	652
22	22	35	139
109	133	262	902
131	155	297	1041
—	—	—	—
—	—	—	—
—	—	—	—
—	—	—	—
—	101	—	—

ber five thousand circulated routinely in various publications and guides. This inflated figure persisted well into the twentieth century. Few scoffed when historians Roger D. Launius and John E. Hallwas wrote, "The Nauvoo Legion had mushroomed . . . attaining an estimated five thousand members."[14] After all, historians argued, the number has merit if the four to six hundred young boys participating in the "Junior League" of the Legion are included in the count.[15]

Did Thomas Sharp and other critics intentionally inflate Legion numbers to suggest a greater Mormon threat? Did Mormons deflate the numbers to minimize the fears of their near neighbors? What is known is that the Legion was a formidable force of recruits, especially when it is remembered that the population of Nauvoo peaked at 11,500 in 1845.

Official records show that the number of recruits in the Nauvoo Legion was somewhere between the estimated high of 3,226 and the lowest estimate of 2,082. The Legion likely had fewer than three thousand recruits.[16] Not an overgrown army, it was a militia that mirrored the growing male population of the city of Nauvoo. Over 90 percent of the recruits identified themselves as Latter-day Saints; the remainder did not report their religious leanings. Although non-Mormons were outnumbered nine to one, they played a key role in the military structure of the Legion. Historian Glen Leonard noted

---

[14] Launius and Hallwas, *Kingdom on the Mississippi Revisited,* 57.

[15] The young boys of Nauvoo were later organized into a "Junior Legion" after the Charter of the Nauvoo Legion had been renounced. Among their number was Joseph Smith III until his mother interceded. However, according to a March 27, 1841, letter from William Niswanger to the Court Martial, it appears that older men were organized into honorific groups, such as "Benjaminite." The letter reads,

> To the Honorable Court Martial
>
> We the officers of Benjaminite Co. in Nauvoo, being duly elected by the same pray your Honorable body to grant us the privilege of assembling with the Nauvoo Legion on the 1st and 6th of April next, being willing to conform to your laws and discipline as laid down by your body. Notwithstanding our age exempts us from doing military duty, we still feel the spirit of seventy-six burning in our bosom, and are willing to grasp the sling and hurl the stone like David of old. (Newell K. Whitney Papers, MSS FM 23, Box 4).

If these were included they would have exaggerated the total size of the Nauvoo Legion.

[16] Available records show only the names of 336 privates and 491 officers. It should be noted that the names of officers are repeats, many being elected to positions more than once.

their presence: "The Legion is not, as has been falsely represented by its enemies, exclusively a 'Mormon military association.' "[17] *Times and Seasons* editors Ebenezer Robinson and Gustavus Hills wrote of their unique contribution to Legion business and added, "A large number of the officers of the Nauvoo Legion . . . are not members of any church."[18] These officers served in Ramus, Seven-mile Mound, Green Plains, and Nauvoo, Illinois, as well as in companies in Keokuk and Fort Madison, Iowa Territory.

The rank of the Legion was filled with men native to the eastern (26 percent), central (22 percent), and southern (6 percent) states. Those who claimed foreign lands as their nativity were also numbered among the recruits, with the British Isles claiming 35 percent. The nativity of the legion recruits mirrors the nativity of the Nauvoo population at the time. All but a few of the soldiers identified themselves as farmers (92 percent). Other occupations represented were carpenters, stock raisers, blacksmiths, merchants, teachers, stonemasons, cattlemen, coopers, gardeners, butchers, and bakers. Even civil servants, such as the justice of the peace, councilman, constable, and policeman found a place in the legion of Nauvoo.[19]

Thomas C. Sharp, editor of the nearby *Warsaw Signal* and increasingly wary of the Legion's growth and its potential uses, wrote to his readership: "How military these people are becoming! Everything they say or do seems to breathe the spirit of military tactics."[20] Though criticized in Mormon circles for ignoring fact and biased military reporting, Sharp brushed the criticisms aside, convinced that the Legion's power and growing number of recruits must be stopped. If not, he contended the Mormon militia would rival in size the Roman Legion and the number of its troops would reach six to ten thousand men. An officer in the U.S. Army or Regular Army passing through Nauvoo thought even Sharp's numbers were low. He believed the Legion would grow to "fifty thousand strong."[21]

---

[17] Joseph Smith and John C. Bennett, "Nauvoo Legion General Orders, May 4, 1841," *Times and Seasons* 2, no. 14, May 15, 1841, 417.

[18] "Officers," *Times and Seasons* 3, no. 5, January 1, 1842, 646.

[19] James E. Smith, "Frontier Nauvoo: Building a Picture from Statistics," *Ensign* 9 (September 1979): 17–19.

[20] Thomas Sharp, "Mormon Visitors," *Warsaw Signal* 2, no. 11, July 21, 1843.

[21] An Officer from the U.S. Artillery, "Highly Important from the Mormon Empire," *The New York Herald* 8, no. 166, June 17, 1842. At the time, the Regular Army of the United States numbered barely eight thousand men.

"Lo! The Chariots of Israel"

The very structure and organization of the Legion refutes the grandiose prediction of 50,000—and Sharp's fear of 10,000—troops. Each enlistee was assigned to one of two units called brigades or cohorts[22]—the first consisting of horse troops, and the second, foot troops or infantry.[23] Cohorts were divided into regiments, regiments into battalions, and battalions into companies; each company consisted of 32 to 64 soldiers. Four companies composed a battalion of 256 men. Two battalions, consisting of 512 soldiers, formed a regiment. Five regiments, or a maximum total of 2,560 men, formed a cohort or brigade, and two cohorts formed the Legion. Thus, if every company, battalion, regiment, and cohort were filled to capacity, the maximum total number of soldiers in the Nauvoo Legion would not have exceeded 5,120. (By comparison, a legion in Republican Rome numbered 4,200 men, and 5,500 in Imperial Rome.)

Ordinances and resolutions accepted as law in Legion courts-martial slightly increased numbers on the rolls, and altered the demographics of the Legion. For example, Section 3 of "Ordinance No. 2" attached 2 musicians to each company. A later resolution added 2 more musicians to each company, raising the total number of soldiers in a company to 68. Smith added 12 chaplains to his staff, and later Brigham Young added 64 personal guards.[24] These additions illustrate that the number of enlistees by 1845 could have exceeded 5,120.

The fact is, however, the Legion never reached its maximum theoretical capacity—although the 5,000 figure was touted for years. To poetess Eliza R. Snow, such a failing was not a problem:

> Should they need re-enforcements, those rights to secure,
> Which our forefathers purchas'd; and Freedom ensure.
> There is still in reserve a strong Cohort above;
> "Lo! the chariots of Israel and horsemen thereof."[25]

---

[22] The term cohort is not found in the military history of the United States. Cohort was a term used in Roman legions.

[23] Headquarters Nauvoo Legion, City of Nauvoo, Illinois, May 25, 1841. Ordinance 2, Section 2: "The Legion shall be and is hereby divided into two cohorts, the horse troops to constitute the first cohort, and the foot troops or soldiers or mounted cavalry to constitute the second cohort."

[24] See Nauvoo Legion, Minutes and Ordinances of Organization, October 20, 1844.

[25] Snow, "The Nauvoo Legion," *Times and Seasons* 2, no. 17 (June 2, 1841): 467.

"A Poll Book of an Election"

From 1841 to 1845, enlistments continued; however, failure to preserve muster rolls and recruitment records has frustrated more than one historian. To compensate, historians have relied on holographic journals and letters, hoping to find the name of a private here or there and create a quasi-list. Unfortunately, their efforts have uncovered only a few names, hardly enough to create a list. Having discovered the names of hundreds of heretofore unknown privates in the Legion (see appendix E), we now present a greater understanding of the character and flavor of the Legion than existed before. These names appeared on forms used in Legion elections.[26] When privates cast their votes, each noted his military assignment. We note seventeen distinct military designations. Cavalry (52), artillery (46), rifle rangers (35), musicians (16), and lancers (11) were the most common assignments designated.[27]

This new information, added to previous research on Mormons residing in Nauvoo in the 1840s, provides the vital statistics of 336 privates and determines their ages at the time of polling. It evidences that, as in many other militias, not all recruits abided by the militia code, which stated that enlistees must be between the ages of eighteen and forty-five.[28] Private Paulinus Harvey Allred, for instance, was aged twelve, and Private David Dort was aged forty-eight at the time of the Legion voting. The majority (107) were between the ages of eighteen and twenty-seven. The median age of the privates was twenty-six.[29]

Other discoveries were that occasionally both father and son served as privates, for instance Albert Clements and his son Alvin; Nathaniel Frampton and his son Samuel; Dimick Huntington and his son

[26] It also proved that Section 14 of the "Revised Laws of the Nauvoo Legion," requiring "[the] clerk shall enter the name of the person voting, and his vote accordingly in a poll book to be provided for that purpose" was carried out. *Revised Laws of the Nauvoo Legion,* Section 14.

[27] It is interesting to note that within a few years the Mormon Battalion was organized (July 16, 1846) and soon assigned privates to military duties. None of the duties assigned to the Mormon Battalion privates were the same as those assigned to the Nauvoo Legion privates. The duties of a Mormon Battalion private were to be a teamster, pioneer, wood chopper, butcher, cattle and mule driver, guard, carpenter, and blacksmith.

[28] According to William Huntington, there were enough men in the Nauvoo Legion over age forty-five to form a Silver Gray Company. He records that "on May 27th 1841 [he] was elected Capt. of a company of Silver Grays in the Nauvoo Legion." William Huntington, MH 1801. Church History Library.

[29] A similar study of the Mormon Battalion reveals that the average age was twenty-five years at the time of enlistment on June 14, 1846. See Black, *Membership of the Church.*

John; and Jeremiah Leavitt and his son Nathaniel. Sibling relationships were common among the privates. Few prominent Mormon leaders were privates or given assignments to be riflemen, archers, and so forth. The notable exceptions were Orrin Porter Rockwell, the famous gun-slinging bodyguard of Smith, and William Weeks, architect of the Nauvoo Temple.[30]

None of the polled privates died while performing militia functions; however, nine privates died between 1841 and 1845.[31] The average private died at age sixty, several years beyond the average age of a man at that time. It could not be supported that these men were more prone to death as a result of being called to duty. In fact, quite the opposite appears to be the norm. The majority (185) died between ages sixty-three and ninety-three.

All enlistees entered the Nauvoo Legion as privates. As shown in the foregoing, there was widespread enthusiasm for the recruitment process. Recruitment into the Nauvoo Legion was taken seriously, as was the right of privates to elect officers.

"To the Best of My Skill and Understanding, So Help Me God"

The Nauvoo Legion was organized into a six-level military structure (see figure 4). Its highest ranking officer, or first tier, was the commander in chief/lieutenant general, and the lowest tier, a private. By February 1841, distinctions between privates and officers were made in an election process. Privates receiving a majority of votes were elected officers. To ensure that the state sanctioned the election of officers, names of elected men were sent to the governor of Illinois to officially commission the soldiers. The governor then approved or disapproved of the Legion election process. Typically he approved, but he did reserve the right to refuse a commission to an elected official.

Electing Legion officers was not a one-time event. Elections, ongoing, vital processes, were held whenever necessary due to a vol-

[30] Another interesting fact is that when the voting privates matured, several held prominent positions in the Mormon Battalion and took a leading role in the militia skirmishes in Utah Territory. Reddick and Reddin Allred, Elijah Averett, George Babcock, and George Dykes were but a few.

[31] The names of the privates who died were Leonard Thornhill, David Dort, William Dudley, Alfred Duzett, William Field, Benjamin Kempton, Ephraim Marks, Newton Olney, and Elisha Pace.

untarily vacated office, terminated office, or illness.[32] Regarding the ongoing process of election and the number of men elected to office, Sharp wrote that "more titles are to be found in the Nauvoo Legion than any one book on military tactics."[33] Eighty commissioned and noncommissioned titled positions were filled in the Legion between 1841 and 1845.[34] A total of 491 appointments were made to these offices (see appendix D). All commissioned officers were required to take an oath of office:

> I do solemnly swear (or affirm) that I will support the Constitution of the United States, and this State, and that I will not be engaged in dueling, either directly or indirectly, during my continuance in office; and that I will faithfully discharge the duties of ______, in the ______, of the Nauvoo Legion of Illinois Militia, to the best of my skill and understanding, so help me God.[35]

Once pledged, officers had the right to organize the Legion within the parameters of their office, provided the framework of instructions or guidelines was in accordance with the militia code of the

---

[32] See Quinn, *The Mormon Hierarchy,* appendix 3, "Danites in 1838: A Partial List," 479–90. In comparing Quinn's partial list of the Danites with the officers of the Legion, we find only 65 of the Legion officers were involved with the Danites. This does not suggest that a position within the Danite organization meant election to office in the Nauvoo Legion.

[33] Thomas Sharp, "Mormon Visitors," *Warsaw Signal* 2, no. 11, July 21, 1843. What Sharp did not disclose, but probably knew, was that many Southern militia units decorated their soldiers with titles.

[34] The names of those filling the positions were compiled from the Illinois Governor's Military Correspondence, the Illinois State Adjutant General's Rosters and Commission Records, the Minutes of the Nauvoo Legion Courts Martial, the Whitney Collection at Brigham Young University, earlier compilations of rank rolls, and other source documents found in the bibliography herein. Where known, birth and death dates, military position, and dates of commission are noted. Years later, Brigadier General Richard W. Young of Utah concurred: "The Nauvoo Legion was a very top heavy corps. The staffs of the general officers were unusually large and somewhat fantastic." Young, "The Nauvoo Legion," 42. Young served as a colonel then brigadier general of the Fortieth Division in France during World War I.

[35] The "Nauvoo League Officer Oath" was similar to the oath required of officers in the national military forces of the United States at that time. See the oath taken by A. P. Rockwood after his election to the Hancock County Fifty-ninth Regiment: "I do solemnly swear (or affirm) that I will support the Constitution of the United States and of this state that I will not be engaged in dueling either directly or indirectly during my continuance in office and that I will faithfully discharge the duties of captain in the 59th Regiment of Illinois Militia to the best of my skill and understanding so help me God." "Papers of Albert Perry Rockwood, 1840–1845."

State of Illinois. Of the men who took the officers' oath, twenty-five-year-old Brigadier General Don Carlos Smith, brother of Smith, was the youngest. Sixty-seven-year-old Adjutant John Haven was the oldest. The median age of an officer was thirty-seven—approximately ten years older than the enlisted privates.

A listing of officers indicates not only that older men served in leading roles within the Legion (most [116] were born between 1810 and 1812), but also that of the 491 men elected to office, 177 were commissioned more than once—that is, for example, promoted from second lieutenant to major. From a military standpoint, the most surprising promotion was that given to Brigham Young. On July 2, 1841 he was commissioned assistant chaplain by Governor Carlin. Four years later, on August 31, 1844, his second commission, signed by Governor Ford, was that of lieutenant general of the Nauvoo Legion (see appendix D).

Other prominent Church leaders holding high-ranking positions were Brevet Major General William Law and Judge Advocate Sidney Rigdon, members of the First Presidency; Aide-de-camp Isaac Morley, patriarch; and Assistant Chaplains Orson Hyde, John E. Page, Orson Pratt, Parley Pratt, George Albert Smith, William Smith, and Wilford Woodruff, were all members of the Quorum of the Twelve Apostles. Lieutenant Anson Call was a member of the Council of the Fifty; Captain Alpheus Cutler, a member of the Nauvoo Temple Committee; Lieutenant Aaron Johnson, high counselor in the Nauvoo Stake and justice of the peace; Herald and Armor Bearer Edward Hunter and Brevet Colonel George Miller, bishops. Often ecclesiastical leaders held religious positions within the Legion. They did not function as combat officers. Also elected and commissioned to leadership roles were Mormons who later turned their heel against Mormonism and lost their military ranking: Major General John C. Bennett, Captain Chauncey Higbee, Surgeon General Robert Foster, and Brevet Major Francis Higbee. Prominent non-Mormons serving in the Legion included Adjutant Jacob B. Backenstos, Brigadier General Davison Hibbard, Major Hiram Kimball, Brevet Brigadier General Hugh McFall, and General Daniel H. Wells. Considering that many privates were also non-Mormons evidences that the Legion was first and foremost a state militia.

The following is a list of titles held by officers in the Nauvoo Legion between 1841 and 1845:

Adjutant general
Aide-de-camp
Assistant adjutant general
Assistant chaplain
Assistant inspector general
Assistant quartermaster general
Battalion adjutant
Brevet brigadier general
Brevet captain
Brevet colonel
Brevet major
Brevet major general
Brigadier chaplain
Brigadier cornet
Brigadier general
Brigadier inspector
Brigadier judge advocate
Brigadier major
Brigadier quartermaster
Brigadier surgeon
Captain of infantry
Chaplain
Chief chaplain
Chief musician
Colonel
Colonel of dragoons
Colonel of infantry
Color bearer
Commander general
Commissary general
Cornet
Corporal
1st corporal
2nd corporal
3rd corporal
4th corporal
Drill officer
Ensign
Fife major
Guard
Herald and armor bearer
Inspector general
Judge advocate
Lieutenant
1st lieutenant
2nd lieutenant
3rd lieutenant
Lieutenant colonel
Lieutenant colonel of infantry
Lieutenant general
Lieutenant major sergeant
Major
Major general
Major sergeant
Musician
Paymaster
Paymaster general
Pioneer
Quartermaster
Quartermaster general
Quartermaster sergeant
Regiment colonel
Regiment drum major
Regiment fife major
Regiment judge advocate
Regiment paymaster
Regiment surgeon
Sergeant
1st sergeant
2nd sergeant
3rd sergeant
4th sergeant
5th sergeant
Sergeant major
Surgeon
Surgeon general
War secretary

Many of the officers served in leadership capacities with family members. Among those having a father-son relationship were Guard Reynolds Cahoon (father) and Quartermaster Sergeant Pulaski Cahoon (son). Those having a sibling relationship included Musician Levi Hancock and Major Solomon Hancock. The Joseph Smith, Sr., family had the greatest number of siblings serving: Brigadier General Don Carlos Smith, Brevet Major General Hyrum Smith, Lieutenant General Joseph Smith, Jr., Guard Samuel Smith, and Assistant Chaplain William Smith.

Some of the commissioned officers were noted tradesmen in Nauvoo: John Bills was a tailor specializing in officers' uniforms; Quartermaster Sergeant Pulaski Cahoon owned a grog shop (tavern); Musician Gustavus Hills was a map maker; Windsor P. Lyon owned a drug and variety store; Adjutant Lucius Scovil was a baker; and Lieutenant Chauncey Webb was a blacksmith.

None of the commissioned officers lost their lives fulfilling a military assignment. However, eighteen Legion officers died between 1841 and 1845.[36] As for whether their service in the Legion affected their age at death, the officers, like the privates, had long lives. Less than one third (126) died between the ages of twenty-four and fifty-six years. The average Legion officer died at age sixty-one.

Of the officers who survived, many played a prominent role in later military affairs. Lieutenant Jacob Abbot, Lieutenant Horace Alexander, Lieutenant George P. Dykes, Colonel Nelson D. Higgins, and Aide-de-camp Jefferson Hunt marched with the Mormon Battalion.[37] Others made notable contributions to the societies in which they lived: Captain Truman O. Angel became the celebrated architect of the Salt Lake Temple, Aide-de-camp Zenos Gurley became a zealous missionary and leader in the Reorganized Church of Jesus Christ of Latter Day Saints, and Brevet Brigadier General Charles C. Rich and Captain Lorenzo Snow served in the Quorum of the Twelve Apostles.

[36] Legion officers who died were Captain Joseph Andrews, Captain George Black, Captain George Clyde, Ensign Salisbury Davis, Lieutenant John DeGraw, Lieutenant Ezra Grant, Major John P. Greene, Guard Elias Higbee, Lieutenant Hiram Kayle, Guard Vinson Knight, Lieutenant Eliphaz Marsh, Captain Luman Shurtliff, Brigadier General Don Carlos Smith, Brevet Major General Hyrum Smith, Lieutenant General Joseph Smith, Guard Samuel H. Smith, Aide-de-Camp Robert Thompson, and Brevet Lieutenant Colonel Benjamin Wilber.

[37] Of the privates elected to be officers in the Nauvoo Legion, fifty-seven later served in the Mormon Battalion.

"Duly Elected to the Office"

The Nauvoo Legion structure, like some other select independent companies, did not mirror the organizational structure of the United States militia.[38] In the 1830s the United States had 159 state and local militias, 370 brigades, 1,629 regiments, 1,775 battalions, and 13,958 companies with a total of 52,625 commissioned officers. The number of noncommissioned officers is not known. By 1839, the total number of men participating in the United States militia, on paper, at least, was 1,029,142.[39] Even at that time, most believed the numbers were grossly exaggerated.

Figure 7 typifies the organization of the state militias within the United States militia. The structure of the Legion also differed from the typical flow chart of state militias and was more like that seen in volunteer companies. A brief examination of the responsibilities and obligations of the offices held within the six-level structure of the Nauvoo Legion follows.

Lieutenant General

The fact that Joseph Smith accepted the rank of lieutenant general is evidence of his support for the Nauvoo Legion (see chapter 5).

> Know ye that Joseph Smith, having been duly elected to the office of lieutenant-general, Nauvoo Legion, of the militia of the State of Illinois, I, Thomas Carlin, governor of said state, do commission him lieutenant-general of the Nauvoo Legion, to take rank from the fifth day of February, 1841.

Illinois Adjutant General Moses K. Anderson recommended that Joseph Smith be appointed a lieutenant general; Secretary of State Lyman Trumbull issued the commission; and Governor Thomas Carlin signed it.

---

[38] The Legion also did not mirror the "Legion of the United States" which was divided into four sub-legions. The legionary staff consisted of 1 major-general or legionary general; 2 aides-de-camp; and 1 adjutant and inspector; 1 major commandant of cavalry, 1 of artillery; 1 quarter master; 1 deputy quarter master; 1 surgeon; and 1 chaplain. Each sub-legion was to have 1,280 non-commissioned officers, musicians, and privates and included one brigadier or "sub-legionary general." Each sub-legion had one troop of dragoons, one company of artillery, two battalions of infantry, one battalion of riflemen, and four other companies. "Organization of the Army in 1792," *American State Papers,* 1:40–41.

[39] "Report from the Secretary of War," submitted February 4, 1840, J. R. Poinsett, Secretary of War, Senate Documents, 26th Congress, 1st Session, 1839.

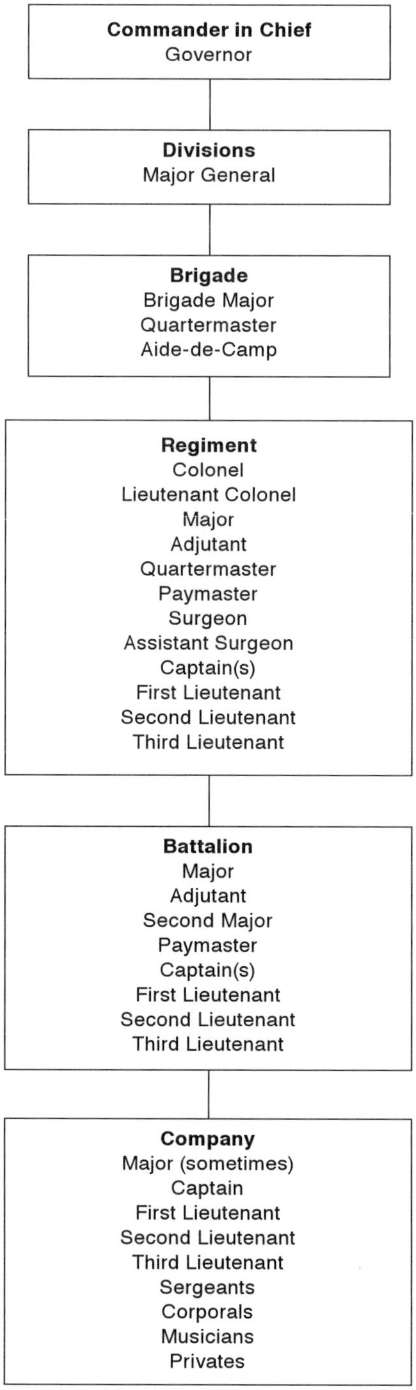

FIGURE 8. Flow chart of officers in a typical state militia in the United States. Officers of the Nauvoo Legion did not feel compelled to follow the "typical state militia" as a model.

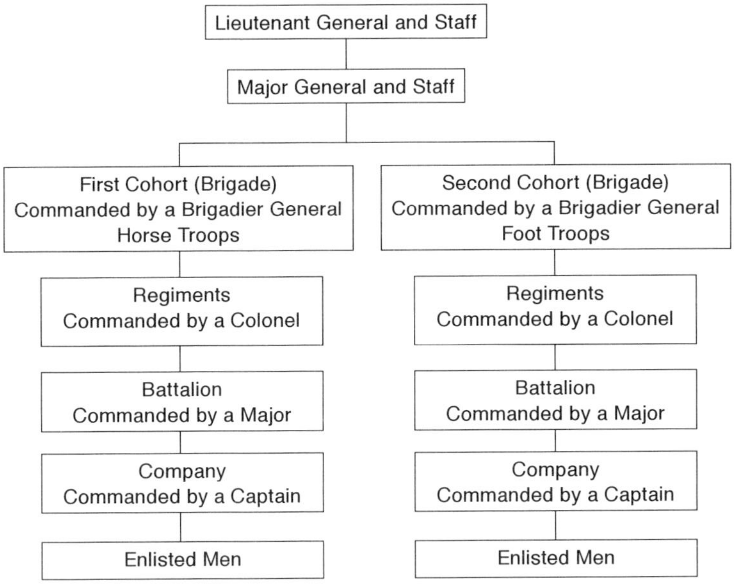

FIGURE 9. Flow chart of officers of the Nauvoo Legion.

As lieutenant general, Smith was the commander, reviewing officer, and leader of the militia unless otherwise directed by the governor of Illinois. He and, later, Brigham Young were commissioned to command all officers and privates in the Legion according to the laws, regulations, and ordinances specified by the state and Legion courts-martial.

Historian Glen Leonard claims that although "in practice Lieutenant General Smith played only a ceremonial role in the Nauvoo militia, his developing role was more central than ceremonial."[40] A staff of able soldiers assisted the lieutenant general. Following the directive of Section 4 of the Legion Charter, the staff consisted of "two principal Aides-de-Camp, a guard, and drill officer." Staff members were selected and appointed by the lieutenant general. The aides-de-camp were given the rank of colonel, meaning they received the rank, pay, and emoluments of a "Colonel of Calvary."

[40] Leonard, *Nauvoo*, 114.

The lieutenant general selected a "guard of twelve Aides-de-Camp, with the rank of Captain of infantry," which title signified that these aides received the pay and emoluments of a captain. Next, the lieutenant general selected "a drill officer with the rank of Colonel of dragoons." The officer received the pay and emoluments of that office.[41]

The "Revised Laws of the Nauvoo Legion," made necessary by the growth of the Legion, added to the lieutenant general's staff an inspector general, a chief chaplain, assistant chaplains, additional aides-de-camp, secretaries, and more guards.[42] These titles reflected the military duties each was expected to perform. For example, aides-de-camp served as secretaries and confidential assistants. The inspector general attended and inspected cohorts during parade exercises. The drill officer, a title not used in other United States militias,[43] supervised the guards and reported irregularities, delinquencies, and other questionable activities. The chief chaplain was responsible for the spiritual well-being of the soldiers. And the herald and armor bearer assumed maintenance and display of Legion, state, and national flags.

Major General

Second in command of the Nauvoo Legion was the major general, who reported directly to the lieutenant general. He also served as secretary of the Legion and as the inspector general. He took command of parades, supervised officer drills, and reviewed officers at the cohort level. Bennett took pride in his election and commission to the office of major general. It appears that poetess Eliza R. Snow shared his view:

> Then Major General Bennett doth next come in command,
> Ever faithful to his leader and strengthening his hand,
> He's a thorough man of war, and of wisdom deep he knew
> He's always added lustre to the "Legion of Nauvoo."[44]

[41] Nauvoo Legion Charter, Section 4. The personal escort of twelve captains for Smith was excessive by the standards of the day. Did it mean protection from real or perceived danger? The answer is probably yes in both cases, as later chapters will show.

[42] See appendix B, Section 14.

[43] It was assumed that many officers were qualified to drill and train soldiers, therefore, the title was not needed at the national military level.

[44] Snow, "The Nauvoo Legion," *Times and Seasons* 2, no. 17 (June 2, 1841): 467.

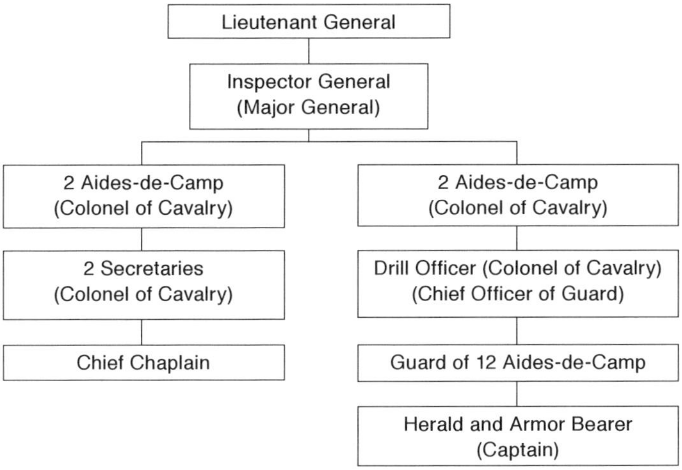

FIGURE 10. Staff of the lieutenant general of the Nauvoo Legion.

But the luster of Bennett was short lived. It ended when he sought to override and undermine decisions made by the lieutenant general. "It is true that I had Joe Smith appointed, or elected, Lieutenant General," boasted Bennett, but he concluded the appointment was "a mere play thing[, for Smith] does not know enough of military matters to tell the difference between a Corporal and a General"[45] (see chapter 8).

After Bennett was dishonorably discharged from the Legion, Wilson Law became major general. When Law, in turn, was cashiered in 1844, Charles C. Rich was elected major general. Each man had different views of the Legion and its military role in Nauvoo. The ever-flamboyant Bennett left no question in the minds of soldiers or observers who was second in command. He sought for and received applause. In contrast, Law showed real interest in weaponry, drills, small effective parading, and in preparing the Legion to defend Nauvoo. Rich gave strict obedience to the orders of the lieutenant general, evidencing his willingness to fulfill the expected role of a major general.

Bennett's staff, like those of Law and Rich, consisted of an adjutant general, surgeon general, cornet, division inspector, quarter-

[45] Bennett, as quoted in Taylor, *Nightfall at Nauvoo,* 137.

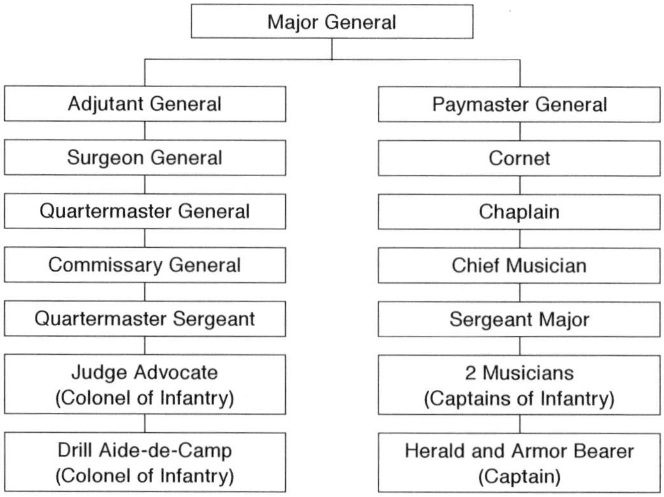

FIGURE 11. Staff of the major general of the Nauvoo Legion.

master general, paymaster general, commissary general, chaplain, judge advocate, cohort surgeon, aides-de-camp, quartermaster sergeant, sergeant major, chief musician, and two musicians.[46] Like the staff soldiers assigned to the lieutenant general, their titles corresponded to their military assignments. For example, the adjutant general was responsible for Legion paperwork. He wrote letters and reports and responded to missives received from regiments, battalions, and companies. He signed orders given by the major general and passed them on to the appropriate military personnel. The paymaster general was the treasurer of the Legion. He received state funding for the Legion and any fines paid by penalized soldiers. He remitted payment for service and other authorized payments as ordered by the major general. The surgeon general, as the title implies, was the chief medical officer. He supervised regimental surgeons, coordinated medical treatments, stored and distributed medicines, and had oversight of all surgical procedures. The quartermaster general was responsible for arming the men with state weapons, applying for additional arms from the state depository, and keeping

[46] See Nauvoo Legion charter. See also Nauvoo Legion, "Minutes and Ordinances of Organization."

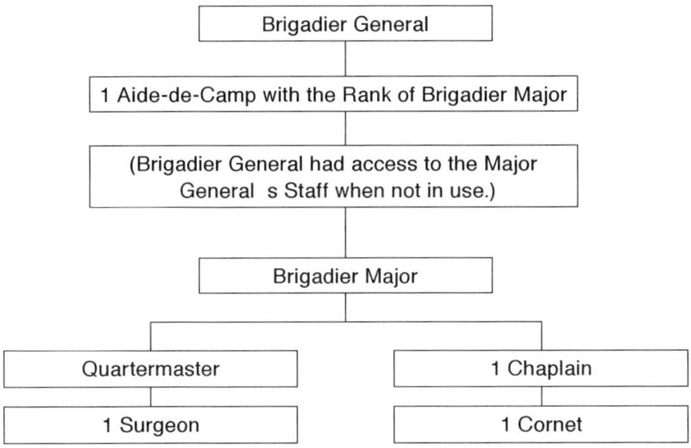

FIGURE 12. Cohort organization of the Nauvoo Legion.

arms in readiness at all times. The commissary general was responsible for procuring and supplying provisions. The judge advocate served as legal counsel; the chief musician selected and orchestrated the presentation of music for parading; and the chaplain, as one might expect, safeguarded the spiritual welfare of the soldiers.[47]

The soldiers appointed to the staffs of the lieutenant general and the major general were respected, obeyed, and honored:

> Their honor and their merits, I cannot now relate,
> We have so many men who are men of honor great;
> We've orators and sages, and priests and prophets too
> And soldiers valiant-hearted in the "Legion of Nauvoo."[48]

The Legion consisted of two brigades, or cohorts. The first consisted of horse troops and the second, foot troops. Each cohort was commanded by a brigadier general, subordinate officers to the major general.[49] The brigadier generals received orders from the major

[47] Twelve assistant chaplains, six in each cohort, were appointed. Eleven of the twelve were members of the Quorum of the Twelve Apostles, the exception being William Marks.

[48] Snow, "The Nauvoo Legion," *Times and Seasons* 2, no. 17 (June 2, 1841): 467.

[49] Davison Hibbard, Wilson Law, George Miller, Charles C. Rich, Don Carlos Smith, and Daniel H. Wells were brigadier generals.

general and, when necessary, had access to his staff to execute the orders.

Brigadier generals were expected to review troops at regimental musters. They were aided in the review process by an aide-de-camp, who held the rank and station of brigadier major. The major accompanied the brigadier general in his changes of station and recorded all orders. He recorded muster rolls issued or received by the brigadier general and served in a secretarial capacity at cohort elections and parades. In addition, the brigadier major inspected weapons at cohort musters and prepared an annual rank roll of the brigade for the major general and state adjutant general. The other members of his staff held subordinate positions. The quartermaster was subordinate to the general quartermaster just as the brigade chaplain, surgeon, and cornet were subordinate to the staff of the major general.

A colonel commanded a regiment of about five hundred soldiers and executed the orders of the brigade general. A colonel represented his troops at regimental and cohort meetings. He had direct supervision of staff officers and military maneuvers at the regimental level, such as drills, inspections, uniforms, and camp appearances.[50]

Assisting the colonel was a lieutenant colonel, who carried out orders issued by the colonel on and off the battlefield. The lieutenant colonel supervised drilling, parading, and inspections. Also serving on the colonel's staff was the quartermaster sergeant, who supplied, when necessary, food, clothing, and equipment. The regimental judge advocate delivered the orders issued by the colonel and performed such secretarial responsibilities as recording dates of commissions, resignations, and preparing rank rolls. He also attended elections and acted as a clerk at regimental parades. The drum major, paymaster, fife major, and color bearer functioned much like their counterparts at the cohort and general levels, but on a smaller scale.

Commanding a battalion was a major.[51] The battalion major was

[50] The following served as colonels in the Nauvoo Legion: Samuel Bent, Titus Billings, George Coulson, Jonathan Dunham, Joseph Hammond, Jesse Harmon, Francis Higbee, Nelson Higgins, Stephen Markham, George Miller, Hosea Stout, and Henry Young.

[51] Men elected to the office of major in the Nauvoo Legion were Samuel Bennett, Samuel Billings, John Bills, Peter Conover, Aaron Golden, John Greene, Solomon Hancock, A. H. Holden, Jesse Hunter, Hiram Kimball, John D. Lee, William Niswanger, Joseph Noble, John Pack, Thomas Rich, Willard Richards, Alanson Ripley, John Scott, George A. Smith, William Smith, Hosea Stout, Lorenzo Wasson, William Wightman, and James Worthington.

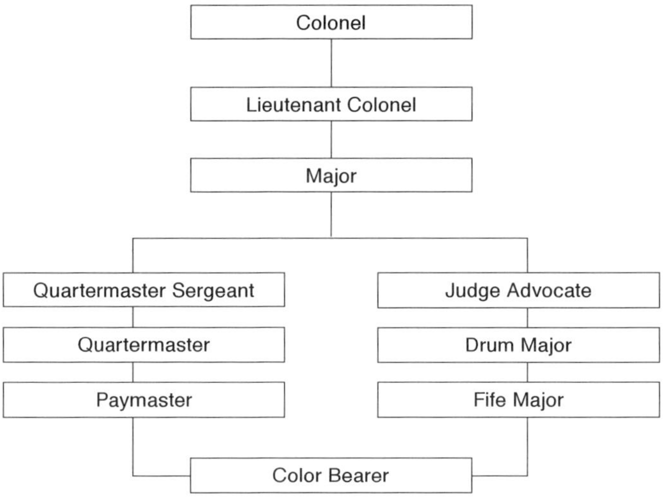

FIGURE 13. Regiment organization of the Nauvoo Legion.

responsible for the respective companies. His organization was composed of not less than two or more than four companies. Although the title of major sounds impressive, in actuality a major was subordinate to officers at the regimental, cohort, and general levels. A major carried out orders issued by his superiors and represented the battalion at the regimental level. Serving with the major was a battalion adjutant, who, like his counterparts at higher levels, functioned as a counselor and secretary. The adjutant sent reports of the battalion's activities and implementations of orders to the colonel.

The captain was the commander of a company—the officer on the "front line." He had the most direct contact with the enlisted soldiers. Whether at company parades, drills, or inspections, he kept the company "in-line."[52] Assisting him were noncommissioned offi-

[52] The following served as captains in the Legion: William Abner, Orvil Allen, Isaac Allred, William Allred, Thomas Anderson, Joseph Andrews, Truman Angel, William Austin, Charles Barnum, Titus Billings, George Black, Levi Bracken, George Brandon, William Burgess, Luman Calkins, Sylvanus Calkins, Nathaniel Case, Darwin Chase, Moses Clawson, George Clyde, Peter Conover, Charles Dana, Edward Darkey, Amos Davis, John Degraw, Nathan Dixon, John Ewell, Thomas Filcher, James Flack, Lysander Gee, John Gleason, Henry Glover, Stephen Goddard, Thomas Grover, Andrew Hamilton, Solomon Hancock, Henry Herriman, Chancey Higbee, Francis Higbee, Joseph Holbrook, Jesse Hunter, William Huntington, Edward Larkey, Alonzo (*continued, next page*)

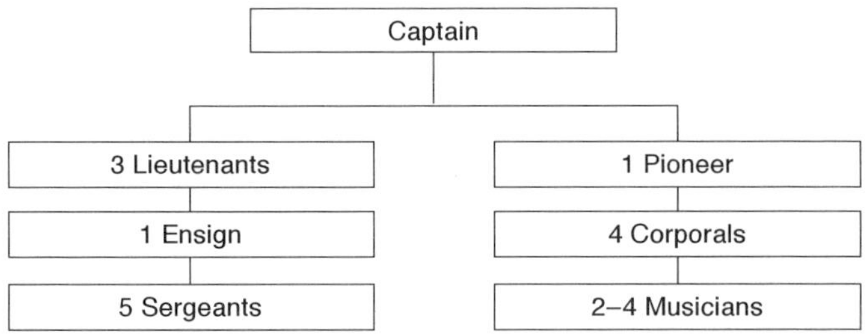

FIGURE 14. Company organization of the Nauvoo Legion.

cers—first lieutenants, second lieutenants, third lieutenants, sergeants, corporals, ensigns, pioneers, and musicians.

Although this six-level organization of the Nauvoo Legion theoretically worked "like clock work," each officer knowing his responsibilities and limits, in actuality the functioning of the Legion on a day-to-day basis was quite inefficient. Mormon officers were expected to put ecclesiastical assignments ahead of their military service. At any given time, assistant chaplains, such as Brigham Young, Heber C. Kimball, Orson Pratt, and Parley P. Pratt, willingly accepted mission calls before military assignments. Likewise, 223 of the Legion officers were members of the Quorums of Seventy and left the Legion from time to time to fulfill various missions for the Church. And the Legion also suffered from those same ailments that plagued other militias—absenteeism, forgetfulness, and all the ills that hamper a large organization. Lest we berate their efforts, it must be remembered that the Nauvoo Legion was composed of citizen soldiers and, as such—for many military exercises were not a high priority—was not unlike most other Illinois militias. Yet as time passed and the city became increasingly threatened from within

LeBaron, John D. Lee, Ira Lincoln, John Loveless, John Luce, Stephen Markham, George Miller, Arthur Milliken, Justus Morse, Samuel Musick, Jesse Nichols, William Niswanger, John Olney, James Pace, John Pack, John Parker, William Parker, Morris Phelps, Charles C. Rich, Thomas Rich, William Riley, W. J. Ritchey, Lewis Robbins, Richard Rushton, John Scott, T. K. Shearer, Luman Shurtliff, Lorenzo Snow, Augustus Stafford, Sylvester Stoddard, Allen Stout, Thomas Thornton, Alva Tippetts, John Tippetts, Theodore Turley, Edward Webb, Edwin Whiting, William Wightman, Benjamin Wilber, T. W. Wilson, Zachariah Wilson, B. B. Wither, and James Worthington.

and without, the value and serious nature of this well-defined militia became increasingly important to the men.

Conclusion

The Nauvoo Legion had a tenuous beginning but mushroomed into the largest militia in Illinois in the 1840s. It never, however, rivaled the size of a Roman legion of six thousand soldiers. Yet approximately three thousand men did enlist who, in turn, elected 491 known officers to lead them on and off the battlefield.[53] The six-level military structure evidences not mere pomp and ceremony but a well-ordered, multi-level leadership structure with a simple but effective design. Each soldier knew his place and the place of each superior officer. From private to officer, responsibilities and duties were clear.

Thus, as early as 1841, the Nauvoo Legion had positioned itself, from an organizational standpoint, to succeed. On May 6, 1843, its lieutenant general proudly said, "The officers did honor to the Legion. . . . [T]hey had made great improvements both in uniform and discipline." Speaking in behalf of the officers, he praised the men: "We felt proud to be associated with a body of men, which, in point of discipline, uniform, appearance, and a knowledge of military tactics, are the pride of Illinois, one of its strongest defenses, and a great bulwark of the western country."[54] Bennett also believed Smith's confidence in the Legion to be well placed, and that with proper management—perhaps himself—"the Legion might . . . be made very useful to the country." He recognized the soldiers as "the most accomplished, brave, and efficient of the corps."[55] But it was not Bennett who would lead the Legion to its greatness. Joseph Smith proved to be more than a figurehead and more capable to lead than Bennett had presumed.

---

[53] The election process was ongoing between 1841 and 1845. As shown in appendix D, one individual could serve for a time as a first lieutenant and later be elected to second lieutenant, sergeant, or captain. Darwin J. Chase served as a first, and then second, lieutenant, and eventually made captain.

[54] *History of the Church*, 5:383–84.

[55] Bennett, *History of the Saints*, 211–12.

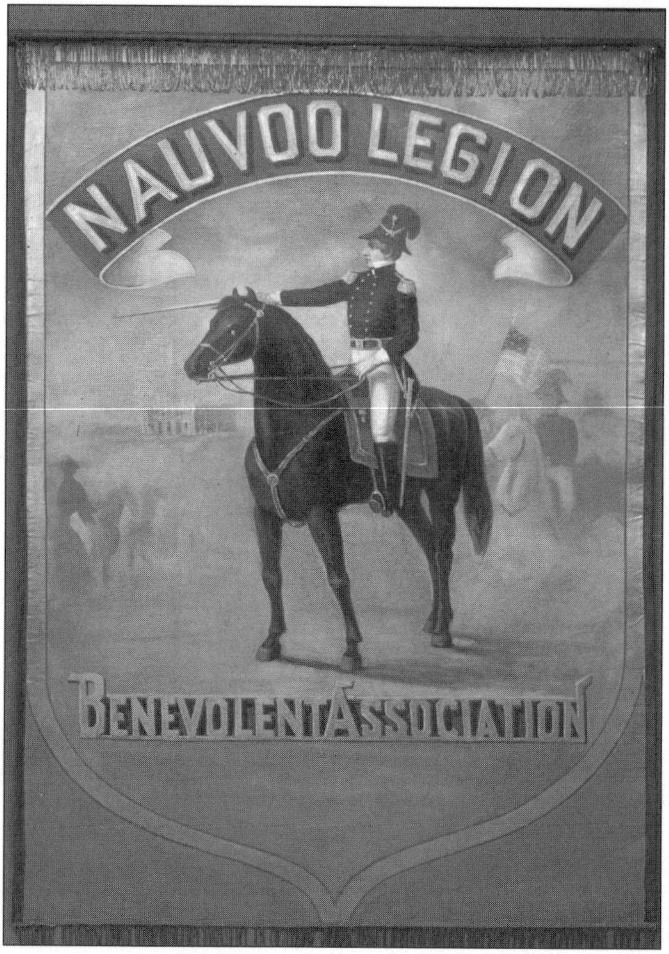

FIGURE 15. Joseph Smith on horseback.
Banner of the Nauvoo Legion Benevolent Association, ca. 1903,
by Danquart A. Weggeland. Paint on silk, with metal fringe and wooden pole,
60 in. × 44 in. *Courtesy of Church History Museum.*

5

Joseph Smith
Prepared to Lead a Militia

This people shall have their legal rights, and
be protected from mob violence or
my blood shall be spilt upon the ground
like water, and my body consigned to the silent tomb.
JOSEPH SMITH

The early 1840s marked a period of astonishing growth in Nauvoo. Not only did Joseph Smith emphasize the importance of building up the Church, but he also directed his followers to build a temple, provide for cultural and educational advancements, and develop Nauvoo into one of the largest cities in Illinois.[1] However, during this time of great prosperity, he was also involved in more than spiritual and community growth. He commanded the largest militia in the state. As one newspaper generously reported, "Lieutenant General Joseph Smith commanded a sizeable force of soldiers which were as well-drilled as regular soldiers."[2]

[1] While it is possible that Nauvoo was the largest city in Illinois in the 1840s, the available numbers are not conclusive. The *Warsaw Signal* reported the population of Nauvoo as 22,599 in 1846. David E. Miller and Della S. Miller put the number closer to 12,000. See Miller and Miller, *Nauvoo,* 64, 75. Mormon military historian Sherman Fleek estimates the population of Chicago at the same time to be 17,832. Letter of Sherman Fleek to Don Cannon, November 26, 2005.)

[2] *Sangamo Journal,* June 3, 1842. Some historians, such as B. H. Roberts, believed that the Nauvoo Legion consisted of "the best body of militia in the State of Illinois." See Roberts, *Rise and Fall of Nauvoo,* 74.

If Smith was a religious leader who preached a gospel of peace, why did he allow himself to lead such a military body? Some historians contend that Smith never intended to use the Nauvoo Legion as an active militia;[3] the Legion existed merely for show—parades and military exhibitions. However, new evidence challenges these theories. It reveals that Smith took the Nauvoo Legion seriously and intended to use it for defensive purposes, if necessary. Although his religious convictions encouraged peaceful coexistence, by the time the Mormons reached Nauvoo, he had grown weary of persecution and suffering resulting from conflicts and misunderstanding. For him, the Legion was not a psychological deterrent created merely for parades and military exercises; rather, it provided the Mormons with a constitutional and state-sanctioned means to defend themselves within legal constraints.

Most studies of Smith have concentrated on his claims of divine revelation and religious thought. Certainly his religious beliefs deeply influenced his personal philosophy—almost to the point that they were inseparable; however, to fully understand his military views it is important to look beyond the religious influences in his life. Although his military thought was in accordance with Book of Mormon defensive military thought and influenced by revelations he claimed to receive, it is imperative to consider his military heritage and personal experiences, which include repeated exposure to mob violence, a march to Jackson County with Zion's Camp, and his Missouri incarceration. The combination of all of these several influences forged his determination to support a militia capable of defending the rights of his people.

"The Duty Which They Owed to Their God"

To what extent the Book of Mormon affected his developing military thought is impossible to gauge; however, it includes detailed

[3] Richard L. Bushman, a leading authority on Joseph Smith, subscribes to this thesis: "Under his direction, the Legion restricted itself to parades, ceremonies, maneuvers, and speeches, a style more to Joseph's taste. No engagements ever occurred." Bushman, *Rough Stone Rolling,* 372. Historians David and Della Miller agree and add that "no such action was ever contemplated." "No such action" refers specifically to Mormon retaliations after the martyrdom of Joseph and Hyrum Smith. For sometime after, many non-Mormons greatly feared that the Nauvoo Legion would seek retribution for its lost leader. Miller and Miller, *Nauvoo,* 101.

accounts of military strategy, battles, wars, and the entire destruction of two ancient civilizations. The book not only reveals a clear warning of the dangers of war and praises to those who threw down their weapons for the cause of peace and Christian obedience, it also stresses the importance of defending freedom even at the cost of war. The book's message that defensive warfare is justified, but only when all other options have failed, may have contributed to Smith's personal views of military affairs.[4]

He may also have been influenced by the revelations which he claimed to have received as Church leader. Many have references to war and are laced with military terminology.[5] Some describe the emergence of a new church as a metaphorical fight between good and evil.[6] Some point to wars to come. For example, in December 1832, Smith said that a civil war would "shortly come to pass beginning at the rebellion of South Carolina." While careful observers are quick to point out that South Carolina threatened secession from the Union in 1832 and that many then felt a civil war was an eventual likelihood, Smith said it would "terminate in the death and misery of many souls"—a chilling statement fulfilled in a conflict that lasted far longer and claimed far more lives than most ever anticipated. Smith also foretold that "war will be poured out upon all nations, beginning at this place."[7] He believed that this and other prophetic statements concerning wars in the last days would inevitably be fulfilled. The very next day he wrote the "olive leaf," a declaration of great and lasting peace, after which he wrote a letter

---

[4] The Nephites, according to the Book of Mormon, were a peaceful civilization in ancient America. Inspired by a better cause than their enemies, they were not fighting for monarchy nor power but

> for their homes and their liberties, their wives and their children, and their all, yea, for their rites of worship and their church.
>
> And they were doing that which they felt was the duty which they owed to their God; for the Lord had said unto them, and also unto their fathers, that: Inasmuch as ye are not guilty of the first offense, neither the second, ye shall not suffer yourselves to be slain by the hands of your enemies.
>
> And again, the Lord has said that: Ye shall defend your families even unto bloodshed. Therefore for this cause were the Nephites contending with the Lamanites, to defend themselves, and their families, and their lands, their country, and their rights, and their religion. (Alma 43: 45–47)

[5] See *Doctrine and Covenants,* 1:13–14 as an example.

[6] See *Doctrine and Covenants,* 5:14, 6:2.

[7] *Doctrine and Covenants,* 87:2.

encouraging the Christian world to repent and avoid the destruction that awaited them.[8]

He claimed that other revelations directed him to defend himself as well as his family. One in particular, received in August 1833, just as the Mormons were experiencing open conflict with their Missouri neighbors, advised patience and, if possible, a peaceful solution to the mounting hostilities. However, they felt authorized to use military action if diplomatic efforts failed. In the context of this revelation, Smith received three laws: the "law of retaliation," the "law of war," and the "law of forgiveness." The "law of war" contains this military solution:

> And again, this is the law that I gave unto mine ancients, that they should not go out unto battle against any nation, kindred, tongue, or people, save I, the Lord, commanded them.
>
> And if any nation, tongue or people should proclaim war against them, they should first lift a standard of peace unto that people, nation, or tongue;
>
> And if that people did not accept the offering of peace, neither the second nor the third time, they should bring these testimonies before the Lord;
>
> Then I, the Lord, would give unto them a commandment, and justify them in going out to battle against that nation, tongue or people.[9]

Thus the Saints were encouraged to "lift a standard of peace" three separate times. If their enemies came against them a fourth time, then they were justified in carrying out a planned military defensive. Joseph Smith's revelations, then, were mixed—one proclaimed peace and another allowed for war. He would have preferred peace but believed himself justified in retaliating when Mormon rights were repeatedly violated.

"Joseph Smith Claimed the Love of Liberty from Both Grandfathers"

How much Smith's heritage influenced patriotic and military feelings is another factor. As scholar Richard Lloyd Anderson explains,

[8] *History of the Church,* 1:312–16. See also Robinson and Garrett, *A Commentary on the Doctrine and Covenants,* 3:86.

[9] See McConkie and Ostler, *Revelations of the Restoration,* 707–18; *Doctrine and Covenants,* 98:33–36.

"Joseph Smith claimed the love of liberty from both grandfathers [Asael Smith and Solomon Mack]."[10] Both men served their country as soldiers, thus demonstrating a strong sense of militarism and patriotism. Asael Smith's views on the subject are contained in his political credo: "Bless God that you live in a land of liberty, and bear yourselves dutifully and conscionable towards the authority under which you live. See God's providence in the appointment of the Federal Constitution, and hold union and order as a precious jewel."[11] True to his conviction, Asael Smith enlisted in the military less than a week after the signing of the Declaration of Independence in July 1776. Smith's maternal grandfather, Solomon Mack, served in the French and Indian War and the American Revolution. Mack's greatest military involvement was during the ill-fated assault against French-held Fort Ticonderoga in 1758. In the failed frontal attack, he saw firsthand the horror and brutality of war. Of a subsequent engagement near Wood Creek in present-day New York, he wrote, "The enemy rose like a cloud and fired a volley upon us, and my being in front brought me into the rear. I turned little to the right, the tomahawks and bullets flying around my ears like hailstones."[12] During the Revolutionary War against Great Britain, Mack served on an American privateer, a nonmilitary naval vessel with legal authority to attack enemy ships and take them as bounties of war. He had several engagements against British merchantmen along the Atlantic Coast.[13]

The influence of these grandfathers is best seen in Smith's well-known "Appeal to the Green Mountain Boys." In this plea to his native state of Vermont, Smith made reference to his ancestors fighting for American liberty: "From the old French War to the final consummation of American Independence, my fathers, fought and bled; and, with the most of that venerable band of patriots, they

[10] Anderson, *Joseph Smith's New England Heritage,* 92.

[11] Anderson, *Joseph Smith's New England Heritage,* 92.

[12] Anderson, *Joseph Smith's New England Heritage,* 39.

[13] For background on the battles at Fort Ticonderoga, see Anderson, *Crucible of War,* 240–49. Solomon Mack also mentions a Major Putnam in his account who is none other than Israel Putnam, who was nearly burned at the stake by Indians during this episode and later commanded American forces at Bunker Hill, striking the now famous legend motto, "Do not fire until you see the whites of their eyes." (Some historians have attributed this phrase to Colonel William Prescott). Solomon Mack also served alongside the famous American Robert Rogers whose guerilla unit "Rogers Rangers" had many daring exploits during the French and Indian war. For interesting accounts of these adventures, see Parkman, *Montcalm and Wolfe,* 375–78.

have gone to rest—bequeathing a glorious country with all her inherent rights to millions of posterity."[14]

Smith may also have been influenced by the War of 1812, which took place during his childhood. Due to tensions over Great Britain's naval blockade and impressment of American sailors into the British navy, disagreements over trade, and territorial expansion into the American Northwest, the United States declared war on Britain.[15] It is difficult to determine the immediate impact of the war on Smith. The general sentiment in New England was opposition to the war,[16] but Smith was very young at the time, and probably more concerned with his leg operation and recovery than what was taking place in the war at the time.[17] However, from early on he had an awareness of war.

"Frequently Beset by Mobs"

Although the United States was not threatened during Smith's adult life as it was during his grandfathers' lives, Smith understood the value of liberty. Repeatedly subjected to personal attacks and mob violence, he recognized the importance of upholding human rights—even if it meant resorting to violence.

He had suffered verbal attacks since 1820, when he shared his visionary experience of seeing God in the woods near his parental home in Palmyra. Later, as these assaults became more physical, he developed a defensive posture. Soon after, the Book of Mormon

[14] Smith, *General Joseph Smith's Appeal to the Green Mountain Boys.* This pamphlet, published in Nauvoo in 1843, was a reprint of the letter he sent to Vermont, originally called "An Appeal to the Freemen of the State of Vermont, the 'Brave Green Mountain Boys,' and Honest Men." The letter reviews many of the sufferings and injustices of the Mormons and solicits help of the Vermont militia to seek redress for the persecutions suffered in Missouri.

[15] Current, Williams, and Freidel, *American History,* 193–201. For more information on the War of 1812, see Borneman, *1812,* and Stagg, *Mr. Madison's War.*

[16] Sherman, Sessions, and Potash, *Freedom and Unity,* 156–57.

[17] Following a devastating outbreak of typhoid fever in the Connecticut Valley, Joseph Smith's leg became seriously infected. Doctors felt it necessary to amputate, but his mother convinced them not to. The doctors were able to treat the infection with surgery and save the boy's leg. Young Joseph Smith was sent to stay with his Uncle Jesse in Salem, Massachusetts, to help his recovery. It is believed that he was exposed to more war while staying with his uncle than he was with his family in New Hampshire. How the war affected him is not recorded, but his inability to serve in the Far West militia was a direct result of this operation. Bushman, *Joseph Smith and the Beginnings of Mormonism,* 32–3[3] See also Wirthlin, "Joseph Smith's Boyhood Operation."

records were in his possession. "No sooner was it known that I had them," wrote Smith, "than the most strenuous exertions were used to get them from me."[18] One evening he was attacked three separate times; each time he was beaten with a gun. Smith made his escape, but not until dislocating his thumb by striking an assailant.[19] Clearly Smith felt justified using force to protect himself, but as time went on and the attacks became more intense, he was unable to defend himself without help.

A particularly severe attack came on the night of March 24, 1832, in Hiram, Ohio. He and his wife Emma had been up much of the night taking care of sick twins they had recently adopted. Smith had just fallen asleep when he was awakened by the screams of his wife. Dragged from his bed by "an infuriated mob,"[20] he tried to defend himself, but the number of men in the home soon overpowered him. After they dragged him from the house, they stripped and scratched him and applied tar to his body. After the mob dispersed, Smith's friends spent the remainder of the night scraping tar and feathers from his body. The next day, a Sunday, Smith recorded, "With my flesh all scarified and defaced, I preached to the congregation as usual."[21] Surrounded by friends and faithful followers at that Sunday meeting, Smith could easily have exacted revenge on the men who had been in the mob the night before. This he preferred not to do.

This encounter illustrates an important aspect of his defensive philosophy. He was determined to defend himself and his rights when under attack, but was neither vengeful nor willing to use force to attack others. He was not by nature a violent man. He reported that "the house was frequently beset by mobs and evil designing persons" and that "several times [he] was shot at, and very narrowly escaped."[22] Weeks before his death Smith rejoiced that in the afterlife "there will be no fear of mobs, persecutions, or malicious lawsuits and arrests; but it will be an eternity of felicity."[23] This perspective helped him bear trials with patience; yet when attacked,

---

[18] *History of the Church,* 1:18.

[19] Bushman, *Rough Stone Rolling,* 60. See also Smith, *History of Joseph Smith by His Mother,* 144; Garrett, "Obtaining and Protecting the Plates," 71.

[20] *History of the Church,* 1:261.

[21] *History of the Church,* 1:261–64. See also Bushman, *Rough Stone Rolling,* 178–79.

[22] *History of the Church,* 4:538.

[23] Cannon and Dahl, *The Prophet Joseph Smith's King Follett Discourse,* 74–75.

he believed all people had the right to defend their homes, families, and religion when called by God to do so.

"Redemption of Zion Must Needs Come by Power"

An opportunity to actuate this principle came in 1833, with the expulsion of the Latter-day Saints from Jackson County, Missouri. On February 24, 1834, Smith made the following proclamation:

> The redemption of Zion must needs come by power; therefore I will raise up unto my people a man, who shall lead them like as Moses led the children of Israel; for ye are the children of Israel, and of the seed of Abraham; and ye must needs be led out of bondage by power, and with a stretched out arm; and as your fathers were led at the first, even so shall the redemption of Zion be.[24]

Subsequently, Zion's Camp came into being (see chapter 2); this provided experience in military organization. The *History of the Church* records that Smith divided "the whole band into companies of twelve, leaving each company to elect its own captain, who assigned each man in his respective company his post and duty."[25] Smith later reorganized the camp, Heber C. Kimball wrote: "Joseph Smith was acknowledged commander-in-chief; Lyman Wight[26] was chosen general of the camp; then Brother Joseph chose twelve men for his life guards. . . . Brother George A. Smith[27] was Brother Joseph's armor bearer; Hyrum Smith[28] was chosen captain of the life guard; the remainder of the camp was organized into companies."[29]

Justus Morse,[30] who "was chosen with nine others out of the

---

[24] *Doctrine and Covenants,* 103:15–18.

[25] *History of the Church,* 2:64.

[26] Lyman Wight (1796–1858) was a military leader and defender of the Latter-day Saints in Missouri; aide-de-camp and brevet major general in the Nauvoo Legion; apostate; led a faction of the Church to Texas.

[27] George A. Smith (1817–75) marched with Zion's Camp; was ordained an apostle in 1838; assistant chaplain and major in the Nauvoo Legion; in the First Presidency of the Church, 1868–75.

[28] Hyrum Smith (1800–1844) was one of the Eight Witnesses to the Book of Mormon; assistant to the President of the Church, 1841–44; chaplain and brevet major general in the Nauvoo Legion; patriarch.

[29] Guthrie, "Joseph Smith as an Administrator," 58. Joseph Smith made the changes halfway through the journey.

[30] Justus Morse (1809–87) was a captain and first lieutenant in the Nauvoo Legion; migrated to Utah; returned to the Midwest; affiliated with the Reorganized Church of Jesus Christ of Latter Day Saints.

'Camp' as sharp shooters," wrote, "[T]he whole company were armed with guns, pistols, and knives, and we expected to deliver said 'lands' from the mob who occupied them, and to avenge the Lord on his enemies as provided in the Prophet's revelations."[31] Joseph Noble noted that "President Smith would have us travel some times with our arms on and then with out it."[32] And Wilford Woodruff recorded that "the men were armed with dirks pistols Swords & rifles For Self defence and according to Brother Joseph's request I delivered him my Sword for his own use."[33]

Regarding the practical aspects of military tactics, Smith wrote, "[I] proposed for a diversion that we divide the camp into three parts and have a sham battle, which was agreed to. . . . Many of our captains showed considerable tact and more acquaintance with military matters than I had expected."[34] Another instance "proved that nearly every man in the camp was ready for battle":

> About eleven o'clock this evening our picket guards reported that they saw the fires of the mob on the southeast of us. I instantly arose and discovered the mistake; but wishing the brethren to enjoy the scene as well as myself, immediately discharged my gun, which was a signal to call all men to arms. When the companies were all paraded and ready for battle, I pointed them to the reflection of the rising moon . . . which gave the appearance of the reflection of the light of a number of camp fires.[35]

After marching to Missouri, Smith claimed that a revelation from God directed the camp to disband. The revelation was a trial of faith for those who anticipated open conflict with the Missourians.[36] Nevertheless camp members complied, little knowing that on that march

[31] Affidavit of Justus Morse, March 23, 1887, Pleasanton, Iowa.

[32] Noble, "Reminiscences of Joseph Bates Noble, 1810–1900."

[33] Woodruff, *Wilford Woodruff's Journal,* 1:9.

[34] *History of the Church,* 2:74.

[35] *History of the Church,* 2:72.

[36] Smith led Zion's Camp with the understanding that the Mormons who had been driven out of Jackson County would be escorted to their homes by the Missouri state militia and that the camp would then offer protection from further attacks. However, when Governor Daniel Dunklin, fearing civil war, refused to provide troops to help the Mormons and negotiations between the opposing sides broke down, Joseph received a revelation stating that God had accepted the sacrifice of the camp, but that the camp would not engage in combat. Chase, "Zion's Camp," *Encyclopedia of Mormonism,* 4:1627–29.

"Joseph [had] instituted his plan to mold the camp into a unified military force."[37]

Zion's Camp, although militarily unsuccessful, may have influenced Smith in several ways. First, it obviously provided him with practical military experience. He was required to oversee the camp and keep the men (many of whom were unhappy and disgruntled) in order. He was also required to make sure his men were armed and prepared for battle. Some have argued that Zion's Camp was a precursor for the Nauvoo Legion;[38] at the very least, it gave him a taste of military leadership. Smith emerged from it better trained and better prepared to lead a future militia.

"Bro[ther] Joseph Has Unsheathed His Sword"

Subsequent events in Missouri would also influence Smith. At the risk of repeating some of the events discussed in chapter 2, it is important to assess their impact on Joseph Smith himself. According to historians Dean Jessee and David Whittaker, "The defensiveness of their [Mormons'] histories from 1839 on, can, in large measure, be attributed to their experiences [in Missouri]."[39] These experiences include the election at Gallatin, the skirmish at Crooked River, Haun's Mill Massacre, and the Mormon expulsion from the state. According to Alexander Baugh, the year 1838 saw an "emergence of a militaristic spirit" among many Latter-day Saints.[40]

Sidney Rigdon's famous "Oration," given on July 4, 1838, illustrates this point:

> In times of peace, it ought to be our aim and our object, to strengthen the bands of the Union by cultivating peace and good will among ourselves. And in times of war, to meet our foes sword in hand, and defend our rights, at the expense of life. For what is life when freedom has fled! . . . We have proved the world with kindness, we have suffered their abuse without cause, with patience, and have endured without resentment, until this day, and still their persecutions and violence does not cease. But from this day and this hour, we will suf-

[37] Launius, *Zion's Camp,* 83.

[38] Launius, *Zion's Camp,* 172. While we see the influence of Zion's Camp, clearly the structure of the Nauvoo Legion was different.

[39] Jessee and Whittaker, "The Last Months of Mormonism in Missouri,"1:5.

[40] Baugh, "A Call to Arms," 36.

> fer it no more. . . . We will never be the aggressors, we will infringe on the rights of no people; but shall stand for our own until death.[41]

The "Oration" is punctuated with Rigdon's fiery rhetoric; it is nonetheless a fact that Smith enthusiastically endorsed his words. In an editorial, he wrote,

> The oration delivered on the occasion, is now published in pamphlet form: those of our friends wishing to have one, can get it, by calling on Ebenezer Robinson,[42] by whom they were printed. We would recommend to all the saints to get one, to be had in their families, as it contains an outline of the suffering and persecutions of the Church from its rise. As also the fixed determinations of the saints, in relation to the persecutors, who are, and have been, continually, not only threatening us with mobs, but actually have been putting their threats into execution; with which we are absolutely determined no longer to bear, come life or come death, for to be mobbed any more without taking vengeance, we will not. EDITOR.[43]

The military engagements between the Mormons and northern Missourians heightened tensions between the opposing groups, but it was not until the fall election in 1838 in the small Missouri town of Gallatin that rising tensions reached an impasse. A few Mormons, residents of Daviess County, had gone to Gallatin to vote, never anticipating that at the polls they would be targets of political and religious persecution. As they approached the polling place, they were surprised to overhear William Peniston, a candidate for office, telling fellow Missourians that the Mormons were rascals and must not be allowed to vote. His cavalier speech and the influence of alcohol led to an argument and fight.[44] "The mob commenced their abuse [striking] one of the brethren, they hollowed out kill him dam kill him the Brethren ran to his relief," wrote Andrew Moore.[45] Outnumbered, the Mormons battled; Smith was upset by the encounter, but praised his followers for defending their rights, recording that they "fought like lions."[46]

---

[41] Crawley, "Two Rare Missouri Documents." One of the documents is a reprint of the published version of Sidney Rigdon's speech. For more on the dramatics of rhetoric in antebellum America, see Largey, "The Rhetoric of Persecution."

[42] Ebenezer Robinson (1816–91), editor of the *Times and Seasons* newspaper in Nauvoo; affiliated with the Reorganized Church of Jesus Christ of Latter Day Saints.

[43] Durham, "Election Day Battle at Gallatin," 58.

[44] *History of the Church,* 3:56–57.

[45] Moore, "Reminiscences of Andrew Moore, 1846."

[46] *History of the Church,* 3:59.

Certainly the conflict at Gallatin fueled Smith's desire to create an effective militia: "the Missourians planned to prevent the Mormons from voting," denying them one of their fundamental Constitutional rights.[47] Smith was determined to protect those freedoms. Professor Baugh states, "The election-day battle at Gallatin on August 6, 1838, was neither a large scale riot nor a military conflict but it essentially marked the beginning of the Mormon War in Northern Missouri."[48] From this time forward, neither Mormon nor Missourian lived without uneasiness or fear.

By October, Mormons and Missourians fought openly.[49] Significant encounters included the Battle of Crooked River and the Haun's Mill Massacre. These tragedies deeply affected Smith. Reading an account of the massacre at Haun's Mill by a mother who lost her husband and a son, he recorded, "Thus are the cries of the widows and the fatherless ascending to heaven. How long, O Lord, wilt thou not avenge the blood of the Saints?"[50] As news of the massacre spread, more violence followed. Government forces surrounded Far West, the largest Mormon settlement in northern Missouri. Hoping to avoid further bloodshed, General Samuel D. Lucas of Jackson County "sent in a flag of truce" to Far West. He wanted to "delay the attack of the City for the night if [Mormons] would surrender Joseph Smith, Sydney Rigdon & P. P. Pratt as hostages until tomorrow morning, 8 o'clock, when they should be returned."[51]

As Joseph Smith and the other Mormon leaders were being led toward the militia camp of General Lucas, they were arrested and taken prisoner. This was followed by an illegal court-martial in which the Mormon prisoners were sentenced to death. As the illicit order was given, General Alexander W. Doniphan of Clay County stepped for-

---

[47] Durham, "Election Day Battle at Gallatin," 49.

[48] Baugh, "A Call to Arms," 102.

[49] Baugh, "A Call to Arms," 185–90. Baugh explains that in response to Joseph Smith's request that the Mormons begin to take matters into their own hands, a company was organized to enter Daviess County and oppose the mob efforts there. However, by the time the company arrived, mobs had burned "several isolated Latter-day Saint homes. At least seven Mormon families . . . were reported to have been among the first victims." Baugh, "A Call to Arms," 191. The Mormons responded by plundering and burning three settlements believed to harbor members of the mob, Gallatin, Millport and Grindstone Fork. Pillaging and burning by both Mormons and anti-Mormons escalated over the next few days. Baugh, "A Call to Arms," 191–217.

[50] *History of the Church,* 3:325.

[51] "Papers of Albert Perry Rockwood, 1838–1839."

ward and defiantly told General Lucas, "It is cold-blooded murder. My brigade shall march for Liberty tomorrow morning at 8 o'clock; and if you execute these men, I will hold you responsible before an earthly tribunal, so help me God."[52] General Lucas did not carry out the planned execution. However, Smith and his party remained in his custody and were subsequently taken to Independence, Jackson County, where they were mocked and paraded before a curious crowd. Transferred to Richmond, Ray County, they were again imprisoned but allowed to attend a courtroom hearing before Judge Austin King, who ordered them to Liberty Jail to await further prosecution.[53]

Thus, over a few short months, Smith and many of his followers saw homes burned, property stolen, and family members murdered. They had come to know much of expulsion from their lands, having been told by the Missouri governor that they were "enemies" in need of "extermination." Smith, himself, had been indicted, ordered to be publicly executed and detained in prison on what some considered false and malicious charges. While in prison in Liberty Jail, he felt more helpless than ever. As he passed months in deplorable conditions, the Mormons were driven from the state. He became resolute in his determination to develop a military force that would protect the rights of his people. Perhaps Albert Rockwood's letter to his father, dated Monday, October 29, 1838, best illustrates his defensive resolve and emerging military leadership:

> You may ask if the Prophet goes out with the Saints to Battle? I answer he is a Prophet to go before the people as in times of old . . . Is not this marvelous? Bro. Joseph has unsheathed his sword & in the name of Jesus declares that it shall not be sheathed again until he can go into any country or state in safety and peace.[54]

Fleeing from persecution in Missouri, the Mormons settled in Illinois. Within nineteen months of their arrival, the Mormons had organized the Nauvoo Legion.

---

[52] *History of the Church*, 190–91.

[53] The jail, called "Liberty" because of its location in the town of Liberty, Clay County, Missouri, was a 22 × 22 foot, two-story limestone structure. It had a single door and small barred windows on both the lower and upper floors.

[54] "Papers of Albert Perry Rockwood." It is interesting that Josiah Quincy understood the impact of these experiences, when, after visiting the prophet, he wrote "The past had shown him that a military organization was necessary." "Josiah Quincy on Joseph Smith," *Cultures in Conflict*, 46.

"In Full Military Suit"

Mormon faithful insisted that Smith be elected to the highest rank, that of lieutenant general in the Nauvoo Legion (see chapter 4). Although the Mormons elected him commander of the Legion, Illinois Governor Carlin "appointed" him to the rank and grade by a state militia commission.[55] In this era, the rank of lieutenant general, whether in the militia or in the Regular Army, was rarely used and was considered a special honor. A commission in the state militia, however, had no bearing or equality in the Regular Army of the United States. Military personnel from the state militias never automatically transferred to the army during war. Officers through the rank of colonel were appointed by state governors. All general officers, whether Regular Army or volunteer, were appointed by the President of the United States.

The fact that Joseph Smith accepted the rank of lieutenant general is evidence of his support of the Nauvoo Legion. Furthermore, it underscores the importance of the Legion in Smith's view. During what would later be termed as "a very large meeting," he stated that "his commission declared that he (General Smith) was the Lieutenant General of the Nauvoo Legion, and of the militia of the State of Illinois, and as such it was not only his duty to enforce the city ordinances, but the laws of the State when called on by the Governor."[56] Not only did Smith honor his rank but he encouraged others to do the same. George Q. Cannon related a circumstance in which a Methodist minister interrupted one of Smith's discourses, saying, "Why, I told my congregation the other Sunday that they might as well believe Joe Smith as such theology as that." The Mormon leader asked, "Did you say Joe Smith in a sermon?" to which the minister replied, "Of course I did. Why not?" To this Smith countered, "Considering only the day and the place, it would have been more respectful to have said Lieutenant General Joseph Smith."[57] This statement demonstrates that Joseph Smith obviously derived personal satisfac-

---

[55] *History of the Church,* 4:309–10; Lieutenant General's commission; in Joseph Smith Papers (box 6, fd. 5), Church History Library. In stating that the State of Illinois commissioned Joseph Smith as Lieutenant General, we are running counter to much that has been written about this matter. Many believe that it was only a rank within the Nauvoo Legion and that it was not a rank in the state militia. See, for example, Bergera, "Joseph Smith and the Hazards of Charismatic Leadership," 35.

[56] "Journal History of the Church," December 9, 1843.

[57] Cannon, *Life of Joseph Smith,* 349.

tion from his position in the Legion. Many Mormons did opt to call him "General" or "Lieutenant General" in their speech and personal journals. Wilford Woodruff[58] was a close personal friend and a member of the Quorum of the Twelve Apostles, and typically referred to him as "President Smith," or "the Prophet," but also deemed it appropriate to call him "General Smith" at times: in describing the arrival of Mormons from England to Nauvoo, he said "they landed near General Smith's place."[59] Clearly the Mormons perceived him as primarily as a prophet, and to a lesser extent, their military leader.

Aside from his rank, Smith's military character was evidenced in his wearing of the Legion uniform. Eunice Billings Snow wrote,

> [S]ome of the most impressive moments of my life were when I saw the Nauvoo Legion on parade with the Prophet (then General Joseph Smith) with his wife, Emma Hale Smith, on horseback at the head of the troops. It was indeed an imposing sight. . . . He in full military suit. . . . His coat was black, while his white pants had red stripes on the outside seams. He also wore a sword at his side.[60]

His wearing of the uniform was not restricted to Legion events. It was also evident in his everyday life in Nauvoo. George Moore, a Unitarian minister from Quincy, Illinois, had an interview with Smith on June 3, 1842. As Moore left Smith's house, the reverend noted, "As I came out, I found two large cannon, mounted in his yard. Can this be a prophet of God, thought I, who must have cannon for a guard, and must convert all his followers into soldiers—into a 'Nauvoo Legion'—and excite in them a warlike spirit?"[61]

---

[58] Wilford Woodruff (1807–98) was an assistant chaplain in the Nauvoo Legion; apostle; first President of the St. George Temple; President of the LDS Church, 1887–98.

[59] Woodruff, *Wilford Woodruff's Journal,* 2:173. In their admiration of Joseph's rank, they were much like other Americans.

[60] Andrus and Andrus, *They Knew the Prophet,* 153.

[61] On November 22, 1840, the *Bloomington Herald* reported a "warlike spirit" stemming from Nauvoo and that militant Mormons were having trouble living peacefully with their neighbors: "From citizens of Montrose, we learned that they [Mormons] paraded for military training weekly, when they are taken through all the exercises in the use of arms. Their purposes for training are not openly avowed, but those who have had much intercourse with them are of the opinion that it is to avenge themselves on Missouri, so soon as their increasing strength will warrant a hope for success. Let their object be what it may, they cannot live long in peace with the neighboring country, it is certain that our southern neighbors may anticipate trouble with them. Their numbers already give them an impudence that free men cannot long quietly submit to and it is increasing to a remarkable degree." Donald Q. Cannon, (*continued, next page*)

"Defensive Rather than an Aggressive Psychology"

It is true that Smith was heavily involved in the Nauvoo Legion, but it is important to consider the actual "spirit" of his military philosophy. As we have tried to show, many factors influenced his military philosophy, including the Book of Mormon, personal revelations, his ancestry, his experience with Zion's Camp, and the difficulties in Missouri. His religious nature may have pushed him toward peace, but his experience led him to head a legal militia to defend the rights of Mormons. His emerging military thought in Nauvoo contains elements of both.

On the Legion, Smith said, "[It] embraces all our military power, and will enable us to perform our military duty by ourselves, and thus afford us the power and privilege of avoiding one of the most fruitful sources of strife, oppression and collision with the world."[62] Addressing members of the Legion, he added:

> We are American citizens. We live upon a soil, for the liberties of which our fathers periled their lives and spilt their blood upon the battle-field. Those rights, so dearly purchased, shall not be disgracefully trodden under foot by lawless marauders without at least a noble effort on our part to sustain our liberties.[63]

Many of Smith's military ideas found their way into his religious and secular rhetoric. Following his arrest at Dixon, Illinois, he said, "But before we bear this unhallowed persecution any longer—before I will be dragged away again among my enemies for trial, I will spill the last drop of blood in my veins, and will see all my enemies in hell! To bear it any longer would be a sin, and I will not bear it any longer."[64] Later in that same address, he added,

> Our enemies have prophesied that we would establish our religion by the sword. Is it true? No. But if Missouri will not stay her cruel hand in her unhallowed persecutions against us, I restrain you not any longer. I say in the name of Jesus Christ, by the authority of the holy priesthood, I this day turn the key that opens the heavens to restrain you no longer from this time forth. I will lead you to the battle; and if you are not afraid to die, and feel disposed to spill your

"Reverend George Moore's Comments," 11. This news article and Reverend Moore's comments reflect the perception that the Mormons had a war-like tendency (see chapter 9).

[62] Cannon, *Life of Joseph Smith*, 363.

[63] Cannon, *Life of Joseph Smith*, 497.

[64] *History of the Church*, 5:467.

> blood in your own defense, you will not offend me. Be not the aggressor; bear until they strike you on the one cheek; then offer the other, and they will be sure to strike that; then defend yourselves, and God will bear you off, and you shall stand forth clear before his tribunal.[65]

In another address, Smith expressed similar ideas: "Always act upon defense but if your enemies oppress you the 2d & 3d time let it come & roar like thunder & you shall stand forth clean before the tribunal of any citizens of Illinois. Deny our right let them go to hell and be damned. I give up my chartered right at the sword and bayonets."[66] Similarly, in September 1838, he said, "We will not act on the offensive, but always on the defensive; our rights and our liberties shall not be taken from us, and we peaceably submit to it, as we have done heretofore, but we will avenge ourselves of our enemies, inasmuch as they will not let us alone."[67] Taken literally, the preceding quotations prove that Smith was determined to use the Legion to defend his followers.

As historian Robert Remini notes, "Joseph fully intended to use this army to *protect* his Church."[68] Defense was his key military concept. In a letter of May 4, 1841, Smith wrote,

> The Legion is not, as has been falsely represented by its enemies, exclusively a Mormon military association, but a body of citizen soldiers organized (without regard to political preferences or religious sentiments) for the public defense, the general good, and the preservation of law and order—to save the innocent, unoffending citizens from the iron grasp of the oppressor, and perpetuate and sustain our free institutions against misrule, anarchy and mob violence.[69]

---

[65] *History of the Church,* 5:468. Smith even described a dream with militant overtones: "I dreamed that a silver-headed old man came to see me and said he was invaded by a gang of robbers, who were plundering his neighbors and threatening destruction to all his subjects. He had heard that I always sought to defend the oppressed, and he had come to hear with his own ears what answer I would give him. I answered, if you will make out the papers and show that you are not the aggressor, I will call out the Legion and defend you while I have a man to stand by me. The man then turned to go away. When he got a little distance he turned around and said I must call out the Legion and go and he would have the papers when I arrived, and says he I have any amount of men which you can have under your command." *History of the Church,* 5:473.

[66] Ehat, *Words of Joseph Smith,* 223.

[67] *History of the Church,* 3:68.

[68] Remini, *Joseph Smith,* 150; emphasis added. Whether the Nauvoo Legion was not exclusively Mormon became an issue for those opposed to the Legion. See chapter 4 on the composition of the Legion.

[69] Roberts, *Rise and Fall of Nauvoo,* 98.

Smith's followers understood his defensive stance. In a letter to his brother George, John S. Fullmer[70] wrote, "And as regards our military, we are to be sure, only a handful, but enough of us to whip any mob that can be started in this country; so you need not fear ever to see the tragedies of Missouri acted over again without a two handed game. That's the object of our Legion."[71] Parley P. Pratt once noted the advantage of the defensive posture of the Legion: "peculiar advantage . . . it affords that security and protection against lawless violence which has been so much needed of late; but which our people could seldom enjoy until thus organized."[72] Pratt's fervor prompted him to predict that the Legion would grow to "fifty thousand strong," and that it would be "led by ambitious and talented officers."[73] William Huntington[74] penned that "everything is in a rapid state of improvement to Guard against the enemy that is that we May be in perfect readiness to defend ourselves with all kinds of weapons of war."[75]

Rank-and-file members saw the Nauvoo Legion as their own militia. They understood its legal status, but also saw it as a Mormon militia. As part of Hosea Stout's history of the Nauvoo Legion, he penned a poem on this theme. Two key verses follow:

> Our "Legion" is all powerful, 'tis a war-like, brave, and grand,
> E're long 't'will prove a terror to Boggs and all his clan,
> 'Tis peaceable and harmless to all who come to view,
> Or, have a mind to settle in the "City of Nauvoo."
>
> Now should our foes be gathered to drive us from our lands,
> Or try to thwart our purposes, to break the Lord's commands,
> The day they come against us, as they before did do,
> They'll feel the weight and power of the "Legion of Nauvoo."[76]

---

[70] John Solomon Fullmer (1807–83), clerk for Joseph Smith; Paymaster General and Brevet Brigadier General of the Nauvoo Legion; served as a Church land agent in Nauvoo.

[71] "Letters of John Solomon Fullmer," April 21, 1845.

[72] Godfrey, "Causes of Mormon Non-Mormon Conflict," 143.

[73] Godfrey, "Causes of Mormon Non-Mormon Conflict," 141.

[74] William Huntington (1784–1846), Second Lieutenant and Captain of the Nauvoo Legion; helped bury the bodies of Joseph and Hyrum Smith; served as the presiding elder in Mt. Pisgah, Iowa, in 1846.

[75] Huntington, "Diary and Autobiography of William Huntington."

[76] "Journal History of the Church," April 6, 1841.

Conclusion

Although Joseph Smith acted primarily as a religious figure, he also functioned as a military leader. His military ideas and activities derived from a variety of sources and influences. He studied and translated scriptures and proclaimed revelations that motivated him to seek peaceful solutions to difficult situations, yet allowed for a military response and action. He was influenced by the patriotic example of his paternal and maternal grandfathers, and he learned the value of freedom for himself when his rights were violated. Having organized, trained, and marched in Zion's Camp to regain control of property lost in Jackson County, he learned much about military tactics and command. He had been an unwilling participant in the violence and brutality of mobs, which caused him to grow weary of repeated violations of constitutional rights. He felt threatened by Missouri and was the target of escalating persecution and religious misunderstanding in Illinois. His military preparation was more experiential than it was academic.

These collective influences led him to accept the rank of lieutenant general of the Nauvoo Legion. As the commander, he insisted that the Legion be trained to defend his people. For him, the Legion existed not only for parades and reviews.[77] He was ready, willing, and able to protect his followers with military might. In his final speech, "drawing his sword and presenting it to heaven," he said:

> I call God and angels to witness that I have unsheathed my sword with a firm and unalterable determination that this people shall have their legal rights, and be protected from mob violence, or my blood shall be spilt upon the ground like water, and my body consigned to the silent tomb. While I live, I will never tamely submit to the dominion of cursed mobocracy.[78]

Having shown in this chapter that Joseph Smith was prepared to lead the Nauvoo Legion, we next turn to the day-to-day operation of this unique Illinois militia. That operation is best seen by reviewing the history of the courts-martial.

---

[77] Interview with Marvin S. Hill, September 19, 2005. See also Hill, "Religion in Nauvoo," 123; and Hill, *Quest for Refuge*, especially chapter 5.

[78] *History of the Church*, 6:499.

6

Courts-martial
Judicial and Lawmaking

The court martial of which shall be composed of the commissioned officers of said Legion and constitute the law making department, with full powers and authority to make, establish, and execute, all such laws and ordinances as may be considered necessary for the benefit, government, and regulation of said Legion.

"An Ordinance Organizing the Nauvoo Legion," Section 25

Buried deep in the archival manuscripts of the Nauvoo Legion are the minutes of courts-martial proceedings. Not always the most exciting material, they have something important to say and we would do well to shine light on these long-neglected records. They confirm the ongoing efforts of the leadership of the Legion to uphold the integrity and reputation of the Legion by disciplining its contrary and wayward members and by controlling all matters pertaining to the Legion. Thus the courts-martial of the Legion had a twofold purpose: to discipline soldiers guilty of personal misconduct unbecoming a member of the Legion; and to regulate the activities of the Legion itself, to insure compliance to state law, to improve efficiencies, and to supervise overall operations.

We begin by examining the role of courts-martial in militias generally. Most readers will appreciate the fact that militias retained the right to discipline their members, to ensure good conduct, and to preserve integrity. Military courts-martial have special provisions to judge the conduct of citizen soldiers, which civil courts are not prepared or empowered to adjudicate. Such courts are essential and the Legion in this regard was unexceptional.

"Unofficer-like and Unbecoming Conduct"

It is clear from the minutes that there existed an unwritten, expected code of behavior for the men of the Nauvoo Legion. Thievery, intoxication, lying, conspiracy, attempted murder or suicide, abuse of women, adultery, usurping another's role, and other forms of unbecoming conduct were unacceptable behaviors. Such actions, either by officers or privates, were not tolerated. Although not unique to the Legion, such displays of misbehavior may have been more easily identified in Nauvoo, for the actions of the Legion courts mirrored the religious practices of the city's dominant religion. Disobedient Mormons were under triple scrutiny: ecclesiastical courts retained and exercised the power of excommunication and virtual expulsion from the community; public courts tried and punished one for criminal activity; and, finally, the Legion itself. It was such a tight community that the findings and rulings in one court sometimes spilled over into the considerations of another. A serious misstep in conduct could deprive one of religious, civic, and military privileges. Secret Danite-like behavior, including defiant lawbreaking and conduct destructive of the Church, would not easily go unnoticed and unpunished in the mixture of judicial reviews functioning in Nauvoo. What impact one court's judgments had on the others is difficult to assess, but it is reasonable to conclude that, as did the notorious cases of John C. Bennett and Wilson Law, an excommunication from the Church often meant a dishonorable discharge from the Legion, and perhaps vice versa.

The examples which follow are not meant to defame the character or reputations of those handled by the Legion, but are presented to evidence its efforts to maintain a standard of conduct. The first Nauvoo Legion adversarial court, held on November 30, 1841, dealt with a charge of thievery against David Smith, assistant to the inspector general, and Joseph Holbrook, a captain in rank.[1] The court

[1] Joseph Holbrook (1806–85), captain in the Nauvoo Legion; policeman in Nauvoo; probate judge in Davis County, Utah. It should be noted that being a policeman did not exempt any officer from serving in the Legion. According to the writings of James Pace, also a policeman, "I was chosen a policeman by Joseph (*continued, next page*)

ruled that both men were guilty as charged. Smith and Holbrook were summarily cashiered from the Legion.[2]

That same year, Captain Sylvester B. Stoddard faced charges of intoxication, which, if not constitutionally illegal, was viewed as unbecoming an officer. Stoddard had charged into the Legion band, picked up a drum, beat the drum, and uttered profane language. He was found guilty as charged and fined five dollars for the offense.[3] Not all charges were upheld. For instance, on May 28, 1842, Brevet Major General Wilson Law[4] was charged with using his sword to "stick Sergeant Major Amasa Bonney." Bonney proferred an additional charge: threatening with abusive language without provocation. Law, however, was found innocent of both charges and Bonney was chastised for bringing unfounded charges before the court.[5]

In 1843 Adjutant L. B. Foote accused Major William Niswanger of ordering company elections without notifying him and appointing an unauthorized soldier to serve in his adjutant position. Niswanger was also charged with spreading falsehoods about Adjutant Foote, claiming that he refused to execute his military responsibilities. In this case Niswanger was found guilty of all charges and cashiered from the Legion.[6] A second trial in 1843 charged Captain Sylvester B. Stoddard with leaving his post under the pretense of illness, then getting drunk, insulting the Regimental Court of Assessment, and refusing to report company delinquents. Although chastised, Stoddard was not fined or cashiered from the Legion.[7]

By far the most famous disciplinary courts-martial dealt with those men—two of whom were major generals of the Legion—who went on to conspire against the life of their lieutenant general. The actions of these men and the consequences stemming therefrom are more fully discussed in chapters 8 and 10; however, the judgments

---

Smith and as such served the remainder of my sojourn in the place. That same season I was elected Captain of the 1st Company of Infantry organization in Nauvoo." See Pace, "Papers of James Pace."

[2] See *Times and Seasons*, December 1, 1841.

[3] Sylvester B. Stoddard (1801–67) captain in the Nauvoo Legion. His tin shop in Nauvoo has been restored. "Manuscript Subject File," 1842.

[4] Wilson Law (1807–77) brigadier general of the Nauvoo Legion; proprietor of the *Nauvoo Expositor*. Law served as a brevet major in general, meaning that he was temporarily authorized to hold the position of a major general.

[5] Amasa Bonney (1804–64) first lieutenant and sergeant major in the Nauvoo Legion. "Manuscript Subject File," 1842. See Winders, *Mr. Polk's Army*, 17, 56.

[6] "Manuscript Subject File," 1843.

[7] "Manuscript Subject File," 1843.

of the Legion in their regard must, of necessity, be shown here. Back in June 1842, the Legion court tried the case and alleged gross misconduct of John C. Bennett. This was no little matter, since Bennett was the co-founder and first major general of the Legion, second only to Smith. The court found Bennett guilty of unofficer-like conduct, conspiracy, gross abusive behavior toward women, attempting to commit suicide by poisoning himself, and disrupting the laws and welfare of the people of Illinois. He was cashiered from the Legion, yet continued to wear the Legion uniform (see chapter 8).

There is further significance to the court-martial of Bennett. After leaving Nauvoo and the Church in a spirit of vindictiveness and disdain, he set out on a wide-sweeping lecture circuit in the East, denouncing Smith and the Mormons while flagrantly wearing his Nauvoo Legion uniform. Since he had been dishonorably discharged, he spoke without the support or consent of the Legion. Appearing without sanction in the trappings of what he once had helped to charter, Bennett mocked the very body he once so ardently promoted.

Then, amidst plots to kill the Mormon leader, General Wilson Law was accused on May 7, 1844, of ungentlemanly and unofficer-like conduct. He also was found guilty and cashiered.[8] Three days later Robert D. Foster, surgeon-in-chief and brevet brigadier general of the Legion, was charged with "unofficer-like and unbecoming conduct." He was also cashiered.[9] Law and Foster were also excommunicated at this time.

The above suggest the ongoing judicial workings of the Nauvoo Legion, and more importantly, an unwritten code of behavior for men of the Legion. They suggest the courts' belief that they needed more than drills, weaponry, and courage—they needed moral fortitude. Yet such strict moral and social codes were not outlined in the Legion Charter. Expectations appear to have been implicit and reflect, in part, the dominant religious practices of the community. Nevertheless, whether written or understood, soldiers of the Legion were required to live up to a higher standard of personal conduct. If conduct were broached, the men became subject to judicial proceedings that determined their military fate.

---

[8] *History of the Church,* 6:362; Nauvoo Legion Proceedings, court-martial trials, fd. 6.

[9] Robert D. Foster (1811–78) was a surgeon general of the Nauvoo Legion, a regent of the University of Nauvoo, a member of the Agricultural and Manufacturing Association, and a Hancock County magistrate. *History of the Church,* 6:355.

"The Court Martial Shall Pass no Law or Act Repugnant to, or Inconsistent with, the Constitution of the United States or of this State"

Differing markedly from the judicial actions of the courts-martial were the lawmaking courts of the Legion. It is important to place them within the military law and context of the time.

On December 10, 1840, Illinois Governor Thomas Carlin granted lawmaking powers to the Nauvoo Legion in "An Act to Incorporate the City of Nauvoo."[10] Section 25 of the act reads, "The court martial of which shall be composed of the commissioned officers of said Legion and constitute the *law making department,* with full powers and authority to make, establish, and execute, all such laws and ordinances as may be considered necessary for the benefit, government, and regulation of said Legion." A proviso within the section insisted that the "court martial shall pass no law or act repugnant to, or inconsistent with, the Constitution of the United States or of this State."[11] Thus, these functions of the Legion were provided by law and protected by long years of American military tradition. They were designed to allow militias to set policies and procedures that would allow it to function successfully on a long-term basis.

As per government sanction and according to the "Nauvoo Legion Minutes and Ordinances of Organization," lawmaking courts continued from 1841 to 1844. Unfortunately, it was not until October 21, 1843, over two years after the first court session, that Colonel Hosea Stout[12] was appointed to compile records of past court proceedings. Stout was authorized "to compile the minutes of the General Court Martial and record them in a book to be provided for that purpose and that all minutes of the General Court Martial since the organizing of the Nauvoo Legion."[13] Stout welcomed the opportunity and began his labors with the intent that Major Willard Richards would include his compilation in the history of Mormonism. From January to August 1844, Stout searched the back streets and byways of Nau-

[10] "Governor's Military Correspondence to the Nauvoo Legion."

[11] "An Ordinance Organizing the Nauvoo Legion," Section 25.

[12] Hosea Stout (1810–89) second lieutenant, captain, colonel, and acting brigadier general of the Nauvoo Legion; fought in the Battle of Crooked River; clerk of the Nauvoo High Council; captain of the Nauvoo police.

[13] "Minutes and Ordinances of the Organization of the Nauvoo Legion," October 21, 1843.

voo, seeking all Legion records. Although frustrated in his efforts, he did not quit until a respectable number of records were compiled. His final product, "Chronological History of the Nauvoo Legion in Illinois," lacks the "spit polish" of today's compilations (see appendix C).

However, historians rely upon his compilation to understand the workings of the lawmaking courts in preparing the Legion to defend its city and fulfill its state obligation.[14] Without his efforts to compile the Legion records, historians could not analyze or recount the events of the lawmaking courts martial. For example, we would assume from the wording of Section 3 of the Legion Charter that the "Lieutenant General, as chief commander and reviewing officer" was always the "President of the Court Martial." From Stout, we learn that the directive of Section 3 was altered. Joseph Smith served as president only from February 4, 1841, until March 12, 1842. When his tenure ended, five other Legion leaders served in that capacity, as detailed in the list below:

Lieutenant General Joseph Smith	February 4, 1841–March 12, 1842
Major General John C. Bennett	June 3, 1842
Major General Wilson Law	August 3, 1842
Major General Wilson Law	October 15, 1842
Brevet General Hyrum Smith	May 20, 1843
Major General Wilson Law	June 10, 1843
Major General Wilson Law	July 8, 1843
Brevet General A. P. Rockwood	October 21, 1843
Brevet General A. P. Rockwood	November 4, 1843
Major General Wilson Law	January 13, 1844
Major General Wilson Law	February 15, 1844
Major General Charles C. Rich	August 31, 1844
Major General Charles C. Rich	October 20, 1844

[14] One should not presume that Stout's secretarial skills used by the Nauvoo High Council, the Revision Committee of the Legion, and the Arsenal Committee, qualified him to be a compiler. A close perusal of his secretarial records in these capacities leave most historians disheartened. For example, of the Revision Committee held on June 15, 1843, Stout records, "They met at 9 A.M. It was not until 6 P.M. that this meeting adjourned." His brevity coupled with self-centered anecdotal reporting, "[Stout] had done one days writing which was accepted," puts him more "front and center" than presiding officers and important resolutions. His preoccupation with reporting the adjourning of meetings rather than the substance of those gatherings also proves unfortunate. For example, Stout reported, "The meeting adjourned until Wednesday July 3, 1844. This meeting adjourned until July 6, and then met again on the 7th and 8th." "An Ordinance Organizing the Nauvoo Legion," Section 3.

Stout also noted the names of secretaries of the courts-martial, which are listed below. Although Section 3 of the Legion Charter designated the major general as the "secretary of the Court Martial," the notations of Stout reveal that only in 1841, when Bennett was secretary, was this directive followed.[15] In 1842 James Sloan,[16] general church recorder and city recorder of Nauvoo, served as secretary. The appointment of Sloan suggests that after 1841 the position of secretary was no longer based on Legion rank. Sloan gave himself the distinction of "war secretary to the Major General."[17] Later secretaries, who were elected Legion officers, did not claim this distinction.

Major General John C. Bennett	February 4, 1841–March 12, 1842
War Secretary James Sloan	June 3, 1842
War Secretary James Sloan	August 3, 1842
War Secretary James Sloan	October 15, 1842
War Secretary James Sloan	May 20, 1843
Major Hosea Stout	June 10, 1843
Colonel Hugh McFall	July 8, 1843
Thomas Bullock	October 21, 1843
Thomas Bullock	November 4, 1843
Thomas Bullock	January 13, 1844
Colonel Hosea Stout	February 15, 1844
Colonel Hosea Stout	August 31, 1844
Colonel Hosea Stout	October 20, 1844

Understanding the role of secretary in these lawmaking courts is crucial, for the secretary recorded elections of officers as directed in Section 7 of the Legion Charter: "No officer shall hereafter be elected by the various companies of the Legion, except upon the nomination of the court martial." Section 8 added, "The court martial shall fill and supply all officers ranking between captains and brigadier general."[18] The election records provide Legion historians with information needed to compile a list of officers (see appendix D).

Secretaries failed to record which officers were present at the

[15] "An Ordinance Organizing the Nauvoo Legion," Section 3.

[16] James Sloan (1792–?) war secretary of the Nauvoo Legion; general church recorder, 1841–43; Nauvoo city recorder, appointed February 1, 1840; Nauvoo notary public, elected September 1842; district clerk of Pottawattamie County, appointed March 1848.

[17] "Minutes and Ordinances of the Organization of the Nauvoo Legion," June 3, 1842; August 3, 1842; October 15, 1842; May 20, 1843.

[18] "An Ordinance Organizing the Nauvoo Legion," Sections 7 and 8.

courts-martial, noting only that the "Officers' Role" was taken and that officers were seated according to rank and distinction. Some historians have wrongfully assumed that "all the military officers commissioned or entitled to commissions, within the City corporation" attended the courts-martial, as this was the directive of Section 9 of the Legion Charter.[19] The mere inclusion of Sloan as "war secretary" discounts this premise.

"Court Martial of the Officers of the Nauvoo Legion"

Although many flaws are apparent in the compiled records of the lawmaking courts, the records are significant. Records for the year 1841 include rulings on parades, military uniforms, and election of officers. The year 1842 saw the Legion mature in the courts; the courts passed a series of ordinances in addition to those specified in the Nauvoo Charter. By 1843 they moved from ordinances to resolutions that gave the Legion power, which their near neighbors feared. Some neighbors considered the resolutions about use of weaponry to be beyond the powers granted in the Nauvoo Charter. In 1844 the courts took a back seat to pressing events, such as the murder of Smith and the daily drills that followed. When pressure from outside Nauvoo subsided, there was one last attempt to resurrect the expansive days of the courts—days in which their rulings became military law—but it was largely unsuccessful.

The Formative Year: 1841

From February to December, commissioned officers met in eleven documented legislative courts-martial. Scant records of these proceedings are available for only seven courts. According to the records, the first court was held at 10 A.M. on February 4, 1841, in Joseph Smith's office.[20] At the court, officers were elected, the most prominent being Joseph Smith as lieutenant general, John C. Bennett as major general, William Law as brigadier general of the First Cohort,

[19] "An Ordinance Organizing the Nauvoo Legion," Section 9.

[20] The meeting was held one day after the Nauvoo City Council passed "An Ordinance Organizing the Nauvoo Legion," which set the pattern for presiding and attendance at the courts.

and Don Carlos Smith[21] as brigadier general of the Second Cohort.[22] On February 20, court was again in session. This court ruled that all men in the city of Nauvoo "between the age of 18 & 45 years, excepting such as one exempted by the laws of the United States" enroll in the Legion. It also designated parade days and levied fines for failure or refusal to appear at the parades.[23] On Tuesday, March 2, court again convened. This court ruled that companies be restricted to forty-six rank-and-file members until further notice. Hoping to prevent men from leaving "one ragged company for a more efficient or preferred outfit," the court advised that soldiers must receive permission to change companies.[24] The court, on March 9, hoping to facilitate the rapid growth of the Legion, concluded that two companies constitute a battalion and two battalions compose a regiment.[25] Proceedings of March 15 "have been lost or mislaid."[26] Without a record, we conclude that the pattern of weekly courts continued. However, existing documents verify only three additional courts in 1841—March 15, and September 2 and 4.[27]

---

[21] Don Carlos Smith (1816–41) brigadier general of the Second Cohort of the Nauvoo Legion; president of the Nauvoo High Priest Quorum; member of the Nauvoo City Council; regent of the University of Nauvoo.

[22] "Minutes and Ordinances of the Organization of the Nauvoo Legion," February 4, 1841.

[23] "Minutes and Ordinances of the Organization of the Nauvoo Legion," February 20, 1841.

[24] "Minutes and Ordinances of the Organization of the Nauvoo Legion," March 2, 1841.

[25] This administrative decision was later modified to meet the changing circumstances of the Legion.

[26] Hosea Stout, "Record of the Nauvoo Legion," December 8, 1843, in "Papers, 1840–1872." Stout alleges that Bennett "mislaid" the records. Without the records, historians are left to surmise that the pattern of weekly courts continued.

[27] Evidence for the March court is found on Smith's written commission, which reads, "Headquarters, Nauvoo Legion, City of Nauvoo, Illinois. March 15, 1841—Oath of office administered by me, the day and year above written. It was then signed John C. Bennett, Major General of the Nauvoo Legion." On September 2, 1841, Wilson Law, William Law, Hyrum Smith, Albert P. Rockwood, and George Miller were commissioned brevet major generals. Similarly, on September 4, 1841, Charles C. Rich was elected brigadier general. According to the Legion Charter, administering office, commissioning an officer, and electing an officer could only be done by the courts. Certificate of Commission of Joseph Smith. "Manuscript Subject File," 1841. Another evidence that the court's martial are active in 1841 is a letter sent by Captain William Niswanger, First Lieutenant Stephen Chase, Second Lieutenant Levi Bracken, and Third Lieutenant Gade Yale to the officers of the court martial. They wrote, "To the honorable Court Martial, We the officers of Benjaminite Co. in (*continued, next page*)

Despite this gap in reporting, the proceedings of the 1841 lawmaking courts reveal that courts-martial were held as specified by the Nauvoo Legion Charter and that the presiding officer conducted court sessions and secretaries kept records of the proceedings. Legion officers were in attendance and seated according to rank and distinction. Passing regulations and amending such regulations were important agenda items, for the regulations specified the size of companies, battalions, and regiments. They designated days of general parades, uniforms, and the Legion seal. Although these may appear as nonessential to the military operations of the city of Nauvoo, they were taken seriously. These formative actions set the pattern and laid a foundation for the extensive lawmaking work that lay ahead.

The Year 1842: "A More Perfect Organization"

It was not until Saturday, March 12, 1842, nearly one year after the last recorded court-martial, that another court session was held. A resolution to divide the city into "Four Company militia districts," mirroring the four ecclesiastical divisions of the city, was discussed and unanimously approved. Also approved was Ordinance No. 1, which specified that "the discipline, drill, rules, regulations, and [officer's] uniform" of the Legion be patterned after that of the U.S. Army;[28] the "duty of every white male inhabitant of the City of Nauvoo, between 18 and 45 years of age [was] to enroll himself in some company of the Legion," and failure to enlist within specified days carried a penalty.

At the court held on June 3, John C. Bennett presided and expressed pleasure when "the thanks of this general court martial

---

Nauvoo [a company composed of men aged forty-five] being duly elected by the same pray your Honorable body to grant us the privilege of assembling with the Nauvoo Legion on the 1st and sixth of April next being willing to conform to your laws and discipline as laid down by your body. Notwithstanding our age exempts us from doing our duty, we still feel the Spirit of Seventy Six burning in our bosom, and are willing to grasp the sling and hurl the stone like David of Old." Whitney "Petition to court martial of Nauvoo Legion," MS 17390, Reel 3, Fd 2. Charles Coulson Rich (1809–83) captain, brigadier general, major general of the Nauvoo Legion; regent of the University of Nauvoo; member of the Nauvoo City Council; member of the Quorum of the Twelve Apostles, 1849–83. See Arrington, *Charles C. Rich.* Certificate of Commission, A. P. Rockwood. "Manuscript Subject File," 1841. "An Ordinance Organizing the Nauvoo Legion," Sections 7 and 10.

[28] "Minutes and Ordinances of the Organization of the Nauvoo Legion," March 12, 1842. The minutes of the court martial of March 12, 1842, are incomplete.

[were] tendered to Major General J. C. Bennett, for the able discharge of his duty since the formation of this Legion."[29] The timing of this court is curious, for Bennett had orchestrated a sham battle on May 7, 1842, during which Joseph Smith's life was imperiled. Ten days later, Bennett resigned as mayor of Nauvoo under a cloud of suspicion (see chapter 8). Yet in June, he presided over a court-martial. The main discussion of this court was Ordinance No. 2, which specified the requisite number of soldiers needed in each company be not less than thirty-two or more than sixty-four privates,[30] officers' pay, and that the ranking officer of the lawmaking court "shall be the president of said court" and that "all laws, or ordinances raised by this court were to be submitted to the lieutenant general for approval or disapproval." If the lieutenant general disapproved of the court's action, a two-thirds vote could override his decision. The passage of this ordinance put in place a check-and-balance system and elevated Joseph Smith to an even higher executive level within the courts.[31]

At its meeting on August 3, the court established Ordinance No. 3, which governed company and general parades, drills, and additional courts and a proviso for treasury bills, bonds, and officers' pay.[32]

The last court of 1842 was held on October 15. Ordinance No. 4 was discussed and approved. It specified that "any private or non-commissioned officer residing without the city corporation" had the right to leave an assigned company to enroll in another and soldiers were to receive pay for accepting calls to duty.[33]

---

[29] Bennett was cashiered from the Legion in mid-June 1842, just days after this court martial. "Minutes and Ordinances of the Organization of the Nauvoo Legion," June 3, 1842.

[30] If companies had less than thirty-two privates, they were to attach to other companies. Likewise, if companies had more than sixty-four privates, their surplus members were to be attached to other companies at the discretion of general officers. The assigning and reassigning of such privates became cumbersome.

[31] "Minutes and Ordinances of the Organization of the Nauvoo Legion," June 3, 1842.

[32] "Minutes and Ordinances of the Organization of the Nauvoo Legion," August 3, 1842. One of the paymasters, Joseph Holbrook, wrote "some of the Nauvoo Legion scrip was paid for fines to me which was in my hands upon leaving Nauvoo and the colonel [Jonathan H. Hale of the Third Regiment, Second Cohort] said [I] could keep it until he should call for it in a future day." It is not known whether Colonel Hale ever asked for the funds back. Holbrook, MS 12158. Church History Library.

[33] "Minutes and Ordinances of the Organization of the Nauvoo Legion," October 15, 1842.

These 1842 courts closely aligned Legion companies with the four Mormon political wards in Nauvoo, the same division used for Mormon ecclesiastical units. The passage of four ordinances strengthened the court's governing power over the Legion. The courts demonstrated that they had the right to dictate Legion policies, procedures, and rules; and that they had the power to pass binding laws effecting Legion discipline, drills, parades, and uniforms. Could anyone doubt that the courts-martial of 1842 showed a marked increase in legislative power, influence, and dominion over the men of the Legion?

The Resolutions of 1843: The Increasing Power of the Courts

Reconvening in May 1843, the court passed a resolution specifying the distribution of public arms, the appointment of a Revision Committee to revise laws governing the Legion,[34] and reimbursement for those who "accrued [expenses] for powder, the use of horses, etc. for the cannon."[35] The next court was held on June 10, and discussed the need for an arsenal for storing Legion weapons. It concluded that the location, purchase, and draft of the arsenal was to be determined by leading Legion officers.[36] The court of July 8 resolved that the Revision Committee continue to revise the Legion laws "as they may seem proper until the printing of the same."[37] The court of October 21 resolved that "Hosea Stout be and is hereby appointed to compile the minutes of the General Court Martial" and that "the form of the rank roll of the Nauvoo Legion be accepted, as presented by the Major John Bills"[38] (see appendix D for an interpolation of the form authorized at this meeting).[39] The last court of 1843 was held on November 4; it resolved to pay travel expenses to Spring-

[34] Colonel Hugh McFall, Major Hosea Stout, Captain Theodore Turley, Brigadier General Charles C. Rich, and Major General Wilson Law were appointed to the Revision Committee.

[35] "Minutes and Ordinances of the Organization of the Nauvoo Legion," May 20, 1843.

[36] "Minutes and Ordinances of the Organization of the Nauvoo Legion," June 10, 1843.

[37] "Minutes and Ordinances of the Organization of the Nauvoo Legion," July 13, 1843.

[38] The rank roll has proven very helpful in the reconstruction of the commissioned and noncommissioned officers of the Legion. John Bills created a form for the rank roll. On the form, names of the officers, current rank, dates and places of their commissions, battalion, regiment, cohort, staff or line were included.

[39] "Minutes and Ordinances of the Organization of the Nauvoo Legion," October 21, 1843.

field, Illinois, allowing the Revision Committee to gather additional arms for the Legion.[40]

The courts-martial of 1843 reflected the growing tension and sense of urgency that was beginning to grip Nauvoo. They targeted the need for resolutions regarding weapons, distribution of public arms, the right to carry additional arms, and the construction of an arsenal. These court rulings caused their near neighbors, especially Thomas Sharp of Warsaw, to sit up and take notice. The Legion courts were no longer ruling on uniforms or parades; they focused increasingly on arming the Legion to defend Nauvoo.

The Year 1844: One Last Ordinance and the Need for State Arms

The courts continued in the fateful year of 1844. At the court on January 13, Hosea Stout was assigned to "arrange the laws of [the] Legion for the press" and publishing the laws "at the lowest price."[41] At the February 10 court, Stout was authorized to publish the laws of the Legion in a small booklet, entitled "Revised Laws of the Nauvoo Legion from the Constitution of the United States" (see appendix B).[42] Two months after the death of Joseph Smith, the Nauvoo Legion courts-martial held August 31 called for the election of a new lieutenant general and major general to fill the vacancies created by the death of its lieutenant general and the defection of Major General Wilson Law. Then, for the first time since 1842, an ordinance was introduced. It was brief—only two sections—and its passage swift. Ordinance No. 5 announced that the election for the above-mentioned officers was to be held at 2 P.M. that very day,[43] and it quoted the words Governor Thomas Ford spoke on 27 June: "as a community of military Saints we will let our religion be our protection with such arms as we can procure for ourselves, until we can receive our proportion of the public arms according to the Charter

---

[40] "Minutes and Ordinances of the Organization of the Nauvoo Legion," November 4, 1843; "Minutes and Ordinances of the Organization of the Nauvoo Legion," November 8, 1843.

[41] "Minutes and Ordinances of the Organization of the Nauvoo Legion," January 28, 1844.

[42] "Minutes and Ordinances of the Organization of the Nauvoo Legion," February 10, 1844.

[43] According to the records of Hugh McFall, clerk of the election, the election was held as directed and Brigham Young was elected lieutenant general and Charles C. Rich, major general.

of said Legion."[44] That afternoon, Brigham Young was elected lieutenant general of the Nauvoo Legion.[45] On October 20, the court convened again and granted the newly elected commander in chief sixty-four bodyguards "armed, and equipped as [Young] may direct."[46] With this, the courts-martial of the Nauvoo Legion adjourned.

Conclusion

A brief recounting of the two types of courts-martial evidences the serious nature of the Nauvoo Legion. If nothing else, the existence of a court-martial mechanism, with Joseph Smith as lieutenant general, allowed Smith to play a supervisory role over matters military that he had not had in Missouri. Legion laws that resulted from court proceedings, whether implicit or explicit, were in force for officer and private alike. Judicial courts were the key to assuring that soldiers adhered to a higher code of behavior. Lawmaking courts were the key to resolutions and ordinances binding on the Legion organization. Failure to comply with laws, resolutions, and ordinances of the courts carried stiff penalties. Did the men of the Legion revolt over such judicial and legislative rulings? A few did, and they found themselves summarily cashiered from the Legion. Most were willing to comply with the courts' decisions. As a result, the courts were able to keep a tight lid on the Legion organization. It is a credit to the courts that such a large group of men functioned so well within the context of the Legion and the constitutional constraints of the United States. One example of their efficient and effective ability to function is the Legion on parade.

---

[44] See appendix C.

[45] "Minutes and Ordinances of the Organization of the Nauvoo Legion," August 31, 1844.

[46] "Minutes and Ordinances of the Organization of the Nauvoo Legion," October 20, 1844.

7

More Than Pomp and Ceremony

Why these weekly parades?
Why all this strictness of discipline?
We pause for reply.
THOMAS SHARP

Nauvoo Legion courts-martial passed ordinances and regulations specifying the need for arms inspections, regular drills, and reviews of companies—or what were called Nauvoo Legion general parades. These governing orders ensured that drills, musters, and inspections were ongoing events in Nauvoo between 1841 and 1845.[1] However, they did not ensure that these events would be crowd pleasing. The simple fact was that these events were ongoing and routine—typical of state-sanctioned militia exercises of the time—and warranted little mention. The pomp and ceremony of the Nauvoo Legion parades, however, reveal a sophisticated city militia, capable of performing military operations.

This chapter shows that there was similarity between the Regular Army officers' uniforms and uniforms worn by Nauvoo Legion officers;[2] the early parades, at least until 1842, reflected much pomp

[1] Section 2, Ordinance. No. 3 stipulated that commissioned officers were to drill one or two days before a Legion general parade. The first drill was held in 1841 near the site later used for the Masonic Hall. "Minutes and Ordinances of the Organization of the Nauvoo Legion," August 20, 1842.

[2] Historians interested in the study of military dress have long (*continued, next page*)

and ceremony; as opposition toward the Mormons intensified, later Nauvoo Legion parades emphasized military preparedness over religious cohesiveness; and numerous small, unannounced parades and military exercises, more than the splendid general parades, helped train members of the Legion to defend Nauvoo.

"Adopt for the Legion, . . . the Discipline, Drill, *Uniform*, Rules, and Regulations of the United States Army"

Contemporaneous critics pointed to Nauvoo Legion uniforms, patterned after those worn by officers in the U.S. Army, to support their concerns about Mormon empire building. However, it is fanciful to suggest that the soldiers' ostentatious regalia evidenced a belief of suggested equality with the U.S. Army or a desire to form a Mormon nation. Scores of militia and volunteer companies elsewhere were known for equally colorful dress. Smith stated that the purpose of the Nauvoo Legion was no more or less than to be obedient to the governing laws of the United States that required the formation of citizen-soldier militias, and to protect and defend the city of Nauvoo from future mobs.[3]

A simple reading of the Illinois militia code reveals that proper officers' uniforms were patterned after those of the national forces. Following the state code with exactness, on February 8, 1841, a Nauvoo Legion court-martial voted to "adopt for the Legion, as nearly as may be, and so far as applicable, the discipline, drill, *uniform*, rules, and regulations of the United States army."[4] Twelve days later, Bennett was ordered to specify the style of uniform—in other words, to designate whether Legion uniforms would resemble the attire worn by U.S. Army officers in 1810, 1820, 1830, or 1840. Having more interest in conformity than in resurrecting retired military styles, Bennett opted to have Legion officers dress like Regular Army officers of the 1840s.

---

recognized the importance of artists as a source for uniform information. For artistic renderings of similar uniforms worn by other state militias, see Nihart, "A New York Regiment in California," 4; Riling, "The Wayne Artillery," 117; Craighead, "Military Art in America," 75; and Curtis, "Some Contemporary Views of the New England Militia,"101.

[3] *History of the Church,* 5:57.

[4] "Minutes and Ordinances of the Organization of the Nauvoo Legion," February 8, 1841. *Emphasis added.*

The basic uniform consisted of a double-breasted blue tailcoat adorned with gold or silver epaulets and twin rows of gold-, silver-, or brass-eagled buttons. The coat was to be worn with pantaloons or tight trousers—generally buff in color, but also were seen in blue, white, and grey on the men of the Legion.[5] A red or wine-colored sash with tassels at the ends was to be draped around the waist of the officer. White gloves were to be worn over the hands. Decorative four-foot swords with elaborately ornamented handles were to be attached to a black belt with a buckle and worn at the officer's side. Also attached to the belt were to be one or two flintlock pistols.[6] High, polished boots that reached the knees were worn by ranking officers; a mid-calf military boot was the footwear of the lower ranks. An ostrich feather atop a black cockade chapeau was the expected headdress. The color of the feather revealed the officer's rank. Thus, from head to toe, the rank of an officer was apparent in the uniform.

The cost of the colorful, flamboyant attire tried most officers' budgets. The coat, pantaloons, epaulets, sash, chapeau, gloves, sword, and belt sold for $208.[7] If the cost for the basic uniform was not prohibitive, the tailor suggested (for an additional charge) adding stripes, gold designs, wings, eagles, chevrons, and varied epaulets.[8] Whether these extras made the officer, no one seemed to care, for each man in uniform caught the eyes of swooning females and concerned critics alike. Critics suggested that the splendid uniforms evidenced the serious, professional expectations of the Legion. But some wondered aloud if officers were trying to rival the military hierarchy of the Regular Army. Their musings deserve an answer.

---

[5] A blue military cape could be worn on inclement days.

[6] Since the Legion received only a small number of arms from the state of Illinois, it is likely that the soldiers carried a hodgepodge of weapons. Rifles, muskets, and shotguns would have been the flintlock variety. These weapons worked by attaching flint to the hammer of the gun and pulling the trigger. Resulting sparks ignited powder in the gun's chamber. Most firearms used by legionnaires were single-shot weapons. Only a few soldiers carried the repeating pepperbox pistol. Other items carried by legionnaires were a cartridge box, a powder flask, a rifleman's pouch, a haversack, and a water canteen. Ganoe, *History of the United States Army*, 150–60; *Revised Statutes of the State of Illinois*, 302. It is interesting to compare other militia uniforms. See Burgess and Walker, "Norfolk Light Artillery Blues," 129; and McMaster, "Military Dress," 173.

[7] The proffering of another $185 was needed for the necessary "horse equipments." In today's dollar, the cost of the uniform would exceed $800. Joseph Smith and John C. Bennett, "Nauvoo Legion, General Orders," *Times and Seasons* 2, no. 14 (May 15, 1841), 417–19.

[8] *Revised Statutes of the State of Illinois*, 302.

(*left*) FIGURE 16. Staff officers, United States Army, 1841–1851.
Plate by H. Charles McBarron, Jr., in *Military Collector and Historian* 15, no. 1 (Spring 1963), 15. *Courtesy of the Company of Military Historians.*

(*right*) FIGURE 17. Norfolk Light Artillery blues, 1838.
From Donald A. Burgess and Carroll H. Walker, "Norfolk Light Artillery Blues," *Military Collector and Historian* 14, no. 4 (Winter 1962), 128. *Courtesy of the Company of Military Historians.*

Credit for the "look alike" military attire goes to John Bills, a Nauvoo tailor. On April 30, 1841, Bills advertised, "He has just received the latest fashions direct from Philadelphia, (through the politeness of President Hyrum Smith) and is prepared to turn out work with dispatch and in the best and most fashionable style. All kinds of military coats made according to the latest pattern."[9] He then named leading officers who endorsed his fine tailoring: "Lt. Gen. Jos. Smith, Major Gen. J. C. Bennett, Brig. Gen. Wilson Law, Brig. Gen. D. C. Smith, and Col. John S. Fullmer."[10] History does not record whether he was motivated by anything other than profit.

[9] Smith and Bennett, "Nauvoo Legion, General Orders," *Times and Seasons* 2, no. 14, May 15, 1841, 417–19. John Bills was born in 1819 in Pennsylvania. He was a personal tailor of Joseph Smith. After Smith's death, Bills migrated west to Utah. Once in Utah, Brigham Young advised him not to continue his trek to California. He defied Young's counsel. Bills died near the Sierra Nevada on February 19, 1850.

[10] Smith and Bennett, "Nauvoo Legion, General Orders," *Times and Seasons* 2, no. 14, May 15, 1841, 417–19.

It is reasonable to suppose that all commissioned and noncommissioned officers rushed to Bills's tailor shop, but such was not the case. Commissioned officers balked at the high price for uniforms and refused to wear them until courts-martial threatened stiff fines for failure to comply. According to Ordinance 3, Section 1, issued at the August 3, 1842, court-martial, the lieutenant general and major general would be fined "thirty dollars; Brevet Major Generals and Brigadier Generals, twenty-five dollars; Colonels, fifteen dollars; Lieutenant Colonels and Majors, ten dollars; Captains, six dollars" for failure to appear on parade grounds in an authorized uniform.[11] Soon commissioned officers were waiting in line at Bills's establishment.

Like their reluctant ranking officers, most noncommissioned officers tried to delay the purchase of a uniform. One excuse after another was accepted until 1844, when a court-martial resolved that a fifty-cent fine be levied against noncommissioned officers for failure to appear on parade in full uniform. These officers were given until September 1, 1844, to obey or have the fine imposed. As begrudging officers paid the price and spruced up, privates took notice. Soon entire companies were wearing simple but consistent attire, what some called "Sunday best." Their new look fulfilled the requisites of Ordinance 3, Section 1, which reads, "[The] uniforms of the United States Army, so far as applicable, be and they hereby are adopted for the Legion; provided, that each company may adopt its own uniform for the non-commissioned officers and privates belonging to it."[12] The makeshift clothing, worn with boots that laced and handheld homemade accoutrements, sufficed for companies in general, but not for aspiring privates and soon not for courts-martial: "Every . . . private who shall appear upon parade without the proper arms, and equipage, as adopted by their respective companies, shall be fined in a sum of twenty-five cents." In August 1842, Ordinance 3 specified that "the sum of one dollar for each company or battalion parade, and two dollars for each cohort or Legion parade" be levied against any soldier out of uniform.[13] By 1844 privates were reporting to the parade

[11] Resolutions passed by courts martial ensured that legionnaires missed few parades. On February 20, 1841, fines were stipulated for nonattendance. "Minutes and Ordinances of the Organization of the Nauvoo Legion," February 20, 1841.

[12] "Minutes and Ordinances of the Organization of the Nauvoo Legion," Ordinance No. 3, Section 1, August 20, 1842.

[13] "Minutes and Ordinances of the Organization of the Nauvoo Legion," Ordinance No. 3, Section 1, August 20, 1842.

grounds in uniforms that resembled those of their commanding officers. With members of the Legion so adorned, the Nauvoo Legion parade was a spectacle, an event not to be missed. It showed, in a very public way, the allegiance that each citizen soldier had for the Legion and for his position within that military body.

"To Honor, Not the World, but Him that is Alive and Reigns"

Hosea Stout captured in verse the significance of the first general Legion parade, held in conjunction with the eleventh anniversary of the Church of Jesus Christ of Latter-day Saints:

"Legion of Nauvoo"

'Tis now the sixth of April in Eighteen Forty-one,
Eleven years exactly since the "Church of Christ" begun;
And then all men did hate us, our numbers being few,
But now we've honor, power; we've a "Legion of Nauvoo."[14]

At the parade, strong underpinnings between the Nauvoo military presence and the Mormon religion were unmistakable. Such an unabashed display of military prowess mixed with religious worship caught some visitors unawares.

In the early morning hours of April 6, 650 men in fourteen companies from Illinois and two adjunct companies from Iowa Territory assembled at the parade grounds. Hancock County courts were canceled, local businesses were closed, and steamboat tickets on the Mississippi River became scarce and even pricy. The citizens of western Illinois were willing to be inconvenienced rather than miss the brightly colored uniforms, waving flags, and lively band music. Hopes of seeing Smith in full military regalia—reviewing his soldiers and orchestrating difficult military maneuvers with a precision that rivaled the coordination and discipline of a well-trained militia—drew all but a few that day.

At first, those gathered at the parade grounds were not disappointed, for at precisely 7:30 A.M. artillery fire announced the arrival of Generals Wilson Law and Don Carlos Smith at the front of their respective cohorts. At 8:00 A.M. a single cannon discharged,

[14] Stout, "Legion of Nauvoo," April 6, 1841.

FIGURE 18. *Joseph Smith Mustering the Nauvoo Legion,* by C. C. A. Christensen, ca. 1880. Tempera on canvas, 6 ft., 6 in. × 9 ft., 9 in. Number 13 in "Mormon Panorama." *Courtesy of Museum of Art, Brigham Young University, Provo, Utah.*

announcing that General Bennett with his staff and field officers had been conducted to their posts and were taking command of the assembled soldiers. After Bennett instructed the men for an hour, the soldiers lined up in formation and made ready to welcome Smith.

The next firing of artillery—again a single cannon blast—announced Smith's coming, or, as reported by the *Times and Seasons,* "gave an appropriate salute."[15] Promptly at 9:30 A.M. he and his guard, staff, and field officers arrived. Their wives followed in an elaborate carriage. When all dignitaries were present, the ladies of Nauvoo presented their commander in chief with a silk national flag—"The 26-Star Flag."[16] The flag was respectfully received and the occasion hailed by more cannon fire; then an official review of the Nauvoo Legion began. Smith passed in front of his soldiers,

[15] Thompson, "Communications," *Times and Seasons* 2, no. 12 (April 15, 1841): 381.

[16] On July 4, 1837 this flag became the official flag of the United States. It was the flag under which four Presidents—Martin Van Buren (1837–41), William Henry Harrison (1841), John Tyler (1841–45), and James Polk (1845–49)—served.

inspecting their formation and uniforms, and nodding his head in approval. Members of the Legion then began the procession or parade toward the temple grounds.

Leading the military processional was Smith, followed by Bennett. Aides-de-camp and conspicuous strangers or invited guests followed. Among the guests was Thomas Sharp, who at the time was not an enemy of the Mormons. Then came the general staff and Second Cohort (foot troops) followed by eight ladies and eight gentlemen walking abreast.[17] Following their lead were twenty musicians under the apt baton of Captain Duzette. The musicians played a lively score composed to honor what Mormons were calling a "Great Day in Israel."

As the band played, flags topped with brass-colored eagles were held aloft. The waving flags—small ones representing military units within the Legion; the large Legion flag;[18] the state flag of Illinois; and the famed red, white, and blue flag of the United States—evoked patriotic pride. But none of the colorful banners was as surprising as that of the Legion band.[19] Although its size, five feet by four feet, was pretentious if not ostentatious, it was not size alone that caused the applauding crowd of eight thousand to pause. It was the single eye, symbolic of the all-seeing eye of God, that caused critics to point and wonder aloud about the true nature of the Nauvoo Legion.

The military entourage moved slowly toward the temple site, where Legion generals and their staffs formed an inner square and the infantry and cavalry formed an outer square to encircle ladies, gentlemen, and distinguished guests between the Legion forces. Once encircled, ranking officers were escorted to the makeshift stand.[20]

The afternoon schedule had not been announced, and to the wonderment of spectators—who had expected only a military display—the events of the day turned religious. Smith, as prophet, seer, and

---

[17] The reason such a walking pattern was chosen is not known.

[18] Questions still remain as to a description of the original Nauvoo Legion flag (1841–45).

[19] To date, an accurate description of the Nauvoo Legion flag of the 1840s is questioned. Brass bands were common. See Todd, "The State Forcibles of New York," 67; McBarron and Todd, "3rd Regiment," 107–108; Barron and Finke, "United States Army Bandsmen," 125; Riling, "Milwaukee Light Guards Music Cover," 118; and Wallace and Finke, "First Regimental Band and Drum Corps," 101.

[20] Thompson, "Communications," *Times and Seasons* 2, no. 12 (April 15, 1841) 381.

revelator of the Mormons, took a leading role in the ceremony—which combined the secular with the sacred—that followed. He announced the singing of a hymn and a speech to be given by Sidney Rigdon, a member of the First Presidency of the Church.

Feeling stronger and clearer of mind than he had for a long time, Rigdon, who had languished in Liberty Jail with Smith, spoke eloquently of the significance of laying cornerstones for the building of the House of the Lord. He recalled tragic scenes that had transpired since the laying of cornerstones for the Kirtland Temple. He spoke of seeing the blood of innocents flow and of hearing the groans of the dying for the witness of Jesus. He assured his listeners that "in all those scenes of tribulation, his confidence, his courage and his joy had been increasing instead of diminishing." He then cautioned members of the Legion "not to usurp authority, but to obey as they are commanded and directed; to honor, not the world, but Him that is alive and reigns."[21] Thus, the principal speaker at the ceremony assured military personnel that when given a choice—military or religious—each soldier must choose God.[22] After Rigdon's remarks, a hymn was sung and a prayer offered.[23]

As if on cue, architects, following the direction of the Presidency of the Church, helped lower the southeast cornerstone of the Nauvoo Temple in its proper place. Smith, as military commander in chief and president of the Church, pronounced a benediction upon the stone:

> This principal corner stone in representation of the First Presidency, is now duly laid in honor of the Great God; and may it there remain until the whole fabric is completed; and may the same be accomplished speedily; that the Saints may have a place to worship God, and the Son of Man have where to lay His head.[24]

President Rigdon added, "May the persons employed in the erection of this house be preserved from all harm while engaged in its construction, till the whole is completed, in the name of the Father,

---

[21] *History of the Church,* 4:328; *Times and Seasons* 2:375–77.

[22] The statement suggests that the Legion is more answerable to God than the state of Illinois.

[23] It was not unusual, especially on a significant date, to end a military parade with the dedication of a building. See Smith, "Militia of the United States," 22; McPherson, *Battle Cry of Freedom,* 317.

[24] *History of the Church,* 4:329; *Times and Seasons* 2:375–77.

and of the Son, and of the Holy Ghost. Even so. Amen."[25] The assembled crowd, including the men of the Legion who had stood in formation, then adjourned for an hour.

Curious onlookers remained near the ceremony site. Perhaps some hoped that when the ceremony reconvened there would be more artillery fire, sword exercises, and a sham battle; but the remainder of the ceremony involved the laying of three more temple cornerstones.[26] The final "amen" marked the close of the day's ceremony as well as the military pomp. Soldiers retired from the temple grounds to the parade grounds, where they were officially dismissed with approbations: Bennett praised their obedience to orders and "soldier-like appearance."[27] Smith extolled their military prowess by stating that "[he had] never witnessed a more imposing spectacle than was presented on this occasion."[28] He wrote of it later,

> April 6, [Tuesday] 1841—At an early hour the several companies comprising the "Nauvoo Legion," with two volunteer companies from Iowa Territory, making sixteen companies in all, assembled at their several places of rendezvous, and were conducted in due order

[25] *History of the Church,* 4:329; *Times and Seasons* 2:375–77.

[26] The southwest cornerstone, laid under the direction of the president of the high priesthood, received the following benediction:

> The second corner stone of the Temple now building by the Church of Jesus Christ of Latter-day Saints, in honor of the Great God, is duly laid, and may the same unanimity, that has been manifested on this occasion continue till the whole is completed; that peace may rest upon it to the laying of the top stone thereof, and the turning of the key thereof; that the Saints may participate in the blessings of Israel's God, within its walls, and the glory of God rest upon the same. Amen.

After laying the northwest cornerstone, this blessing was pronounced: "The third corner stone is now duly laid; may this stone be a firm support to the building that the whole may be completed as before proposed." When the final or northeast cornerstone was lowered in place, Bishop Newel K. Whitney prayed, "The fourth and last corner stone, expressive of the Lesser Priesthood, is now duly laid, and may the blessings before pronounced, with all others desirable, rest upon the same forever. Amen." *History of the Church,* 4:330; *Times and Seasons* 2:375–77.

[27] Thompson, "Communications," *Times and Seasons* 2, no. 12 (April 15, 1841): 381, recognized the military prowess of the major general on that occasion: "Too much praise cannot be given to Maj. General Bennett for his active service." It is of interest that the following day, at the Church's general conference, "President Rigdon arose and stated that, in consequence of weakness from his labors of yesterday, he would call upon General John C. Bennett to officiate in his place." *History of the Church,* 4:339; *Times and Seasons* 2 (April 7–8, 1841): 384–88.

[28] *History of the Church,* 4:331; *Times and Seasons* 2, no. 12 (April 6, 1841): 12, 14.

> to the ground assigned for general review. The appearance, order and movements of the Legion were chaste, grand and imposing, and reflected great credit upon the taste, skill and tact of the men comprising said Legion. We doubt whether the like can be presented in any other city in the western country.[29]

The Mormon faithful concurred, but not all others did. Some guests viewed it as something sinister or un-American, and criticized the employment of Illinois State Militia for an avowedly ecclesiastical purpose (see chapter 2).

Among their number was Thomas Sharp. He admitted his admiration for the military procession and believed it comparable to that of the U.S. Army, yet he could not tolerate military power intertwined with religious zeal. The military and religious pomp and ceremony not only troubled him, it terrified him. He returned to Warsaw with one thought in mind—the need to warn his readership about rising Mormon military power.

At first, Sharp's comments seemed little more than an annoyance to those in Nauvoo. During the general conference of the Church, held on the temple grounds over the next two days, the mood was distinctly upbeat, and the tone one of cautious optimism. "Peace and prosperity attend us," reported the First Presidency. "The time was when we [were] looked upon as deceivers, and that 'Mormonism' would soon pass away, come to naught, and be forgotten. But the time has gone by when it is looked upon as a transient matter, or a bubble on the wave."[30]

Indeed there was much for the Saints to cheer about that April. Although their efforts at seeking redress from Washington for Missouri's wrongs had been maddeningly rebuffed and would sorely agitate the Mormons for years to come, at least in Nauvoo they had found safety, security, and opportunity: "We hope that those scenes of blood will never more occur." More than a refuge, Illinois offered new hope, freedom, legal protection, and a strong measure of self-rule. Thanks to the liberality, humanitarianism, and understanding of its citizens and legislature, the Mormons enjoyed "several liberal

---

[29] *History of the Church,* 4:326–27; Rough draft notes of History of the Church, 1841–007. Church History Library. Despite the glowing description, most of the citizen soldiers were not yet in uniform. There is also some question whether there were indeed sixteen companies in 1841.

[30] *History of the Church,* 4:337; *Times and Seasons* 2:384–86.

charters . . . by which [they hoped] to prosper until [their] city became the most splendid, [their] University the most learned, and [the] Legion the most effective of any in the Union."[31]

With hopes high, Legion officers enthusiastically planned another military and religious parade to be held in conjunction with the Independence Day celebrations of 1841. They appear to have been much satisfied with the pomp of the April parade, for on July 3, men of the Legion were once again gathering on the parade grounds at an early hour. Each soldier's attire and armaments were carefully inspected. Adjustments were made, where needed, before artillery fire announced the arrival of senior officers. Once officers had arrived and Smith had reviewed the troops, a gala processional began. Uniforms, horses, flags, and the band drew high praise; as did an imposing display of spears, lances, bayonets, and cavalry.

The ceremony that followed the processional was military in nature with a national ritual (Independence Day) at its core. Smith gave an impressive patriotic address in which he spoke of his love for America and his willingness to defend its constitution at all costs: "I would ask no greater boon, than to lay down my life for my country."[32] Men of the Legion were then dismissed and the crowd was encouraged to leave. Curiously, only officers were invited to remain. Soon they were joined by Mormon leaders. In a grove near the temple grounds, the military and religious leaders, along with their wives, enjoyed a sumptuous feast. Of this feast, Smith penned, "An elaborate dinner was got up in the grove, of which I partook, in company with the officers of the Legion, President Rigdon and many others, with their ladies."[33]

The separate, exclusive dining arrangement and the social mixing of military officers and religious leaders did not sit well with lingering onlookers. The pivotal role of Smith in both camps was not lost on anyone. An anonymous commentator from the *Quincy Whig* perhaps said it best: "The spectacle presented in Smith's case of a civil, ecclesiastical, and military leader, united in one and the same person, with power over life and liberty, can never find favor in the minds of sound and thinking Republicans."[34]

---

[31] *History of the Church,* 4:338; *Times and Seasons* 2:384–86.

[32] *History of the Church,* 4:382.

[33] *History of the Church,* 4:382.

[34] "The Mormons," *The Nauvoo Expositor* 1, no. 1, June 7, 1844. The term "Republican" did not refer to a political party but to rule by the people through elected representatives.

"A Well-organized and Efficient Force"

In 1842 Legion officers dropped all hints of religion in their military displays, perhaps a deliberate strategy to avoid the controversy caused by mixing secular with the religious in earlier parades. To reassure onlookers, parade-day programs were clearly outlined.[35] Conspicuously absent were the ceremonial cornerstones laying and sumptuous dinners. These were replaced with drilling, field exercises, and a sham battle. Was the dramatic change a response to Sharp's haranguing editorials? Perhaps. However, the clearer answer lies in the fact that the Nauvoo Legion was coming of age as a defensive military presence that was proud of its prowess and weaponry skills.

---

[35] The lieutenant general on April 28, 1842, asked Major General John C. Bennett to set up the program (*History of the Church,* 4:601). The program was as follows:

April 28, A.D. 1842.

Headquarters, Nauvoo Legion,

City of Nauvoo, Illinois, April 28, 1842

General Orders—

The Lieutenant-General directs that a *programme militaire* issue from the office of his commanding general for the 7th of May *proximo,* which I now proceed to consummate.

1st. The Adjutants will form the lines of their respective regiments, and the Colonels of the line assume command at nine o'clock, A.M.

2nd. The Adjutant-General will form the line of the Legion, and the Brigadier-Generals assume the command of their respective cohorts at half-past nine o'clock A.M.

3rd. The Major-General will assume the command of the Legion at ten o'clock, A.M.

4th. At a quarter past ten o'clock A.M., the Lieutenant-General will be escorted to the field at the review station.

5th. General review and inspection will follow, accompanied by such evolutions and exercises as the time will admit of.

6th. At half-past twelve o'clock P.M. the forces will be dismissed until a quarter before two o'clock P.M.

7th. At two o'clock P.M. the Major-General will resume the command and perform such military movements and field exercises as the Lieutenant-General may direct.

8th. At three o'clock P.M. the cohorts will separate and form the line of battle, the Brigadiers assume their respective commands and General Law's command will make a descent upon that of General Rich's in order of sham battle.

9th. At half-past three o'clock P.M. the cohorts will resume their positions in the line of the Legion, and a sham battle will be fought between the mounted riflemen under the immediate command of Lieutenant General Smith and the Invincibles under the immediate command of Major-General Bennett.

10th. At half-past four o'clock P.M. the forces will be dismissed for the day.

11th. Every officer, musician and private will be required to be at their respective posts at the hours specified throughout the day, under the most severe penalties of the law.

John C. Bennett
Major-General

By parade days of 1842, most soldiers had prepared their armaments "in the best possible condition" and were ready for the closest inspection and review. Each enlistee knew that officers would not allow "deficiency [to] be countenanced, overlooked, or suffered to pass without fine."[36] Legion officers, too, honed their military tactics and skills. They participated in mandatory drill practices for two days before each general parade. Among those who worked to improve military skills was the prophet himself. "Friday, May 6, 1842, I attended the Legion officers' drill in the morning," he recorded.[37] His ambition was to show "a well organized and efficient force . . . in point of good order, neat uniforms and equipment, and a well organized and thoroughly disciplined Legion."[38]

Feeling confident in his own military skills and that of the legionnaires, the commander in chief sent invitations to famous state and local leaders to attend yet another day of Legion pomp and ceremony:

> His Excellency the Governor of Illinois, the circuit judge of the judicial circuit, and the members of the bar, the officers of Hancock County, Colonel Williams and Colonel Deming, with their respective field and staff officers of the Illinois militia, and General Swazey and Colonel Fuller, with their respective field and staff officers, and Captain Davis and Avery's companies of cavalry of Iowa militia, are respectfully invited to attend and participate in the general parade on May 7.
>
> Joseph Smith, Lieutenant General[39]

Responses to the invitation were overwhelmingly positive; they even lured a surprise guest, Judge Stephen A. Douglas, who, having learned about thc upcoming parade, adjourned the Carthage Circuit Court to be in Nauvoo, a city that now touted a Legion of some two thousand soldiers in twenty-six different companies. Douglas was joined by thousands who streamed into Nauvoo in wagons, carriages, skiffs, river boats, and steamers before sunup on May 7, 1842. Upward of eleven thousand visitors, reported the *Wasp,* stood near the parade grounds awaiting command from the major general for the program to commence.[40]

---

[36] *History of the Church* 4:502; Smith, "Nauvoo Legion, General Orders," *Times and Seasons* 3, no. 8 (February 15, 1842): 700.

[37] *History of the Church,* 5:3; Law of the Lord, 95.

[38] *History of the Church,* 4:583; *Times and Seasons* 3:761–62.

[39] *History of the Church,* 4:502; *Times and Seasons* 3:8, 700–701.

[40] *Nauvoo Wasp,* July 9, 1842.

FIGURE 19. "'Lieutenant-General' Joseph Smith Reviewing the Nauvoo Legion," by unknown artist. Engraving printed with watercolor highlights on paper. From J. H. Beadle, *Life in Utah* (Philadelphia: National Publishing, 1870), facing p. 76. *Courtesy of Church History Museum.*

At 10:00 A.M. sharp, Bennett made a grand entrance and then took command of the Legion. With his brightly colored uniform and plume atop his chapeau, Bennett ordered the soldiers into formation. Near 1:00 P.M., Bennett dismissed the soldiers, advising them to make ready for a sham battle to be held at 3:00 P.M. During the two-hour recess, ranking officers (major generals, brigadier generals, musicians and their staffs) dined at the home of Joseph and Emma Smith. Following the exclusive luncheon, Legion officers took their positions on the battlefield. The First Cohort of soldiers on horseback was placed under the able guidance of General Law. Law's troops challenged the foot soldiers of the Second Cohort, led by General Rich. Emotions likely ran high when the Second Cohort agreed to engage the First Cohort in battle. It is further presumed that as privates in each cohort spoke of certain victory, officers concurred aloud, but in whispered tones expressed the greater desire to witness proficiency and precision in the battle.

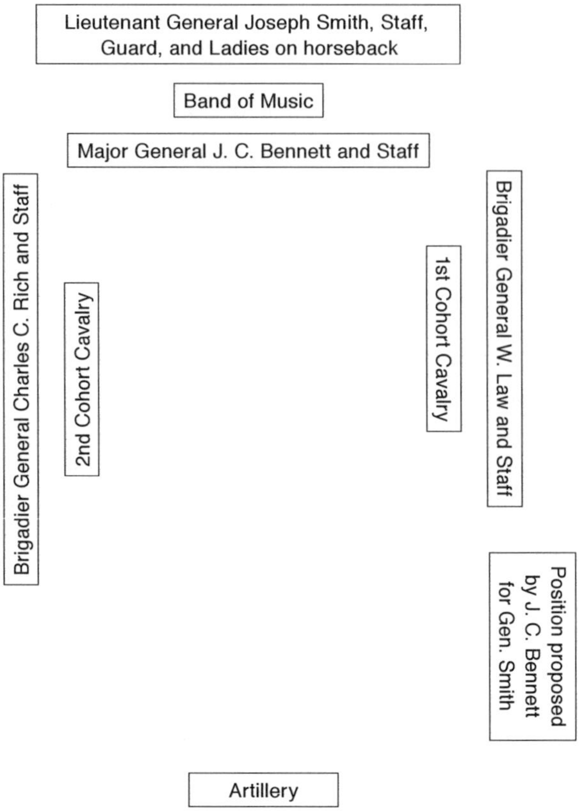

FIGURE 20. Sham battle formation of the Nauvoo Legion, May 7, 1842.

The sham battle had all the trappings of a great contest (see fig. 19). As each cohort took its station, surprisingly, Smith did not move. "I was solicited by General Bennett to take command of the first cohort during the sham battle; this I declined," he later wrote.[42] "General Bennett next requested me to take my station in the rear of the cavalry, without my staff, during the engagement; but this was counteracted by Captain A. P. Rockwood, commander of my life guards, who kept close to my side, and I chose my own position."

---

[41] The First and Second Cohorts were referred to as cavalry in the Nauvoo Legion on the day of the sham battle.

[42] *History of the Church,* 5:4 (see chapter 8).

This was the climax of several disagreements between Bennett and Smith. Was Bennett planning to use the Legion to perform a political assassination? Smith thought such was the case, for he penned, "And if General Bennett's true feelings toward me are not made manifest to the world in a very short time, then it may be possible that . . . a short time will determine the point."[43] Smith added, "Let John C. Bennett answer at the day of judgment, 'Why did you request me to command one of the cohorts, and also to take my position without my staff, during the sham battle, on the 7th of May, 1842, where my life might have been the forfeit, and no man have known who did the deed?' "[44] Whether Smith's dark premonitions were correct is debatable. But there was no question such thoughts colored the battle and spelled the end for the once promising military career of Bennett (see chapter 8).

Yet the parade, the battle, and the pomp and ceremony were viewed by onlookers as a great, unprecedented spectacle. By all accounts it was a grand day; three times as many men—some two thousand organized into twenty-six different companies—were on parade as in the year before. The Legion had become ten times the size of the Fifty-ninth Regiment of Hancock County, and of most other county regiments in Illinois. Smith said, "[My] soul was never better satisfied than on this occasion."[45] General Swazey of Iowa expressed admiration and gratitude for the Legion's learned discipline, and parade precision, and sham battles. In a letter written to the *New York Herald* another Regular Army officer penned,

> Yesterday was a great day among the Mormons. Their Legion, to the number of two thousand men, was paraded by Generals Smith, Bennett, and others, and certainly made a very noble and imposing appearance. The evolution of the troops directed by Major General Bennett, would do honor to any body of armed militia in any of the States, and approximates very closely to our regular forces. What does all this mean? Why this exact discipline of the Mormon corps. . . . [T]here are no troops in the States like them in point of enthusiasm and warlike aspect, and warlike character.[46]

---

[43] *History of the Church*, 5:4.

[44] *History of the Church*, 5:4.

[45] *History of the Church*, 5:3; Nauvoo Legion paper, fd. 10.

[46] An Officer from the U.S. Artillery, "Highly Important from the Mormon Empire," *The New York Herald* 8, no. 166 (June 17, 1842), as cited in Allaman, "Uniforms and Equipment," 326–27. The officer did not reveal his religious preference.

Other parades in 1842 and 1843 echoed the confidence exhibited by the men of the Legion in this May parade. It was obvious to one and all that the Legion, whether on parade or on the battlefield, was a well-equipped and capable fighting force, yet the number of onlookers diminished from parade to parade. The reason for the declining attendance was that plaudits of once-pleased crowds had turned to fear. Unfounded rumors, once ignored, were embraced and shouted in the press. Only a few spoke in favor of the Nauvoo Mormons, but like the contributor to the *Quincy Whig,* they chose to remain anonymous: "The Mormons have been most grossly slandered, and that they respect, cherish and love the free institutions of our country, and appreciate the sacrifice and bloodshed of those patriots who established them. I never saw a more orderly, gentlemanly and hospitable people than the Mormons, nor a more interesting population."[47]

The May 6, 1843, parade—held near Smith's farm and in which ladies rode horses and waved white feathers and plumes—attracted small numbers from outside Nauvoo. The only dignitaries present were "two United States officers and General Swazey, of Iowa."[48] Although they "expressed great satisfaction at [their] appearance and evolutions," times were changing.[49] The Legion had become more than pomp and ceremony—the men of the Legion were capable and prepared to defend Nauvoo and respond to the governor's call for military help. Smith acknowledged their strength and his willingness to call the Legion to arms: "that when we have petitioned those in power for assistance, they have always told us they had no power to help us. Damn such traitors! When they give me the power to protect the innocent, I will never say I can do nothing for their good: I will exercise that power, so help me God."[50]

"This Was the Day for the Training of the Companies"

Invitations to dignitaries and sumptuous feasts were now only memories of past parade days. Waving Legion flags and precision

---

[47] Quoted in *History of the Church,* 5:491; *Nauvoo Neighbor,* 1: 12.

[48] *History of the Church,* 5:384.

[49] *History of the Church,* 5:383–84.

[50] *History of the Church,* 5:384.

marchers no longer delighted throngs of well-wishers. Spectators, once pleased, were afraid to come to Nauvoo. Hoping to assure peace and goodwill to surrounding neighbors, the grand pomp and ceremony of the parades was quietly replaced by small events—company drills, company inspections, and company parades.[51] Conspicuously absent from these minor events was the commander in chief and his staff. The fear of arrest had forced Smith into hiding. On September 10, 1842, he wrote, "This was the day for the training of the companies of the Nauvoo Legion; and lest I should be observed by the multitude passing and repassing, I kept very still. After dark, my wife sent a messenger and requested me to return home, as she thought I would be as safe as there as anywhere; and I went safely home undiscovered."[52]

Without the lieutenant general reviewing the troops in splendid military regalia, most small parades attracted little attention.[53] Although Smith was present at some of these small events, he was a passive observer: "At one P.M. [on December 19, 1843] I was present when the Legion paraded near the Temple, were inspected by the officers, and instructed to prepare themselves with arms and ammunition and to hold themselves in readiness, for a moment's notice."[54] Yet to him, these small gatherings that prepared the militia to defend Nauvoo were more significant than all the grand parades combined. After one such event, he penned, "I was highly gratified with the officers and soldiers, and I felt extremely well myself." He then added, "I rode home with my staff, highly delighted with the day's performance, and well paid for my services."[55]

It wasn't just the men of the Legion who were rising in their military station, it was Joseph Smith himself. Recognizing Smith's maturing military stature, Surgeon General Robert D. Foster remarked in October 1843, "General Joseph Smith, whether we view

[51] Levi Richards recalled on two separate occasions being at a small parade in 1843: May 6, "Marched to the prairie about three miles where the Legion were assembled—acted as First Lieut. through the day—very cool windy day"; September 16, "attended Legion Parade on the Prairie out of the city 1st Lieut. commanding the company. Weather fine." Levi Richards, MS 1284, box 1, Fd 5, vol. 20, Church History Library.

[52] *History of the Church,* 5:161.

[53] Lieutenant General Joseph Smith occupied himself with other business on that date. The Legion troops were reviewed by Major General Wilson Law. See *History of the Church,* 5:165.

[54] *History of the Church,* 6:121.

[55] *History of the Church,* 6:34.

him as a Prophet at the head of the Church, a General at the head of the Legion, a Mayor at the head of the City Council, or as a landlord at the head of his table, if he has equals, he has no superiors."[56]

"The Commander in Chief, with His Staff, Is Respectfully Solicited to Accept an Escort from the Legion"

It was not until June 18, 1844, that Smith emerged from the sidelines to put on his military regalia and retake command of a Nauvoo Legion parade.[57] "I took the command, and with my staff rode in front of the Legion, marched up Main Street, and returned to our former parade ground," Smith recorded. "The number on parade was very large, considering the number of Elders who had been sent on missions."[58] This was the last Legion parade Smith led, for nine days later, on June 27, 1844, he was murdered in Carthage, Illinois.[59]

---

[56] *History of the Church,* 6:42.

[57] Before the June 18 gathering, Albert P. Rockwood, commander of the lifeguards of the Lieutenant General had each guard make a list of the accouterments they possessed which belonged to the United States. The list made by Henry G. Sherwood has survived: "One rifle, one holster and pistol, one sword without trimmings, one cartridge box with belt, one bullet pouch and strap, one powder flask with the muzzle off—all in good condition except as is above named and valued at forty dollars, which aforesaid arms or accouterments I promise the said Col. A. P. Rockwood to deliver to him, or his successor in office all or any part thereof in like good condition when officially disarmed." H. G. Sherwood, guard of the said Lieut. Gen. Jan. 13, 1844. A similar list made by Thomas Grover and James Allred has also survived. "Papers of Albert Perry Rockwood, 1838–1839."

[58] *History of the Church,* 6:500. Among those ordered into action was Heber Hale. He wrote, "On account of their repeated threats by the mob and inhabitants of Hancock County, the Legion was ordered to parade on the morning of the 18th of June, 1844. We paraded at the Masonic Hall and drilled, during the four noon; then marched on the Arsenal grounds, and dismissed at 2:00 P.M. We came together again at 4:00 P.M.; but in consequence of a show of rain, we adjourned until the next morning. Wednesday, the 19th, Legion met according to order and drilled on the Arsenal ground. Adjourned for dinner, and at night adjourned until the next morning at 8:00." Hale, *Bishop Jonathan H. Hale of Nauvoo,* 89–90. In "Jonathan H. Hale Papers."

[59] Aroet Lucius Hale was well aware of the problems plaguing Nauvoo. He penned, "At one time, when General Smith and the Officers of the Legion was going through a general review and inspection of arms, our drums was stacked. We were at rest, watching their review. When we returned to our drums, there was a drop of fresh blood on nearly all of our drums. Shortly after this mobbings commenced and finally the Prophet Joseph and Hyrum Smith was killed. I was with the Band when General Smith made his last speech on the housetop by the mansion when he drew his sword for the last time." Hale, "Aroet Lucius Hale Papers."

Although the men of the Legion sorely missed their commander in chief, his death did not halt the parades. In fact, history records more parades, drills, and musterings held in the weeks following his death than in the preceding two years. From June 27 until July 7, legionnaires drilled, exercised, and paraded daily—as if their very lives and those of their loved ones depended upon their military skills. The *History of the Church* records, "The Legion paraded at the Masonic Hall field one day . . . then moved for drilling to 'the ground near Spencer's northeast of the Temple'" the next day.[60] It was not until threats of invasion subsided that the daily mustering stopped.

For Mormons and neighbors alike, when mustering ended all assumed that the grand days of Legion parades were over. But there was to be one more parade. On September 27, 1844, as Governor Ford arrived in Nauvoo to present certificates of commission to Brigham Young, the newly appointed lieutenant general of the Legion, and Charles Rich,[61] major general. Ford received the following invitation: "Sir: The review of the Nauvoo Legion will take place this day [September 28] at twelve P.M., at which time the commander in chief, with his staff, is respectfully solicited to accept an escort from the Legion and be present at the review."[62] The surprised governor accepted the invitation.

For this last parade, Young attired himself in the uniform so often worn by Smith. From Smith's ornate sword to his favorite horse, Jo Duncan, Young looked like his slain predecessor.[63] As he reviewed the soldiers, "the governor, General J. J. Hardin and staff" looked on.[64] For the dignitaries and the curious but cautious witnesses, the

---

[60] Hale, *Bishop Jonathan H. Hale of Nauvoo* 88–91, as cited in Leonard, *Nauvoo,* 118.

[61] It appears that Charles C. Rich had the assignment as major general to be a part of issuing shares in the Nauvoo Legion Association. Information about the issuance of such shares and the association itself is lacking. In the Higbee papers is found the following statement: "May the 24th received of E. Elsworth secretary of the Nauvoo Legion Association a 5 Dollar share No. 88 signed Brigham Young Lieut. General of the Nauvoo Legion Charles C. Rich, Maj. Gen. of the Nauvoo Legion this day May the 24th 1845." "Higbee Papers," MS 1742, Fd 1.

[62] *History of the Church,* 7:277.

[63] Twelve-year-old Joseph Smith III recalled fitting out the horse for the occasion. The horse was fitted with a "saddle, housings, holsters, and bridle." It appears after the parade, a clerk of Brigham Young's "rode the horse to exhaustion, which infuriated young Joseph, who resolved never again to put a saddle on a horse for Brigham Young." Anderson, *Joseph Smith III and the Restoration,* 74–75.

[64] *History of the Church,* 7:277.

Legion made a credible and soldier-like appearance, with one notable flaw. Although Legion staff officers appeared well groomed and in proper uniform, they were not carrying arms.[65] The soldiers wanted to remind the governor that he had ordered the disarmament of the Legion before Smith's murder, putting him on notice that his actions in June 1844 crippled the Legion in the very hour that their commander in chief fell.[66]

Few men of the Legion at this, their last parade and review, walked with heads held high, and even fewer recalled the boastful days when Hosea Stout's poem of greatness seemed appropriate:

> They'll find that Illinois firm in her place will stand,
> And, faithfully, sustain us, in peace upon her land.
> They'll find that she doth sanction, all that we want to do
> And, especially she'll strengthen the "Legion of Nauvoo."[67]

Conclusion

The grand parades of the 1840s reveal a level of military sophistication within Legion ranks. Soldiers on parade appeared to onlookers to be more than a ragged, inefficient militia dutifully fulfilling prescribed state guidelines. In colorful, flamboyant attire, the soldiers of Nauvoo gave new meaning to parading near the Mississippi. They dressed in their finest, many in uniforms like those of the Regular Army, and proudly displayed their wide array of weaponry. They marched in time to the drums of their own band and followed the orders of their elected leaders to spruce up, stand erect, or about-face. On parade, the soldiers exhibited a training component sure to impress and entertain onlookers.

---

[65] Three cannons and two hundred and twenty small arms were surrendered following Ford's order. See Gayler, "Governor Ford and the Smiths," 398. In spite of the surrender on June 27, 1844, Colonel A. P. Rockwood received the following correspondence: "Headquarters Nauvoo June 27 by order of Maj. Gen. Jonathan Dunham, You are hereby ordered to assemble the Lieut. Gen. Staff under your command to assemble at the Temple by Eleven o'clock with arms and accouterments—but no gun or pistol must be loaded or discharged without further order. Jonathan Dunham Maj. Gen., by Thos. Bullock sec." "Papers of Albert Perry Rockwood, 1838–1839."

[66] According to William Huntington, "Sept. 28th Legion on parade Reviewed by the Governor same evening shot one of there men in a sham Fight. Sept. 30th Governor and troops to the Amount of 400 left Nauvoo for Warsaw to arrest the murders of Joseph & Hyrum Smith." Huntington, "Papers of William Huntington."

[67] "Legion of Nauvoo," "Journal History of the Church," April 6, 1841.

Their parades, like those in other Illinois towns, attracted spectators; parading was part of the American culture. The citizens of Nauvoo saw patriotism at its finest and the fulfillment of duty in the parading of the Nauvoo Legion. Only a few, like Thomas Sharp, saw kingdom building (see chapter 9); parading did, however, evidence some relationship between the Nauvoo military presence and the Mormon religion, especially early on. The laying of temple cornerstones and exclusive ("by invitation only") dinners that combined religious and military personnel are but two examples. Smith was not just the commander in chief of the Legion but also the leader of a growing religious moment, and as such he functioned in both offices even on parade days.

However, Smith attempted to dispel future fears stemming from his dual roles—a strategy that had agitated his enemies—by restructuring parade days (see chapter 9). It was obvious that he did not want a repeat of events that had happened in Missouri. In 1843 he ordered Legion parades to be toned down, suggesting a conscious strategy not to excite near neighbors. In response to Smith's directive, small, unannounced parades replaced the grandiose events that had brought thousands of spectators to Nauvoo. The small, unobtrusive company parades—although not crowd pleasing—effectively trained the men of the Legion to defend Nauvoo and to prepare for a call to arms, and were not just mere pomp, ceremony, and applause.

8

The Call to Arms, 1842–mid-1843

In case of any mob coming upon us,
I wish to be informed by the Governor
what will be the best course for us to pursue.

JOSEPH SMITH

Ever since the deaths of Joseph and Hyrum Smith in June 1844, there has been much debate concerning the place and role of the Nauvoo Legion. In fact, since the charge of treason against the Mormon leader involved his declaring martial law and his alleged abuse of Legion power, it is incumbent that this history carefully analyze this pivotal sequence of events. More than mere parades, regimental drills, and military pageantry, the history of the Nauvoo Legion is one of personalities. Prominent members of the Legion became sharply divided in their loyalties and actively either defended or defamed the life and leadership of Joseph Smith. In the process, the Legion became a militia of divided loyalties and torn allegiances. If the growing outside pressure for the Mormons to leave Illinois was primarily politically motivated, then the work of intrigue and conspiracy that ended in Carthage Jail sprang from disaffected Latter-day Saints, most of whom had once served in the ranks of the Legion.

This chapter will discuss the disaffection and intrigue of John C. Bennett, co-sponsor and major general of the Legion; the fallout from the attempted assassination of Lilburn W. Boggs; Joseph

Smith's arrest in 1843 by Missouri sheriff Joseph Reynolds, and his release by the Nauvoo Municipal Court; and the role of the Legion in the Daniel and Philander Avery kidnappings of late 1843.

"An Opportunistic Convert"

Whether Bennett intended to kill his superior officer that spring day in 1842 may never be proven.[1] What is known is that from that time forward, he became Smith's chief antagonist and conspired with deliberate vengeance to overthrow his former leader and destroy the religion of the Latter-day Saints.

The unscrupulous Bennett will ever pose a challenge to faithful Mormon scholars. To disparage him too roundly is to question his leader's judgment of character; to defend him too blindly is to deny his gross deficiencies. Yet, as Mormon historian B. H. Roberts admitted, "it must be confessed that President Joseph Smith and the people of Nauvoo erred greatly in their treatment of [him], by being too indulgent and long suffering." Smith's trust in and sometimes blind loyalty to his friends, coupled with a willingness to forgive became—at least in this instance—a virtue run to seed.[2]

Perhaps it was the return of members of the Quorum of the Twelve Apostles and their suspicions of Bennett's rapid rise to power and influence as mayor of the city and special assistant to the First Presidency that stopped Smith short.[3] Or perhaps it was Emma Smith's persistent questioning of Bennett's true intentions or Hyrum Smith's revelations that Bennett had abandoned his wife and family for a life of profligate living. Even before Bennett's arrival in Nauvoo, Illinois Governor Thomas Carlin knew of his dishonest, disreputable intentions.[4] Likewise, Thomas Ford, one of the state supreme court justices and later governor, called Bennett "the great-

---

[1] John Sweeney Jr., in his thesis on the history of the Nauvoo Legion, believes Bennett had sinister intents: "It is clear that Bennett attempted to kill or have someone kill Joseph Smith during this battle." However, Sweeney gives no concrete evidence for his conclusion. Sweeney, "A History of the Nauvoo Legion," 58.

[2] Roberts, *Comprehensive History of the Church,* 2:146–47; see also Draper, "Prophets Are Human Too."

[3] Bennett's biographer argues that Bennett's fall from grace began "shortly after [Brigham] Young's return from the mission of the Twelve to Great Britain." Smith, *Saintly Scoundrel,* 84.

[4] *History of the Church,* 5:49–50.

est scamp in the western country . . . he was everywhere accounted the same debauched, unprincipled and profligate character."[5]

Smith knew of Bennett's philanderings as early as May 19, 1842. Yet after Bennett cried "like a child" and begged "that he might be spared," Smith once more "plead for mercy for him," likely hoping that he would do less damage within the Church than without.[6] But as evidence of Bennett's unchaste conduct mounted, Smith excommunicated him and cashiered him from his high-ranking position as major general.[7] "Had he only been guilty of adultery, that was sufficient to stamp disgrace upon him," Smith wrote, but that "he must needs make use of my [Smith's] name in order to effect his purpose" was clearly the last straw.[8]

For his part Bennett sought to excuse his behavior on the grounds that his leader was secretly practicing plural marriage and had directed some of his closest associates to do the same. As Bennett's biographer argues, he claimed that Smith "taught and acted in the same manner" but publicly proclaimed against it for fear of opposition and "of trouble in his own house with his wife Emma Smith." And as Fawn Brodie put it, "Callous, profligate, and too wise in his profession as physician and instructor of midwifery, [Bennett] was eager to exploit polygamy."[9] "Although polygamy was still denied in public," wrote one of Smith's biographers, "in the realization that the Gentiles [non-Mormons] and most of the Saints were not yet prepared for such a radical change in the social structure, several high leaders in the church . . . were already participating."[10] Yet once his true reputation had been revealed, Bennett abruptly left town in a rage, "swearing to drink the heart's blood of his enemies" and determined to defend his character by launching a personal vendetta against Smith, plural marriage, and the alleged evils of Mormonism.[11] Knowing full well Bennett's formidable political and promotional skills as well as his malicious intent, Smith wasted little time informing his

[5] Thomas Ford, *History of Illinois,* 263.

[6] *The Papers of Joseph Smith,* 2:387–88.

[7] Bennett was excommunicated on June 24, 1842, and cashiered from the Legion six days later. He was also expelled from the Masonic Lodge in Nauvoo earlier that same month. See *History of the Church,* 5:22, 35–39, 49.

[8] *Times and Seasons,* 3: 839–43.

[9] Brodie, *No Man Knows My History,* 309.

[10] Hill, *Joseph Smith,* 298.

[11] Hill, *Joseph Smith,* 300.

commander in chief and governor of the state, Thomas Carlin, of Bennett's sudden resignation as major general and sought his advice:

> I have been credibly informed that he is colleaguing with some of our former cruel persecutors, the Missourians, and that he is threatening destruction upon us. . . . It is rumored, and strong evidence exists, that Dr. Bennett and [others] have posted bills in Galena, calling upon the people to hold meetings . . . and come here and mob us out of the place, and try to kidnap me. . . . In case of any mob coming upon us, I wish to be informed by the Governor what will be the best course for us to pursue.[12]

Carlin responded that he thought Smith was overwrought and that his apprehensions about Bennett were unfounded. He, therefore, refused to authorize putting the Nauvoo Legion on a state of readiness to be called out in defense. Carlin could not "conceive of the least probability, or scarcely possibility, of an attack of violence upon the citizens of Nauvoo from any quarter" and advised his military subordinate not to exaggerate the threats from his former major general.[13] If such an attack were to occur, however, Carlin said the Mormons had no other option than to "resort to the first law of nature, namely, to defend [their] rights."[14] Nevertheless, many in Nauvoo were more than a little concerned that a confidante-turned-renegade was on the loose.[15]

Bennett soon embarked upon an ambitious journey that took him throughout Illinois and Missouri and eventually to the East Coast where, dressed in his Nauvoo Legion uniform, he lectured (for a considerable fee) to large audiences in New York, Philadelphia, Boston, and elsewhere—broadcasting his own merits while defaming the Mormons. Eager to capitalize on his newfound fame and chance for fortune, in 1842 he hurriedly published a stinging diatribe entitled *The History of the Saints; or, An Exposé of Joe Smith and Mormonism:* a collection of affidavits, half-baked commentaries, and assorted statements previously published by various enemies of the

[12] *History of the Church,* 5:43–44; "Joseph Smith Letter Books," 2:233–35.

[13] *The Papers of Joseph Smith,* 2:424–25. See also "Joseph Smith Letter Books," 2:240–41; and *History of the Church,* 5:82–83.

[14] *History of the Church,* 5:51.

[15] As Joseph Smith admitted: "Bennett had given him more trouble than any man with whom he had ever been associated." "Joe Smith," *Sangamo Journal* 10, no. 48 (July 22, 1842), as cited in Godfrey, "Causes of Mormon Non-Mormon Conflict," 118.

Church, along with his own opinions. Although the New York media denounced his book as "obscene and licentious in the highest degree," Bennett's denunciations of Mormonism attracted large audiences.[16]

His book took special aim at the alleged evils and designs of Mormonism as a murderous and immoral society and at Smith's claims as prophet, but Bennett used much of his ammunition to denounce the Nauvoo Legion and his former commander's supposed intention to establish a great despotic empire in the West. "It is a notorious fact that they are gathering from every part of the world," Bennett quoted from William Harris, author of *Mormonism Portrayed,*

> and they have obtained an act of the Legislature, organizing the "Nauvoo Legion," . . . have obtained arms of the government, and are at this time more than one thousand strong, and increasing continually. Now, I ask, why all this gathering, so different from every other denomination, unless they have designs against the rights and liberties of others? Why are they using their best exertions for, and actually raising up, a large, well-drilled, well-armed, standing army? There can be no religion in this, every one knows; and hence it follows that they are not only contemplating, but actually preparing for, the execution of some murderous design.[17]

Unwilling to abide by facts when rumors made for a far more sensational story, he proposed that "Nauvoo, garrisoned by twenty or thirty thousand fanatics, armed to the teeth, and well supplied with provisions, would be one of the most formidable [forces] in the world." Furthermore, Bennett stated, the Danites in Nauvoo, which he called the "Destructives," were at Smith's beck and call and "in their capacities of spies and informers, are of great service to the Prophet and assist materially in extending and confirming his influence over the Mormons."[18]

According to Bennett, the real purpose of the Legion, as an extension of the Danites, was "to execute a daring and colossal scheme of rebellion and usurpation throughout the Northwestern States of the Union . . . and [erect] upon the ruin of their present governments a despotic military and religious empire."[19] Specifically its aim was

[16] Smith, *Saintly Scoundrel,* 126; Brodie, *No Man Knows My History,* 317.

[17] Bennett, *History of the Saints,* 141.

[18] Bennett, *History of the Saints,* 192, 270.

[19] *History of the Church,* 5:80; Bennett, *History of the Saints,* 300, 306, 321.

> to conquer Independence, in Jackson County, Missouri. . . . Independence they consider their Zion, and they there intend to rear their Great Temple, the corner-stone of which is already laid. There is to be the great gathering-place for all the Saints, and in that delightful and healthy country they expect to find their Eden, and build the New Jerusalem.[20]

If such were the designs of the Legion, no one else in the Legion knew it. Ever and always more extreme and militaristic than his leaders, Bennett, "Joab, General in Israel" proclaimed that the Legion would soon be strong enough to go on the offensive to right any wrong, whether in Illinois or Missouri. The truth is, Bennett believed in military force as a way to achieve his goals and desperately wanted to be at the forefront of any such deliberate actions. Why Smith never used the Legion as a force for revenge against the enemies of the Church continued to puzzle him. Why have force and not use it? And if Bennett baited his leaders to use the Legion in such a way, they never bought into it. Scorned and now spurned by those who once trusted him, Bennett turned against his former friends, accusing them of not doing the very things he himself desired, and doing so in the uniform of the Nauvoo Legion that he could no longer lead.

"Peace We Must Have, If We Have to Fight for It"

The immediate fear among the Mormons was that Bennett would instigate yet another effort at extradition. As one contemporary Mormon, John Lowe Butler, indelicately put it, "The Missourians were red hot mad, their blood thirsty souls were boiling over to get hold of [Smith] to tare [*sic*] him to pieces like dogs upon their prey, and so it went on."[21] Smith and his lawyers had already successfully countered an 1840 and then an 1841 attempt to have him deported to Missouri to stand trial for treason against the state. Bennett's task was made infinitely easier after the night of May 6, 1842, when Lilburn W. Boggs, former Missouri governor, suffered gunshot wounds in his Independence, Missouri, home, in a blatant assassination attempt. Orrin Porter Rockwell, one of Smith's most trusted body-

[20] Bennett, *History of the Saints*, 192–93.
[21] Butler, "Autobiography of John Lowe Butler," 28.

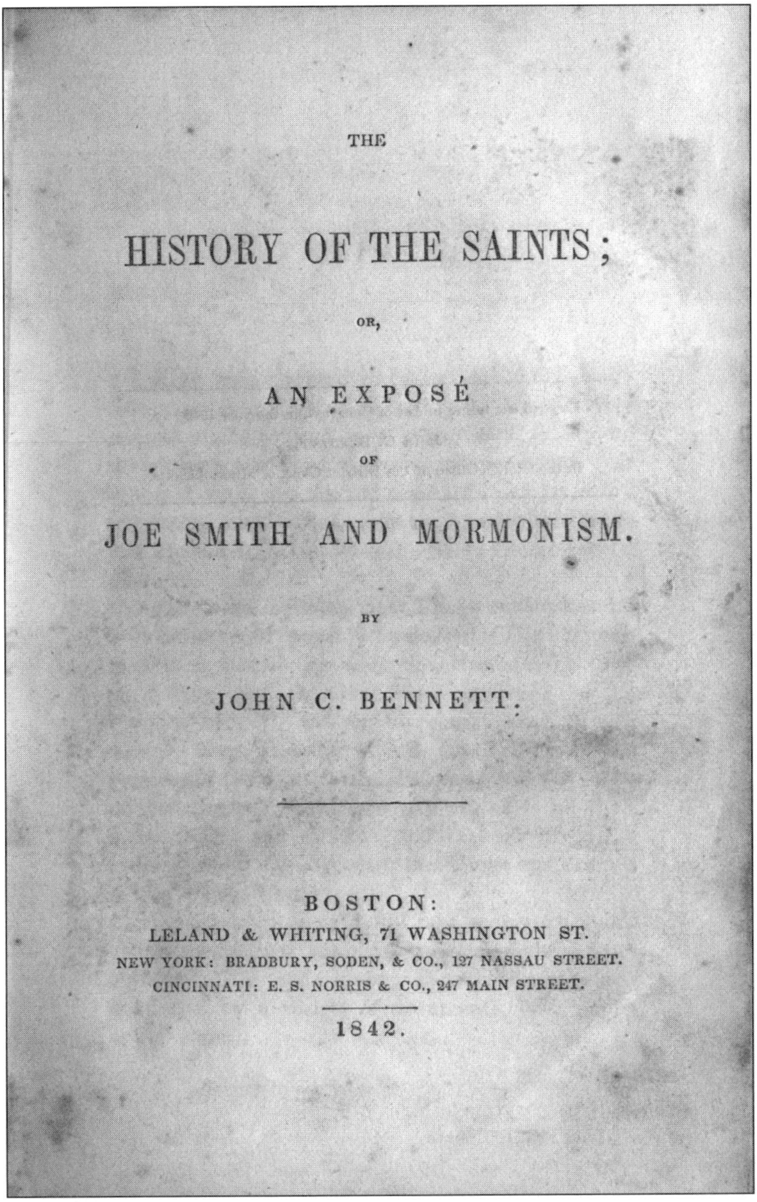

THE

HISTORY OF THE SAINTS;

OR,

AN EXPOSÉ

OF

JOE SMITH AND MORMONISM.

BY

JOHN C. BENNETT.

BOSTON:
LELAND & WHITING, 71 WASHINGTON ST.
NEW YORK: BRADBURY, SODEN, & CO., 127 NASSAU STREET.
CINCINNATI: E. S. NORRIS & CO., 247 MAIN STREET.

1842.

FIGURE 21. Title page of *The History of the Saints; or, An Exposé of Joe Smith and Mormonism,* by John C. Bennett (1842)
Courtesy of Church History Library.

guards and lifelong friends—and who was in Independence at the time—was soon arrested on suspicion of the crime.

As soon as Boggs had recovered sufficiently, Bennett persuaded him to sign an affidavit charging Smith with "being accessory before the fact of the intended murder."[22] Bennett also persuaded Governor Thomas Reynolds to seek Smith's extradition on the grounds of his being a fugitive from justice. In Reynolds's words, "General Bennett has pledged himself to prove that Rockwell is the person who endeavored to assassinate ex-Governor Boggs, and that the Mormon prophet was the instigator of the deed."[23] Furthermore, Bennett was busy confirming fears and fanning the flames of prejudice among the Missourians. "It is not doubted here in the least," wrote one worried postmaster in July 1842,

> that the information which he [John C. Bennett] intends to convey to you is literally correct. . . . Nearly [Smith's] whole conversation and thoughts are taken up by planning the destruction of Missouri and unless checked, depend upon it, he will some day and that before long give your state more trouble than you are aware of . . . Smith's word is law . . . and could you attend one of their military parades (And you could not miss one any day in the year . . . for their city is constantly a military encampment) you would be satisfied that my remarks are not groundless.[24]

Three months later, on August 8, 1842, Smith (then mayor), was arrested in Nauvoo by Adams County, Illinois, sheriff Thomas King "on a requisition from Governor Reynolds of Missouri based on an affidavit from Boggs," for alleged complicity in the shooting. Smith immediately applied to the Nauvoo Municipal Court for a writ of

---

[22] *History of the Church,* 5:86. No evidence has yet shown that Joseph Smith had anything to do with the murder attempt. However, there was enough "circumstantial evidence" to cast suspicion on Rockwell—his hatred of Boggs, his presence in Independence the night of the shooting, and his veiled threats. See Arrington, *Brigham Young,* 103. Certainly Boggs believed Rockwell had pulled the trigger.

[23] *Bloomington Herald,* March 27, 1842.

[24] L. B. Fleak to Governor Reynolds, July 12, 1842, as quoted in Jennings, "Two Iowa Postmasters View Nauvoo," 278–79. In a later letter, this same individual wrote: "Depend upon it, those fanatiks will one day give your state a great deal of trouble, their whole thought is how they shall injure or destroy Missouri and the first thing taught their new members is to despise Missouri." L. B. Fleak to Governor Reynolds, December 4, 1842, "Two Iowa Postmasters View Nauvoo," 287.

habeas corpus, which was granted. Taken by surprise by this legal maneuver, King returned empty-handed. Thomas Carlin, governor of Illinois, who had acted on Governor Reynolds's behalf, was incensed by this news and told King that the Nauvoo Municipal Court had no authority to override a warrant issued by the governor. Meanwhile, Smith deemed it wise to go into hiding until competent legal authority could be obtained.[25]

Fearful that Nauvoo's court and ordinances would not protect him against another extradition attempt, Smith went into hiding for three months. From somewhere down the Mississippi River or over in Iowa, and acting in his capacity as head of the Nauvoo Legion, Smith ordered Bennett's successor and new major general, Wilson Law, to take a proactive, though still defensive, stance with respect to the Legion and his personal safety.[26] "I have come fully to the conclusion both since this last difficulty commenced as well as before," Smith explained, "that I never would suffer myself to go into the hands of the Missourians alive." Fearing mob action against the city, Smith directed further:

> You will see, therefore, that the peace of the city of Nauvoo is kept, let who will endeavor to disturb it . . . you will also see that force or violence is immediately dispersed and brought to punishment; or meet it, or contest it, at the point of the sword with firm, undaunted and unyielding valor; and let them know that the spirit of old Seventy-Six and of Washington yet lives . . . and let no man, woman or child be intimidated, or suffer it to be done . . . Go ahead, David Crockett like, and lay down our lives like men, and defend ourselves to the best advantage we can to the very last.[27]

An obedient soldier, Wilson Law replied no less firmly: "Peace we must have if we have to fight for it. . . . The world will justify us in fighting for our rights, and then you can come out like a lion and lead your people to victory and glory in the name of the Lord of Hosts."[28]

Convinced that Missouri would not cease its extradition efforts and certain that Bennett was still stirring the mix, Smith reacted

---

[25] For a comprehensive new study on Joseph Smith's expanded use of habeas corpus, see Thurston, "The Boggs Shooting and Attempted Extradition."

[26] Wilson Law narrowly defeated Lyman Wight for the post on August 3, 1842.

[27] *The Papers of Joseph Smith*, 2:407–11.

[28] *History of the Church*, 5:96, 110–12.

indignantly. While in hiding that August, he viewed the Legion as far more than mere decoration; indeed, if all else failed, it would become the arm of his defense. He ordered Law and the Legion to be ready to defend the city against possible attack. Smith hoped to "be able to triumph gloriously over those who seek our destruction and overthrow which I believe we shall."[29] It would be a pattern repeated often over the next two years.

Rhetoric aside, Smith would use force only as a last resort, and then only in a defensive capacity. It was one thing to speak, but quite another to act. Writing to James Arlington Bennett[30] in New York, he said, "Our enemies shall not have it to say that we rebel against government or commit treason. However much they may lift their hands in oppression and tyranny, when it comes in the form of government we tamely submit, although it leads us to the slaughter and to beggary."[31] Smith would eventually submit to the governor's demands, even at the expense of his life; these words are characteristic of the man: carry the threat of action, but employ it only to defend against illegal aggression.

By the end of August he hesitantly returned to Nauvoo, keeping careful watch. Governor Carlin, in an earlier letter to Emma Smith, had reiterated his belief that the Nauvoo Municipal Court had overstepped its bounds in releasing her husband. As late as September 3, Missouri agents "were again on the move" and almost arrested him, but on a last-minute tip, he "passed out the back door, and through the corn in his garden to Bro. Newel K. Whitney's."[32]

Eager to clear his name and prove the illegality of Governor Reynolds's latest extradition efforts, Smith, on the advice and assurance of Justin Butterfield, an eminent Chicago lawyer and U.S. Attorney for the District of Illinois, determined to surrender to Wilson Law—who, as general of the Nauvoo Legion, was the highest ranking lawman in Nauvoo—and be tried before the United States District Court in Springfield. Meanwhile, Illinois' new governor, Thomas Ford, a former justice of the state supreme court, likewise believed in Smith's innocence and was anxious to clarify the matter and per-

---

[29] *The Papers of Joseph Smith,* 2:425–26; See also *History of the Church,* 5:105–106.

[30] James Arlington Bennett (1787–1863), inspector general, major general of the Nauvoo Legion.

[31] *History of the Church,* 5:158.

[32] *History of the Church,* 5:145.

haps solve the "Mormon problem" while still early in his administration. At the conclusion of the trial, Judge Nathaniel Pope ruled in favor of the defense, stating that the Missouri affidavit was faulty in that Smith could not have been a fugitive from justice, since it could not be proven that he had committed a crime or was even in Missouri at the time of Boggs's shooting. Smith was freed on January 5, 1843. Rockwell, who had been in a Missouri jail for nine months awaiting trial, too, was released because of insufficient evidence.[33]

The Mormon prophet may have won this latest legal battle but almost lost the political war. The Nauvoo Legion had become an issue in the earlier 1842 gubernatorial election between the Whig candidate, Joseph Duncan, and the Democratic contender, Adam W. Snyder, who had pushed the Nauvoo Charter legislation through the legislature some two years before. The Whigs, who felt betrayed when Smith's support waned, had turned against the Mormons and tried to make it appear that Illinois was sanctioning a religion. During the election campaign, which Duncan had expected to win quite handily, he promised to repeal the Nauvoo Charter, recall all the public arms given to the Legion, and require members of the Mormon militia to rejoin other nearby units of the state militia.[34]

In late 1842 some prominent Whigs urged the repeal of the Nauvoo Charter, and with it the Nauvoo Legion. Anxious not to lose the Mormon vote, the Democrats stalled. Finally, in December 1842, the Senate Judiciary Committee reported that the powers granted the Nauvoo Legion were "not exceptional" and that "the public mind has been grossly abused by falsely colored and highly exaggerated representations of powers in the Nauvoo Charter."[35]

In one of those strange twists in politics, Snyder died late in the campaign and his replacement—the forty-two-year-old Thomas Ford, an unprepossessing candidate but firm defender of the law—won the election. He garnered not only the Mormon vote but that of most other constituencies as well. Although never a strong supporter of the Nauvoo Charter and what he felt were its excesses, Ford, inaugurated on December 8, 1842, just before Smith went on

[33] Hill, *Joseph Smith,* 323.

[34] Ford, *History of Illinois,* 269. Joseph Duncan, governor of Illinois from 1836 to 1838, ran on a strong anti-Mormon platform and, in part, expected to win because of it.

[35] Report of the Committee on the Judiciary, December 19, 1842, Senate, 13th Assembly, 2, as cited in Hampshire, *Mormonism in Conflict,* 107.

trial at Springfield, would not have favored its renunciation; rather, Ford's aim was "to reform rather than repeal the charters."[36]

But the public clamor would not go away. In the ensuing session of the new state legislature, legislators came very close once again to repealing the Nauvoo Charter. On March 3, 1843, the House voted for repeal, but the Senate, by only a single vote, decided not to do so. Representative Owen had spoken eloquently in defense of the Legion and called attempts to repeal the Charter "obnoxious." He showed convincingly that the powers of the Legion were not exceptional, that the Invincible Dragoons of the Second Division of Illinois "had virtually identical powers to the Nauvoo Legion."[37] Though a vote to repeal passed the House, thanks to Stephen A. Douglas, the Democratic-controlled Senate refused to advance the bill to a third reading. Though Nauvoo retained its charter, such actions did not bode well for the future of the state's most controversial city and militia.[38]

---

[36] Hill, *Joseph Smith,* 309. Responding to Ford's misgivings over the charter, the *Times and Seasons* article "Remarks on Chartered Rights" countered as follows:

> His Excellency seems to think that our Charters are objectionable on many accounts; but particularly of the powers granted. . . . We say that it [the Nauvoo Legion] is equipped, officered and organized, in a manner that not only does credit to the city of Nauvoo, but the state of Illinois . . . All who have seen its numbers . . . witnessed it . . . to be one of the most efficient military bodies in this state; have they transcended their power, been negligent in their duties, or violated the law? They have not. . . . If found among other citizens, then the Mormons, would be lauded to the skies. (*Times and Seasons* 4, no. 3 [December 15, 1842]: 41–42)

[37] The reader may recall from chapter 3 that Bennett was the inspiration behind the Invincible Dragoons. Thus, his imprint upon the Charter of the Legion looms ever larger in history. *Illinois State Register,* March 31, 1843, "Speech of Mr. Owen," Sheet 1, cols. 3–5, as cited in Hampshire, *Mormonism in Conflict,* 110.

[38] On December 9, 1842, a Mr. Davis of Bond County introduced a resolution to the House of Representatives urging the repeal of the Nauvoo charter and the taking away of all state arms from the Nauvoo Legion.

William Smith, Joseph's younger and often outspoken brother and elected representative from Nauvoo, helped save the day for the Latter-day Saints. "Much feeling exists upon the subject of the extraordinary powers granted to the Mormons; and a strong effort is on foot to bring about a repeal of the Nauvoo charter; but the brother of Joe Smith, who is a member of the House, rehearsed to the locofocos [Democrats] the great help they have derived from Mormon votes, and it is thought the charter will be sustained." *Iowa City Standard,* December 29, 1842, 2.

And to the charges made that the Legion's arms be confiscated, William Smith argued that the Legion had "no more than their quota" and in fact, as with virtually every other militia in the state, "had received but a small portion of that to which it is entitled." *History of the Church,* 5:201. The truth is, the Nauvoo Legion, like virtually every other militia in the state, was significantly under-provisioned. (*continued, next page*)

"The Whole Country Was Swarming with Men"

Their leader exonerated, the citizens of Nauvoo looked upon 1843 with a spirit of guarded optimism. Temple construction received renewed emphasis, missionary work expanded, and the emigration of new Mormon converts in England and elsewhere continued apace. Bennett's attacks had fallen on deaf ears, among most of the Mormons at any rate, and the future looked brighter than it had for a long time.

As this history has shown earlier, the Legion grew from a base number of 1,490 in one cohort in 1841 to 1,751 in the same cohort in 1843 (see chapter 4). And it seemed more alive than ever before, ramping up its musters and drills in direct proportion to the threats upon its leader's life and upon the city and its citizens. More than a motley crew of state militiamen, it saw itself increasingly as the first line of defense against whatever troubles lay ahead. At the May 6 Legion parade, Emma Smith and several other ladies, mounted on horseback and wearing white feathers or plumes and black velvet, joined Smith as he inspected the ranks on the prairie ground east of his farm.[39] "The Legion looked well," Joseph Smith proudly remembered. "[B]etter than on any former occasion, and they performed their evolutions in admirable style." He went on to say,

> The officers did honor to the Legion, many of whom were equipped and armed, cap-a-pie. Many ladies on horseback honored us with their presence and we observed that the men were in good spirits; that they had made great improvements, both in uniform and discipline, and from what we saw, we felt proud to be associated with a body of

---

The *Wasp* applauded the senate vote. An excerpt dated March 15, 1843, reads:

> The house, in the dignity of its standing, passes a bill, at the request of the people, telling them that they shall have a charter granting them several privileges, and telling them that it shall be *perpetual,* without any repealing clause. It is made a law, and the grand seal of state appended to it. The people, on the good faith of the state, go to work and improve under the provisions of that charter. Companies are formed, buildings are erected, and money expended; but by-and-by they find out that they have been leaning upon a broken reed, that there is no dependence to be placed in government, that they (the legislature) have broken their most sacred promises, violated their plighted faith, and wantonly and wickedly sought to injure thousands of men who relied on their promises, by an unprecedented, unconstitutional, and tyrannical law, trampling under foot the faith of the state, and virtually saying that the members of the legislature that granted the charter were all fools or knaves, and that we, the pure representatives of the people, must break the plighted faith of the state to set them right! (1:46)

[39] Newell and Avery, *Mormon Enigma,* 139.

> men which in point of discipline, uniform, appearance, and a knowledge of military tactics, are the pride of Illinois, one of its strongest defenses and a great bulwark of the western country.[40]

In a speech Smith gave that day to the Legion, he said, "When we have petitioned those in power for assistance they have always told us they had no power to help us, damn such power. When they give me power to protect the innocent I will never say I can do nothing. I will exercise that power for their good. So help me God."[41]

In mid-June, fearful of yet another arrest of its leader, Legion officers organized an elite bodyguard regiment called the "Escort Regiment of Light Infantry" under the direction of Charles C. Rich,[42] and placed Colonel Jonathan Dunham[43] in charge of the construction of an arsenal for the city , even though the Legion was, like most other companies and regiments, insufficiently provisioned.[44] In July the Legion began issuing the short-lived Nauvoo Legion scrip—in amounts of $1 to $500—as a way, apparently, for paying overdue fines of those otherwise too poor or unable to do so. For special services rendered, officers and men were issued scrip that was accepted "in payment of debts due the Legion, and redeemable by the Paymaster General on demand."[45]

Smith's temporary respite from lawsuits ended abruptly on June 23, 1843, when in Dixon, Illinois, some two hundred miles north of Nauvoo, he was once again arrested; this time by Joseph H. Reynolds, sheriff of Jackson County, Missouri, and constable Harmon T. Wilson of Carthage, Illinois, on a writ of extradition reluctantly issued by Governor Ford.[46] The charge was that of treason arising out of the Missouri Mormon War of 1838, during which Smith had undeniably fled the state. "When Reynolds of Missouri and Wilson of

---

[40] Ehat and Cook, *Words of Joseph Smith,* 200.

[41] Ehat and Cook, *Words of Joseph Smith,* 199.

[42] *History of the Church,* 5:430–31. See also *Nauvoo Neighbor,* 30–31. This escort was to be Joseph Smith's own "Life Guards." See *History of the Church,* 5:458.

[43] Jonathan Dunham (1800–1845) colonel, brigadier general of the Nauvoo Legion; missionary in New York and Indiana.

[44] *History of the Church,* 5:422, 430.

[45] Original Certificate, glued into the "Manuscript History of the Church," July 25, 1843. See also *History of the Church,* 5:518. It is not known whether other independent militia in Illinois or anywhere else in the country used such scrip. It appears to be a rare action and may have been issued as an inducement to attract more recruits at this, an increasingly dangerous time, when there was a real fear of invasion. Such new recruits, many of whom had spent everything just to gather to Nauvoo, were otherwise too poor to pay fines in real money.

[46] Bushman, *Rough Stone Rolling,* 504.

Carthage came to take me," remembered Smith, "the first salutation was (instead of tapping me on the shoulder and saying you are my prisoner) with two cocked pistols to my head 'God damn you I will shoot you I will shoot you god damn you I will shoot you' nearly 50 times first and last. I asked them what they wanted to shoot me for. 'If you made any resistance.' 'O very well,' says I. 'I have no resistance to make.' They then dragged me away."[47]

Bennett had once again plotted with a recovering Lilburn Boggs to issue a new, carefully redrafted writ on the four-year-old charge of treason against Missouri and complicity in the shooting of Boggs.[48] While Colonel Stephen Markham,[49] a member of the Legion, galloped to Nauvoo for help, Smith, fearing for his life should he be carried to Missouri, sought immediate legal counsel. Cyrus Walker, the new leader of the Illinois Whig Party and one of the best criminal lawyers in the state, happened to be in the neighborhood electioneering for the upcoming congressional and county elections. On condition of a substantial legal fee and Smith's pledge of his vote in the coming election, Walker arranged for a countersuit from the circuit court of Lee County, Illinois, against sheriffs Reynolds and Wilson on charges of battery and false imprisonment, and sought $400 in bail. In a case of captured captors, the two officers of the law were themselves arrested and placed in the custody of the sheriff of Lee County, Illinois. The complicated entourage then set out for Quincy for a proposed hearing before state supreme court justice and leading Democrat, Stephen A. Douglas.

Meanwhile, having heard the news of Smith's arrest, two companies of the Nauvoo Legion—some 175 men under the command of Brigadier Generals Wilson Law and Charles Rich, the latter likely acting in his added capacity as leader over the newly formed Escort Regiment—set out on June 25 to bring sufficient force to prevent their leader "from being kidnapped and taken into Missouri," as it was rumored about that "the whole country was swarming with men anxious to carry [him] there and kill [him] there."[50] Another 75 men

---

[47] Ehat and Cook, *Words of Joseph Smith*, 219.

[48] Brodie, *No Man Knows My History*, 348.

[49] Stephen Markham (1800–1878): captain, brevet major, lieutenant colonel, brevet colonel, colonel of the Nauvoo Legion; body guard for Joseph Smith.

[50] "Manuscript History of the Church," Book D, 2:1586; see also *History of the Church*, 5:448. It is not known whether Markham acted on his own in calling up the Legion or whether he was carrying out orders from Lieutenant General Joseph Smith.

sailed up the Mississippi River on the *Maid of Iowa* to intercept possible river runners. Rushing at breakneck speed, one vanguard company of the Legion caught up with the Smith party on June 27. Careful not to use violence but rather the intimidation of sheer numbers, the rescue party captured both captives and captors and compelled Wilson and Reynolds to surrender their arms. Smith, very much relieved, said, "Gentlemen, I think I will not go to Missouri this time! These are my Boys!"[51] Acting, in part, on the recommendation of Walker who did not want his arch political rivals, Judge Douglas and the Democrats, to take credit for freeing Smith, the entire party headed for Nauvoo not by steamboat, as Reynolds had wanted, but by land. Welcomed by the sounds of the marching Nauvoo Brass Band, firing cannons, and cheering crowds lining the streets, the posse, now over 140 men in size, trotted into an embracing Mormon capital. On Friday, June 30, at dinner in his own home, Smith placed his arresters, Reynolds and Wilson, "at the head of the table," with about fifty other invited guests.[52]

The following day a jubilant, if exasperated, Smith spoke at length to a crowded assembly about his recent ordeal and thanked those who had secured his rescue. Speaking freely, if not indelicately—as he was often prone to do in such moments of deliverance—he defended the Nauvoo Charter and the Legion: "The time has come when forbearance is no longer a virtue," he proclaimed,

> and if you or I are again taken unlawfully, you are at liberty to give loose to blood and thunder. But be cool, be deliberate, be wise, act with almighty power. . . . But before I will bear the unhallowed persecution any longer—before I will be dragged away again among my enemies for trial, I will spill the last drop of blood in my veins, and will see all my enemies in hell! To bear it any longer would be a sin.[53]

Yet once again such militant words were almost immediately tempered by a plea for nonviolence, as if he himself recognized when he had gone too far: "However indignant you may feel about the high handed oppression which has been raised against me by these men," Smith counseled, "use not the hand of violence against them, for they could not be prevailed upon to come here till I pledged my honor and

[51] Mace, "Journal of Wandle Mace," 63.

[52] *History of the Church,* 5:460.

[53] As taken from a composite of the Joseph Smith and Wilford Woodruff journals, 1843. See also *History of the Church,* 5:467.

my life that a hair of their heads should not be hurt."[54] Two days later, the Nauvoo Municipal Court discharged Smith "for want of substance in the warrant upon which he was arrested."[55] In the meantime, two very disappointed, embarrassed lawmen had already left town.

Choosing to regard the entire Dixon arrest matter as another flagrant miscarriage of justice, a shameful extension of habeas corpus, and an affront to the honor of the state of Missouri, Governor Reynolds wasted little time expressing his displeasure. He believed that the Legion had acted improperly, that the Nauvoo Municipal Court had overreached its authority in freeing Smith, and that Governor Ford had failed to fulfill his responsibilities as commander in chief of the state's militia. Reynolds insisted that Ford call out the state militia immediately, arrest the Mormon leader, and turn him over to Missouri officials.[56]

Faced with the growing possibility of outright civil war in his state, a nervous Governor Ford commissioned a special agent—Mason Brayman, Esq.—to conduct a thorough investigation of the recent events: "The imprisonment of the agent of Missouri," he wrote, "and the array of citizens of Nauvoo in military force, if true, may so excite the already combustible state of public feeling . . . and lead to collision of hostile forces. Feeling it my duty to cause the laws to be respected and by all means to prevent any invasion from abroad I . . . propose that I should avail myself of the means of acquiring, as early as I can, correct information of the events."[57] Specifically, Ford asked Brayman to find out the truth of the rumors, "how far the citizens of Nauvoo may be disposed to act with military force," and the probability of Missouri's sending an invading force to Nauvoo.[58]

Although it is tempting to argue that Ford's refusal to turn Smith

---

[54] Joseph Smith Papers, MSS 155, Box 4, Fd 5. Church History Library. *History of the Church,* 5:467–68. For several different accounts of this speech, see Ehat and Cook, *Words of Joseph Smith,* 216–23. See also Hill, "Carthage Conspiracy Reconsidered," 113. Hill argues that Joseph Smith's mood became more militant because of the Dixon arrest.

[55] Joseph Smith Papers, MSS 155, Box 4 Fd. 13 Church History Library See also History of the Church, 5:474.

[56] *Nauvoo Neighbor,* 1:18. See also *History of the Church,* 5:533. It is not perfectly clear whether it was Governor Thomas Reynolds or Sheriff Joseph H. Reynolds who wrote the letter. Ford referred to the demand of Joseph H. Reynolds but his letter of August 14, was to Governor Thomas Reynolds. Furthermore, it is not clear what influence, if any, John Bennett or other political influences may have been at work.

[57] *History of the Church,* 5:533.

[58] Governor Thomas Ford to Mason Brayman, July 3, 1843. Governor's Correspondence, Executive Sub-Series, 1843.

over to Missouri was, in part, politically motivated by the fear of losing the Mormon vote in the pending congressional elections, his August 14, 1843, letter of explanation to Governor Reynolds gave other reasons, and offered insights into how he perceived his role as commander in chief of the Illinois State Militia, including the Nauvoo Legion.[59] Relying heavily on Brayman's findings, Ford admitted that although most of the rescuing party were members of the Nauvoo Legion, there was no evidence, he argued, that they acted in a military capacity since "there was no exhibition of arms of any description, nor was there any military or warlike array, nor was there any actual force used, though Mr. [Joseph H.] Reynolds testifies that he felt under constraint."[60]

Governor Ford, generally averse to the use of military force, defended his actions by a close reading of the state's militia laws. He believed the law allowed him to call out the militia under only three circumstances: "there must be either a requisition from the president [of the United States], an actual or threatened invasion, or some extreme emergency, to warrant the governor in exercising this power." "No one of these exigencies has arisen," he concluded, admitting that the Nauvoo Municipal Court may not have acted in Missouri's best interest, but based on a strict interpretation of the facts nothing illegal had occurred.[61]

Arguably a better judge than a governor, Ford continued in his characteristically strict reading of the law:

> If we allow that force was exhibited and threatened to compel your agent to carry his prisoner before the Municipal Court of Nauvoo,

[59] According to several Democratic newspapers, including the *Illinois State Register,* the whole episode of Joseph Smith's recent arrest was "a Whig conspiracy to compel a Democratic governor to issue a writ against Smith, pending the Congressional election, so as to incense the Mormons, create a necessity for Walker's and perhaps Browning's professional services in favor of Smith, to get him delivered out of the net of their own weaving, and thereby get the everlasting gratitude of the Mormons and their support for the Whig cause." *History of the Church,* 5:515. While it is reasonable to conclude that politics played a role in Ford's thinking, Bennett's motivations were more than merely rabidly political. His collaboration with Whig interests had a far more sinister objective in mind.

[60] *Nauvoo Neighbor* 1:18. *History of the Church,* 5:534. Letter of Governor Ford to Governor Thomas Reynolds, August 14, 1843. In his later history, Ford wrote that a "number of armed Mormons" interrogated the party but stops short of admitting they were from the Nauvoo Legion and that they used force. Ford, *History of Illinois,* 314–15.

[61] *History of the Church,* 5:535.

> that the court there took cognizance of the cause without jurisdiction and against the consent of your agent, it would amount at most to a riot; and to a resistance of authority in a single case, and that, too, under color of law and legal process. To constitute an extreme emergency, so as to justify a call for the militia, there ought, in my opinion, to be something more than a mere illegal act—something more than a design to resist the law in a single instance. The design ought to be general, as in treason, rebellion, or insurrection.[62]

He concluded thus: "There has been no warlike array in the proceedings of Smith and his friends, no exhibition or arms, and no actual force of an illegal character."[63]

Governor Ford's careful reasoning aside, the Legion's leaving its area of jurisdiction without order of the governor could only find justification in the heated temper of the times. For if this was not a direct or official deployment of the Legion, it certainly had all the markings, excepting uniforms: two general officers in charge, two companies deployed, a roster call, and assembling, organizing, and executing. Wilson and Reynolds were likely acting legally when they set out with a signed writ of arrest to take Smith back with them to Missouri to stand trial for alleged treason. However, their duplicity in disguising themselves as Mormon elders, the brutal way they handled their prisoner, and their failure to read the writ invalidated the legality of their arrest.[64]

The Nauvoo response to the news of Smith's capture was swift in coming, for most believed that if Wilson and Reynolds were successful, Smith would never live to see Illinois again. Feelings on all sides reached a fever pitch virtually overnight, and desperate times called for desperate measures. If companies of the Legion transformed themselves temporarily into an illegal posse, they did so to prevent perceived injustice and the abuse of its leader. Furthermore, those members of the Legion who responded acted without violence or bloodshed, a point Ford relied upon to support his own inaction.

Response from Missourians on both sides of the river was predictably quick in coming. Wrote one furious observer, "It will be

---

[62] *History of the Church,* 5:536.

[63] *History of the Church,* 5:536.

[64] Anderson, *Lucy's Book: A Critical Edition of Lucy Mack Smith's Family Memoir,* 732.

but a small matter to raise volunteers enough here to raze the city of Nauvoo to the ground; if the governor of Illinois fears to deliver up Jo Smith, there will be something serious between the two states"; and "[i]f the governor of Illinois is so imbecile as to allow his warrant to be disregarded by the Mormons . . . then let him be impeached. . . . The Mormons are only a lawless banditti, and I fear the pestilence has contaminated the whole community."[65]

Amid growing tensions, a large and very animated gathering met at Carthage, Illinois, in early September 1843 and enumerated their primary grievances against the Mormons and Governor Ford's recent inaction, and determined on a course of action. Agreeing with Missouri Governor Reynolds in nearly every matter of the Dixon arrest episode (going so far as to request Reynolds "to make another demand upon the authorities of this state for the body of Joseph Smith"), they believed the Mormon threat was fundamentally political, blending the powers of church and state in one man. Such fears were heightened when it became evident that the Mormons held the balance of political power in Hancock County and significant political influence in several western Illinois counties. As Ford later put it, "The great cause of popular fury was that the Mormons at several preceding elections had cast their vote as a unit. . . . They [are] fearful that if division should be encouraged in politics, it would soon extend to their religion, and rend their church with schism and into sects."[66] Mormon voters in Hancock County outnumbered non-Mormons by 1843 and controlled county elections and influenced the selection of state legislators from that multi-county district.

Furthermore, many Hancock County residents could not and would not disassociate the military power of the Legion from its lieutenant general. They believed Joseph Smith was "absolutely a despot" with virtually total control over the executive, legislative, and judicial power in the city, and claimed he had proven himself to be a dangerous character (see chapter 9). More incensed by the power and actions of the Nauvoo Municipal Court than any specific action of the Legion, they nevertheless believed Smith held too much sway

[65] *Warsaw Message*, 1:29. See also *History of the Church*, 5:539. The *Nauvoo Neighbor* responded: "No wonder a negro could be burned alive in Missouri! No wonder a criminal could be taken out of jail and murdered while the sheriff held a respite in his hand, in Missouri; and no wonder that a Mormon will not risk his life in Missouri." *History of the Church*, 5:540.

[66] Ford, *History of Illinois*, 330.

over the Legion: "[He] has caused large bodies of his ragamuffin soldiery to arm themselves, and turn out in pursuit of officers legally authorized to arrest himself." To their way of thinking, the Legion was a military expression of Mormon authority run amok.[67]

The Carthage conference ended ominously, resolving to resist all Mormon wrongs "peaceably if we can, but forcibly, if we must"; to request Governor Reynolds "to make another demand upon the authorities of this state for the body of Joseph Smith"; and, in a barely veiled censure of Governor Ford, to contend against any politicians, of either party, who "truckle to the heads of the Mormon clan."[68]

Such threats soon ricocheted throughout the dusty streets of Nauvoo and contributed directly to an unmistakable fear of invasion. The Legion's customary September drills became more intense than ever. On September 11, 1843, Smith appointed W. W. Phelps, Henry Miller,[69] and Hosea Stout to "a committee to wait on Governor Ford" to increase the number of state arms provided the Legion—a request that fell on deaf ears (almost every militia in the state was at least as poorly provisioned as the Nauvoo Legion; however, this did not prevent militiamen from acquiring their own private arms).[70] At the general Legion parade five days later, Smith once again inspected the troops and "requested the officers to increase the Legion in numbers."

In response to the recent Carthage gathering, the citizens of Nauvoo, at an elaborate dinner at the new Mansion House on October

---

[67] In the earliest account of the conflict in Hancock County, historian George T. M. Davis put his slant on things when he wrote: "The church, the military, and the judiciary, as well as the Common Council of Nauvoo were solely and entirely under [Smith's] unlimited control . . . Nauvoo was, to all intents and purposes, a separate and distinct government, acknowledging no superior power to their own and assuming to themselves the power to make their own laws and administer them in their own way." Davis, *An Authentic Account of the Massacre of Joseph Smith* as cited in Hallwas and Launius, *Cultures in Conflict,* 107.

[68] *History of the Church,* 6:5–8. For a fine discussion, if not defense, of the "enormous fear of despotism" that animated the anti-Mormon sentiments of many in Hancock County, see Hallwas, "Mormon Nauvoo from a Non-Mormon Perspective," 53–70. At base, he argues that the conflict was an ideological one over the perception that Nauvoo was "a deviation from democracy" (58), that the well-beloved concept of the separation of church and state was nonexistent in Nauvoo city, and that far too much political, military, and ecclesiastical power rested in one man. This is much the same interpretation as offered by Winn, *Exiles in a Land of Liberty,* especially chapter 8.

[69] Henry William Miller (1807–85): major, aide-de-camp, brigadier general of the Nauvoo Legion; marched with the Mormon Battalion.

[70] Leonard, *Nauvoo,* 114–15.

3, passed several resolutions of their own. First, with respect to their leader, "whether we view him as a Prophet at the head of the Church, a General at the head of the Legion, a Mayor at the head of his table, if he has equals, he has no superiors." In response to the animadversion "ragamuffin soldiery," they declared that the "Nauvoo Legion [is] a well disciplined and faithful band of invincibles, ready at all times to defend this country with this motto, 'Vive La Republique.'" The Nauvoo Charter was again honored as "an unalterable decree by a patriotic band of wise legislators" and Governor Ford praised as "fearless and faithful" in his duties—"long may he live."[71]

Neither side seemed inclined to pursue the path of dialogue, accommodation, or diplomacy. The Latter-day Saints were as committed to building up the church as their antagonists were to tearing it down and driving them from the state. Without quick intervention, Governor Ford would inevitably lose control over a very explosive situation.

Smith was sufficiently concerned that he sought Ford's advice on what action he should take in the case of an attack upon the city. The governor downplayed any such eventuality: "I am of opinion that there is but little danger of any such invasion. It is altogether more likely that some other mode of annoyance will be adopted";[72] he may have expected instead a series of disturbances or attacks on outlying Mormon farms and settlements.

"Keep Cool as a Cucumber"

As if to make good on their threats, late in 1843 a company of Missourians and Illinois settlers kidnapped young Philander Avery and, soon afterward, his father, Daniel Avery, near Warsaw, Illinois, on the grounds that the two men were horse thieves. Both men were hurried off without trial to a Monticello, Missouri, jail. Smith, fearing that this was the start of worse acts to follow, sent a letter to Governor Ford asking, "Shall any portion of the Legion be called out?"[73] While waiting for orders, he directed city marshal Henry G. Sherwood[74] to watch for further kidnapping threats. Sherwood was to call

[71] *Nauvoo Neighbor,* October 3, 1843, 1:23; See also *History of the Church,* 6:42–43.

[72] *History of the Church,* 6:35.

[73] Manuscript copy of Thomas Bullock, December 6, 1843. Church History Library. See also *History of the Church,* 6:101.

[74] Henry Garlie Sherwood (1785–1862) guard in the Nauvoo Legion; marshal in Nauvoo; surveyor; missionary to Louisiana.

"for a suitable portion of the Nauvoo Legion to protect the rights of the citizens" to compel "obedience to the ordinances of said city and secure the peace of the citizens."[75] Sherwood in turn ordered the Legion to be ready.

Recognizing that the Legion should not be called into armed action without the governor's direct order, the Nauvoo City Council chose to enact a provision in the city charter that allowed for the establishment of a city police force. Likewise, the city council was sensitive to charges from some surrounding communities that Nauvoo housed its share of criminals—horse thieves, counterfeiters, and worse—and needed to take effective investigative action. Thus, at a meeting on December 12, 1843, the city council passed an ordinance establishing a company of forty men to act as a municipal police force, with Hosea Stout as chief of police.[76]

It is important to differentiate between those men serving in the Legion as an arm of the state militia and the same men serving in other capacities at the request of the city mayor. Since Nauvoo had no civil police force until 1843, members of the Legion were sometimes called upon by the mayor for police purposes.[77] In this capac-

[75] Order of Joseph Smith, MSS 5201, Church History Library. Original letter is in the files of the Department of Interior, Washington, D.C.

[76] *History of the Church,* 6:110, 149. Some have argued that the new Nauvoo police force was nothing more than a revived Mormon Danite body intent on threatening the lives of Mormon dissidents. The facts suggest otherwise. In part, the organization of the Nauvoo city police was a belated recognition that the Legion was neither equipped for, nor commissioned to, handle criminal activity. It was a militia, not an investigative, security body. Nor could the Legion be called out without Springfield's approval. Furthermore, some of the outside criticisms were true. With growing recognition that there were ne'er-do-wells in a rapidly growing city of over ten thousand inhabitants, city leaders recognized the need for a police force.

[77] The Nauvoo police, formally organized in early 1843, were captained by Jonathan Dunham with twenty-two men in the First Guard and eighteen in the Second Guard. An expansion in December 1843 retained Dunham. According to Hosea Stout, however, "this was only a temporary arrangement of the police organization, while the regular police, who were mostly officers in the Legion were in actual service which lasted until the Legion was disbanded." "June 26, 1844, meeting of police—Nauvoo Legion." Church History Library.

Legally constituted municipal police forces were slow to develop in America. Very few such forces existed in the 1840s, not even in the largest cities in the country. In many communities, police protection was furnished by the sheriff, marshal, or other authorities invested with the safety and security concerns of each community. From 1841 to 1844, Hosea Stout acted as chief of police, an informal collection of security officers. Leonard, *Nauvoo,* 469.

ity, they acted not as a Legion force but as individuals commissioned to protect the public peace. Since the early days of settlement, it was well known that theft was a major crime in communities along the Mississippi. River towns were known to attract drifters, escapees, and criminals, and Nauvoo had its share. As the city grew it became a greater target for thieves, counterfeiters, heavy drinkers, and other ne'er-do-wells. Remembered Hawkins Taylor, sheriff of Lee County, Iowa, just across the Mississippi River from Nauvoo, "Nauvoo was infected at that time with a great number of thieves, who would cross over to Iowa and commit depredations and embark to Nauvoo. I would go over and arrest them and bring them back, the Mormons allowing me to do it."[78] There was a great enough criminal element among the Mormons themselves to cause concern. Indeed, in December 1841 several members had been cut off from the Church for stealing.[79] To minimize this threat, from time to time members of the Legion were called upon to find and arrest such individuals and help bring them to justice.[80]

On rarer occasions the Legion itself responded to the call of city officials. For instance, on October 30, 1841, "in obedience to an order from the mayor," Smith, acting in his military capacity, "called out two companies of the Nauvoo Legion, and removed a grog shop, kept by Pulaski S. Cahoon, and which had been declared a nuisance by the city council."[81] This order set a precedent for future action. As expected, in a letter dated December 12, 1843, Governor Ford refused to call out the Legion on the very same grounds that he had denied Governor Reynolds's earlier request—no invasion, no insurrection,

---

78 Archives Special Collections, Western Illinois University Library, Macomb, Illinois, as quoted by Hallwas and Launius, *Cultures in Conflict,* 52.

79 Roberts, *Comprehensive History of the Church,* 2:116. Church leaders tried vigilantly to bring such criminals within the Church to justice. Joseph Smith said, "The Church must be cleansed, and I proclaim against all iniquity." *History of the Church,* 4:588.

80 The criminal problem in Nauvoo was as real and difficult as in other river towns. The Quorum of the Twelve Apostles was so concerned with it that they wondered why a police force had not been established earlier. "As there are gangs of robbers up and down this river, from whom we have suffered much, having had many horses, cattle and other property stolen, we purpose instituting a police for the protection of our property, and the rigorous enforcement of the laws of our county and should any, who call themselves Latter-day Saints, be found in their midst, they will be cut off from the Church, and handed over to the law of the land." *Times and Seasons,* 616–17. See also *History of the Church,* 4:465.

81 *Times and Seasons,* 599. See also *History of the Church,* 4:442–44.

and no extreme emergency. "I would advise your citizens to be strictly peaceable towards the people of Missouri," he said. "You ought to be aware that in every country individuals are liable to be visited with wrong, which the law is slow to redress, and some of which are never redressed in this world. This fact, however, has never been held to be a justification for violence, not warranted by law."[82]

On December 18, hearing that a large mob was gathering at Warsaw, a few miles south of Nauvoo, Smith ignored Ford's reply and instructed Major General Wilson Law to "order out such a portion of the Nauvoo Legion as may be necessary to repel any such mobocratic or hostile design . . . to secure the peace of the citizens"—but not to take overt action.[83] The following day, the Legion paraded near the temple grounds, where the men were "instructed to prepare themselves with arms and ammunition and to hold themselves in readiness for a moment's notice."[84]

Fortunately for all sides the Averys were freed by their Missouri captors on Christmas Day, 1843. Their return temporarily defused a potentially explosive situation. In speaking to the newly organized police force—some of whom admittedly had volatile dispositions—Joseph Smith wisely advised a peaceful approach. "Let Missouri alone," he cautioned. "Our best policy [is] to acquaint the Executive, by affidavits, of every violation of our rights, so that when the onset comes, he will be obliged by law to send the militia to our support. Let us keep cool as a cucumber on a frosty morning. Do not be excited." As for town criminals, he said, "Have the ordinances of the city always in your possession, and study them, and ferret out all grogshops, gambling houses, brothels, and disorderly conduct; and if a transgressor resists, cuff his ears."[85]

The immediate danger now past, Smith wrote to Governor Ford to apprise him of the situation and of his decision to put the Legion on alert. "I thought it advisable to have a portion of the Legion ready to resist a mob," he wrote. "A burnt child dreads the fire, and when my old friends, men, women and children, look to me in the hour

[82] Governor Thomas Ford to Joseph Smith, December 12, 1843. Original letter in Joseph Smith Correspondence, Joseph Smith Collection. Church History Library. See also *History of the Church,* 6:114.

[83] *History of the Church,* 6:120.

[84] "Joseph Smith Journal," 203–204. See also *History of the Church,* 6:121.

[85] Nauvoo City Council Minutes, Booklet #3, 30–32. See also *History of the Church,* 6:151.

of danger for protection . . . I am bound by my oath of office and by all laws human and divine to grant it."[86] He further penned, "I am happy to say none were ordered to march, as it was deemed most advisable to let Colonel Levi Williams and his mob [at Warsaw] flourish until indictments could be made at the Circuit Court of Hancock County."[87]

That John C. Bennett, the "opportunistic convert" who turned spiteful and vengeful toward his former friends and people, helped motivate Governor Thomas Reynolds of Missouri to seek Joseph Smith's extradition cannot be denied. Bennett would play an incendiary role in causing Mormon difficulties wherever and whenever he could, by force of pen or personality. While the Mormon prophet was cleared of one set of charges in late 1842, he faced more extradition attempts in mid-1843. The Nauvoo Legion's role in defending and rescuing its leader prompted Governor Ford to make a thorough investigation of the matter and eventually to reject Missouri's various well-defined points of legal argument. Such efforts served only to further inflame passions among Mormon enemies—and worsen the negative perceptions they held.

---

[86] Joseph Smith to Governor Thomas Ford, January 1, 1844, *Personal Writings of Joseph Smith*, 588.

[87] *History of the Church*, 6:153.

9

Perceptions and Fears

Is an army necessary to propagate religion?
Is it necessary to protect their civil rights?
THOMAS SHARP, JUNE 9, 1841

We pause to consider the sentiments, perceptions, and fears about the Mormons and Joseph Smith that nearly led to the repeal of the Nauvoo Charter in 1843. Recognizing that perceptions, accurate or no, often have very powerful consequences, it is vital that we stop and evaluate the prevailing perceptions and fears of the time. Some fears were legitimate. In his excellent study of the 1840s conflict between Mormons and non-Mormons in Hancock County, historian Kenneth Godfrey showed that perceptions often were more important than facts. For example, in the case of lawlessness in the greater Nauvoo area, some non-Mormons believed that the Mormons were responsible for every crime committed. Conversely, Mormons believed that their non-Mormon neighbors were responsible for the lawlessness. In fact, both sides bore responsibility for the situation.[1]

Some nineteenth-century Americans, who valued separation of church and state, had negative reactions to Joseph Smith and Mormonism. Smith, being the founder of a religious movement, mayor of a large community, and now lieutenant general of a growing city militia, represented too much power vested in one man. Was Joseph Smith like Muhammad—a religious lawgiver, Oracle of God, judge of the people, and military leader?

[1] Godfrey, "Causes of Mormon Non-Mormon Conflict," 173–75.

As questions arose about the connection between Smith and Muhammad, the most disturbing, if not the most vehement, were hurled against Smith's leadership of the Nauvoo Legion. But these attacks were "brush fires" for those wanting to see a negative. The Legion was a scapegoat for the intended target—Joseph Smith and Mormonism. Although the Legion's role in the history of Mormonism in Illinois was relatively brief—and some would say insignificant—a disproportionate number of criticisms attacked its foundation, its pomp and ceremony, and its calls to arm. Print media characterized Smith as unpatriotic and ambitious, and those who followed his lead, dupes of a military despot. Visitors to the heartland of Mormonism enjoyed a certain celebrity upon returning home and sharing stories of the militant Mormons and their arsenal.

Venues of Criticisms

Most criticisms of the Legion appeared in newspaper articles and editorials. Thomas C. Sharp, editor of the *Warsaw Signal,* was the most critical. Sharp, a native of New Jersey, was born in 1813. He graduated from Dickinson College in Pennsylvania before studying law. Sharp moved to Warsaw, Illinois, where he hoped to make his fortune. Warsaw then had a population of five hundred and was enjoying a season of prosperity. Sharp liked what he saw, acquired a newspaper, the *Western World,* and changed its name to the *Warsaw Signal.*[2]

During Nauvoo's first year (1839–40), the *Signal* was free of anti-Mormon sentiment. That began to change on April 6, 1841, when Sharp attended the military parade and cornerstone laying of the Nauvoo Temple. Most spectators applauded the events of that day, but Sharp did not. On July 21, 1841, he penned, "Every thing they say or do seems to breathe the spirit of military tactics. . . . Truly fighting must be a part of the creed of these Saints." Sharp had previously exhorted his readers thus:

> Ask yourselves what means this array of military force which is paraded under the direction of this church. Is an army necessary to

[2] Launius, "Anti-Mormonism in Illinois," 27–31. Because the *Warsaw Signal* was the only newspaper in the county not under Mormon control, it became very influential as the exclusive newspaper voice in Hancock County opposing Mormonism.

> propagate religion? Is it necessary to protect their civil rights? Why then this parade? Are they so patriotic as to have no other end than the safety of the state in view? Why these weekly parades? Why all this strictness of discipline? We pause for a reply.[3]

Such questioning caused more than one reader to fear. Other editorials threatened the peace of Nauvoo. Sharp called for the abolition of the Legion, and even gave space in the *Signal* to competitive newspaper editors who made unfavorable comments about the Legion.[4] On August 13, 1845, Sharp reprinted a *Saint Louis Reveille* article calling the Legion a "playing soldier affair on the part of the boys, big and little of the town."[5] Although the article failed to qualify or support its criticisms, Sharp had no qualms in trumpeting the attacks as the genuine truth.

Thomas Sharp was not the only resident in Warsaw who spoke out against Mormonism and its military force. In 1843 townsfolk organized the popular Warsaw Legislature, a forum for anti-Mormon discussion led by William Grover. Grover, a native of New York, had a law practice in Warsaw. He was reputed to be a "sought after" public speaker who could engage, if not incite, a crowd. Grover's speeches before the Warsaw Legislature and his sarcastic comments about "Nephites" (a people in the Book of Mormon; Grover used the term to refer to Nauvoo residents), added fuel to the smoldering hatred of the Legion.[6]

These criticisms of Sharp and Grover were echoed in Springfield, the state capital. Springfield's leading paper, the *Sangamo Journal*, asked, "What would be thought if Baptists, Methodists, Presbyterians or Episcopalians of this state had military organizations?"[7] A month later, the *New York Herald* printed an anonymous letter from a regular artillery officer, who labeled the Nauvoo Mormons "warlike fanatics." He asked if "they intend[ed] to conquer Missouri,

---

[3] Thomas Sharp, "The Mormons," *Warsaw Signal* 2, no. 5, June 9, 1841.

[4] The May 28, 1845, issue, for example, contained unfavorable articles from the *Quincy Whig*, *Sangamo Journal*, and *Cleveland Herald*.

[5] *Warsaw Signal*, August 13, 1845.

[6] Hallwas and Launius, *Cultures in Conflict*, 97–98.

[7] "We were not the Aggressors," *Sangamo Journal* 10, no. 41, June 3, 1842. This question was asked shortly after the attempted assassination of Lilburn W. Boggs, former governor of Missouri. Fearing that Missourians would blame the Mormons and retaliate, Joseph Smith called upon the legion to stand guard in Nauvoo. Their guard duty attracted attention and was the subject of the article's criticism.

Illinois, Mexico?"[8] The questions raised in the *Journal* caused many in Springfield, especially politicians, to take a stand. Most believed that religious leaders should not meddle in political or military affairs and that Smith was "a dangerous man."[9]

The *Bloomington Herald* concurred, and suggested that militant Mormons had trouble living in peace with their neighbors:

> We learned that they [Mormons] paraded for military training weekly, when they are taken through all the exercises in the use of arms. Their purposes for training are not openly avowed, but those who have had much intercourse with them are of the opinion that it is to avenge themselves on Missouri, so soon as their increasing strength will warrant a hope for success. Let their object be what it may, they cannot live long in peace with the neighboring country, it is certain that our southern neighbors may anticipate trouble with them. Their numbers already give them an impudence that free men cannot long quietly submit to and it is increasing to a remarkable degree.[10]

The *Logansport Telegraph* compared Smith to Muhammad and asked whether Mormonism was spreading by the sword.[11] The *Quincy Herald* reported that the Legion was an armed militia defiant of government authority.[12] In Alton, *The Peoples Miscellany and Illinois Herald* printed their opposition to the Legion's public display of military power.[13]

In the Iowa Territory, the *Davenport Gazette* linked the Legion to Nauvoo civil courts, claiming that it was used to enforce civil law.[14] The *Gazette* hinted at problems that arose from improper use of military power, especially when citizens were bearing arms and

[8] "An Officer of the U.S. Artillery," *New York Herald* 8, no. 16 (June 17, 1842); "An Ordinance in Relation to Religious Societies," *Wasp* no. 6 (May 21, 1842).

[9] "Citizens of Illinois—Read and Consider," *Sangamo Journal* 10, no. 22 (January 21, 1842).

[10] "Mormons," *Bloomington Herald* 1, no. 4 (November 20, 1840): 2. In the quotation by Hajicek, the date is given as November 20, 1840. It should be noted that the Legion was not organized until 1841. Hajicek, *Newsclippings from Iowa and Illinois,* 3.

[11] *Logansport Telegraph,* July 30, 1842.

[12] *Quincy Herald,* August 25, 1842, as cited in Godfrey, "Causes of Mormon Non-Mormon Conflict," 144.

[13] *The Peoples Miscellany and Illinois Herald,* July 27, 1842. The article suggested that Joseph Smith and his Legion would be welcome in Iowa.

[14] "Joe Smith," *Davenport Gazette* 3, no. 26 (February 15, 1844).

preparing to fight.[15] On June 22, 1844, the *Lee County Democrat* reported that the followers of "Joe" Smith were determined to fight until the last drop of blood was shed.[16]

The Saint Louis *Reporter* newspaper claimed that a Mormon force of five thousand was armed and ready to attack Missouri.[17] In Ohio, the *Franklin Times* announced Mormonism was increasing by military force.[18] In Washington, D.C., the *Daily National Intelligencer* asserted that Smith used the Legion to rid himself of unwanted followers.[19] And in the *New York Sun* there were reports of a military despot living in the West—a thinly veiled reference to Smith and the Nauvoo Legion.[20]

Scorned and ridiculed by journalists, the Legion also came under attack in books. *An Authentic Account,* by George T. M. Davis of Alton, Illinois, thus criticized the Legion: "Joe further stated, that God revealed to him, that the Indians and Latter Day Saints, under Joe as their King and Ruler, were to conquer Gentiles, and that their subjection to this authority was to be obtained by the sword."[21] And John C. Bennett's *The History of the Saints; or an Exposé of Joe Smith and Mormonism,* declared Smith planned to conquer Ohio, Indiana, Iowa, Illinois, and Missouri and establish a militant Mormon empire (see chapter 10).[22]

In addition, some visitors to Nauvoo disseminated tales of Smith

---

15 "Mormon Troubles," *Davenport Gazette* 3, no. 5 (June 27, 1844): 2.

16 *Lee County Democrat,* June 22, 1844. This article discusses the destruction of the *Expositor* and affirms as fact that the Mormons are ready to fight if any attempt is made to take Joseph Smith or other Church leaders out of Nauvoo.

17 See *Niles' National Register,* December 9, 1843.

18 *Franklin Times,* May 22, 1841.

19 *Daily National Intelligencer,* June 10, 1844.

20 *Sun,* July 1843, as cited in Miller and Miller, *Nauvoo,* 132.

21 Davis, "An Authentic Account of the Massacre of Joseph Smith, the Mormon Prophet, and Hyrum Smith, His Brother, Together with a Brief History of the Rise and Progress of Mormonism, and All the Circumstances which Led to Their Death," in Hallwas and Launius, *Cultures in Conflict,* 103. Davis spent much of June 1844 in Hancock County studying the Mormon conflict. He sent information to the Alton newspaper about his findings on Mormonism. His book focused on the political issues surrounding Joseph Smith. His perspective of the Legion places it somewhat separate from its religious context.

22 Smith, *Saintly Scoundrel,* 125. As stated previously, John Bennett held important positions in the Church and in Nauvoo city government, and he had been instrumental in establishing the Legion. Bennett viciously attacked the Church and the Legion after his excommunication and court martial.

and his Legion. One such visitor was Reverend George Moore of Quincy, Illinois. A native of Sudbury, Massachusetts, Moore came of age in Concord, and in spite of friendships with literary types such as Ralph Waldo Emerson and Henry David Thoreau, he found his temperament was more suited to the ministry. Lured to the West, Moore, like other clergymen of the 1840s, hoped to tame more than a wilderness. He traveled from town to town spreading his version of the gospel and recording his ministry. One interesting reference was of a visit to Nauvoo, during which he saw cannons near the doorstep of Smith's home.[23] His comments were these:

> As I came out [of the Smith home] I found two large cannons, mounted in his yard. Can this be a prophet of God, thought I, who must have cannons for a guard, and must convert all his followers into soldiers into a Nauvoo Legion and excite them in a warlike spirit? What return is this to Judaism, nay to Judaism, but to barbarism? And yet this imposter (for I cannot call him any thing else) has his thousands of followers. Nauvoo contains a population of from 5 to 10,000 being variously estimated and the converts to this system, if system it may be called, are coming in by hundreds.[24]

Such accounts, whether real or imagined, found eager audiences in such remote communities as Oquawka, Illinois. When members of the Legion rode their horses into the small village in search of their commander, who had been arrested in Dixon, town residents saw soldiers raise swords and grasp cocked pistols, primed and ready for attack. Although no damage was done, Oquawka's residents quickly labeled the soldiers "Destroying Angels."[25] Such labels sold newspapers, elevated storytellers, and led opportunist politicians to seize the moment and speak out.

By 1843 the Nauvoo Legion was being discussed in halls of government. To many politicians, the Legion had become a growing cancer on the western border of the United States. Illinoisans, Iowans, Missourians, and government officials as far away as Wash-

---

[23] Cannon, "Reverend George Moore's Comments," 8.

[24] Cannon, "Reverend George Moore's Comments," 11.

[25] Allaman, "Joseph Smith's Visits to Henderson County," 51. Joseph Smith had been taken prisoner by a "posse." Many Mormons feared that he would be killed if transported from Illinois to Missouri. Believing Joseph to be in Oquawka, soldiers charged into the town in hopes of preventing the posse from crossing the river to Missouri.

ington, D.C., insisted that Governor Ford resolve the menacing threat. Would he speak out? And if he spoke, which way would he turn? Would he follow the growing tide of opposition or defend the right of Nauvoo citizens to have a city militia?

Once Ford had taken action to assess the rumors from a variety of society's sectors, other critics clamored to be heard. The American Home Missionary Society expressed open contempt of Mormons' organizing and equipping military companies.[26] Hancock County historian Thomas Gregg would later write of the dangerous power of the Legion, "Thus was set going at Nauvoo, if not with unusual and dangerous powers, at least under unusual circumstances, two engines capable of wielding a powerful influence—an influence which was subsequently wielded and felt thro [*sic*] out the county and the State."[27]

Major Perceptions and Criticisms

Opposition to the Legion had its desired effect. It put Joseph Smith and his soldiers on notice that their military structure, and even their very lives, were in danger. Such opposition also represented the genuine fears of some of the non-Mormon population. What follows is an attempt to identify at least the major critical perceptions many had of the Saints in Nauvoo and of the Legion.

Mormons Were Warlike Fanatics

There are now approximately 30,000 of these war-like fanatics.
SANGAMO JOURNAL, MAY 6, 1842

The time Mormons devoted to Nauvoo Legion matters constituted a mere fraction of their overall activities. Although Mormons did participate in Zion's Camp, Smith's followers were busy with many other things. They felt more comfortable proclaiming themselves to be law-abiding citizens rather than training for defense. However, after being harassed, mobbed, and persecuted in the state of Missouri, some were willing to fight back. The Nauvoo era, however, emphasized peaceful coexistence with neighbors as a higher priority than mustering, drilling, and conducting parades.

---

[26] Launius, "American Home Missionary Society Ministers," 22.
[27] Gregg, "Historical Sketches of the Mormon Era," 75.

A Church Should Not Sponsor a Military Organization

What would be thought if the Baptists, Methodists, Presbyterians, or Episcopalians of this state had military organizations?

SANGAMO JOURNAL, JUNE 3, 1842

Churches in the United States usually did not sponsor a militia unit. Although the majority of Legion members were Mormons, faith was not the only reason for their enlistment. Recruitment followed state regulations, which required all able-bodied males aged eighteen to forty-five to enlist. Unlike the Catholic and Jewish militia, the Nauvoo Legion included non-Mormons. The so-called Mormon Legion was born of a state requirement. Nevertheless, some onlookers were suspicious, and some members of the Legion *did* view it as a Mormon militia (see chapter 5).

Legionnaires Were Improperly Used to Protect Smith and Other Mormon Leaders

The citizens of that place are a lawless banditti, gathered together for the purpose of protecting one another.

DEBATES ON THE NAUVOO CHARTER, DECEMBER 1844, SPRINGFIELD, ILLINOIS

This criticism has some validity, since the Legion was used for such purposes—the prime example being the rescue of Smith from sheriffs Reynolds and Wilson in 1843. In this instance, it was not Smith who called the Legion to duty, but one of his subordinates. The issue, however, is clouded. Smith was the leader of the Mormons, mayor of Nauvoo, and lieutenant general of the Nauvoo Legion. Was the Legion called to rescue its commander in chief, a civic leader, or the Mormon prophet? Determining the capacity in which Smith was functioning at the time of the rescue is vital to determining whether the Nauvoo Legion was used improperly. Such determinations had to be made each time the Legion was called to arms.

The Mormons Planned to Attack Missouri

Do they intend to conquer Missouri, Illinois, or Mexico?

NEW YORK HERALD, JUNE 17, 1844

Bennett certainly encouraged such action. The Legion, however, was primarily a defensive military force and remained so during its brief existence. Using the defensive definition to describe the Legion counters its critics' accusations of aggressive schemes. The Latter-day Saints did not have the monetary resources, equipment, or arms to take aggressive action, even if they desired to do so.

Smith Was Like Muhammad and Spread Religion by the Sword

Building a military church
like Mohammed of old [he] was going to
spread the gospel with his sword.
LOGANSPORT TELEGRAPH, JULY 30, 1842

This criticism reflects a strong nineteenth-century American interest in Muhammad. Among the most popular biographies of the time were Humphrey Prideaux's *The True Nature of Imposture, Fully Displayed in the Life of Mohammet;* William Muir's *Life of Mohammed;* George Bush's *Life of Mohammed—Founder of the Religion of Islam, and of the Empire of Saracens;* Washington Irving's *Mohammed and His Successors;* and George Miles's *Mohammed, the Arabian Prophet: A Tragedy in Five Acts.*[28] Familiarity with Muhammad made it easy, if not natural, for critics to compare Smith with the self-proclaimed prophetic/military leader. Such comparisons began in Palmyra, New York, when attorney Abner Cole printed excerpts of the Book of Mormon in the *Reflector.*[29] Mormon missionary work had been going on since the spring of 1830. The diaries, letters, and reminiscences of hundreds of missionaries and their converts make it very clear that compulsion was not part of their message. Nor was violence condoned in any way.

The Legion Was Too Well Armed

5 pieces of Cannon—6 pounders! 500 muskets!!—460 pistols!!!
85 rifles!!!! 113 yeagers!!!!!—123 swords!!!!!!
ALTON TELEGRAPH AND DEMOCRATIC REVIEW, JULY 23, 1842

A proper response to this charge must take into account the total number of weapons in the Legion's possession. Governor Ford

[28] Fluhman, "An 'American Mahomet,'" 27.

[29] It was not until Eduard Meyer's *Ursprung und Geschichte der Mormonen, mit Exkursen über die Anfänge des Islâms und des Christentums* that a favorable comparison was made between the men. Meyer pointed out that both religious leaders brought forth new scripture—Joseph Smith the Book of Mormon, and Muhammad the Qur'an.

claimed the Legion possessed 3 cannons and 250 small arms.[30] The basis for this claim is unknown, and the count does not factor in the weapons personally owned by members of the Legion. The Legion was certainly no better outfitted than any other militia in the state. In fact, there is evidence to suggest that the Legion did not have enough arms. A military document dating from 1843 shows this lack of weapons, as explained in this scholarly commentary:

> With the minor exception of six rifles listed in the First Artillery, only the three rifle companies carried state-provided rifles, though they were unevenly distributed. The Second and Third Rifle Regiments held 59 and 40 each and between them had four pistol pairs, while the Fourth's 28 rifles were supplemented by a third (21) of the muskets. The Fifth Infantry Regiment shouldered state-provided muskets solely. Since no such weapons are listed for members of the general staff, it can be assumed that these officers were expected to procure their own arms (swords and pistols)—likely a common practice throughout the United States at the time. To this day, all officers procure their own swords. All in all, the "General Return" essentially corroborates reports of the small numbers of arms provided to the Legion by the state. It was not much. Rather it was apparently, a token allotment.[31]

Mormons Cannot Live Peacefully with Their Neighbors

They cannot live long in peace
with the neighboring country.

BLOOMINGTON HERALD, NOVEMBER 20, 1841

In communities from New York to Illinois, good relationships were built and amicable associations established between Mormons and non-Mormons. Mormons were instructed by their leaders to "let your love and moderations be known unto all men."[32] Most Mormons followed this counsel, and welcomed strangers and those of other religious persuasions into their cities and homes. Nevertheless, sometimes problems with their neighbors arose due to misunderstandings.

---

[30] Ford, *History of Illinois*, 235.

[31] Saunders, "Officers and Arms," 145.

[32] *History of the Church*, 4:339.

The Legion Was Growing Too Large

The St. Louis Reporter states that the Nauvoo Legion numbers some four or five thousand men.

NILES' NATIONAL REGISTER, DECEMBER 9, 1843

Admittedly, comments by some leading Mormons caused others to fear. Apostle Parley P. Pratt, writing in boosteristic fashion to encourage British migration to Nauvoo, had predicted in September 1842 that the Legion would someday be "fifty thousand strong" and would be led by talented officers.[33] He had also argued that it provided a

> peculiar advantage to the Saints. . . . [I]t afforded that security and protection against lawless violence which has been so much needed . . . but which our people could seldom enjoy until thus organized. . . . Nauvoo, then, is the nucleus of a glorious dominion of universal liberty, peace and plenty; it is an organization of the government of which there shall be no end.[34]

Notwithstanding such exaggeration and rhetoric, the size of the Legion reflected the population of the Nauvoo and the encouragement of church leadership. Despite the above claim and that of the *Sangamo Journal* that the Legion numbered "30,000," it was but a fraction of that size. True, the Legion was larger than other militia units in Illinois, but if size were the issue, the state had the right to intervene. There is no record of the state of Illinois attempting to change the size of the Nauvoo Legion. Nevertheless, its size caused consternation among non-Mormons in nearby towns and villages with smaller and less enthusiastic militias. They feared what the leaders of such a sizable militia might be planning.

The Military Prowess of the Legion Was Feared

Lieutenant General Joseph Smith commanded a sizable force of soldiers which were as well-drilled as regular soldiers.

SANGAMO JOURNAL, JUNE 3, 1842

Determining the combat effectiveness of the Legion is difficult. Historian B. H. Roberts believed that the "Legion became the best

---

[33] *The Millennial Star*, September 1842.

[34] *The Millennial Star*, August 1842.

body of militia in the State of Illinois," But others disagreed.[35] Most Legion activities, such as parades and drills, never gave cause for such widespread fear. However, many residents of Illinois perceived the Legion's power could be used improperly.

The Legion Eliminated Dissenters

The "Prophet" is despatching companies in other directions under similar orders, in order to get rid of a portion of the disaffected of his followers.

DAILY NATIONAL INTELLIGENCER, JUNE 10, 1844

This was of greater concern among dissenting Mormons such as Bennett, the Laws, and the Higbees than to those outside the faith. The claim has some validity, since legionnaires did destroy the *Nauvoo Expositor*, which was owned and operated by Mormon dissidents (see chapter 10). There is no record, however, of any Legion soldier called to arms to eliminate a given individual or group for any reason, including disaffection from the faith.

The Legion as Empire Builder

Foreign conquest will most certainly follow.

NEW YORK HERALD, MAY 8, 1842

Some believed that a Mormon empire was planned owing to their perceptions of the Council of Fifty (see chapter 10).[36] This criticism relates, at least in part, to fears of Mormonism spread by the sword. Records do not indicate this was ever intended by Smith or the men under his command. Smith did colonize parts of western Illinois and eastern Iowa, but beyond protecting the settlements in those areas, the Nauvoo Legion did not play a role in his colonization efforts.

Men of the Legion Were "Destroying Angels"

The Mormons, or "the destroying angels."

PEOPLE OF OQUAWKA, ILLINOIS, 51

This label stemmed from an unfortunate, oftentimes deliberate, and incorrect comparison of the Nauvoo Legion to the Danites of Mis-

[35] Roberts, *Rise and Fall of Nauvoo*, 74.

[36] See Hansen, *Quest for Empire*.

souri. Although vague similarities do exist, the comparison is generally not valid. The Legion was an authorized state militia; the Danites were not. Smith wanted to avoid problems such as those caused by Danites in Missouri. He would not allow extralegal activities.

Conclusion

Specific criticisms of the Legion are so intricately intertwined with a broader objection to Mormonism that it is difficult to separate the part from the whole. The Nauvoo Legion was only one issue on a long list of contentions between the Mormons and their critics. Yet it became the scapegoat for Mormonism and its prophetic leader. Although most winked at the idea of a prophet living in Illinois, the thought of a self-proclaimed Muhammad wielding a sword and leading a growing army did not sit well with Americans who wanted the United States to attain its Manifest Destiny—to stretch from sea to sea—and a democratic republic with a separation of church and state. To those who traced their roots to the founding fathers, the Continental Congress, and the Constitutional Convention, the idea of a religious leader with a strong military presence on the frontier was unacceptable.

10

The Gathering Storm, 1843–1844

Boys, don't be cast down. I will come back again.

JOSEPH SMITH

Resolutions and counter-resolutions, realities and perceptions aside, Mormon leaders sensed the gathering storm. This chapter will examine those events and causes that led to the deaths of Joseph and Hyrum Smith in June 1844, but with special emphasis on the Nauvoo Legion and its role in this well-known chapter of Mormon history.

Unwilling to risk war and civil bloodshed or surrender their sense of Zion and separateness, the Mormon leaders began exploring a wide range of other options. As part of his Great Western Measure, Joseph Smith sent several unannounced proselyting missionaries to American Indians, hoping to learn of a possible refuge for the Latter-day Saints in the West.[1] In July 1843 Jonathan Dunham, a leading member of the Legion, scouted out much of Iowa, where he met with the Pottawattamies and various other tribes as far west as the Missouri River. Among other things this expedition was an effort to ascertain Indian sentiments toward the Mormons, determine possible evacuation travel routes, and identify potential new locations if the Mormons were forced to resettle at short notice.[2]

---

[1] Leonard, *Nauvoo,* 323. See also Esplin, "'A Place Prepared': Joseph, Brigham, and the Quest for Promised Refuge in the West," in Prete, *Window of Faith,* 71–96.

[2] Leonard, *Nauvo,* 324. See also *History of the Church,* 5:509.

Later, in February 1844, Smith requested that the Western Exploration Company explore as far west as California and Oregon "with the view of finding a location to which the church could remove after the temple at Nauvoo was completed."[3] Some of Smith's advisors, including Apostle Lyman Wight and Bishop George Miller, strongly suggested that the Church, or at least new members from the southern states, consider resettling in southern Texas.[4]

To what extent Smith anticipated a full-scale western exodus is debatable; however, it is fair to presume that he foresaw some future western movement.[5] Church authorities were well aware of the intensifying interest of Congress in the West, particularly Oregon and California. Since federal officials had not yet paid any reparations for the Missouri atrocities, perhaps the Mormons could capitalize financially in other ways. This was surely one reason for three debatable, if not radical, memorials to Congress passed by the Nauvoo City Council in late 1843 and early 1844. On November 8, 1843, the council petitioned Congress "to receive the City of Nauvoo under the protection of the United States Government" and to "acknowledge the Nauvoo Legion as United States troops, and to assist in fortifications and other purposes."[6]

This attempt to federalize the city and its militia may also have been a response to recent political clamor. Repeal of the city's charter, and with it the Nauvoo Legion, was becoming a real possibility. Just one week before, in an attempt to pacify loyal Illinois Democrats displeased with Governor Ford's unwillingness to renounce the Nauvoo Charter, Attorney General Josiah Lamborn took critical, albeit careless, aim at the Nauvoo Legion. Lamborn, denying a Legion request for more arms, took issue with state Senate Judiciary Committee conclusions that the Legion was not "exceptional": "They occupy a novel position, disconnected from the military communities of the whole State, and in no way subject to

[3] Roberts, *Comprehensive History of the Church,* 2:210.

[4] For the most recent study on Lyman Wight, see Johnson, *Polygamy on the Pedernales.*

[5] Richard L. Bushman argues that Joseph Smith may have been considering California "as early as 1842" when he realized that Nauvoo could never possibly support the incoming tide of British immigrant converts. Bushman, *Rough Stone Rolling,* 518. For a detailed, if not critical, study of the British migration to Nauvoo of some five thousand souls, see Woods, *Gathering to Nauvoo,* especially chapters 3 and 4.

[6] Nauvoo City Council Minutes, December 8, 1843. See also *History of the Church,* 6:107.

the regular military officers, [and] possess an exemption even from subjection to the general military laws, with a law-making power invested in their own Legion."[7] Such talk may have represented a genuine difference in interpretation of Smith's calling the Legion to duty, but more likely it was mere pretext, a political argument aimed at distancing the Ford administration from the Mormons; it was well known in the state's adjutant general's office that the Legion was legally a part of the state militia, and fundamentally no different in its relationship to the state than any other independent militia in Illinois. Even State Auditor W. L. D. Ewing disagreed with Lamborn: "I am not satisfied of myself, entirely, of the correctness of the opinion of the Attorney General."[8] Nonetheless, the Legion was the immediate whipping post, a political liability, and politicians on both sides of the aisle increasingly tried to distance themselves from it.

Two weeks later, Nauvoo leaders petitioned federal officers for the territorialization of Nauvoo—that is to say, that it be granted territorial status so that the mayor could "call to his aid a sufficient number of U.S. forces, in connection with the Nauvoo Legion to repel the invasion of mobs."[9] Soon afterwards came yet another memorial, more bold than the first, proposing that Smith be "authorized and empowered to raise a company of one hundred thousand armed volunteers . . . and marching and transporting the same to the borders of the United States and Territories."[10]

---

[7] *Nauvoo Neighbor,* EXTRA, December 9, 1843, 2:33. See also *History of the Church,* 6:96–97.

[8] *Nauvoo Neighbor,* EXTRA, December 9, 1843, 1:33. See also *History of the Church,* 6:96–97. Of Lamborn's posturing, Joseph Smith said: "Your Excellency's opinion that the Nauvoo Legion are part of the Militia of the State of Illinois, seems so consistent with the spirit and genius of the Charter and the common law of the land, as well as the intention of our constitution, that the Attorney General's opinions, to the contrary notwithstanding, are somewhat like an eclipse on the opposite side of the earth, 'to us invisible.'" Joseph Smith to Governor Thomas Ford, January 1, 1844, in *Personal Writings of Joseph Smith,* 589.

[9] Photocopy of the National Archives copy in "Joseph Smith Papers," Box 4, Fd 3. Church History Library. See also *History of the Church,* 6:131.

[10] "Joseph Smith Papers," Box 4, Fd 3. Church History Library. See also *History of the Church,* 6:277. This recommendation of raising an army of 100,000 men looked very much like that of Secretary of War J. R. Poinsett's plan put forth three years previously of establishing an army of 100,000 young men to be the "moveable force" of the Regular Army (see chapter 1). If the state of Illinois had previously encouraged the establishment of the Nauvoo Legion to help fulfill its requirements (*continued, next page*)

The impossibility of such requests being granted was not lost on the petitioners; however, it communicated to the government how grave the Latter-day Saints believed their situation had become. Such pleas for help did little to ameliorate local ill will and suspicion; some saw them as confirmation of Bennett's accusations of Mormon empire building.

It was in this deteriorating climate of fear and frustration that Joseph Smith announced his candidacy for the presidency of the United States. Having exhausted all legal means for redress and worried over the future welfare of his people, Smith felt his only remaining option was to try the court of public opinion. The inspiration for such action extended back to the Missouri expulsion and Smith's unsuccessful visit with Martin Van Buren in fall 1839. Continued rejection of Mormon petitions and a perceived attitude of indifference toward Mormon fears of invasion culminated in the October 1843 *Times and Seasons* article "Who Shall Be Our Next President?" probably penned by John Taylor. "We have hitherto adopted every legal measure," he stated:

> First, we petitioned the State of Missouri, but in vain. We have memorialized Congress, but they have turned a deaf ear to our supplication. . . . [Many] find it difficult to believe that such enormities could be practiced in a Republican government. But our wrong cannot slumber. Such tyranny and oppression must not be passed over in silence. Our injuries, though past, are not forgotten by us; they still rankle in our bosoms, and the blood of the innocent yet cries for justice. . . . We make these remarks for the purpose of drawing the attention of our brethren to this subject, both at home and abroad, that we may fix upon the man who will be most likely to render us assistance in obtaining redress for our grievances.[11]

The man the Mormons fixed upon after receiving little to no hope of redress from the major presidential candidates of the day was their prophet leader, whom they formally nominated as their candidate for president on January 29, 1844. Although he likely never

---

to the military laws of the United States, might not the federal government, in need of military manpower to police the West, accept this new Mormon offer which was virtually Poinsett's plan revisited? Mormon leaders thought it worth the chance. Neither recommendation, however, found acceptance in Congress.

[11] As quoted in *Times and Seasons,* October 1, 1843, 4:22, 343–44. See also *History of the Church,* 6:40.

expected to win the election, Smith hoped to undo some of the damage inflicted by Bennett and others by gaining a measure of sympathy on the national scene and thereby bring attention to their cause. As he once remarked, "I do not care half so much about the Pres[idential] election as I do the office I have got. We have as good a right to make a political party to gain power to defend ourselves as for demagogues to make use of our religion to get power to destroy ourselves. We will whip the mob by getting up a president."[12]

Smith's candidacy and his petitions to Congress earlier in 1844 were interpreted by many outsiders as an excessive blending of the powers of church and state and a further effort to combine in himself full religious and political power, and added fuel to the growing fire of discontent and suspicion in Hancock County. As Willis G. Swartz contended, it was the "bold announcement for the presidency" that led to later persecution at the hands of "surrounding Gentiles."[13] What intensified was the increasing foreboding of pending conflict, an exaggerated sense of "them versus us."

All such actions—secret expeditions west, memorials to Congress to redress Missouri wrongs, a run for the presidency—were designed to attract national attention to their worsening plight. However, they were bound to be misconstrued by the many Hancock County residents who were increasingly convinced that Mormons were enemies of the state.[14]

---

[12] Ehat and Cook, *Words of Joseph Smith,* 325. Gary Bergera has argued that the Council of Fifty "underscores the sobriety with which Joseph took his calling as a prophet and leader as well as the pre-emptive legitimacy his calling afforded him in execution of God's will." Bergera, "Joseph Smith and the Hazards of Charismatic Leadership," 35. No evidence exists to show that the Council of Fifty exercised any control over the Nauvoo Legion. Hill, "Counter-Revolution," 29–30. Klaus Hansen has argued, rather radically, that Smith's candidacy, as well as the purpose and designs of the Council of Fifty and the military power of the Nauvoo Legion, were all part of a grand design among the Latter-day Saints to establish a political Kingdom of God upon the earth by taking over the reins of the United States government. See Hansen, *Quest for Empire,* 77–81.

[13] Swartz, "Mormonism in Illinois," 100.

[14] Governor Ford later said that Joseph Smith's candidacy did him much more harm than good, bringing him into "conflict with zealots and bigots of all parties and . . . that this was the prophet's crowning error" for it turned "all parties against them." Ford, *History of Illinois,* 319–21. For a brief overview of Joseph Smith's candidacy, see Garr, "Joseph Smith—Candidate for President of the United States," in Garrett, *Regional Studies in Latter-day Saint Church History: Illinois,* 151–68.

Council of the Kingdom

Shortly after declaring his candidacy, Joseph Smith announced the creation of the Council of Fifty in March 1844. Although one of the issues behind its creation was, as historian Glen Leonard has argued, establishing a Mormon sanctuary in Texas,[15] this body of fifty men, which included a few non-Mormons, chiefly sought financial redress from state and federal governments for the Missouri depredations of the decade before, assisted with Smith's campaign for the presidency, and made plans for a possible exodus to the West.[16]

The full role and purpose of the Council of Fifty may never be understood unless additional primary sources are found, most especially the minutes kept by the Council itself. Extensive arguments and conclusions about what it stood for without the requisite critical sources seem injudicious. However, this has not kept some scholars from asserting that it was a culmination of the essential "revolutionary ideology" latent in the Mormon message of religious superiority and of separating itself from the world into a "quasi-totalitarian society" that found expression in Nauvoo. Such interpreters see in Nauvoo the beginning of a Mormon political kingdom of God in anticipation of the Second Coming. As Klaus Hansen has argued, "Mormonism provided the essential ingredients for a potentially successful movement of revolutionary dimensions in this world—a realistic means for achieving not only a religious but a social, economic and political millennium"; the Nauvoo Legion would be the military instrument for building such a Kingdom of God.[17]

Others maintain that the Council of Fifty—or Council of the Kingdom, or Kingdom of God, as it was variously called—which held power over the Legion, manifested Smith's militant desires to establish a theocratic empire. Under Smith, the Council of Fifty would set its own laws, declare that the United States Constitution and congressional law were irrelevant, and that their new "system of government" would "set aside at will the laws of the United States" and all other secular governments.[18] In language reminiscent of John C. Bennett's accusations, they argue that the Council of Fifty, with

[15] Leonard, *Nauvoo,* 332.

[16] Quinn, "The Council of Fifty and Its Members," 164. For a contrasting view, see Hill, "Counter-Revolution," 29.

[17] Hansen, *Mormonism and the American Experience,* 120, 122.

[18] Quinn, *The Mormon Hierarchy,* 121.

its Masonic-like system of secrecy and penalties, was an expansion of the earlier Danites—militant, single-minded, and theocratic.[19] For these scholars the Council of Fifty would be the political engine to mastermind the establishment of a Mormon theocratic government that would spread throughout the world. In the meantime, running roughshod over the Quorum of the Twelve Apostles, it would order the excommunication of disaffected apostates and cashier from the Legion those perceived to be enemies of the Kingdom.

The relevance of arguments for militarism and theocracy invites respectful commentary. Klaus Hansen, in his argument for "militant" and "revolutionary" Mormonism, asserts that although the revolutionary seeds of Mormonism are latent in its claims of exclusivity as the only true and living church upon the earth, its first manifestation of militancy began in 1834 with Zion's Camp: "It set a precedent for the establishment of the military arm of the Kingdom." Indeed, "All future Mormon military organizations, including the Nauvoo Legion, as well as the militia of that same name organized by Brigham Young in Utah and the Army of Israel that directed the exodus to the Great Basin, were patterned after Zion's Camp."[20]

If the Legion took orders from the Council of Fifty after March 1844, nothing in available records indicate as much. It never functioned as an arm of a would-be government under the rule of the Council of Fifty. In pattern, style, and organization, it was entirely different from either Zion's Camp or the Danites; in fact, it was a conscious effort to distance itself from such organizations. It never crossed state boundaries and never burned down villages or homes. And there are no records to show that the Council of Fifty ever directed the Legion or, for that matter, the later Mormon exodus westward; in fact, George Miller, James Emmett, Peter Haws, and other members of the Council broke with the Church at Winter Quarters over Brigham

---

[19] Quinn, *The Mormon Hierarchy,* 128.

[20] Hansen, *Mormonism and the American Experience,* 136–37. That comments by some leading Mormons caused non-Mormons to fear must be admitted. As mentioned earlier, Apostle Parley P. Pratt, writing in his usual colorful style in the London-based *Millennial Star* back in September 1842, had predicted that the Legion would be "fifty thousand strong" and would be led by talented officers. He also argued that it provided a "peculiar advantage to the Saints. . . . [I]t afforded that security and protection against lawless violence which has been so much needed . . . but which our people could seldom enjoy until thus organized. . . . Nauvoo then, is the nucleus of a glorious dominion of universal liberty, peace, and plenty; it is an organization of the government of which there shall be no end." Quinn, *The Mormon Hierarchy,* 121.

Young's Word and Will of the Lord revelation (D&C 136) that firmly re-established the Twelve Apostles in charge of the Church in the absence of a First Presidency. There may have been confusion in 1844 over the focus of ultimate leadership in the Church, especially following the death of Joseph Smith, but by 1847 it had been put to rest by the Quorum of the Twelve, who viewed the Council of Fifty as an advisory board and not a governing body.[21] As Kenneth Godfrey has argued, "Many people seem to have thought the Prophet was going to attempt to establish a secular kingdom by using force and violence. This, of course, aroused some anxiety especially in view of the increasing strength of the city's militia. In reality, there was little reason for the general populace to be overly concerned regarding the prophet's political activities in this regard."[22]

The Council of Fifty may have seen itself as a government in waiting, a provision for authority if, indeed, God was about to "vex" the nation with war, pestilence, and suffering. As Richard Bushman has argued, it "may have considered itself the incipient organization for millennial rule, a shadow government awaiting the demise of worldly political authority and the beginning of Christ's earthly reign."[23] Not a military arm of the Council of Fifty, the Legion was, at least until its charter was repealed, an authorized part of the Illinois State Militia.[24]

"We Have a Judas in Our Midst"

As much as he feared his enemies from without, Smith recognized that his greatest threats came from within Nauvoo. "My life is more in danger from some little dough-head of a fool in this city than from all my numerous and inveterate enemies abroad," he said near the end of 1843. "I am exposed to far greater danger from traitors among ourselves than from enemies without. . . . We have a Judas in our midst."[25] And once again, as Bennett did the year before, one

---

[21] Bennett. *Mormons at the Missouri,* 156–57.

[22] Godfrey, "Causes of Mormon Non-Mormon Conflict," 66.

[23] Bushman, *Rough Stone Rolling,* 521.

[24] For a full discussion of the Council of Fifty as a Mormon call to political kingdom building and empire, see Hansen, *Quest for Empire,* chapters 2–4 in particular.

[25] Nauvoo City Council Minutes #3, 30–32. See also *History of the Church,* 6:152. On another occasion, Joseph Smith said with exasperation, "This Gospel gathers up some of [the] meanest of all God's creations. . . . Yes and some of the finest fellows that ever lived." "Autobiography of Wandle Mace," 89.

of Smith's closest officials in the Legion turned against him. There is little question that the introduction of plural marriage among the leadership of the Church, and the secretive way it was presented, was a source of dissent. As Glen Leonard phrased it, "Many members of the church found it necessary to sort out for themselves the conflicting claims about whether plural marriage did or did not exist within the Church."[26] Polygamy became both a crucible of faith and a catalyst for opposition. Brigham Young, for instance, said that upon hearing the doctrine for the first time he wished for the grave. And some, like Bennett, applied the practice to justify their own desires. Still others simply could not bring themselves to accept it and lost faith in their spiritual leaders. Few took a neutral stand with respect to plural marriage. It became, for many, the ultimate indicator of allegiance.

Unquestionably, rumors of its practice contributed to external opposition. The Carthage gathering hinted that it was a contributing factor in their resolutions of resistance. The Mormons, it charged, were setting aside "all those moral and religious institutions which have been established by the Bible, and which have in all ages been cherished by men as the only means of maintaining those social blessings which are so indispensably necessary for our happiness."[27]

Among those Mormons most opposed to what some termed "the spiritual wife system," was William Law, second counselor in the Church's First Presidency since 1841. Once a strong supporter of the Church, who had even served a mission countering Bennett's allegations, Law balked at plural marriage. "I had the fortitude to tell Joseph," he recorded in his journal, "that it was of the Devil and that he should put it down and I feel that I have opposed a base error and that the eternal God is on my side, and if I am persecuted it is because I vindicate principles of virtue and justice, not that I wish to injure any man."[28] Dropped from the First Presidency in January

---

[26] Leonard, *Nauvoo,* 354.

[27] *Warsaw Message,* 1:29. See also *History of the Church,* 6:5. For a full treatment of the "Moral Crusade" which Bennett and others launched against the Mormons, an effort that amounted to a "vilification campaign" see Hampshire, *Mormonism in Conflict,* 138.

[28] "Diary of William Law," 4; Launius, "The Murders in Carthage," 18. In Governor Ford's estimation, Law was "a deluded but conscientious and candid man." Ford, *History of Illinois,* 323. For a balanced study on Law, see Cook, "William Law, Nauvoo Dissenter."

1844, Law was soon joined by others who felt the same way—including his brother Wilson, then major general of the Legion; Dr. Robert D. Foster, surgeon general of the Legion; William Marks, president of the Nauvoo Stake; Francis Higbee[29] and Chauncey L. Higbee;[30] and a few others. For protection and support they turned to such rogues as the notorious killer Joseph H. Jackson.[31]

Matters came to a head early in 1844. On February 7, General Wilson Law published an article in neighboring Warsaw titled "Buckeye's Lamentations for the Want of More Wives." Ten days later, fueled by ever more obloquy from disaffected Mormons, local residents held another convention at Carthage, "the object being to devise ways and means of expelling the Saints from the State." The convention chose March 9 as "a day of fasting and prayer" for "Almighty God [to] . . . bring the false Prophet Joseph Smith to deep repentance, or that He will make a public example of him and his leading accomplices."[32]

While Smith was proclaiming his famous discourses on the nature of God and of baptism for the dead, some of his closest followers were coming out against him. On April 18, Church authorities excommunicated Robert D. Foster, William and Wilson Law, Jane Law, and others "for unchristian like conduct." The court-martial of the Legion soon followed suit by suspending Wilson Law as major general "for ungentlemanly conduct," and cashiering both him and Foster from the Legion a few days later.[33] On April 28, William Law proclaimed himself president of a new splinter group that formed themselves into the "Reformed Mormon Church" with Austin Cowles and Wilson Law as his counselors.

On May 23, a Carthage grand jury indicted Smith on charges of adultery and perjury, based on the testimony of William Law and Joseph H. Jackson. Smith and other members of the Legion

[29] Francis Marion Higbee (1820–?) brevet major, captain, colonel of the Nauvoo Legion; publisher of the *Nauvoo Expositor*.

[30] Chauncey Lawson Higbee (1821–84) aide-de-camp to major general, captain, first lieutenant of the Nauvoo Legion; state representative, state senator, circuit court judge in Illinois; publisher of the *Nauvoo Expositor*.

[31] Joseph H. Jackson (1807–53).

[32] *The Warsaw Signal*, February 21, 1844.

[33] *History of the Church*, 6:348, 362. See also Sweeney, "A History of the Nauvoo Legion," 112.

promptly traveled to Carthage to deny such allegations, but the court deferred the case. Nothing more was ever heard of the charges.

At last the disaffected parties purchased and imported a press to Nauvoo and founded a newspaper, the *Nauvoo Expositor.* Among its declared intentions were to expose the practice of plural marriage and the alleged immoralities of Church leaders; to portray Smith as "King, Priest and Ruler over Israel on Earth"; to cast aspersions on the doctrine of plurality of gods; and to seek repeal of the Nauvoo Charter and, with it, the Nauvoo Legion.[34] A thousand copies of the first and only issue were printed June 7. Whether the *Expositor* was a ploy to provoke a swift and deliberate destructive response may never be known, but in a decision that has ever sparked debate, Mayor Joseph Smith and the city council declared it a nuisance and a threat to the peace and good order of the community, and—failing, perhaps, to grasp the full consequences of destroying a press—ordered its immediate destruction.[35]

On June 12, David Bettisworth, a local constable, arrested Joseph Smith and many others, and charged them with promoting a "riot" by destroying the press. The following day's acquittal by the Nauvoo Municipal Court of Smith and the others charged succeeded only in convincing infuriated non-Mormon onlookers that justice could not be expected in Nauvoo. As much as the destruction of the press itself, the Municipal Court's decision fanned the rising flames of fear and suspicion.

The precise role the Legion played in this episode bears careful scrutiny. The city council did, in fact, order Jonathan Dunham, acting major general, "to assist the Marshal with the Legion, if called upon so to do."[36] It appears that the destruction of the press was the work of both the Legion and the police, as "two companies under command of Dunham and Markham retired in perfect order" and

[34] "Prospectus of the Nauvoo Expositor," *The Nauvoo Expositor,* June 7, 1844, sec. I, p. 4.

[35] "Joseph Smith Journal," 151. See also *History of the Church,* 6:342. The destruction of a printing press was not an uncommon event in America at this time. There are some sixteen recorded instances of mob violence against the press in the United States between 1832 and 1867, perhaps the most famous of which was the destruction just seven years before in Alton, Illinois, of Elijah Lovejoy's abolitionist newspaper, *The Alton Observer,* and with it, Lovejoy's murder. See Oaks, "The Suppression of the *Nauvoo Expositor,*" 874.

[36] "Joseph Smith Journal," 151. See also *History of the Church,* 6:432.

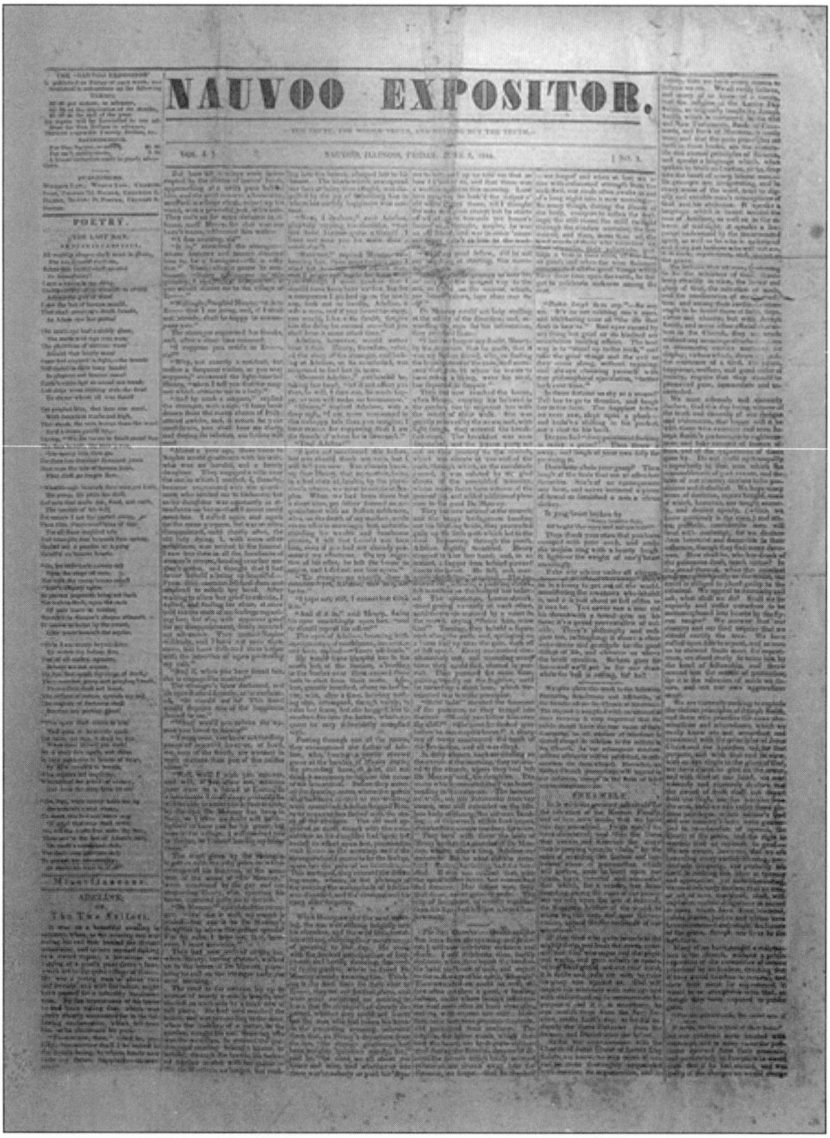

NAUVOO EXPOSITOR.

FIGURE 22. Masthead, *Nauvoo Expositor,* Friday, June 7, 1844.
Courtesy of Church History Library.

supervised the ordered action which, as one testified, was done "as peaceably as people move on a Sunday."[37] Isaac Haight, a participant, wrote, "The City Council considered it a nuisance and ordered the mayor to call on the police and Legion to abate the nuisance. It was done according to order. We burnt the fixtures and papers and destroyed the press."[38]

The events surrounding the destruction of the *Expositor*'s press sparked the conflagration that claimed the life of the Mormon leader later that month. In Warsaw, Thomas C. Sharp roundly condemned the move, describing it as an "unparalleled outrage" and demanding his readers "carry the war into the enemy camp."[39] He further wrote, "War and extermination [are] inevitable! CITIZENS ARISE, ONE AND ALL!!! Can you stand by and suffer such INFERNAL DEVILS! to rob men of their property rights without avenging them. We have no time for comment! Every man will make his own. LET IT BE WITH POWDER AND BALL."[40] On June 13, a mass meeting of 700 concerned citizens at Warsaw described the action as "an outrage of an alarming character" and resolved that "if [Smith was] not surrendered, a war of extermination should be waged to the entire destruction . . . of his adherents."[41] Wrote one local citizen, "Such excitement I never witnessed in my life"; "we all felt that the time had come where either the Mormons or old citizens had to leave."[42] Adding to these perceptions were rumors that fifteen hundred armed Missourians were gathering in Warsaw and that mobs were threatening Mormons in outlying areas. An attack on the city, or at least on more vulnerable outlying Mormon settlements, seemed imminent.

---

[37] *History of the Church,* 6:490. According to one eyewitness, Markham carried out the press and type. Other members of the Legion walked "quietly along as though they were walking to the 'Dead March in Saul.'" Twelve others assisted in the actual operation. *Nauvoo Neighbor,* EXTRA, EXTRA, June 21, 1844. See also *History of the Church,* 6:490. William Law, however, a part owner of the press, says nothing about the Legion's participation. See "Diary of William Law," 10. Certainly the governor was convinced that the Legion played an active role. Ford, *History of Illinois,* 323.

[38] Haight, Biographical Sketch and Diary," typescript, 13.

[39] Knox et al., "Extra. Preamble and Resolutions," *Warsaw Signal,* June 14, 1844; C. A. Foster, "The Time is Come!" *Warsaw Signal,* June 11, 1844, as cited in Hill, "Carthage Conspiracy Reconsidered," 117.

[40] *Warsaw Signal,* June 12, 1844, 1.

[41] *Warsaw Signal,* June 19, 1844. See also *History of the Church,* 6:463–64.

[42] Samuel Otho Williams to John Prickett, July 10, 1844, "Mormon Collection," as quoted in Launius, "The Murders in Carthage," 20.

As it was his custom to prepare the Legion for action pending approval from the governor, Smith ordered Isaac Morley,[43] who was then living in the Morley Settlement a few miles south of town, to ready the militia residing there: "And if the mob shall fall upon the Saints by force of arms, defend them at every hazard unless providence dictate the retreat of the troops to Nauvoo . . . and if the mob move towards Nauvoo, either come before them or in their rear and be ready to co-operate with the main body of the Legion."[44] Several companies from outlying communities, such as La Harpe, Illinois, and Augusta, Iowa, arrived in the city "for the protection of the same."[45] Smith urged town marshal John P. Greene "to take such measures as shall be necessary to preserve the peace of said city according to the provisions of the Charter and the laws of the state, and with the police and Legion see that no violent act is committed."[46] Once again, Smith wrote Ford for advice: "The Nauvoo Legion is at your service to quell all insurrection. . . . I wish, urgently wish, your Excellency to come down in person with your staff and investigate the whole matter without delay."[47]

Without promise of help from the governor and fearing an imminent attack and widespread bloodshed, Smith took the unauthorized measure of declaring martial law within the city. On Tuesday, June 18, he ordered the Legion to assist the police with picket duty, block all roads and alleys leading into the city, and patrol along the river banks. Work began with the fortifying of trenches. Drills were multiplied and sentries were posted throughout the city; residents could reach their homes or other destinations only with a pass. Almost overnight Nauvoo turned into an armed camp. The "Nauvoo Guard"[48] as some began to call the Legion, "soon swelled to between three and five thousand men ready to defend their families and firesides, and also their own lives. All passes to and from the city

[43] Isaac Morley (1786–1864): aide-de-camp of the Nauvoo Legion; veteran of the War of 1812; patriarch; served in the Utah Territorial Legislature, 1851–55.

[44] "Joseph Smith Papers," MSS 155, box 2, fd 8. See also *History of the Church,* 6:482. A similar directive was sent to John Smith and the Latter-day Saints living near Ramus advocating similar rearguard action on the mob when it should attack the city.

[45] "Journal of S. W. Richards," 19 and June 20, 1844, typescript, 33.

[46] Joseph Smith to John P. Greene, June 17, 1846, vault MSS 36, L. Tom Perry Special Collections.

[47] *History of the Church,* 6:480.

[48] "Journal of Philo Johnson," 1.

FIGURE 23. *Genl Joseph Smith Addressing the Nauvoo Legion*, study for oil mural by William W. Major, 1845. Watercolor and ink on paper, 11⅞ in. × 16¾ in. *Courtesy of Church History Museum.*

were guarded and every suspicious looking person going to or from was made to give an account of himself, and this for our safety."[49]

At 2:00 P.M., before an assembly of thousands, Legion soldiers lined up in front of the Mansion House. Smith, in full uniform and standing atop the frame of a nearby building, spoke for ninety minutes, delivering what is still regarded as one of his most famous and most prophetic speeches. "I shall never forget this occasion," Wandle Mace, a member of the Legion, vividly recalled, "nor the power manifested by the Prophet in this his last address. How noble, how

[49] Letter of John S. Fullmer, 1844, John S. Fullmer Letters. Vilate Kimball confirmed this account when she wrote on June 9, 1844, "Between three and four thousand brethren have been under arms here the past week. Expecting everyday they [the mob] would come, the brethren were called in from all the branches round to help defend the city." Vilate Kimball to Heber C. Kimball, June 9, 1844, as cited in Esplin, "Life in Nauvoo," 235. The swelling in numbers referred to may account for later exaggerations of the actual size of the Nauvoo Legion. At the height of the Nauvoo crisis and the declaration of martial law, men younger than eighteen and older than forty-five not ordinarily eligible for Legion duty took up arms and joined in with it.

grand he appeared, dressed in his full uniform as Lieutenant General he addressed us, the Nauvoo Legion."[50]

"Will you all stand by me to the death, and sustain at the peril of your lives, the laws of our country?" Smith asked. "Aye!" shouted the vast assemblage. Smith continued,

> It is well . . . I call God and angels to witness that I have unsheathed my sword with a firm and unalterable determination that this people shall have their legal rights, and be protected from mob violence, or my blood shall be spilt upon the ground like water. . . . I do not regard my own life. I am ready to be offered a sacrifice for this people. . . . God has tried you. You are a good people; therefore I love you with all my heart. . . . You have stood by me in the hour of trouble, and I am willing to sacrifice my life for your preservation. May the Lord God of Israel bless you forever and ever.[51]

Smith's remarks electrified his listeners, particularly members of the Legion. "No man ever spoke as he did," one legionnaire's wife recorded, "and never was a company of soldiers more determined to live or die for him."[52]

Smith's enemies lost little time responding. "Joe is evidently much alarmed," reported the *Warsaw Signal* the next day, "but he has gone too far to back out. He must toe the mark or run. Compromise is out of the question. . . . An injured and insulted community [Warsaw] suffering under their long-borne grievances, are determined by an appeal to arms, as a last resort, to redress wrongs that have become insupportable."[53] On June 20, still awaiting word from the governor, an exasperated Joseph Smith wrote an urgent letter to U.S. President John Tyler in which he recited the grave circumstances existing in Nauvoo and pleaded for federal protection.

These were exceedingly tense days in the history of Nauvoo. Every morning the Legion assembled at the parade grounds at 8:00 A.M. and remained at the ready till late in the afternoon. Several other military companies, including two from La Harpe, Illinois, and Augusta, Iowa, arrived to offer further protection.[54] One false step by either

[50] "Autobiography of Wandle Mace," 90.

[51] "Manuscript History of the Church," Book F, 118–19. See also *History of the Church,* 6:499–500; and Ehat and Cook, *Words of Joseph Smith,* 383–84.

[52] Hess, "Life Sketch of Caroline Holland Steed," typescript, 1.

[53] "The Preparation," *Warsaw Signal* no. 19, June 19, 1844. See also "Autobiography of Wandle Mace," 90.

[54] "Journal of S. W. Richards," June 19, 1844.

side may well have brought on civil war, which likely would have cost the lives of hundreds, if not thousands, of people. One member of the Legion, who came into the city from the Morley Settlement, remembered: "I was in the city [of Nauvoo] at that time about two weeks during which time every man almost slept on his arms and walked armed by day, ready at a moment's warning to lose their lives, or lay them in jeopardy in defense of our rights."[55]

Governor Ford finally responded by letter, which a messenger delivered to Joseph Smith at 10:00 P.M. on June 22. Ford had tried carefully to walk a neutral path and to do everything possible to prevent bloodshed. He had turned a deaf ear to those who were demanding that he disarm the Legion. He had not ordered state militia intervention on either side. Believing that the destruction of the *Expositor* "was a very gross outrage upon the laws and liberties of the people," and convinced that Smith had no authority to declare martial law, Governor Ford counseled Smith to accept arrest and come to Carthage for trial. To Ford's mind, an all-out civil war could only be averted by Smith's submission to trial: "If you, by refusing to submit, shall make it necessary to call out the militia, I have great fears that your city will be destroyed, and your people many of them exterminated."[56]

At midnight Smith replied in his capacity as both mayor and lieutenant general. Defending his actions against the *Expositor,* he nevertheless struck a distinctly conciliatory tone: "If we have erred in judgment, it is an official act, and belongs to the Supreme Court to correct it. . . . If lawyers have belied their profession to abuse us [i.e., bad legal counsel] the evil be on their heads"; "If we have erred, we again say we will make all right if we can have the privilege."[57] Regarding his declaration of martial law, Smith wrote, "we suppose your Excellency is well aware by this time that the mass-meetings of the county declared utter extermination of the Mormons, and that the Legion was not called out until complaints were made to the Mayor, and the citizens were afraid of their lives." Nevertheless, at the governor's request, Smith ordered the immediate disband-

---

55 "Diary of Oliver B. Huntington," part 1, typescript, 45.

56 "Joseph Smith Papers," MSS 155, Box 3, Fd 8. See also *History of the Church,* 6:533–36. Ford later commented on the city council's ruling to destroy the *Expositor:* "It was altogether the most curious and irregular trial that ever was recorded." Ford, *History of Illinois,* 523.

57 During a later conversation with Governor Ford at Carthage Jail, Joseph Smith offered to pay for the loss of the press. See Leonard, *Nauvoo,* 385.

FIGURE 24. Governor Thomas Ford, ca. 1840. *Courtesy of Church History Library.*

ment of the Legion, leaving the city, as he put it, "open and unprotected." He concluded, "We again say, if anything wrong has been done on our part, and we know of nothing, we will make all things right if the Government will give us the opportunity."[58]

At a moment when he could have commanded an army to defend their rights—the very thing Bennett and others had been promoting before the Legion was even organized—he bowed to the orders of his commander. As one eyewitness and member of the Legion put it: "At the word we would gladly have marched and met the mob in battle but that was not Joseph's way."[59]

Smith did not immediately surrender himself, believing that "there was no mercy" in the governor's letter. "As sure as we fall into their hands we are dead men," his brother, Hyrum, declared.[60] That night, Saturday, June 22, the two men and a few trusted friends crossed the river and made ready to start for the Rocky Mountains, in hopes that their departure might lessen tensions. However, upon further reflection, they returned and surrendered, recognizing that this was the only way to save the city and "all the men, women and children

[58] *History of the Church,* 6:540–41. See also "Journal of S. W. Richards," June 23, 1844.

[59] "Biographical Sketch of Luman A. Shurtliff," typescript, 2.

[60] "Manuscript History of the Church," book F, 147. See also *History of the Church,* 6:545.

that were in it" from certain conflict. As he turned back across the river he reportedly said, "We are going back to be slaughtered."[61]

Early the morning of Monday, June 24, Joseph and Hyrum Smith left for Carthage, with a company of some thirty friends and bodyguards, to face the charge of riot—based on the destruction of the *Expositor*'s press. Four miles outside of Carthage they met James A. Dunn, captain of the Volunteer Horse Company of the Union Dragoons (Carthage),[62] and some sixty cavalry who presented them with an order from the governor for the surrender of all state arms held by the Legion. Quick to obey, Smith scratched out his final order, to Major General Dunham, to comply with the governor's wishes.[63]

The two brothers then returned to Nauvoo with Captain Dunn "to see that they were given up according to the Governor's order."[64] "And while they were taking our arms," one member of the Legion painfully recalled, Joseph said to the officers near him, " 'These men are too good, too quiet and law abiding for this rough generation,' and looking around him, at his friends the Nauvoo Legion, and seeing our red faces he said, 'Boys.' He always called us boys, His Boys. 'Don't be cast down, I will come back again.' After a little hesitation he added, 'As soon as I can.' That expression, 'As soon as I can,' sank deep into my heart and confirmed my fears. I never expected to see him again alive. The sad expression upon his face as he looked upon us, 'His Boys' for the last time I shall never forget."[65]

---

[61] *History of the Church,* 6:549. Said Nauvoo resident Vilate Kimball to Heber C. Kimball, on June 9, 1844, "Their giving themselves up is all that will save our city from destruction." June 9,Cited in Esplin, "Life in Nauvoo," 235. Emma Smith also bade him to return and give himself up. *History of the Church,* 6:549.

[62] Letter of W. D. Abernathy to Governor Ford, July 2, 1843, "Governor-Correspondence, Military."

[63] Original manuscript of this final order is in possession of Brent Ashworth, Provo, Utah, document collector. Used by permission of the owner.

[64] "Journal of S. W. Richards," June 24, 1844. See also the account by Hale in "Jonathan H. Hale Papers."

[65] "Autobiography of Wandle Mace," 99. It should be pointed out that the governor was ordering the return only of government-issued weapons and that the Saints were careful not to surrender their private weapons. "The morning Joseph received the orders from the Government [that] all the Mormon troops [be] disbanded," remembered Oliver B. Huntington. "I went with father to the Masonic Hall which was used as a commissary headquarters and took away some provisions and loaded some hundreds of stands of arms belonging to the Church, to have them hid to prevent the governor from seizing them." "Diary of Oliver B. Huntington," part 1, typescript, 45. Obviously the Church itself had purchased an unknown quantity of weapons, much as it did wagons, teams, and other supplies for the good of the whole community.

Governor Ford gave similar orders to opposing forces in and around Carthage, including militias at Warsaw. Some fifteen hundred to two thousand men responded with displeasure at his commands. Many obeyed and began to leave for home, but some, believing in the "higher law of popular sovereignty" and the need to take the law into their own hands, formed themselves into their own vigilante groups. According to John Hay, whose father was a part of these forces,

> Colonel Williams read the Governor's order. . . . Capt. Grover soon found himself without a company. Aldrich essayed a speech, calling for volunteers for Carthage. . . . Sharp came up and took it off his hands. Sharp, being a spirited and impressive talker, soon had a respectable squad about him. . . . The speeches of Grover and Sharp were rather vague; the purpose of murder does not seem to have been hinted. They protested against being made the tools and puppets of Tommy Ford.[66]

Whether or not Ford, as Mormon historian Kenneth Godfrey intimates, was "a part of the conspiracy," knowing "the Mormon people well enough to be convinced that they would not retaliate," may never be known.[67] The fact remains that Ford knew that the Nauvoo Legion, over which he wielded ultimate authority, would obey his directive. Furthermore, he knew that the surrender of arms might lessen mounting tensions. Ford later wrote, "A large portion of the people by pure misrepresentation had been made to believe that the Legion had received of the state as many as 30 cannons and a 6,000 stand of small arms. I was of the opinion that the removal of these arms would tend much to allay this excitement and prejudice."[68] It is true that even after surrendering their stacks of state arms Nauvoo's militiamen still owned private weapons, but their surrender was more than a mere symbolic gesture of peace and compliance. In obedience to their commander in chief, the Legion disarmed itself, at least of its public weapons, and dismissed. In response Governor Ford ordered Captain Singleton of the Brown Company to take a company of troops from McDonough County to help the Nauvoo police maintain order and, if necessary, to mobilize the now

---

[66] As quoted in Huntress, "Governor Thomas Ford and the Murderers of Joseph Smith," 50. It should be noted that Colonel Levi Williams, a local farmer, was the commanding officer of the "Green Plains Minute Men" of Warsaw and attached to the Fifty-ninth Regiment of the Illinois militia. See letter of Levi Williams to the Governor of Illinois, October 23, 1843, "Governor Correspondence, 1843 Military Affairs."

[67] Godfrey, "Non-Mormon Views," 15.

[68] Ford, *History of Illinois,* 335–36.

FIGURE 25. *Joseph Smith and the Nauvoo Temple,*
by Valoy Eaton, 1989(?). Oil on board, $13^{3}/_{4}$ in. × $19^{1}/_{2}$ in.
Courtesy of Church History Museum.

privately armed Nauvoo Legion to protect the city.[69] Addressing the residents of Nauvoo, Singleton said he saw that "harmony and peace" prevailed in the city, and on the morning of June 27, he ordered the Legion to assemble at noon, "when he informed them that they were under his command by order of the Governor."[70]

In truth Ford faced an almost impossible dilemma. To side with the Mormons would incite antagonisms further. To support the local citizenry would risk losing the obedience of Nauvoo. To prevent all-out civil war, he had to act prudently and disarm contending opponents, using a neutral force from McDonough County to do so. In doing so he was condemned by both sides. As Keith Huntress has argued, "A more forceful and less legalistic chief executive would have been likely, in those times, to have been more violently anti-Mormon than was Ford. Gov. Boggs of Missouri would probably not have hesitated to override a magistrate, but neither would he have hesitated to authorize the killings of the Smith. . . . The governor tried almost everything in his endeavor to keep the peace; it was not his fault that nothing worked."[71] Nonetheless, Ford's actions reveal a man who lacked the courage to assert full control when it was needed most.

[69] Leonard, *Nauvoo,* 383. [70] "Journal of S. W. Richards," June 27, 1844.
[71] Huntress, "Governor Thomas Ford and the Murderers of Joseph Smith," 49, 51.

After the charge of riot was dismissed, Smith was charged by private citizens with the capital crime of treason for illegally calling out the Legion. Ford considered the treason charge groundless, since the city had a right to defend itself. However, this charge was a non-bailable offense and one of the few for which one could be kept in jail without trial. It consisted in the "alleged levying of war against the state [of Illinois] in declaring martial law in Nauvoo and in ordering the Legion to resist the posse comitatus."[72] Not surprisingly Smith devoted much of his time in Carthage Jail writing about his actions regarding the Legion and defending his decision to destroy the *Expositor*. Although he may have acted without explicit order of his commanding officer, he believed he did so as "the last resort, and only defense, in the absence of executive protection, against a large, organized military and mobocratic force."[73] Did the Legion ever act in an offensive way against the state? Did it not obey the orders of the commander in chief? Was it involved in armed rebellion against the state? Such were some of many questions meant for the impending trial—a trial which never came.

What then transpired is well known. Joseph and Hyrum Smith were placed in Carthage Jail to await trial under the protection of the local militia unit, the Carthage Greys—an old independent company, well armed and uniformed—the members of which were the elite of the region. Meanwhile Governor Ford, with a small band of militia, on the morning of June 27, rode to Nauvoo, where at about 4:00 P.M. he was escorted into the city by an armed guard. Captain Singleton ordered the dismissal of the Legion beforehand, "because the Governor was a coming into Nauvoo from Carthage and he did not want any military show."[74] Ford guaranteed the safety of the city and urged the citizens of Nauvoo to lay down their private weapons. He then left town for Quincy before hearing any further news. Back in Carthage, shortly after 5:00 P.M., an angry mob of about two hundred men with painted faces—a collection of Missouri malcontents, Mormon dissenters, and Warsaw agitators (many of whom were militia from Green Plains and Warsaw) in the guise of a militia—stormed the jail.

[72] Ford, *History of Illinois*, 337. See also Hampshire, *Mormonism in Conflict*, 203.

[73] "John S. Fullmer Diary," November 27, 1854. See also *History of the Church*, 6:577.

[74] Report by Hale, "Jonathan H. Hale Papers."

II

The Struggle to Survive
The Repeal of the Charter

Where now is the Prophet Joseph? Where now is the Prophet Joseph?
Where now is the Prophet Joseph? Safe in Carthage jail!

For Joseph and Hyrum Smith, Carthage, Illinois, was a scene of broken promises, arraignments, and incarceration. Accusations of riot stemming from the *Nauvoo Expositor* incident had turned to charges of treason. Rumors once whispered in secret now were shouted in public. Smith's enemies boasted that the two men would never leave Carthage: "There was nothing against these men; the law could not reach them but powder and ball would, and they should not go out of Carthage alive."[1]

Around 5:00 p.m. on June 27, 1844, men began running around the corner of the jail. John Taylor described them as "an armed mob—painted black—of from 150 to 200 persons."[2] They easily overpowered the jailor, rushed the stairs, and began shooting into the east bedroom. Despite their initial attempts to protect themselves, the captives were no match for the disguised attackers. Hyrum Smith was the first to fall to an assassin's bullet. As he backed away from the door to the center of the room, one bullet pierced the upper panel of the door and struck him on the left side of the nose. Falling to the floor, he exclaimed, "I am a dead man!" Bending over the

[1] *History of the Church*, 6:566.

[2] John Taylor (1801–87): assistant chaplain, judge advocate of the Nauvoo Legion; president of the Church of Jesus Christ of Latter-day Saints, 1880–87.

body of his lifeless brother, Smith cried, "Oh, dear brother Hyrum!"[3] He then moved toward the east bedroom window; two balls hit him from the doorway, and two others struck him from the outside. He fell from the second-story window to the ground below and was heard to exclaim, "O Lord, my God!"[4] The assailants had accomplished their goal: Joseph Smith, the Mormon prophet, was dead.

Fearing that the Nauvoo Legion would pillage and destroy Carthage in retaliation, Governor Ford "advised all who were present [in Carthage] to disperse, as he expected the Mormons would be so exasperated that they would come and burn the town."[5] Retaliation was not the issue for most Mormons, however, although Captain Allen Stout's[6] journal entry may typify the anguish of some: "I knew not how to contain myself. . . . I feel like cutting their throats."[7] The most pressing issue for most Nauvoo residents was one of grief and lamentation and preparation for the return of the cortège to Nauvoo. The Legion was never used for retaliation.

About 8:00 A.M. on Friday, June 28, the remains of the Smith brothers were placed in rough boxes, put into two wagons, and covered with prairie hay, blankets, and bushes to protect them from the hot sun. A guard consisting of eight members of the Legion—led by Third Lieutenant Samuel Smith,[8] brother of the fallen men—escorted the remains from Carthage to Nauvoo. Other soldiers remained in Nauvoo to muster under the command of Major General Dunham[9] on the parade grounds east of the temple. They then

---

[3] The prisoners used weapons to defend themselves in the jail. *History of the Church,* 6:618.

[4] *Doctrine and Covenants,* 135:1. This was an eye-witness account by John Taylor, who was wounded during the attack. For additional information on the death of Joseph and Hyrum Smith, see Cannon and Largey, "The Martyrdom." One recent study puts this event in a broader context. See Wicks and Foisteg, *Junius and Joseph.*

[5] Although the Saints made no effort to retaliate, Governor Ford displayed genuine concern. After advising the citizens of Carthage to disperse, "the Governor and his *posse* fled towards Quincy, and did not consider themselves safe until they had reached Augusta, eighteen miles distant from Carthage." *History of the Church,* 6:625.

[6] Allen Joseph Stout (1815–89): third lieutenant, captain of the Nauvoo Legion; bodyguard for Joseph Smith and Brigham Young.

[7] "Journal of Allen Joseph Stout," 19. The fact that the Legion was not called out is evidence of the restraint on the part of the Mormons. Although many non-Mormons feared an attack by the Nauvoo Legion, it did not occur, then or later.

[8] Samuel Harrison Smith (1808–44): guard, second lieutenant of the Nauvoo Legion; first missionary for the LDS Church; one of Eight Witnesses to the Book of Mormon.

[9] Jonathan R. Dunham (1800–45): colonel, brigadier general of the Nauvoo Legion.

marched to the east end of Mulholland Street, where they met the wagons bearing the bodies of their slain leaders.[10] Dunham and his staff, Brigadier General Hosea Stout and his staff, and other commanders were among the thousands of mourners.

Between 2:30 and 3:00 P.M. the military processional traversed Main Street to the Mansion House, where Willard Richards, William W. Phelps, Smith's attorney James Wood, and town marshal Stephen Markham[11] urged members of the Legion and the people of Nauvoo to remain calm.[12] Meanwhile, the remains of the slain were taken inside the Mansion House and the door closed. "The wagon was driven inside of the back gate and the gate was locked," penned Mary Rich. "No one was allowed in the yard except the guards and the Prophet's special friends."[13] Those assembled heard messages of comfort from their leaders. Most memorable were the words of Willard Richards, who "pledged his honor, and his life for their good conduct." The people "with one united voice resolved to trust to the law for a remedy of such a high-handed assassination, and when that failed, to call upon God to avenge them of their wrongs." Richards concluded, "O, Americans, weep, for the glory of freedom has departed!"[14] The assembled thereupon quietly dispersed, but were promised that beginning at 8:00 A.M., June 29, the remains of the martyrs could be viewed by all.

Exactly at 8:00 A.M., the public viewing began. "Thousands came from all quarters to take a last look; and steamboats loaded with strangers came from Burlington, Quincy and many other places, to look upon their dead bodies," reported Sarah Rich.[15] An estimated "ten thousand persons visited the remains," entering at the west door and exiting at the north door of the Mansion House.[16] Following the viewing mourners assembled to listen to a funeral sermon by William W. Phelps. Paying tribute to the slain leaders, he said, "Two of the greatest and best men who have lived on earth since the Jews crucified the Savior, have fallen victims to the popular will of mobocracy."[17]

---

[10] *History of the Church,* 7:134.

[11] Stephen Markham (1800–1878): brevet major, lieutenant colonel, brevet colonel, colonel of the Nauvoo Legion; private courier for Joseph Smith.

[12] Leonard, *Nauvoo,* 401.

[13] "Autobiography of Mary Rich," 17.

[14] *History of the Church,* 6:626; See *Times and Seasons* 5, no. 12, 561.

[15] "Autobiography of Sarah Rich," 29–30.

[16] *History of the Church,* 6:627.

[17] Van Wagoner and Walker, "Joseph/Hyrum Smith Funeral Sermon," 9.

After the membership of the Church voted to approve temporary leadership of the Church by Brigham Young and the Twelve Apostles rather than accept the claim of guardianship by Sidney Rigdon, on August 31 the Legion elected Brigham Young as its new lieutenant general, assuming the command and influence earlier held by Joseph Smith.[18] Taking up his military responsibilities, Young attended a Nauvoo Legion court-martial where resolutions calling for the construction of an arsenal and a gunsmith's shop were presented and passed.[19] By mid-September he broke ground for the arsenal and dedicated the site to the "God of the Armies of Israel."[20]

Meanwhile, the Legion went through the motions of the occasional parade and sham battle but seemed to sense its days as a state-sanctioned militia were numbered, despite the fact that in fall 1844 it was apparent that Governor Ford had once again taken a personal interest in the Nauvoo Legion. In coming to Nauvoo to present commissions to Young and Charles Rich, Ford also reviewed the troops and authorized members of the Legion to suppress mob activity in Hancock County. He also authorized the procurement of two hundred additional muskets. His conciliatory actions were surprising, if not suspicious, to the Mormons. Did the governor recognize the risk of trying to achieve a compromise given the volatile atmosphere? Did he want the Legion to shoot it out with their neighbors? Governor Ford attempted to explain his actions by stating, "As to myself, I shared the fate of all men in high places who favor moderation, who see that parties in the frenzy of their excitement are wrong espousing the cause of neither; which fate always is to be hated by both parties."[21]

But it was all political posturing; soon after Ford had commissioned and armed the Legion again, the state legislature once more debated whether to repeal the Nauvoo Charter. As discussed in earlier chapters, opponents of the charter had sought for its repeal, believing that the Legion had been granted too much power. Others had wanted to weaken it by amendment and modification.[22]

---

[18] "Journal History of the Church," August 31, 1844.

[19] "Journal History of the Church," September 10, 1844.

[20] "Journal History of the Church," September 16, 1844.

[21] Ford, *History of Illinois,* 255. Governor Ford wrote to Brigham Young authorizing him to work "under the direction of the said sheriff [Backenstos]" to "suppress mobs." "Journal History of the Church," October 9, 1844.

[22] Leonard, *Nauvo,* 465–66.

Ford now joined those seeking repeal. In a letter published in the *Warsaw Signal* on February 14, 1844, he expressed dissatisfaction and frustration with the state Senate for not taking decisive action on the charter.[23] In fall and winter 1844, several legislators pressed hard for the repeal. Almon W. Babbitt, a Mormon serving in the state House of Representatives, wrote Brigham Young to warn him that opponents of the charter were stirring up votes in favor of the repeal.[24] Babbitt's letter, although informative, did nothing to stem the tide.

By January 1845 the issue resurfaced. Those in favor of repealing the charter spoke vigorously of its alleged evils, including the concentration of power in one place.[25] It appears that the lightning rod of dissent was not so much the Nauvoo Legion as it was the other powers granted in the charter—especially the provision for the Nauvoo Municipal Court to issue writs of habeas corpus. As Governor Carlin had said earlier,

> From my recollection of the Charter it authorizes the municipal court to issue writs of habeas corpus in all cases of imprisonment or custody arising from the authority of the ordinances of said city; but that power was granted, or intended to be granted, to release persons held in custody under the authority of writs issued by the courts or executive of the state, is most absurd and ridiculous; and to attempt to exercise it is a gross usurpation of power that cannot be tolerated.[26]

Babbitt delivered two highly reasonable speeches before the legislature arguing for the need to retain the charter.[27] Especially important was the need to retain a police force to ensure the safety of Nauvoo's several thousand citizens. Rather than outright appeal of what he termed a "general impeachment" of the Mormons, Babbitt argued, "Why not amend the charter [of] all its objectionable features?"[28] Babbitt's pleas, however, fell on deaf ears. Non-Mormon

---

[23] *History of the Church,* 6:189. In this letter, Governor Ford responded to the urgings of the citizens of Hancock County to repeal portions of the Nauvoo Charter. Ford explained that he has no power as governor to repeal the laws. He had presented the matter before the state legislature in the previous session, and they had determined not to act.

[24] *History of the Church,* 7:325.

[25] Flanders, *Nauvoo,* 285.

[26] Letter of Governor Carlin to Emma Smith, September 7, 1842. See *History of the Church,* 5:154. See also "Journal of Wandle Mace," 170–80.

[27] *History of the Church,* 7:363. See also Roberts, *Comprehensive History of the Church,* 2:483–85.

[28] "Journal of Wandle Mace," 172–75.

sheriff Jacob Backenstos of Hancock County argued for much the same thing. An excerpt from his speech shows the logic, if not the passion, of a doomed cause:

> I have been sorry, Mr. Speaker, to witness the manifestation of prejudice which has been exhibited during this discussion. Men occupying the high and responsible seats of legislators should never suffer themselves to be moved by excitement, or influenced by so base a passion as prejudice; these are the elements of feeble minds and ungenerous hearts, and should never be suffered to enter the sacred retreats of liberty and laws—the hall of legislation.
>
> Mr. Speaker, one very important reason in my mind why we should not repeal the city charter of Nauvoo is, that you strip the largest and most populous city in this State of all her police regulations. Why not amend the charter in all its objectionable features? Why not leave them powers sufficient to maintain an efficient city organization?
>
> The peace of the people of Hancock [County] hangs upon the action of this house.[29]

One might ask why Backenstos would risk his political capital to speak on behalf of the Latter-day Saints. Backenstos had become intimately acquainted with the Mormons and their leader, Joseph Smith. In fact, in 1841 he had loaned money to Smith and in 1842 was inducted into Freemasonry under Smith's sponsorship. Furthermore, the two families were linked by marriage—Smith performed the marriage ceremony for William Backenstos, the sheriff's brother, and Clara Wasson, a niece-in-law of the lieutenant general. On a visit to the Backenstos house in Carthage, Smith once preached a five-hour sermon to him and some of his friends. Although Backenstos never joined with the Mormons, he was an avid friend and a champion of their cause, and wished to protect them by preserving the Nauvoo Charter.[30]

Nevertheless, neither Babbitt nor Backenstos changed the minds of the legislature. On January 29, 1845, the Illinois House of Representatives voted overwhelmingly (seventy-five to thirty-one) to

---

[29] It should be noted that Backenstos investigated his case. Several other cities in Illinois also had their charters repealed. See "The Nauvoo Charter." Said Backenstos of the eventual repeal, "It is an act of wanton legislation unwarranted by circumstances and without a parallel in the history of our country." See "Journal of Wandle Mace," 178–79.

[30] Whitman and Varner, "Sheriff Jacob B. Backenstos," 153–56.

approve the senate bill and repeal the charter.[31] The ramifications of their action were immediate and devastating to the Mormon community in Nauvoo—a city still of some twelve thousand people—now without a legalized city, militia, university, police force, judicial system, legislative system, or mayor. The city of Nauvoo physically remained, but without a sanctioned government and with a legion or militia without support of the law.

Backenstos's affirmative statements about Mormonism prompted Governor Ford to warn him to be careful. Said Ford, "If they ever get hold of you they will murder you."[32] His words were not far from the truth. In September 1845 Backenstos called upon individual members of the former Nauvoo Legion to aid him when a mob drove him and his family from their home. The first men to respond were the well-known Orrin Porter Rockwell and Return Jackson Redden.[33] Rockwell's biographer noted their assistance:

> No sooner had he spoken than two horsemen appeared on the crest of the hill and raced down on them. Worrell was well ahead of the closest man; the other had been thrown when his horse stumbled. Once the two were within hailing distance the Sheriff shouted an order to stop. In answer, Worrell reached for his pistol. Before he could bring the gun to bear, a ball from Rockwell's rifle tore into his abdomen and catapulted Worrell from the saddle. At the sound of the shot the second rider frantically wheeled his horse and galloped to the wagon and buggy now arriving on the scene. The men gazed in disbelief at Worrell's crumpled form on the ground. Under Rock-

[31] The charter was repealed because sentiment in the Illinois legislature had now turned against the Mormons. The repeal of the charter meant that the residents of Nauvoo were operating without a government authorized by the state. As such the Legion could no longer function as it had in the past. Hampshire discusses the repeal of the Nauvoo Charter in her chapter "The Triangle of Mobocracy, 1844–1847," *Mormonism in Conflict,* 234–37. Her chapter title underscores her thesis. Concerning the arguments against the charter, she wrote: "In the debates which followed in both Houses, the old arguments concerning alleged Mormon abuse of the law, the possible influence of religious prejudice on the question of repeal, the effect of repeal on Nauvoo's creditors and investors, the precedent which repeal would set and the consequent effect upon other city charters, the advisability of merely cutting or reforming those obnoxious sections—were all well aired. There were few new issues." (235).

[32] Letter of Thomas L. Ford to J. B. Backenstos, September 21, 1845.

[33] Whitman and Varner, "Sheriff Jacob B. Backenstos," 153–56. There is some confusion as to the actual name of Return Jackson Redding. It has been spelled Jack Redding, Jack Redman, and John Redding, see Schindler, *Orrin Porter Rockwell,* 139.

well's cold gaze they gathered up their wounded leader and carried him to the wagon; he died before they reached Warsaw.[34]

Following Worrell's death, Backenstos warned the Mormons, "Defend your lives and your property with force of arms against any and all persons who may molest you in the shape of a mob or by whatever name they may call themselves and be in readiness and hold yourselves subject to my further orders."[35] He then urged them to raise troops to assist him in defending their rights. Some of the unchartered Nauvoo Legion responded with daily preparations for war; their commanding officer, Brigham Young, responded by appealing to famed orator Daniel Webster for help: "Believing you to be a man of erudition and great legal attainments, we have thought it advisable to address you on the subject, asking for your opinion as to the most expedient course to be taken—which court would be the most proper tribunal—whether there is any precedent to be found in this or any other civilized nation."[36]

The Legion continued to function as if it were still an authorized, state-sanctioned militia. It did so out of the necessity of protecting Nauvoo and its citizens. The Nauvoo Whittling and Whistling Brigade, composed of boys with jackknives and sticks, was but one example. The bishops of each ecclesiastical ward in Nauvoo organized other young men into designated militia units with specific patrol duties. When a suspicious stranger entered Nauvoo, youths were ordered to follow while whistling and whittling on wood. This menacing procedure, viewed as harassment of unwelcome outsiders, caused many undesirables to leave town.[37]

---

[34] Schindler, *Orrin Porter Rockwell*, 139. After an unsuccessful attempt to recruit a posse to challenge the mobs that were burning outlying Mormon homes, Sheriff Backenstos returned to his home in Carthage only to be driven out by a mob disgusted by his sympathy for the Latter-day Saints. He stayed the night at a friend's house in Warsaw where he was informed of a plot against his life. Backenstos took extra caution returning to Carthage the next morning but was spotted and pursued by Lieutenant Frank Worrell of the Carthage Greys and a small gang. While fleeing, Backenstos asked Rockwell and Redden for help.

[35] "Journal History of the Church," September 16, 1845.

[36] Letter of Brigham Young et al. to Daniel Webster, February 1, 1845.

[37] The Mormons employed such extralegal activities because they had no other choice. They had to defend themselves with whatever means they could devise. Moody, "Nauvoo's Whistling and Whittling Brigade," 480–90. Some local citizens believed they had unjustly been forced out of Nauvoo by the brigade. See, for example, "Robert Atherton's Grievance," in Hallwas and Launier, *Conflicts in Culture*, 73–74.

Members of the Legion also felt obligated to participate in military operations while completing assigned religious tasks; for example, John Brown recorded, "Two Elders, viz: Wm. Hyde and Elam Luddington came from Nauvoo with an epistle from the Twelve calling in all young, middle aged and able bodied men, to Nauvoo to defend the place and help build the Temple, carry with them their arms and ammunition."[38] The traditional and expected actions, such as new military appointments, of the Legion continued; on May 7, 1845, Hosea Stout met with various officers "to regulate matters in case we should be attacked by our enemies. I was appointed to act as Brigadier-General second cohort."[39]

This was the military posture in Nauvoo when Major William B. Warren of the Illinois Supreme Court, having been appointed by Governor Ford to act as a mediator, entered the city, in company with the state militia, on October 25, 1845. Unlike Backenstos, Warren did not fully understand the antagonism many felt toward the Mormons and their loyal friends. He expressed disgust at seeing fifteen soldiers on patrol. Mormon apostle John Taylor, who had been severely wounded at Carthage, bluntly apprised Warren of the situation:

> We lack confidence in the governor's troops under your command while hundreds of murderers, robbers, and house burners roam at large unwhipped of justice. We shall take measures to protect ourselves. I, sir, have been shot all to pieces under the "protection" of the governor's troops. Our leading men have been murdered in Carthage and we shall not trust ourselves unprotected again until the state gives some evidence more than it has done of its justice and humane intentions to enforce its laws.[40]

Taylor's words fell on deaf ears. To Warren's mind, the Nauvoo Legion had been officially disbanded and was acting outside the precincts of the law. The Mormons felt that, with or without state approval, the Legion was a necessity, since Nauvoo was still very much threatened. They felt they not only needed to muster, drill, and parade, but also to prepare to defend themselves. The Mormons believed Warren and the state militia and other hostile elements

[38] "Journal History of the Church," March 2, 1845.

[39] "Journal History of the Church," May 7, 1845. Many other militias, especially "crack" volunteer companies, had often operated outside formal state chartering.

[40] *History of the Church,* 7:488.

posed an imminent danger to the city and other communities on both sides of the Mississippi River.

At greatest risk were those in the outlying settlements of Hancock County. Mobs found these isolated villages and farms easy prey for their crimes. On November 15, 1845,

> A considerable party of the mob set fire to a stack of straw near Solomon Hancock's barn and concealed themselves. Hancock and others went out to put out the fire which was the only way to save the building, when they were fired upon by the burners, and Elder Edmund Durfee killed on the spot, many balls flew around the rest of the brethren, but none of the rest were hurt.[41]

Such bloodshed led the Mormons to step up their military maneuvers, much to Warren's dismay. Encouraging their removal from Illinois to Iowa, Warren offered little advice regarding defense. Amid preparations for their exodus to the West, several Mormons, in a kind of rear-guard action, vigilantly patrolled and protected Nauvoo. They marched, mustered, paraded, made leadership changes, and devised plans for defending their city. They went on military expeditions to prevent enemies from attacking them. One such operation occurred near Warsaw under the command of Colonel J. H. Hale and John D. Lee.[42]

By early 1846 some neighbors believed that Mormonism and its Legion had survived the death of the Smith brothers and were stronger than ever. Rumors circulated that the Mormons and the Legion, under Young's leadership, were in Illinois to stay. Other rumors hinted that the Mormons were about to leave Illinois and join another nation, threatening the stability of the United States. While such hearsay went unchecked, the number of government troops under the command of Warren increased. As one observer noted,

> Quite a number of the governor's troops are prowling around our city; I am informed that they are seeking to arrest some of the leading men of the church. This evening I read a letter from S. [Samuel] Brannan in which he said he had ascertained from Amos Kendall, the late postmaster-general, that the government intended to intercept our movements by stationing strong forces in our way to take from

[41] *History of the Church,* 7:523.

[42] *History of the Church,* 7:577.

us all firearms on the pretense that we were going to join another nation.[43]

Having no other choice, and acting under a growing cloud of persecution and oppression, Brigham Young directed the first vanguard companies of Latter-day Saints to quit Nauvoo for the West on February 4, 1846. The advance party, commanded by Charles Shumway, crossed the icy Mississippi River into the Iowa Territory. Others soon followed. On flatboats, old lighters, and skiffs, the Latter-day Saints formed a makeshift fleet to carry the exiles. Their exodus to the West had begun in earnest.[44] Brigham Young joined the early companies departing that February and March, and encouraged the rest of the city to leave by fall of that year.

The remaining members of the Legion were given two primary assignments—to protect those crossing the Mississippi and to ensure the safety of as many of those temporarily remaining behind as possible. The Nauvoo Legion successfully provided the needed manpower for both assignments. Those who remained in the city felt free to participate in the dedication of the Nauvoo Temple on April 30, 1846, knowing that the Legion was standing guard. As Wilford Woodruff noted,

> We dedicated the Temple of the Lord built by the Church of Jesus Christ of Latter Day Saints, unto His Most Holy name. We had an interesting time. Notwithstanding the many false Prophesies of Sidney Rigdon and others that the roof should not go on nor the House be finished, and the threats of the mob that we should not dedicate it yet we have done both and we had an interesting time.[45]

The summer of 1846, however, was another story. Showing inexcusable behavior reminiscent of the worst scenes of Missouri, Hancock County mob activity intensified against the poor, sick, and otherwise unprepared citizens who delayed their departure to the West.[46] On June 9, Alexander Neibaur recorded, "The mobbers renewed hostilities in Hancock County, Illinois."[47] Threats and vio-

[43] John D. Lee, MSS 1253.

[44] Leonard, *Nauvoo,* 574–75.

[45] Because of recurring mob threats, the Legion had to stand ready to defend the Saints. Woodruff, *Wilford Woodruff's Journal,* 3:41.

[46] By the summer of 1846 many Mormons had moved out of Nauvoo. Only a rear guard remained.

[47] "Journal History of the Church," June 9, 1846.

FIGURE 26. *The Battle of Nauvoo,* by C. C. A. Christensen, ca. 1865. Tempera on muslin, 76½ in. × 113½ in. *Courtesy of Museum of Art, Brigham Young University, Provo, Utah.*

lence increased steadily in late summer, reaching a climax on September 10: Colonel Thomas Brockman[48] of the Illinois State Militia led several hundred men on a march toward Nauvoo. That evening, Brockman's men camped near Joseph Smith's farm east of town. Recognizing the imminent threat this action posed to the community, Nauvoo defenders set up fortifications at the east end of town. Brockman's soldiers chose to outflank the defensive positions, and entered the town at its unprotected flank. Rallying to prevent further encroachment into the city, sharpshooters from the Nauvoo Legion engaged Brockman's artillery in a volley of fire, delaying the advance of the artillery company for a time.

Fighting broke out again the next day. On Saturday, September 12, Brockman's forces called for surrender but were met with stiff

[48] Colonel Thomas S. Brockman (1811–67) was a Campbellite preacher, commissioner of Brown County, Illinois, a tax collector, and commander of the posse that attacked Nauvoo in September 1846.

resistance instead. In the ensuing battle, three Nauvoo defenders were fatally wounded—William Anderson, August Anderson, and David Morris.[49] Still the battle continued. Wrote one Mormon eyewitness,

> The little band of brethren and some of the new citizens made a brave stand against the mob, sometime the cannon balls from the mob would be picked up and loaded into our steamboat shaft cannon and fired back at them, ammunition was scarce with us: and we were but a handful, some said not more than one hundred men against one thousand of the mob. In the midst of these scenes a committee of the citizens of Quincy arrived, and viewing the battle from the top of the Temple declared they were the bravest little band of men that ever lived, they came to Nauvoo for the purpose of acting as Mediators.[50]

Nevertheless, the small "Spartan Band," or remnant of the once powerful Nauvoo Legion, could not defend the largely vacated city against a vastly superior force, nor did Church leaders or Legion commanders advise it to do so any longer. Daniel H. Wells pleaded for them to take the wiser course and surrender: "What interests have the Saints to expect from its defense? Our interests are not identified with it, but in getting away from it. Who could urge the propriety of exposing life to defend a place for the purpose of vacating it?"[51]

The city surrendered soon afterward. A citizen committee from Quincy negotiated the following terms of surrender:

1. The City of Nauvoo would surrender, and Colonel Brockman, who led the militia, would enter and take possession of the city with his force.
2. The Mormon population must leave the state or disperse as soon as they could cross the river.
3. Nauvoo citizens' arms would be turned in, and the Quincy Committee would return them to the Saints when they crossed the river.
4. Ten men from the Quincy Committee and the occupation forces pledged to protect all persons and property from violence.

[49] None of the three were soldiers in the Nauvoo Legion. Leonard, *Nauvoo,* 608–11.

[50] "Journal of Wandle Mace," 101–102. Of course the Legion had been depleted just as the general population had been depleted by the exodus.

[51] William Pickett to Brigham Young, December 27, 1847. Brigham Young Papers. Church History Library.

> 5. The sick and helpless would be protected and treated with humanity.
>
> Five men with their families, including the trustees of the Church, and five clerks would be permitted to remain in the city for the disposition of property, free from all molestation and personal violence.[52]

"Farewell Nauvoo, the Beautiful! The City of Joseph!" wrote Second Lieutenant Wandle Mace.[53]

A few agents remained behind to dispose of real estate, but within days the remaining Mormons crossed the river, leaving behind most of their worldly possessions. These so-called "poor camps" suffered terribly, waiting on the Iowa side for rescue parties from much further west to come and carry them along. Wrote Brigham Young,

> Our homes, gardens, orchards, farms, streets, bridges, mills, public halls, magnificent temple, and other public improvements we leave as a monument of our patriotism, industry, economy, uprightness of purpose, and integrity of heart; and as a living testimony of the falsehood and wickedness of those who charge us with disloyalty to the Constitution of our country, idleness, and dishonesty.[54]

Those who had built Nauvoo now turned their "hearts and all their labours towards the setting sun, for they desire[d] to be so far removed from those who had been their oppressors that there should be an everlasting barrier between them and future persecution."[55] An entire community moved itself and its shopkeepers, artisans, mechanics, and skilled laborers to the West. It may well be argued that no other city in American history had ever undergone such an extreme transformation in so short a time and under such trying, painful circum-

[52] Leonard, *Nauvoo,* 612–13. Looking at all of this activity from the standpoint of non-Mormon "Illinois Volunteers," one hears a different story. In *Illinois Volunteers in the Mormon War,* Hyneman and Lute make clear that the "Illinois Volunteers," did not speak with one voice. In fact, there were serious disagreements among those pitted against the Mormons. Some were vehemently anti-Mormon, others either sympathized with the Mormons or lent support for their cause. Regarding the role of Governor Thomas L. Ford, this study argues that he tried to resolve the issues and to be fair to all concerned.

[53] Wandle Mace (1809–90) second lieutenant of the Nauvoo Legion; millwright; missionary to Orange County, New York. "Journal of Wandle Mace," 105.

[54] *History of the Church,* 7:603.

[55] General Epistle from the Council of the Twelve Apostles to the "Church dispersed Throughout the earth," December 23, 1847, in Clark, *Messages of the First Presidency,* 1:328.

stances. One wonders how many other people closed the doors of their homes and abandoned their once flourishing city to wander in a wilderness in search of safety, peace, and religious freedom.

On December 7, 1846, before the general assembly of the state of Illinois, Governor Ford announced, "It is with much satisfaction that I am enabled to state, that the people called Mormons have been removed from the state. The great body of them removed voluntarily, but a small remnant of them were barbarously expelled with force, and in a manner which reflects but little credit on the state or its institutions."[56] That the Nauvoo Legion would again serve to meet the needs of the Mormons in the Utah Territory is another story, to be told at another time, and in another place.

---

[56] *Monmouth Atlas,* December 18, 1846. In reference to those expelled with force, Leonard records "Even though the Saints left quickly, and despite promises not to molest residents, the occupying forces harassed many who were frustrated by their own lack of preparations for the forced evacuation. The militia seized fleeing citizens at random and threw them into the river, shouting obscenities at some in mock baptisms. They held courts-martial for others, condemned them to die, and then expelled them from the city. The soldiers searched for arms in wagons and homes, burst open trunks and chests, and tore up floors." Leonard, *Nauvoo,* 613. Governor Ford was clearly embarrassed by the violence and his inability to control the situation.

12

Conclusion

Let their objective be what it may,
they cannot live long in peace with the neighboring Country.

So what are we to make of the Nauvoo Legion? Clearly there is much more to the story than previously assumed. Sharing the spotlight in Mormon history with the later Mormon Battalion that served in Stephen W. Kearny's Army of the West during the Mexican-American War, the Nauvoo Legion will forever be remembered, despite its short existence, as one of the most colorful and certainly most controversial militias in U.S. history. Having deliberately restructured and restricted this study to the history of the Legion in Illinois from 1841 to 1846, we believe that we have provided as careful a study of the Legion as possible.

We approached this topic first of all by placing it in the larger context of American military history. We have tried to show that in origin, makeup, and operation, the Nauvoo Legion was an arm of the Illinois State Militia. We have likewise argued that it was not a static or moribund militia, like so many of the militias of the time; it grew in activity and intensity in accordance to local invitation and also in direct proportion to the mounting anti-Mormon sentiment and opposition from Warsaw, Quincy, and other nearby communities. Increasingly, it took on the enthusiasm and avidity of independent, uniformed regiments, for whom military service was an optional, though exciting, avocation. Finally, we have also tried to show that the Legion took on the appearance of a religious, church-sponsored Mormon militia. Consequently it had the legitimacy of a state militia, the trappings of a private regiment, and the enthusiasm and uniqueness of a religious force—a blending of legal requirement, civic duty, and religious fervor. Obeying the governor, it would respond to Joseph Smith, the Mormon prophet and city's mayor all in one and to defend family and kin when called upon. What the Legion was depended on the differing viewpoints and interpretations of either its participants or detractors.

Yet the fact remains: the Nauvoo Legion, like the city of Nauvoo itself, began as a bona fide legal entity, but as time passed became part of a much greater drama—that of a religion under suspicion and attack. The Legion became so inextricably part of the larger maelstrom of conflict that to study it in isolation is like taking a brick out of a wall or a single scene out of a three-act play. It has far less meaning on its own than it does in the greater collective story. We have tried to show the Legion for what it was—a militia of the state of Illinois and therefore of the United States of America—but we have also attempted to place it in the difficult context of Mormon–anti-Mormon relations, which collapsed in turmoil.

Our major findings and arguments may be summarized as follows:

The formation of the Nauvoo Legion grew out of a longstanding American tradition. The Militia Act of 1792 called for every able-bodied man between the ages of eighteen and forty-five to serve in a local militia. This was the law of the land, although it was often ineffectively and unequally enforced. Thus, in origin and design, the Nauvoo Legion was an American construct.

The Nauvoo Legion came into being by statutory provision of the Illinois state legislature and functioned as a legitimate arm of the Illinois State Militia. When first authorized it fulfilled not only the provisions of state and federal law, but began at the express encouragement of the state at a time when the Illinois State Militia suffered, like so many other state militias, from acute neglect and disrepair. As much as the Legion may have derived from the needs of a church and people under fire, it owed it beginnings to the exigencies of a state under federal scrutiny.

By judicial review, the citizens of Nauvoo were allowed to form a city militia—its own legion—in form and structure not unlike the Invincible Dragoons or the proposed Illinois Legion. It was independent not of the state, but only in the sense that it was not a part of nearby county regiments, particularly the Hancock County Fifty-ninth Regiment.

Law and precedent alone do not fully explain the provenance of the Nauvoo Legion; bitter lessons do—lessons the Latter-day Saints learned from their recent and torturous Missouri past. What started in 1831 with eager anticipation among a people anxious to establish Zion—their New Jerusalem—in Jackson County, Missouri, ended in October 1838 with a solemn proclamation of expulsion by a governor convinced that they had to leave the state to prevent civil war. The Mormons had tried to establish a new Zion in a place most difficult and in a culture most unreceptive. They had also tried to do so at a time in American history marked by riot and insurrection. And they had done it as a people not fully prepared for so great a task.

The Nauvoo Legion was not a resurrection of Mormonism's problematic Zion's Camp of 1834, nor was it a reincarnation of the Danites. The Legion was a deliberate, conscious effort to improve upon the inadequacies and shortcomings of Zion's Camp and the irregularities and illegalities of the Danites. That some former members of Zion's Camp and members of the Danites served in the Legion was inevitable and to be expected. But unlike either group, the Legion was legally sanctioned by the state, and drilled and paraded in public.

Securing the charter for the city of Nauvoo, and with it a provision for a militia, represented a deliberate effort by Church authorities to secure legitimacy. The two men most responsible for the charter were Joseph Smith and John C. Bennett. Immediate friends, the two represented a people's pressing needs on one side and an individual's private ambitions on the other. Smith too eagerly entrusted Bennett with securing for the Legion what Bennett had tried but failed to attain in his proposed "Illinois Legion"—a potentially formidable force composed of militias from three counties. Extremist in his militant views, anxious to command, and hoping to use the Legion to advance his own ambitions, Bennett was a successful but destabilizing force in the creation and development of the Nauvoo Legion.

As lieutenant general, Joseph Smith was in many ways uniquely prepared by ancestry, religious conviction, training, and personal experience as leader of the Zion's Camp expedition to lead a militia. He felt confident advising the Legion on tactical, practical, and immediate matters of military importance. As its commander he insisted that the Legion be well trained and prepared to defend the city and its people. Yet he was by no means a professional soldier, and, by disposition, arguably less equipped for military leadership than other men in Nauvoo. His rank of lieutenant general may have sounded grandiose but was equal to that of a major general in other state regiments. In his military capacity Joseph Smith answered to the governor of the state of Illinois. What he gained by actively controlling the city's militia he lost by contributing to rising public perceptions of a prophet-leader intent on blending the powers of church and state.

An accurate count of the numbers who served in the Legion has been difficult to precisely determine. Its size reflected the changing population growth of Nauvoo. As thousands of new converts migrated to the Mormon capital, the ranks of the Legion rose proportionately. The discrepancy noted in Legion statistics may simply be a matter of faulty and incomplete records. It probably never reached three thousand men; however, it grew quickly and, as anti-Mormon sentiment intensified, remained a single unit, never breaking into small extralegal groups. The Legion's readiness improved in direct response to the rising tide of opposition.

The Legion was organized into a six-level military structure. The highest ranking officer, or first tier, was the commander in chief/lieutenant general, and the lowest tier, a private. By February 1841 distinctions between privates and officers were made in an election process. By election privates often became officers, as was the case in other militias in the state. Such elections were sanctioned by the state, and names of those elected were sent to the governor of Illinois to officially commission the officers. Typically the governor approved the election of each officer, but reserved the right to refuse a commission. Elections were an ongoing, vital process and were held when necessitated by a voluntarily vacated office, terminated office, or illness. Eighty commissioned and noncommissioned positions were filled in the Legion between 1841 and 1845. Of the 491 men elected, 177 were commissioned more than once.

Military courts-martial played a significant role in the Legion. First, the adversarial courts, like those held in other militia units of the state, tried members for their behavior, kept men in check, and ensured that separate interest groups like the Danites did not take the law into their own hands. Second, the law-making courts-martial played a central role in the revision of laws, election of officers, and the development of rules that governed citizen soldiers in military settings. The very nature of their rulings bespeaks the obvious—the Nauvoo Legion was a vibrant military organization bent on defending its citizens and fulfilling its legal obligation to the State of Illinois. These legislative powers were explicitly provided in the Constitution of the United States for all militias. Legion courts could not pass any law inconsistent with the military laws or constitutions of either the State of Illinois or the United States.

The Nauvoo Legion maintained a very impressive public image. Legion drills, musters, and inspections were ongoing and routine, and even typical of state-sanctioned militia exercises of the time. The Nauvoo Legion musters and parades led anti-Mormons to form a negative perception of the military leanings of their Mormon neighbors. The parades were a deliberate attempt by leaders of the Legion to make public the military preparedness of the Legion. The pomp and ceremony associated with these early (1841–42) parades revealed a sophisticated city militia capable of performing military operations. It also revealed a similarity between the Regular Army officers' uniforms and those of Nauvoo Legion officers. As opposition toward the Mormons in Nauvoo intensified, later Legion parades evidenced military preparedness. Numerous small, unannounced parades and military exercises, rather than the splendid general parades, helped train the Legion to defend Nauvoo.

Like most other contemporary state militias, the Legion was inadequately armed and equipped. Soldiers often had to use their own weapons. And although they were expected to be in uniform and were sometimes fined if they were not, many could not afford it.

The Nauvoo Legion was called to duty more often and for more purposes than perhaps previously believed. In most cases the Legion acted in obedience to the militia laws of Illinois. Some of its actions, however, are open to question and debate. The Legion was never used as an offensive weapon against the states of Missouri or Illinois. Smith did order the Legion to protect the city in times of perceived emergency; however, major deployments waited upon word from Springfield. In the destruction of a grog shop and the *Nauvoo Expositor*, the Legion followed the directions of local authority. It cannot be said that it ever acted in a mobocratic fashion. Governor Ford believed that even the Legion's activities to free Smith from arresting parties were in accordance with law. And in the most poignant moments leading up to the events at Carthage, the Legion surrendered and disbanded in accordance with the governor's requests. Since Nauvoo did not have a civil police force until 1843, members of the Legion were sometimes called upon by the mayor to perform police actions. In this capacity, they acted not as a Legion force but as individuals committed to preserve the public peace.

As a consequence of the intensifying conflicts within Nauvoo, several prominent, high-ranking officers, including major generals John C. Bennett and Wilson Law, were cashiered from the Legion. Eventually distrusted and disliked by most Mormons, as well as many non-Mormons, Bennett waged a vicious and vindictive campaign against Joseph Smith, spreading rumors about the power and intent of the Legion. Never able to understand why Smith did not use the Legion as an engine of war, "General Joab" did all in his power to defame and destroy the Saints. The actions Bennett and others associated with him have compelled us to place a very human face on the Legion.

The eventual legislative repeal of the Nauvoo Charter, and with it the Nauvoo Legion, in 1845 was the culmination of a recurring debate among Illinois Whigs and Democrats. Compelling evidence was never raised to show that the powers of the Legion, as originally vouchsafed by the state in 1841, were strange or "exceptional." The repeal came because of escalating Mormon rhetoric, threats of force, mounting opposition, and prejudice. The focal point of anti-Mormon sentiment was not just the Legion itself, but the concentration of political and religious power in Joseph Smith himself, a lack of separation of church and state, and fear of what the Mormons might do. In the end, Mormonism lost the battle of public opinion, and with it the Nauvoo Legion as a legitimate arm of the state militia.

Until more is known about the Council of Fifty, the Legion's role therein is purely speculative. There is no evidence that the Legion played any part in the Council, innuendos notwithstanding. The Council had an advisory role in Joseph Smith's candidacy for president of the United States and his plans for moving the Latter-day Saints westward. The Council of Fifty may also have been the political arm for the eventual establishment of a Mormon theocratic version of the Kingdom of God, but the Council had no jurisdiction over the Legion itself.

Participation in the Legion was often spotty and difficult. Many were called to interrupt their military service to fulfill missionary assignments. The sporadic involvement in military affairs was not unlike that in other Illinois state militias. But as time passed and storm clouds gathered, the men of the Nauvoo Legion took their military duties more seriously. It became a better drilled, better prepared, and more disciplined militia as the threat of persecution and eventual invasion loomed larger. By June 1844 the Nauvoo Legion was at its peak of readiness.

The repeal of the Nauvoo Charter in 1845 did not prevent the Nauvoo Legion from mustering, parading, or drilling. Out of the need to protect the citizens of Nauvoo, who were awaiting the inevitable exodus west, the Legion functioned as if it were still an authorized, state-sanctioned militia. The only difference was that it existed outside of the law and solely under Mormon church leadership. Those members of the Legion who fought in the "Battle of Nauvoo" against overwhelming numbers of Illinois State Militia troops did so believing that such was in the best interests of the city, and until they were advised by their own leaders to surrender and move on.

WE CONCLUDE WITH THREE FINAL POINTS. ALTHOUGH THE Nauvoo Legion is a well-known force in Mormon history, we have been persuaded to revisit and re-examine this topic. We now know the names of several hundreds of previously unknown privates who once proudly enlisted. Their service is well worth remembering (see appendix E).

Evidence that the Legion created or represented a greater spirit of militancy than ever before among the Mormons seems lacking. Although a great many served in the Legion, many were new citizens who knew nothing from personal experience of Zion's Camp or the earlier Danites. Participation was a legal requirement and defense became the order of the day.

Finally, it may well be argued that the greatest contribution of the Nauvoo Legion was in preventing what *never* occurred—extradition, mass killings, and eventual civil war. Strong and formidable, the Legion was a worthy deterrent to wanton persecution, unjust attack, and very real threats of extermination. As such it deserves an honorable place in the military history and tradition of Illinois and of the United States.

Appendix A

An Ordinance Organizing the Nauvoo Legion

Section 1. Be it ordained by the City Council of the City of Nauvoo, that the inhabitants of the City of Nauvoo, and such citizens of Hancock County as may unite by voluntary enrollment, be, and they are hereby organized into a body of independent military men, to be called the "Nauvoo Legion," as contemplated in the 25th section of "An act to incorporate the City of Nauvoo," approved, December 16, 1840.

Section 2. The Legion shall be, and is hereby, divided into two Cohorts; the horse troops to constitute the first Cohort, and the foot troops to constitute the second Cohort.

Section 3. The general officers of the Legion shall consist of a lieutenant general, as the chief commanding and reviewing officer, and president of the court martial, and Legion; a major general, as the second-in-command of the Legion, the secretary of the court martial, and Legion, and adjutant and inspector general; a brigadier general, as commander of the first cohort; and a brigadier general, as commander of the second cohort.

Section 4. The staff of the lieutenant general shall consist of two principal aides-de-camp with the rank of colonels of cavalry; and a guard of twelve aides-de-camp, with the rank of captains of infantry and a drill officer, with the rank of colonel of dragoons, who shall likewise be the chief officer of the guard.

Section 5. The staff of the major general shall consist of an adjutant, a surgeon-in-chief, a coronet, a quarter master, a pay-master, a commissary, and a chaplain, with the rank of colonels of infantry;

a surgeon for each cohort, a quarter-master sergeant, a sergeant-major, and chief musician, with the rank of captains of light infantry; and two musicians, with the rank of captains of infantry.

Section 6. The staff of each brigadier general shall consist of one aid-de-camp, with the rank of lieutenant-colonel of infantry; provided that the said brigadiers shall have access to the staff of the major general when not otherwise in service.

Section 7. No officer shall hereafter be elected by the various companies of the Legion, except upon the nomination of the court martial; and it is hereby made the duty of the court martial to nominate at least two candidates for each vacant office, whenever such vacancies occur.

Section 8. The court martial shall fill and supply all officers ranking between captain and brigadier generals, by granting brevet commissions to the most worthy company officers of the line, who shall thereafter take rank and command according to the date of their brevets; provided that their original place in the line shall not thereby be vacated.

Section 9. The court martial consisting of all the military officers, commissioned or entitled to commissions, within the limits of the city corporation, shall meet at the office of Joseph Smith, on Thursday the 4th day of February, 1841, at ten o'clock, A.M., and then and there, proceed to elect the general officers of the Legion as contemplated in the 3rd section of this ordinance.

Section 10. The court martial shall adopt for the Legion, as nearly as may be, and so far as applicable, the discipline, drill, uniform, rules and regulations, of the United States army.

Section 11. This ordinance shall take effect, and be in force, from and after its passage.

Passed, February 3rd, A.D. 1841.

JOHN C. BENNETT, Mayor.
JAMES SLOAN, Recorder.

Appendix B

Revised Laws of the Nauvoo Legion, from the Constitution of the United States by Authority

The Powers of Congress

Article 1 Sec. 8. Paragraph 14. To provide for calling forth the militia to execute the laws of the union, suppress insurrections, and repel invasions.

Paragraph 15. To provide for organizing, arming and disciplining the militia, and for governing such parts of them as may be employed in the service of the United States, reserving to the states respectively, the appointment of the officers, and the authority of training the militia according to the discipline prescribed by Congress.

Paragraph 17. To make all laws which shall be necessary and proper for carrying into execution the foregoing powers, and all other powers vested by the constitution in the government of the United States or in any department or officer thereof.

Amendments to the Constitution of the United States

Article 2. A well regulated militia being necessary to the security of a free state the right of the people to keep and bear arms shall not be infringed.

Constitution of Illinois

Article 5. Paragraph 1. The militia of the state of Illinois shall consist of all free male able-bodied persons, (negroes, mulattoes and Indians excepted,) resident of the state, between the age of eighteen and 45 years, except such persons as now are, or hereafter may be exempted by the laws of the United States, or this state, shall be armed, equipped, and trained as the general assembly may provide by law.

Paragraph 2. No person or persons, constitutionally [conscientiously] scrupulous of bearing arms, shall be compelled to do military duty in times of peace, provided such person or persons shall pay an equivalent for such exemption.

Paragraph 3. Company, battalion and regimental officers, staff officers excepted, shall be elected by the person composing their several companies, battalion and regiments.

Paragraph 4. Brigadier and Major-Generals shall be elected by the officers of their brigades and divisions respectively.

Paragraph 5. All militia officers shall be commissioned by the Governor, and may hold their commission during good behavior, or until they arrive at the age of 60 years.

Paragraph 6. The militia shall in all cases, except treason, felony or breach of the peace, be privileged from arrest during their attendance at musters and election of officers, and in going to and returning from the same.

City Charter

Section 25. The city council may organize the inhabitants of said city, subject to military duty, into a body of independent military men, to be called the "Nauvoo Legion," the court martial of which shall be composed of the commissioned officers of said Legion, and constitute the law-making department, with full powers and authority to make, ordain, establish and execute all such laws and ordinances as may be considered necessary for the benefit, government and regulation of said Legion. *Provided,* said court martial shall pass no law or act repugnant to, or inconsistent with, the Constitution of the United States or of this State; and provided, also, that the officers of the Legion shall be commissioned by the Governor of the State. The said Legion shall perform the same amount of military duty as is now or may be hereafter required of the regular militia of the State, and shall be at the disposal of the Mayor in executing the laws and ordinances of the City Corporation and the laws of the State, and at the disposal of the Governor for the public defense, and the execution of the laws of the State or of the United States, and shall be entitled to their proportion of the public arms; and provided, also, that said Legion shall be exempt from all other military duty.

Any citizen of Hancock county, may, by voluntary enrollment, attach himself to the Nauvoo Legion, with all the privileges which appertain to that independent military body.

An Ordinance Organizing the Nauvoo Legion

Section 1. Be it ordained by the City Council of the City of Nauvoo, that the inhabitants of the City of Nauvoo, and such citizens of Hancock county as may unite by voluntary enrollment, be, and they are hereby organized into a body of independent military men, to be called the "Nauvoo Legion," as contemplated in the 25th section of "An Act to Incorporate the City of Nauvoo," approved, December 16, 1840.

Sec. 2. The Legion shall be, and is hereby, divided into two Cohorts,—the horse troops to constitute the first Cohort, and the foot troops to constitute the second Cohort.

Sec. 3. The general officers of the Legion shall consist of a Lieut. General, as the chief commanding and reviewing officer, and President of the Court Martial, and Legion; a Major General, as the second in command of the Legion, the Secretary of the Court Martial, and Legion, and Adjutant and Inspector General; a Brigadier General, as commander of the first Cohort; and a Brigadier General, as commander of the second Cohort.

Sec. 4. The Staff of the Lieutenant General shall consist of two principle Aides-de-Camp, with the rank of Colonels of Cavalry, and a guard of twelve Aides-de-Camp, with the rank of Captains of Infantry and a Drill Officer, with the rank of Colonel of Dragoons, who shall likewise be the chief officer of the guard.

Sec. 5. The staff of the Major General shall consist of an adjutant, a Surgeon-in-Chief, a Coronet [Cornet], a Quartermaster, a Paymaster, a commissary, and a Chaplain with the rank of colonels of infantry, a surgeon for each cohort, a Quartermaster Sergeant, Sergeant Major, and Chief Musician, with the rank of captains of Light Infantry; and two Musicians, with the rank of captains of Infantry.

Sec. 6. The staff of each Brigadier General shall consist of one Aide-de-Camp, with the rank of Lieutenant Colonel of Infantry; provided that the said Brigadiers shall have access to the staff of the Major-General when not otherwise in service.

Sec. 7. No officer shall hereafter be elected by the various companies of the Legion, except upon the nomination of the Court-Martial, and it is hereby made the duty of the Court-Martial to nominate at least two candidates for each vacant office, whenever such vacancies occur.

Sec. 8. The Court-Martial shall fill and supply all officers ranking between Captain and Brigadier Generals, by granting brevet commissions to the most worthy company officers of the line, who shall thereafter take rank and command according to the date of their brevets; provided that their original place in the line shall not thereby be vacated.

Sec. 9. The Court-Martial consisting of all the military officers, commissioned or entitled to commissions, within the limits of the city corporation, shall meet at the office of Joseph Smith on Thursday the 4th of February 1841, at 10 o'clock A.M. and then and there, proceed to elect the general officers of the Legion as contemplated in the 3rd section of this ordinance.

Sec. 10. The Court-Martial shall adopt for the Legion, as nearly as may be, and so far as applicable, the discipline, drill, uniform, rules and regulations, of the United States army.

Sec. 11. This ordinance shall take effect, and be in force, from and after its passage.

Passed, February 3rd. A.D. 1841.

JOHN C. BENNETT, Mayor.
JAMES SLOAN, Recorder.

Section 1. Be it ordained by the Court-Martial of the Nauvoo Legion in general court assembled. That all free while male inhabitants, resident in the city of Nauvoo, who are or shall be of the age of 18 and under the age of 45 years, except as may be hereinafter excepted, shall severally and respectively be enrolled in the militia, of the Nauvoo Legion, by the captain or commissioned officer of the company within those bounds such citizen shall reside, within 20 days after he shall be informed of such residence; and also, those who may, from time to time, arrive at the age of 18, who shall reside in the bounds of his company; and shall without delay, notify such person by an officer or non-commissioned officer of the company.

Provided, that it shall be the privilege of any such person, within the aforesaid 20 days, to volunteer into any of the independent companies of the Legion.

Sec. 2. That the staff of the Lieutenant General, shall consist of a Chief Chaplain, four Aides-de-Camp, a drill officers, and secretaries not exceeding two, each to have the rank of Colonels of Cavalry, and a guard of twelve Aides-de-Camp with the rank of Captain. The drill officer likewise to be the chief officer of the guard.

Sec. 3. That the staff of the Major-General, shall consist of an Adjutant-General, to act as Division Inspector, a Quarter Master General, a Chaplain, a Judge Advocate, a Cornet and drill Aides-de-Camp [a Cornet and two Aides-de-Camp], each with the rank of Colonels of Infantry; a Quarter Master Sergeant, a Sergeant Major and a Chief Musician, each with the rank of Major.

Sec. 4. That the staff of the Brigadier General shall consist of one Cohort, or Brigade Inspector, to act as Brigade Major, one Quarter Master, and one Aide-de-Camp. The Aide-de-Camp to perform the duties of Cohort or Brigade Judge Advocate, one Surgeon, one Chaplain, and one Cornet, each with the rank of Major.

Sec. 5. That to each regiment their shall be one Colonel, one Lieutenant Colonel, and one Major, with a regimental staff to be appointed by the Colonel to consist of one Adjutant, who shall act as Regimental Judge Advocate, one Quarter Master and one Pay-Master, each to rank as Captains: one Surgeon, one Sergeant Major, one Quarter Master Sergeant, one drum and one Fife Major, and one Color Bearer.

Sec. 6. That to each company there shall be one Captain, three Lieutenants, one Ensign, five Sergeants, one Pioneer, four Corporals, and not less than two nor more than four appropriate musicians. The Sergeants, Pioneer and Corporals to be appointed by the Captains, respectively, and to hold their appointments by certificate.

Sec. 7. That each Cohort or Brigade, Regiment, Battalion and Company of the same grade when in the field, shall take rank from right to left in the following order: first, fifth, fourth, seventh, third, eighth, sixth, second, according to the rank of the captains.

Sec. 8. That each cohort or brigade shall consist of not less than two regiments, each regiment of two battalions or squadrons, as the case may be, each battalion or squadron of not less than two nor more than four companies; each company shall consist of not less than thirty-two or more than sixty-four rank and file; and no private shall be permitted to leave the company to which he belongs, without the permission of his Captain, unless in case of promotion; and no Captain shall give such permission unless his company shall consist of more than sixty-four, rank and file, and each member over that number, may claim a discharge from his captain by producing evidence that he has attached himself to another company.

Sec. 9. That every officer commissioned by virtue of this act, shall within thirty days after receiving his commission and previous to entering upon the duties of his office, take an oath to support the Constitution of the United States, and of this State, also, an oath of office; an endorsement or certificate of which shall be endorsed on the back of his commission by the person administering the same, and if any person receiving such commission, who was elected by his own consent, shall fail to take the oaths as aforesaid, within the time herein provided and give notice thereof within twenty days thereafter to the proper officer whose duty it shall be to direct such vacancy to be filled; he shall be fined in the sum of ten dollars, by sentence of the appropriate court-martial, and forfeit his office; which shall be filled as in other cases. Provided, that any officer declared duly elected, may received a certificate of any superior officer, which shall entitle him to command, until his commission can be procured, and in all cases the officer giving such certificate, shall administer to such officer the necessary oaths of office. Provided, also, that when it shall be necessary to administer oaths to carry into effect any of the provisions of this act, any judge, justice of the peace, or officer of the legion, duly commissioned and sworn, shall be authorized to administer such oaths.

Sec. 10. That for good cause shown, the Commander in Chief of the legion, may receive the resignation of a Major General, a Major General may accept the resignation of a Brigadier General under his command; a Brigadier General may accept the resignation of a Colonel under his command, and Colonels may accept the resignations of the commissioned officers under their respective commands, and in all cases when a resignation is accepted, the cause of such resignation shall be given in writing by the officer so resigning which shall be endorsed on the back of the commission, or if the commission be not surrendered the letter of resignation shall be preserved by the officer receiving it, and it shall be the duty of all officers authorized to accept resignations as aforesaid, to order elections to fill such vacancies, within twenty days, as may occur by resignation or otherwise, giving at all times sufficient notices of such election, and except in cases of emergency, the order for an election of a Major or Brigadier General shall be given, at least twenty days previous; stating the time and place of holding such election; for the election of any field or company officer, the order for the same shall be given at least ten days previous, stating the time and place of holding such election. It shall be the duty of all officers ordering elections as aforesaid to attend the place of holding such election and organize the board.

Sec. 11. That all returns of elections so held, shall be made to the officer ordering the same, who shall make returns thereof, within thirty days thereafter, to the Adjutant-General of the legion, the names of all officers who may have thus been duly elected.

Sec. 12. That it may be lawful for any field or company officer to be elected, without previous notice, whenever the regiment, battalion or company, as the case may be, have been called out to do military duty according to law, provided returns be made as aforesaid.

Sec. 13. That it shall be the duty of all officers authorized to appoint staff-officers by virtue of this act to accept their resignations as above, and fill all vacancies in their own staff by appointment and make returns thereof to the proper officers as in cases of election.

Sec. 14. That the manner of voting shall be, by the elector addressing the Judges of election in his own proper person, and with an audible voice, to be heard by the Judges and Clerk, name the person he votes for, and the Clerk shall enter the name of the person voting, and his vote accordingly in a poll-book to be provided for that purpose; which poll-book shall be, as near as may be, in the following form, to wit:

A poll-book of an election held at ——, in the county of Hancock, in the ——, of the Nauvoo Legion, of the Illinois Militia, on the ——, day of ——, 18——.

When all the votes shall be given, they shall be examined and counted, the Judges shall cause the clerk to make out a return thereof as near as may be, in the following form, to wit:

At an election held at ______, in the county of Hancock, in the

______ of the Nauvoo Legion, of the Illinois Militia, on the ______ day of ______, 18______, the following named persons received the number of votes annexed to their names, for the following described offices, to wit:

A. R. had votes for &c.
O. D. had votes for &c.
(And in like manner of all other officers,)
Certified by us,

O. P. Judges
Q. R. of
S. T. election.

Attest,
U.V. Clerk

Which return when so made out and certified, shall be transmitted by the Judges to the officer ordering the election, also a poll-book as aforesaid shall be kept by the officer whose duty it shall hereafter be made, to act as clerk of election; and in cases of a contested election, it shall be the duty of the said clerk, to transmit the same to the presiding officer of the court of inquiry in which such contest shall be tried; and the person having the greatest number of votes shall be declared fully elected.

Sec. 15. That all contested elections, shall be tried by a board of officers, to be appointed for that purpose by the officer ordering the same. Provided, that in all cases the numbers composing such board ordering the same. Provided, that in all cases the numbers composing such board of officers as aforesaid, shall be as near as may be, the rank of the officer whose election shall be contested; and shall consist of not less than three nor more than seven members.

Sec. 16. That the officer appointing the board of officers, as aforesaid, shall notify each member thereof in writing, of the time when, and place where such board is to be held; and if any officer when so appointed and notified as aforesaid, shall neglect or refuse to attend at the time and place of holding such board, he shall be liable to be fined as in other cases for neglect of duty, and the decision of all such boards of officers, which may at any time be instituted as aforesaid, shall be final and conclusive.

Sec. 17. That when any election shall be contested, as aforesaid, it shall not be lawful for any officer, whose duty it may be to certify the same, to make returns thereof, until a decision shall be had thereon, as aforesaid, after which the presiding officer of the board shall certify to the officer who may have appointed the same, which of the contending parties are entitled to the office; and such successful party shall then be commissioned as in other cases. Provided, that no exceptions shall be allowed to be taken to the election of any officer, unless the same be done within ten days after such election shall [have] been held.

Sec. 18. That the presiding officer of any board, which may, at any time, be appointed, to pass upon a contested election, as aforesaid, shall have power, at the request of either party, to send for and examine witnesses; and if such board, as aforesaid, without the reasonable excuse, it shall be the duty of the presiding officer as aforesaid, to turn such witness over as a delinquent to the next regular court of inquiry, having proper jurisdiction, who shall thereupon proceed to acquit, or to assess the fine of such witness, as circumstances shall require, in like manner as is prescribed against delinquents for failing to attend general muster, when legally required so to do.

Sec. 19. That all oaths of office, to be taken by the officers of this legion, shall be as near as may be, in the following form, to wit: "I do solemnly swear (or affirm,) that I will support the constitution of the United States, and of this State, and that I will not be engaged in dueling, either directly or indirectly, during my continuance in office; and that I will faithfully discharge the duties of ______, in the ______, of the Nauvoo Legion of Illinois militia, to the best of my skill and understanding, so help me God;" which said oath shall be certified on the back of the commission or certificate (as the case may be,) by the officer administering the same.

Sec. 20. That the Legion shall parade in the following manner to wit: each company in the legion shall hold a company parade on the first Saturday, each battalion a battalion parade on the second Saturday, and each regiment a regimental parade on the third Saturday of May, annually, at such place as the commandants of said companies, battalions, and regiments respectively may direct, by giving at least ten days public notice, by advertising the same in three public places: Provided the parades as aforesaid be in the bounds of the said companies, battalions or regiments; and, provided also, that the Brigadier General of each cohort or brigade may have the power to change the days of the regimental parades to suit his own convenience, as a reviewing officer, and, provided also that the time of such parade shall be not less than one week before the court of assessment and the court of assessment of fines shall be held on the first Saturday in June.

Sec. 21. That there shall also be a company parade on the first Saturday, a cohort or brigade parade on the second Saturday, and a legion parade on the fourth Saturday in September, annually, and in officer drills for said cohort and legion parades shall be on the days previous thereto respectively, and all officers in the city of Nauvoo, or within ten miles thereof shall be required to attend said drills except such officers as reside beyond said limits, who shall be exempted from duty on the day of the cohort officer drill, except commandants of companies and held officers, . . . shall be exempt from duty on the days of the officer drills as aforesaid.

Sec. 22. That companies, battalions, and regiments, shall [be] formed for parade at 10 o'clock, A.M. at which hour the roll shall be called and shall be required to perform not less than four nor more than six hours duty each day, as aforesaid; Provided, however, that on days of cohort and legion parades the commandants thereof may have power to order the time and place of holding the parades, as aforesaid, as they may deem proper.

Sec. 23. That there shall be a legion or division court of inquiry and assessment of fines, to be composed of the Major General as president, the Brigadier Generals, and drill officer, as members; and the Adjutant General as Secretary. It shall be the duty of said court to assess fines on all delinquent officers, non-commissioned officers on all officer drill parades, and also all delinquent general officers, or any of their staff, on all cohorts of legion parades, in conformity to the provisions of this act.

Sec. 24. That there shall be a regimental court of inquiry and assessment of fines, in each regiment, to be composed of the Colonel as president, the Lieutenant, Colonel, Major, and Captains as members, and the Adjutant as Secretary. It shall be the duty of said court to assess fines on all delinquent officers, noncommissioned officers, musicians and privates belonging to such regiment, in conformity to the provisions of this act.

Sec. 25. That it shall likewise be the duty of each court of assessment to fine any member of said court who does not attend the same according to the provision of this act.

Sec. 26. That each court of assessment shall meet at 10 o'clock, A.M. and continue in session from time to time, by adjournment, until all the business shall be finished, at such places as the presidents respectively may appoint on the regimental and legion parades, and it shall be the duty of all delinquents so returned, to appear without further notice at said court; to make a lawful excuse if any they have; and should any person feel themselves aggrieved by the decision of said court, they may appeal to the president of the board who shall have to remit the fine [who shall have power &c.].

Sec. 27. That it shall not be lawful for any officer to remit fines unless upon the testimony of the person applying upon oath, or other satisfactory evidence, it shall appear that he was out of the county on the day on which he was required to do duty, or in case of sickness with himself or family; or that he was detained by the requirements of the civil law, or that he was not subject to do duty in the company, staff, or corps, in which he was returned as a delinquent, or that he did duty in the company, staff, or corps, in which he was returned as a delinquent, or that he did duty in the company to which he belongs according to law. And it shall be the duty of all officers authorized to remit fines aforesaid, to cause the secretary of the board of assessment to keep record of the same in a book kept for that purpose, in which shall be recorded the testimony given by or in behalf of the person so applying, and any officer who shall wilfully remit any fine except as above provided, shall be cashiered by the decision of a court martial detailed by the officers having proper jurisdiction.

Sec. 28. That the presiding officers [officer] of each board shall cause the Secretary of the same, to keep a record of the proceedings of the court, in a book kept for that purpose and make out therefrom a certified list of the names of the persons fined with the fine or fines annexed to each name, upon which list it shall be the duty of the presiding officers to issue, and furnish to the collector, the following warrant within thirty days from the court of assessment, which shall be his authority for collecting and paying over the same, to wit:

STATE OF ILLINOIS ss. To A. B. Collector for the Nauvoo Legion, Hancock County.

Greetings:

In the name of the people of the State of Illinois, you are hereby required and commanded to collect from each person named in the foregoing list, the several sums of money set opposite their names, and within ninety days after receiving this warrant, to pay over to the Paymaster of the Legion (or Regiment as the case may be,) the amount so collected, and take his receipt for the same, and if any one or more of said persons shall neglect or refuse to pay the same, you are hereby further commanded to levy on the personal goods and chattels of each delinquent and make sale thereof according to the law regulating the collection of debts of a similar amount by execution in this State. Given under my hand, this ______ day of ______, 18______

C. D. Maj. Gen. or Col.
(as the case may be,) and president of the court

And the collector, or any person authorized to collect fines under the provisions of this act, who shall neglect or refuse to pay over the amount so collected, as required by the foregoing warrant, after deducting twenty per cent which shall be his fees for collection. It shall be the duty of the Paymaster to whom the returns were to be made, to proceed against such collector, as aforesaid, or his securities, before any Justice of the Peace of said county or any court having proper jurisdiction; and the said collector or his securities shall only be exonerated from the payment of the amount of such fines, by showing to the satisfaction of said Justice or court, as aforesaid, that there was no property whereon to levy, of which such fine or fines could be made, or that the fine or fines had been remitted by the president of the court issuing the same in conformity to the provisions of this act.

Sec. 29. That the following forfeitures and penalties shall be incurred for delinquents on cohort or legion parade days, to wit: the Lieutenant and Major General, twenty dollars; Brevet Major Generals and Brigadier Generals, fifteen dollars; Brevet Brigadier Generals and Colonels and Majors or any officer holding the rank thereof, eight dollars; Captains or any officer holding the rank thereof, five dollars; Lieutenants and Ensigns or any officer holding the rank thereof, three dollars; Non-Commissioned officers Musicians and privates, two dollars; and for delinquencies at officer drills, or any regimental, battalion or company parade or for neglect of any orders of a superior officer, they shall be fined in proportion to rank, as recited in the foregoing part of this section, in one half the sums aforesaid.

Sec. 30. That fathers shall be bound for the payment of fines incurred by their sons under twenty-one years of age, guardians for the payment of fines incurred by their wards; and masters for the payment of fines incurred by their apprentices, to be charged and collected accordingly.

Sec. 31. That on complaint of a commissioned officer, in writing, to a superior officer, charging any officer, under the command of such superior, with neglect of any of the duties enjoined on them by this act, of disobedience of orders, or of being guilty of any conduct unbecoming an officer or gentleman, such superior officer shall, if he thinks the complaint sufficient cause for an arrest, cause the officer against whom such complaint is made, to be arrested by notifying such officer in writing, that he is suspended from command until acquitted from such arrest, stating at the same time, the grounds of such arrest, and the time and place of trial; and at the same time notify the officer next in command, that in consequence of such arrest, he is required to do the duties which were enjoined on the officer so arrested. Provided, that when any superior officer shall consider the charges made against any officer of insufficient consequence to cause his arrest, he shall, on application of the officer preferring the charges, give his reasons in writing for his refusal to cause the arrest, which reasons the complaining officer may send, together with the charges, to the next common superior, who may, if he thinks correct, order the arrest and trial of such officers.

Sec. 32. That in all cases when an officer is arrested, the officer who orders the arrest shall issue any summons (subpoenas,) that may be applied for by either of the parties, or which he may think necessary to compel the attendance of witnesses; and the party so applying, or any person whom the officer granting the summons (subpoenas,) may appoint, may serve the same, and endorse the time of such service thereon, which shall be at least three days previous to the sitting of the court martial, except in cases of emergency, and shall make a return thereof to the president of said court the first day thereof, who shall, if necessary, administer an oath or affirmation to the person returning the summons (subpoena,) relative to the service thereof; and any person who neglects or refuses to attend a court martial, after being summoned, (subpoenaed,) shall be fined in a sum not exceeding fifty dollars, which fine shall be collected and applied as other fines under the provisions of this act; and any court martial appointed under the provisions of this act, shall have power to issue compulsory process to compel the attendance of witnesses who neglect or refuse to attend after being duly summoned.

Sec. 33. That the Major General shall be tried by courts [court] martial appointed by the Lieutenant General, where a Major General shall preside. Brigadier Generals shall be tried by courts martial appointed by the Major General, where a Brigadier General shall preside. Colonels, Lieutenant Colonels, Majors and Captains, shall be tried by courts martial, appointed by the Brigadier General, where a Colonel shall preside; and subalterns shall be tried by courts martial appointed by a Colonel, where a Lieutenant Colonel or a Major shall preside; and all commissioned staff officers shall be tried by courts martial detailed by their respective superior officers as in other cases under the provisions of this act. Each courts martial shall consist of not less than five nor more than thirteen members, and to be of rank as near as can conveniently be had, of the officer tried; all court martials so ordered, shall have power to punish any officer for neglect of duty, disobedience of orders, contempt, or any conduct unbecoming an officer or a gentleman, by suspension, fining, cashiering and disqualification to hold any office in the Nauvoo Legion, and in all cases where fines may be assessed against any person by the sentence of such court martial, they shall be collected by warrant from the president as in cases of delinquents by the provisions of this act.

Sec. 34. That when any court martial is met agreeably to the provisions of this act, the president shall administer the following oath or affirmation to the Judge Advocate: "You do solemnly swear (or affirm,) that you will not disclose or discover the vote of any particular member of this court martial, unless required to give evidence thereof as a witness by a court of justice, nor divulge the sentence of the court to any but the proper authority, until it shall be disclosed by the same;" and the Judge Advocate, or person acting as such, shall administer the following oath to each member of such court martial: "You do solemnly swear, (or affirm,) that you will truly determine, according to evidence the matter now before you, between the United States, the State of Illinois, or the Nauvoo Legion (as the case may be,) and A. B. (the person to be tried,) and that you will truly administer justice, according to law, without partiality, favor or affection, according to your conscience and the best of your understanding, and the customs of war in like cases, and that you will not divulge the sentence of the court, until it shall be published by the proper authority; neither will you discover the vote or opinion of any member of the court, unless required to give evidence thereof in a court of justice." The Judge Advocate shall prosecute in the name of the United States, the State of Illinois, or the Nauvoo Legion, (as the case may be,) but shall so far consider himself council for the person accused as to object to any leading question being put to them or any witness which might tend to eliminate himself; he shall also see that right and justice shall be done to the accused. All persons giving evidence before a court martial are to be examined on oath, in the following manner: "You do swear (or affirm,) that the evidence that you give, shall be the truth, the whole truth, and nothing but the truth." The court shall have power to punish its members, or any persons attending the same, or disorderly conduct, as in other cases; and in giving their votes on any subject, to begin with the lowest in rank: Provided, that the party tried by such court martial shall be entitled to a copy of the sentence, and the proceedings of the court in his case, after the decision and sentence, upon demand thereof, whether such sentence be approved or not: Provided, also, that all sentences of any such court martial shall be submitted to the officer ordering the same, who shall have power to approve or disapprove of the sentence of any such court; also to pardon or mitigate the sentence.

Sec. 35. That the Adjutant General or Division Inspector, be allowed the sum of five dollars for each regiment he shall actually inspect, by order of the Major General of the Legion, on the certificate of the Major General: the Cohort or Brigade Major the sum of ten dollars, annually for each battalion in the cohort or brigade to which he belongs on the certificate of the Brigadier General to be paid out of the State treasury.

Sec. 36. That it shall be the duty of every officer belonging to the Legion, who may have occasion to leave the bounds of the Legion for more than one month, at any time to notify the officer next in command in writing on the subject, ordering him that in consequence of his absence, he is required to do the duties which were enjoined on himself until he shall return; also, the post of any staff officer merely acting by appointment and not commissioned, be considered vacated in consequence of neglect of duty, and another may be appointed to fill his post.

Sec. 37. That each Regimental or Battalion Adjutant, shall receive annually, from the treasury of the legion, two dollars for each company in their respective regiments or battalion, on condition of the faithful performance of their duty, on the certificate of their Colonel or Major, and that the record books of the Adjutant shall be open to the inspection of their respective field and General officers.

Sec. 38. That the Adjutant General or Division Inspector shall be allowed thirty dollars, annually in consideration of the faithful performance of his duty on the certificate of the Major General.

Sec. 39. That the officers composing the courts of inquiry and assessment of fines, shall be allowed for their services one dollar and fifty cents each, per day, to be certified by the presiding officer of the board.

Sec. 40. That all disbursements, made pursuant to this act, shall be paid out of any money in the treasury not otherwise appropriated.

Sec. 41. That the Major General may issue bills of credit to the amount of five hundred dollars, to be signed by himself or the Lieutenant General or both, at their discretion, and countersigned by the Paymaster General of the legion, and redeemable out of any money in the treasury not otherwise appropriated.

Sec. 42. That each collector of fines be required to give bonds with approved security to the Paymaster of the legion or regiment, as the case may be, to twice the amount of the fines which are put into their hands for collection, before entering upon the duties of their office.

Sec. 43. That there shall be a general court martial of the Nauvoo Legion held on the third Saturday in October, annually, to continue in session by adjournment, until all business before it shall be finished, at such time and place as the Lieutenant and Major Generals, shall appoint.

Sec. 44. That the Lieutenant and Major Generals, may have power to call a special session of the general court martial of the Nauvoo Legion, and also, to order out the legion at any time when they may deem proper; and for non-attendance on such order, delinquents shall be fined as in other cases of general parade.

Sec. 45. That it shall be the duty of the commandants of the several parades as above provided, to give at least ten days notice thereof by advertisement in three public places, except in cases of a special call.

Sec. 46. That any collector of fines may apply to any Alderman or Justice of the Peace for garnishee, in any case where he may see proper, where he may not be able to find property or levy on, according to the law regulating the collection of debts by garnishee in this state.

Sec. 47. That it shall be the duty of the Lieutenant General, to review the legion at least once every year.

Sec. 48. That it shall be the duty of the Major General to take command on all legion parades, and all legion officer drills, also to act as reviewing officer at cohort parades at least once each year, to cause the Adjutant General or Division Inspector to record all general orders, also all reports and rank rolls received, annually, from the several cohorts or Brigades, and when required by the Commander in Chief, of the State to make out legion or division returns and rank-rolls to be forwarded to the Adjutant General of the State; also, to issue enlisting orders for the raising of new companies, at his discretion; to cause the Adjutant General of the legion to apply for and receive commissions, at least every six months; and do and perform all other duties that in anywise appertain to the office of Major General.

Sec. 49. That it shall be the duty of the Brigadier Generals, to review the several regiments and odd battalions composing their respective cohorts or brigades, annually, at the regimental musters, and to cause their respective brigade Majors to record all reports received annually from the several regiments and odd battalions composing their commands and make out a consolidated cohort or brigade return therefrom and forward one to the Major General of the legion or division and one to the Adjutant General of the State on or before the first day of December, annually, and to do and perform all other duties which may be necessary to the perfection of discipline, or which may in anywise appertain to the office of Brigadier General.

Sec. 50. That it shall be the duty of the Colonels commanding regiments and Majors commanding odd battalions, to make from the several officers commanding battalions or companies, a complete return of their respective commands, on the day of the regimental parades, annually, to cause their Adjutants to record all returns so received, also all orders received or issued by themselves, and to make out a Regimental return and rank-roll and forward it to the Brigadier General of their respective cohorts or brigades by the first day of October, annually, also to be responsible for the good order of their respective regiments or odd battalions and cause to be executed the laws and orders applicable to their commands, and to do and perform all other duties belonging to their respective offices.

Sec. 51. That it shall be the duty of the Lieutenant Colonel and

Major commanding battalions, to assume the command at all musters of their respective battalions, to require of the officers commanding companies, annual returns on the day of the battalion parades, and on the day of the regimental muster, deliver said returns to their respective Colonels, and do and perform all other duties which may in anywise appertain to their office.

Sec. 52. That it shall be the duty of Captains or commandants of companies to take command of their respective companies at all company, battalion, regimental, cohort, brigade, and legion, or division parades at the hour specified by the provisions of this act; and to cause the roll of their respective companies to be called under their immediate inspection, noting all delinquents at any such muster upon the company roll or report of delinquents, made out by them for that purpose, which roll or list shall be returned by them to the appropriate court of assessment of fines also, to read or cause to be read, so much of the laws of the legion as relates to the duties of companies, at the head of their respective companies at every company parade, and to do and perform all other duties appertaining to the office of Captain.

Sec. 53. That in all cases of the death, removal, absence, or resignation of any superior officer, it shall be the duty of the next officer in rank attached to the same corps to assume the command and perform all the duties that would have devolved on any such commanding officer were he present, and to exercise the same until such superior shall return, or the vacancy be filled, agreeably to the provisions of this act, in like manner if it should happen at any time that there is no commissioned officer belonging to any company, it shall be the duty of the senior non-commissioned officer of such company to assume the command, under the same penalties that any superior officer of a company would be were he present, for any neglect of duty.

Sec. 54. That it shall be the duty of the drill-officer to take command of the Lieutenant General's guard at all times when they are called out, and note and return all delinquents under his command according to the provisions of this act.

Sec. 55. That it shall be the duty of the Adjutant General or Division Inspector to distribute all orders from the Major General of the legion or Adjutant General of the State; attend all reviews with the Major General, to act as drill-officer at all legion or division officer drills, under the Major General; to record all orders received or issued by the Major General, all returns and rank-rolls received, annually, from the cohorts or brigades also to make out division returns when required by the Major General's staff under his inspection at all legion parades, and perform such other duties as may in anywise appertain to his office.

Sec. 56. That it shall be the duty of the Quarter Master General of the legion to apply for and receive all arms that are or may become due to the legion, from the State; to deposit all arms so received, or which may have heretofore been received and not otherwise disposed of, in some safe place, also to employ means to preserve all such arms from damage, as in his opinion may, from time to time become necessary, to furnish when required so to do by his superior officer, a full exhibit of all arms in his possession, belonging to the State, also to do and perform all other duties that may in anywise appertain to the office of Quarter Master General.

Sec. 57. That it shall be the duty of the Paymaster General of the legion, within twenty days from the passage of this act, to give bonds, with sufficient security, to the amount of five thousand dollars to the general court[s] martial of the Nauvoo legion, for the due performance of his duty. It shall also be his duty, to receive all monies belonging to the legion, according to the provisions of this act, which shall only be paid out upon the certificate of the Major General, or by an act of the general courts [court] martial, except as provided above, to attend all general court martial, and lay before it an account[s] of the finances of the legion, stating particularly all monies received and paid out, with his several proceedings relative to the duties of his office, and all account so exhibited and settled by the court martial, shall be entered by the secretary on the record book of the court martial, and do and perform such other duties as may in anywise appertain to his office.

Sec. 58. That it shall be the duty of the Brigade Major, to attend all regimental musters composing their respective cohorts or brigades, to inspect the arms and equipments of all officers and privates at every such muster, also, to record all orders received or issued by the Brigadier General, also, all returns and rank-rolls received, annually, from the several regiments composing their respective cohorts or brigades in a general order-book kept for that purpose, to consolidate the annual returns and rank-rolls received from the several officers commanding regiments in their cohorts or brigade, into a brigade return agreeably to the requirements of the State law, and on or before the first day of December, annually, transmit one copy to the Major General of the legion, and one to the Adjutant General of the State, also attend all elections ordered by the Brigadier General as clerk of the same, also to form their respective cohorts or brigades and call the roll of the Brigadier General's staff under his inspection, at all cohort and legion parades; also to act as drill officer at all cohort or brigade officer drills, under the Brigadier General, to distribute all general orders, and do and perform all duties as may in anywise be necessary for the perfection of discipline, and all other duties that appertain to his office.

Sec. 59. That it shall be the duty of the Quarter Master of each cohort to apply for and receive all arms from the Quarter Master General of the legion that are or may become due to their respective cohorts or brigades, from the Quarter Master General of the legion, and give bonds for the same to the Quarter Master General of the legion, and to do and perform all other duties that in anywise appertain to his office.

Sec. 60. That it shall be the duty of the Adjutants of regiments, to deliver all regimental orders, also to record all orders received or issued by their respective commanding officers, also, all annual returns received by them and the date of each officer's commission belonging to their regiment, noting all resignations, removals, or deaths of any officer, in an order-book kept for that purpose, also, to make out, under the direction of the commanding officer, regimental returns and rank-rolls, also, to attend all elections, ordered by their respective commanders, as Clerk of the same, to form the regiment at all regimental, cohort and legion parades, and immediately thereafter to inform the commanding officer that the parade is ready, also, to call the roll of the field and Staff officers at all such parades, under the inspection of the commanding officer, and note all delinquents, and to do and perform such other duties as may be required of them by their superior officer.

Sec. 61. That it shall be the duty of the Quarter Master of each regiment to apply for and receive all arms from the Quarter Master of their respective cohorts, or brigades, that are, or may become due to their respective companies, and to give bonds for the same, to the Quarter Master of their respective companies, and to give bonds for the same, to the Quarter Master of their respective cohorts or brigades, and to do and perform all other duties that in anywise appertain to his office.

Sec. 62. That it shall be the duty of the Paymaster of each regiment before entering upon the duties of his office to give bonds to the Paymaster General of the legion, to the amount of two hundred dollars, with approved security, for the due performance of his duty, also, to receive all monies, collected in their respective regiments, from the person authorized to collect fines, and give his receipt for the same, and pay over the same to the Paymaster-General of the legion, except as otherwise provided, within ten days after the receipt thereof and take his receipt for the same, and do and perform all such other duties as in anywise appertain to his office.

Sec. 63. That it shall be the duty of the Sergeant Major to assist the Adjutant in forming the regiment, at all parades; also, to assist him in delivering all orders to the regiment, and do and perform such other duties as he may be required by his superior officer, or that may belong to the station of Sergeant-Major.

Sec. 64. That it shall be the duty of regimental Surgeons, to grant certificates to persons for inability to do military duty according to law.

Sec. 65. That all officers belonging to the general or regimental staff, whose duties are not defined particularly by this act, shall attend all musters held by their respective commanding officer to obey all orders from them or any superior officer, and do and perform such other duties as may in anywise appertain or belong to their respective stations.

Sec. 66. That any non-commissioned officer, musician, or private, who shall disobey orders, or be guilty of any kind of insubordination on parade, shall be returned in the list of delinquents, and fined not exceeding five dollars by the proper court of assessments.

Sec. 67. That any commissioned or non-commissioned officer or private who shall appear on parade with loaded fire-arms, or loading the same on the field without orders from their respective commanding officers, shall be returned as above and fined in any sum not exceeding twenty dollars, at the discretion of the proper court of assessment.

Sec. 68. That any commissioned or non-commissioned officer or private, who shall appear on parade without his proper arms and accoutrements, shall be fined in the sum of fifty cents; Provided, that no one shall be compelled to appear on parade with arms unless he actually has them, and that the oath or affirmation of the person shall be evidence on the case, and from and after the first day of September next, if any commissioned, non-commissioned officer or private, shall appear on parade without some instrument of war and necessary accoutrements, he shall be fined in the sum of one dollar by the proper court of assessment.

Sec. 69. That the band shall consist of two divisions, the martial portion, to be called the first division, and the brass portion, the second division, and to be commanded by the Chief Musician, whose duty it shall be to dispose of said band among the legion, appropriating a proper portion of music to each company and regiment beginning at the oldest company and regiment first; and further that said Chief Musician be empowered to increase said band to a sufficient number to meet all demands of the legion: Provided, that Colonels and Captains may provide their own music by attaching it to said band.

Sec. 70. That there shall be added to the staff of the Brigadier General of the first cohort, one musician, and to the staff of the Brigadier General of the second cohort, two musicians to rank as Captains.

Sec. 71. That each company shall be supplied with not less than two nor more than four appropriate musical instruments, and each regiment in the first cohort a trumpet, and each regiment in the second cohort with a bass drum.

Sec. 72. That the commander of each regiment, be authorized to retain sufficient means in his own hands to defray the necessary expenses of the same and buy the prescribed instruments for his regiment.

Sec. 73. That any officer, authorized to remit fines, shall be allowed the sum of twenty-five cents for each fine remitted, to be paid by the person applying.

Sec. 74. That no property which has been levied on by any collector for fines, shall be released until all costs arising thereon shall have been paid, in consequence of the person having obtained a remission of his fine, after said levy.

Sec. 75. That the following property shall be exempt from execution for fines due the legion, to wit: fifteen dollars worth of household furniture, necessary cooking utensils, bed and necessary bedding for each two in [a] family, and bedsteads, necessary wearing apparel for the family, one cow and calf, and three months provisions; Provided that the wearing appearel of the delinquent shall not be exempt.

Sec. 76. That all laws and parts of laws heretofore passed and not embraced in this act, be, and they are, hereby repealed.

Sec. 77. This act to take effect and be in force from and after its publication.

WILSON LAW,
President of the Court.
HOSEA STOUT, *Secretary.*

Approved, February 14, 1844.

JOSEPH SMITH,
Lieut. General, Nauvoo Legion.

Resolutions

Passed by the General Court Martial of the Nauvoo Legion

Resolved, That an Arsenal be built in the city of Nauvoo, to be located in any part of the city, where the Lieutenant and Major Generals may direct, who are also authorized to make, or caused to be made a draft of the same, and also to purchase any piece of ground for the aforesaid purpose, which they may deem proper.

Resolved, That any Constable or Collector of fines, be, and is hereby authorized, if he cannot obtain money, to take property in payment of fines, at a fair valuation, at his own discretion, and make returns thereof to the proper officer as in other cases. Passed June 10, 1843.

Resolved, That the Major and Lieutenant Generals, be, and are hereby authorized to regulate the building of the Arsenal, and make such other improvements on the ground on which it is to be built, as they may deem necessary, with full power to carry into effect any order or regulation which they may deem proper for the peace and benefit of the legion and the security of the public arms. Passed October 21, 1843.

Resolved, That a committee of seven, be and are hereby appointed, whose duty it shall be to meet at such times as may be appointed, and deliberate upon all matters, relative to the benefit, government, regulation and good order of the legion, and make report thereof to the general court martial from time to time, and said committee to be governed by their own by-laws, and that said committee be allowed each one dollar and fifty cents for each day's services; the committee to be chosen annually by the general court martial. Passed January 13, 1844.

Rank Roll of the Nauvoo Legion of the Illinois Militia, for the Year 1843

Names of Officers.	Rank of Officers.	Staff of Line.	Date of Commissions.	Place of Residence.	Remarks.
	Legion. Cohort. Regiment. Battalion. Company.				
Joseph Smith,	Lieut. General	N. L. line.	March 4, 1841.	Nauvoo.	
Wilson Law,	Maj. General.	N. L. line.	July 8, 1842.	"	Elected in place of J. C. Bennet, Cashiered.
Charles C. Rich,	Brig. General.	2 " line.	July 8, 1842.	"	Elected in place of D. C. Smith, deceased.
George Coulston,	Colonel.	2 1 " line.	July 8, 1843.	La Harpe, Hancock Co.	
John Parker,	Lieut. Colonel.	1 1 1 " line.	July 8, 1843.	Nauvoo.	
Jesse Harmon,	Major.	2 4 2 " line.	July 8, 1843.	"	
Lewis Robins,	Captain.	2 1 1 2 " line.	Aug. 4, 1842.	"	Elected in place of John Pack, Promoted.
Geo. W. Crouse,	Adjutant.	5 2 " line.	July 28, 1843.	"	
William Law,	Aid to Lt. Gen.	N. L. " line.	July 28, 1843.	"	
John G. Loose,	1st. Lieutenant.	2 1 4 2 " line.	July 28, 1843.	"	
R. D. Foster,	Sur.-in-Chief.	N. L. " line.	Sept. 4, 1841.	"	

Articles of War

An Act for Establishing Rules and Articles for the Government of the Armies of the United States

Sec. 1. *Be it enacted by the Senate and House of Representatives of the United States of America, in Congress assembled,* That from and after the passing of this act, the following shall be the rules and articles by which the armies of the United States shall be governed;

Art. 1. Every officer now in the army of the United States, shall, in six months from the passing of this act, and every officer who shall hereafter be appointed, shall, before he enters on the duties of his office, subscribe these rules and regulations.

Art. 2. It is earnestly recommended to all officers and soldiers diligently to attend divine service; and all officers who shall behave indecently, or irreverently, at any place of divine worship, shall, if commissioned officers, be brought before a general court martial, there to be publicly and severely reprimanded by the president; if non-commissioned officers or soldier, every person so offending, shall, for his first offence, forfeit *one sixth of a dollar,* so deducted out of his next pay; for the second offence, he shall not only forfeit a like sum, but be confined twenty-four hours; and for every like offence shall suffer and pay in like manner; which money, so forfeited, shall be applied by the captain or senior officer of the troop or company, to the use of the sick soldiers of the company or troop to which the offender belongs.

Art. 3. Any non-commissioned officer or soldier who shall use any profane oath or execration, shall incur the penalties expressed in the foregoing article; and a commissioned officer shall forfeit and pay for each and every such offence, one dollar, to be applied as in the preceding article.

Art. 4. Every chaplain commissioned in the army or armies of the United States, who shall absent himself from the duties assigned him (except in cases of sickness or leave of absence,) shall, on conviction thereof before a court martial, be fined not exceeding one month's pay, besides the loss of his pay during his absence; or be discharged, as the said court martial shall judge proper.

Art. 5. Any officer or soldier who shall use contemptuous or disrespectful words against the President of the United States, against the Vice-President thereof, against the Congress of the United States, or against the chief magistrate or legislature of any of the

United States in which he may be quartered, if a commissioned officer, shall be cashiered, or otherwise punished, as a court martial shall direct; if a non-commissioned officer or soldier, he shall suffer such punishment as shall be inflicted on him by the sentence of a court martial.

Art. 6. Any officer or soldier who shall behave himself with contempt or disrespect towards his commanding officer, shall be punished according to the nature of the offence, by the judgement of a court martial.

Art. 7. Any officer or soldier who shall begin, excite, cause or join in any mutiny or sedition in any troop or company in the service of the United States, or in any party, post detachment, or guard, shall suffer death, or such other punishment as by a court martial shall be inflicted.

Art. 8. Any officer, non-commissioned officer, or soldier, who, being present at any mutiny or sedition, who does not use his utmost endeavor to suppress the same, or coming to the knowledge of any intended mutiny, does not, without delay, give information thereof to his commanding officer, shall be punished by the sentence of a court martial with death or otherwise, according to the nature of his offence.

Art. 9. Any officer or soldier who shall strike his superior officer, or draw or lift up any weapon, or offer any violence against him, being in the execution of his office, on any pretense whatsoever, or shall disobey any lawful command of his superior officer, shall suffer death, or such other punishment, as shall, according to the nature of his offence, be inflicted upon him by the sentence of a court martial.

Art. 10. Every non-commissioned officer or soldier, who shall enlist himself in the service of the United States, shall, at the time of his so enlisting, or within six days afterwards, have the articles for the government of the armies of the United States, read to him, and shall, by the officer, who enlisted him, or by the commanding officer of the troop or company into which he was enlisted, be taken before the next justice of the peace, or chief magistrate of any city or town corporate, not being an officer of the army, or, where recourse cannot be had to the civil magistrate, before the judge advocate and in his presence, shall take the following oath or affirmation: "I, A. B., do solemnly swear, or affirm (as the case may be) that I will bear true allegiance to the United States of America, and that I will serve them honestly and faithfully against all their enemies, or opposers, whatsoever; and observe and obey the orders of the President of the United States, and the orders of the officers appointed over me, according to the rules and articles for the government of the armies of the United States." Which justice; magistrate, or judge advocate, is to give the officer a certificate, signifying that the man enlisted, did take the said oath or affirmation.

Art. 11. After a non-commissioned officer or soldier shall have been duly enlisted and sworn, he shall not be dismissed from the service without a discharge in writing; and no discharge granted to him shall be sufficient, which is not signed by a field officer of the regiment to which he belongs, or commanding officer, where no field officer of the regiment is present; and no discharge shall be given to a non-commissioned officer or soldier, before his term of service has expired, but by order of the President, the Secretary of War, the commanding officer of a department, or the sentence of a general court martial; nor shall a commissioned officer be discharged the service, but by order of the President of the United States or by sentence of a general court martial.

Art. 12. Every colonel, or other officer commanding a regiment, troop, or company, and actually quartered with it, may give furloughs to non-commissioned officers or soldiers, in such numbers, and for so long a time as he shall judge to be most consistent with the good of the service; and the captain or other inferior officer commanding a troop or company, or in any garrison, fort or barrack, of the United States, (his field officer being absent) may give furlongs to non-commissioned officers or soldiers, for a time not exceeding twenty days in six months, but not to more than two persons to be absent at the same time, excepting some extraordinary occasion should require it.

Art. 13. At every muster, the commanding officer of each regiment, troop, or company, there present, shall give to the commissary of musters, or other officer who musters the said regiment, troop, or company, certificates signed by himself, signifying how long such officers shall not appear at the said muster, have been absent, and the reason of their absence. In like manner, the commanding officer of every troop, or company, shall give certificates, signifying the reasons of the absence of the non-commissioned officers and private soldiers, which reasons, and times of absence, shall be inserted in the muster-rolls opposite the name of the respective absent officers and soldiers.

The certificates shall, together with the muster-rolls be remitted by the commissary of musters, or other officer mustering, to the department of war, as speedily as the distance of the place will admit.

Art. 14. Every officer who shall be convicted, before a general court martial, of having signed a false certificate, relating to the absence of either officer or private soldier or relative to his or their pay, shall be cashiered.

Art. 15. Every officer who shall knowingly make a false muster of man or horse, and every officer or commissary of musters, who shall willingly sign, direct, or allow the signing of muster rolls, wherein such false muster is contained, shall, upon proof, made thereof by two witnesses, before a general court martial, be cashiered, and shall be thereby utterly disabled to have or hold any office or employment in the service of the United States.

Art. 16. Any commissary of musters or other officer, who shall be convicted of having taken money or other thing, by way of gratification, on the mustering any regiment, troop, or company, or on signing the muster-rolls, shall be displaced from his office, and shall be thereby utterly disabled to have or hold any office or employment in the service of the United States.

Art. 17. Any officer who shall presume to muster a person as a soldier who is not a soldier, shall be deemed guilty of having made a false muster, and shall suffer accordingly.

Art. 18. Every officer who shall knowingly make a false return to the department of war, or to any of his superior officers, authorized to call for such returns, of the state of the regiment, troop or company, or garrison, under his command, or of the arms, ammunition, clothing, or other stores thereunto belonging, shall, on conviction thereof, before a court martial, be cashiered.

Art. 19. The commanding officer of every regiment, troop, or independent company, or garrison, of the United States, shall, in the beginning of every month, remit, through the proper channels, to the department of war an exact return of the regiment, troop, independent company, or garrison under his command, specifying the names of officers then absent from their posts, with the reasons for, and the time of their absence. And any officer who shall be convicted of having through neglect or design, omitted sending such returns, shall be punished according to the nature of his crime, by the judgment of a general court martial.

Art. 20. All officers and soldiers who have received pay, or have been duly enlisted in the service of the United States, and shall be convicted of having deserted the same, shall suffer death, or such other punishment as by sentence of a court martial shall be inflicted.

Art. 21. Any non-commissioned officer or soldier, who shall, without leave from his commanding officer, absent himself from his troop, company, or detachment, shall, upon being convicted thereof, be punished according to the nature of his offence, at the discretion of a court martial.

Art. 22. No non-commissioned officer or soldier, shall enlist himself in any other regiment, troop, or company, without a regular discharge from the regiment, troop, or company in which he last served, on the penalty of being reputed a deserter, and suffering accordingly. And in case any officer shall knowingly receive and entertain such non-commissioned officer or soldier, or shall not, after his being discovered to be a deserter, immediately confine him, and give notice thereof to the corps in which he last served, the said officer shall, by a court martial, be cashiered.

Art. 23. Any officer or soldier who shall be convicted of having advised or persuaded any other officer or soldier to desert the service of the United States, shall suffer death, or such other punishment as shall be inflicted upon him by the sentence of a court martial.

Art. 24. No officer or soldier shall use any reproachful or provoking speeches or gestures to another, upon pain, if an officer, of being put in arrest; if a soldier, confined, and of asking pardon of the party offended in the presence of his commanding officer.

Art. 25. No officer or soldier shall send a challenge to another officer or soldier, to fight a duel, or accept a challenge, if sent, upon pain, if a commissioned officer, of being cashiered; if a non-commissioned officer or soldier of suffering corporeal punishment, at the discretion of a court martial.

Art. 26. If any commissioned or non-commissioned officer commanding a guard, shall knowingly or willingly suffer any person whatsoever, to go forth to fight a duel, he shall be punished as a challenger; and all seconds, promoters, and carriers of challenges, in order to duels, shall be deemed principals, and punished accordingly. And it shall be the duty of every officer commanding an army, regiment, company, post, or detachment, who is knowing to a challenge being given, or accepted by any officer, non-commissioned officer, of soldier, under his command, or has reason to believe the same to be the case, immediately to arrest and bring to trial such offenders.

Art. 27. All officers, of what condition soever, have power to part and quell all quarrels, frays, and disorders, though the persons concerned should belong to another regiment, troop, or company; and either to order officers into arrest, or non-commissioned officers or soldiers into confinement, until their proper superior officers shall be acquainted therewith; and whosoever shall refuse to obey such officer, (though of an inferior rank,) or shall draw his sword upon him, shall be punished at the discretion of a general court martial.

Art. 28. Any officer or soldier who shall upbraid another for refusing a challenge, shall himself be punished as a challenger: and all officers and soldiers are hereby discharged from any disgrace or opinion of disadvantage which might arise from their having refused to accept of challenges, as they will only have acted in obedience to the laws, and done their duty as good soldiers, who subject themselves to discipline.

Art. 29. No settler shall be permitted to sell any kind of liquors or victuals, or to keep their houses or shops open for the entertainment of soldiers, after nine at night, or before the beating of the revillers, or upon Sundays, during divine service or sermon, on the penalty of being dismissed from all future settling.

Art. 30. All officers commanding in the field, forts, barracks, or garrisons of the United States, are hereby required to see that the persons permitted to settle, shall supply the soldiers with good and wholesome provisions, or other articles, at a reasonable price, as they shall be answerable for their neglect.

Art. 31. No officer commanding in any of the garrisons, forts, or barracks of the United States, shall exact exorbitant prices for houses or stalls, let out to settlers, or connive at the like exactions in others; nor by his own authority, and for his private advantage, lay any duty or imposition upon, or be interested in, the sale of any victuals, liquors, or other necessaries of life, brought into the garrison, fort, or barracks; for the use of the soldiers, on the penalty of being discharged from the service.

Art. 32. Every officer commanding in quarters, garrisons, or on the march, shall keep good order, and, to the utmost of his power, redress all abuses or disorders, which may be committed by any officer or soldier under his command; if, upon complaint made to him, of officers or soldiers beating or otherwise ill treating any person, of disturbing fairs or markets, or of committing any kind of riots, to the disquieting of the citizens of the United States; the said commander, who shall refuse or omit to see justice done to the offender or offenders, and reparation made to the party or parties injured, as far as part of the offenders' pay shall enable him or them, shall, upon proof thereof, be cashiered or otherwise punished, as a general court martial shall direct.

Art. 33. When any commissioned officer or soldier shall be accused of a capital crime, or having used violence, or committed any offence against the persons or property of any citizen of the United States, such as is punishable by the known laws of the land; the commanding officer, and officers of every regiment, troop, or company, to which the person or persons, so accused, shall belong, are hereby required, upon application duly made by, or in behalf of, the parties injured, to use their utmost endeavors to deliver over such accused person, or persons, to the civil magistrate, and likewise to be aiding and assisting the officers of justice in apprehending and securing the person or persons so accused, in order to bring him or them to trial. If any commanding officer or officers, shall wilfully neglect, or shall refuse upon the application aforesaid, to deliver over such accused person or persons, to the civil magistrates, or to be aiding and assisting the officers of justice in apprehending such person or persons, the officer or officers so offending, shall be cashiered.

Art. 34. If any officer shall think himself wronged by his colonel, or the commanding officer of the regiment, and shall, upon due application being made to him, be refused redress, he may complain to the general commanding in the State or Territory where such regiment shall be stationed, in order to obtain justice; who is hereby required to examine into the said complaint, and take proper measures for redressing the wrong complained of, and transmit, as soon as possible, to the department of war, a true statement of such complaint, with the proceedings thereon.

Art. 35. If any inferior officer or soldier, shall think himself wronged by his captain, or other officer, he is to complain thereof to the commanding officer of the regiment, who is hereby required to summon a regimental court martial, for the doing of justice to the complainant; for which regimental court martial, either party may, if he thinks himself still aggrieved, appeal to a general court martial. But if, upon a second hearing, the appeal shall appear vexatious and groundless, the person so appealing, shall be punished at the discretion of the said court martial.

Art. 36. Any commissioned officer, storekeeper, or commissary, who shall be convicted at a general court martial, of having sold, without a proper order for that purpose, embezzled, misapplied, or wilfully, or through neglect suffered any of the provisions, forage, arms, clothing, ammunition, or other military stores belonging to the United States, to be spoiled or damaged, shall, at his own private expense, make good the loss or damage, and shall moreover forfeit all his pay, and be dismissed from the service.

Art. 37. Any non-commissioned officer or soldier who shall be convicted at a regimental court martial, of having sold, or designedly, or through neglect, wasting the ammunition delivered out to him, to be employed in the service of the United States, shall be punished at the discretion of such court.

Art. 38. Every non-commissioned officer or soldier who shall be convicted before a court martial of having sold, lost or spoiled, through neglect, his horse, arms, clothes, or accoutrements, shall undergo such weekly stoppages (not exceeding the half of his pay) as such court martial shall judge sufficient, for repairing the loss or damage; and shall suffer confinement, or such other corporeal punishment as his crime shall deserve.

Art. 39. Every officer who shall be convicted before a court martial, of having embezzled, or misapplied, any money with which he may have been entrusted, for the payment of men under his command, or for enlisting men into the service, or for other purposes, if a commissioned officer, shall be cashiered, and compelled to refund the money; if a non-commissioned officer, shall be reduced to the ranks, be put under stoppages until the money be made good, and suffer such corporeal punishment as such court martial shall direct.

Art. 40. Every captain of a troop, or company, is charged with the arms accoutrements, ammunition, clothing, or other warlike stores belonging to the troop or company under his command, which he is to be accountable for to his colonel, in case of their being lost, spoiled, or damaged, not by unavoidable accidents, or on actual service.

Art. 41. All non-commissioned officers and soldiers who shall be found one mile from the camp, without leave in writing, from their commanding officer, shall suffer such punishment as shall be inflicted upon them by the sentence of a court martial.

Art. 42. No officer or soldier shall lie out of his quarters, garrison, or camp, without leave from his superior officer, upon penalty of being punished according to the nature of his offence, by the sentence of a court martial.

Art. 43. Every non-commissioned officer and soldier shall retire to his quarters or tent, at the beating of the retreat; in default of which he shall be punished according to the nature of his offence.

Art. 44. No officer, non-commissioned officer, or soldier, shall fail in repairing at the time fixed, to the place of parade, of exercise, or other rendezvous, appointed by his commanding officer, if not prevented by sickness or some other evident necessity; or shall go from the said place of rendezvous, without leave from his commanding officer, before he shall be regularly dismissed or relieved, on the penalty of being punished according to the nature of his offence by the sentence of a court martial.

Art. 45. Any commissioned officer who shall be found drunk on his guard, party or other duty, shall be cashiered. Any non-commissioned officer or soldier so offending, shall suffer such corporeal punishment as shall be inflicted by the sentence of the court martial.

Art. 46. Any sentinel who shall be found sleeping upon his post, or shall leave it before he shall be regularly relieved, shall suffer death, or such other punishment as shall be inflicted by the sentence of a court martial.

Art. 47. No soldier belonging to any regiment, troop, or company, shall hire another to do his duty for him, or be excused from duty, but in cases of sickness, disability, or leave of absence; and every such soldier found guilty of hiring his duty, as also the party so hired to do another's duty, shall be punished at the discretion of a regimental court martial.

Art. 48. And every non-commissioned officer conniving at such hiring of duty aforesaid, shall be reduced; and every commissioned officer, knowing and allowing such ill practices in the service, shall be punished by the judgment of a general court martial.

Art. 49. Any officer belonging to the service of the United, States who, by discharging of fire arms, drawing of swords, beating of drums, or by any other means whatsoever, shall occasion false alarms in camp, garrison, or quarters, shall suffer death, or such other punishment as shall be ordered by the sentence of a general court martial.

Art. 50. Any officer or soldier who shall, without urgent necessity, or without the leave of his superior officer, quit his guard, platoon, or division, shall be punished according to the nature of his offence, by the sentence of a court martial.

Art. 51. No officer or soldier, shall do violence to any person who brings provisions or other necessaries to the camp, garrison, or quarters, of the forces of the United States, employed in any part of the United States, upon pain of death, or such other punishment as court martial shall direct.

Art. 52. Any officer or soldier who shall misbehave himself before the enemy, run away, or shamefully abandon any fort, post or guard, which he or they may be commanded to defend, or speak words inducing others to do the like; or shall cast away his arms or ammunition, or who shall quit his post or colors to plunder and pillage; every such offender being duly convicted thereof, shall suffer death, or such other punishment as shall be ordered by the sentence of a general court martial.

Art. 53. Any person belonging to the armies of the United States, who shall make known the watch word to any person who is not entitled to receive it, according to the rules and discipline of war, or shall presume to give a parole or watch word different from what he received, shall suffer death, or such other punishment as shall be ordered by the sentence of a general court martial.

Art. 54. All officers and soldiers are to behave themselves orderly in quarters, and on their march; and whosoever shall commit any waste, or spoil, either in walks of trees, parks, fish-ponds, houses or gardens, cornfields, enclosures of meadows, or shall maliciously destroy any property whatsoever, belonging to the inhabitants of the United States, unless by order of the then commander-in-chief of the armies of the said States, shall (besides such penalties as they are liable to by law) be punished according to the nature and degree of the offence, by the judgement of a regimental or general court martial.

Art. 55. Whosoever belonging to the armies of the United States, employed in foreign parts, shall force a safe guard, shall suffer death.

Art. 56. Whosoever shall relieve the enemy with money, victuals, or ammunition, or shall knowingly harbor or protect an enemy, shall suffer death, or such other punishment as shall be ordered by the sentence of a court martial.

Art. 57. Whosoever shall be convicted of holding correspondence with, or giving intelligence to the enemy, either directly or indirectly, shall suffer death, or such other punishment as shall be ordered by the sentence of a court martial.

Art. 58. All public stores taken in the enemy's camp, towns, forts, or magazines, whether of artillery, ammunition, clothing, forage or provisions, shall be secured for the service of the United States; for the neglect of which, the commanding officer is to be answerable.

Art. 59. If any commander of any garrison, fortress, or post, shall be compelled, by the officers and soldiers under his command, to give up to the enemy, or to abandon it, the commissioned officers, non-commissioned officers, or soldiers, who shall be convicted of having so offended, shall suffer death, or such other punishment as shall be inflicted upon them by the sentence of a court martial.

Art. 60. All settlers and retainers to the camp, and all persons whatsoever, serving with the armies of the United States, in the field, though not enlisted soldiers, are to be subject to orders, according to the rules, and discipline of war.

Art. 61. Officers having brevets, or commissions, of a prior date to those of the regiment in which they serve may take place in courts martial and on detachments, when composed of different corps, according to the rank given them in their brevets, or dates of their former commissions; but in the regiment, troop, or company, to which such officers belong, they shall do duty, and take rank, both in courts martial and on detachments, which shall be composed only of their own corps, according to the commissions by which they are mustered in the said corps.

Art. 62. If upon marches, guards or in quarters, different corps of the army shall happen to join, or do duty together, the officer highest in rank of the line of the army, marine corps, or militia, by commission there, on duty, or in quarters, shall command the whole, and give orders for what is needful to the service, unless otherwise specially directed by the President of the United States, according to the nature of the case.

Art. 63. The functions of the engineers, being generally confined to the most elevated branch of military science, they are not to assume, nor are they subject to be ordered on any duty beyond the line of their immediate profession, except by the special order of the President of the United States; but they are to receive every mark of respect, to which their rank in the army may entitle them respectively, and are liable to be transferred, at the discretion of the President, from one corps to another, regard being paid to rank.

Art. 64. General courts martial may consist of any number of commissioned officers from five to thirteen inclusively; but they shall not consist of less than thirteen, where that number can be convened without manifest injury to the service.

Art. 65. Any general officer commanding an army, or colonel commanding a separate department, may appoint general courts martial whenever necessary. But no sentence of a court martial shall be carried into execution, until after the whole proceedings shall have been laid before the officer ordering the same, or the officer commanding the troops for the time being; neither shall any sentence of a general court martial, in time of peace, extending to the loss of life, or the dismission of a commissioned officer, be carried into execution, until after the whole proceedings shall have been transmitted to the Secretary of War, to be laid before the President of the United States, for his confirmation or disapproval and orders in the case. All other sentences may be confirmed and executed by the officer ordering the court to assemble, or the commanding officer for the time being, as the case may be.

Art. 66. Every officer commanding a regiment or corps, may appoint, for his own regiment or corps, courts martial, to consist of three commissioned officers, for the trial and punishment of offences, not capital, and decide upon their sentences. For the same purpose, all officers commanding any of the garrisons, forts, barracks, or other places, where the troops consist of different corps, may assemble courts martial, to consist of three commissioned officers, and decide upon their sentences.

Art. 67. No garrison or regimental court martial shall have the power to try capital cases or commissioned officers, neither shall they inflict a fine exceeding one month's pay, nor imprison, nor put to hard labor, any non-commissioned officer or soldier, for a longer time than one month.

Art. 68. Whenever it may be found convenient and necessary to the public service, the officers of the marine shall be associated with the officers of the land forces, for the purpose of holding courts martial and trying offenders belonging to either; and in such cases, the orders of the senior officer of either corps, who may be present and duly authorized, shall be received and obeyed.

Art. 69. The judge advocate, or some person deputed by him, or by the general or officer commanding army, detachment, or garrison, shall prosecute in the name of the United States, but shall so far consider himself as counsel for the prisoner, after the said prisoner shall have made his plea, as to object to any leading question to any of the witnesses, or any question to the prisoner, the answer to which might tend to criminate himself; and administer to each member of the court, before they proceed upon any trial, the following oath, which shall also be taken by all members of the regimental and garrison courts martial:

"You, A. B. do swear, that you will well and truly try and determine, according to evidence, the matter now before you, between the United States of America and the prisoner to be tried, and that you will duly administer justice according to the provisions of 'An act establishing rules and articles for the government of the armies of the United States,' without partiality, favor, or affection; and if any doubt shall arise, not explained by said articles, according to your conscience, the best of your understanding and the custom of war in like cases; and you do further swear, that you will not divulge the sentence of the court until it shall be published by the proper authority; neither will you disclose nor discover the vote or opinion of any particular member of the court martial, unless required to give evidence thereof as a witness, by a court of justice, in a due course of law. *So help you God.*"

And as soon as the said oath shall have been administered to the respective members, the president of the court shall administer to the judge advocate, or person officiating as such, an oath in the following words:

"You A. B. do swear, that you will not disclose or discover the vote or opinion of any particular member of the court martial, unless required to give evidence thereof, as a witness, by a court of justice, in due course of law. Nor divulge the sentence of the court to any but the proper authority, until it shall be duly disclosed by the same. *So help you God.*"

Art. 70. When a prisoner, arraigned before a general court martial, shall, from obstinate and deliberate design, stand mute, or answer foreign to the purpose, the court may proceed to trial and judgment as if the prisoner had regularly pleaded not guilty.

Art. 71. When a member shall be challenged by a prisoner, he must state his cause of challenge, of which the court shall, after due deliberation determine the relevancy or validity, and decide accordingly; and no challenge to more than one member at a time shall be received by the court.

Art. 72. All the members of a court martial are to behave with decency and calmness; and in giving their votes, are to begin with the youngest in commission.

Art. 73. All persons who give evidence before a court martial, are to be examined on oath or affirmation, in the following form:

"You swear or affirm (as the case may be,) the evidence you shall give in the cause now in hearing, shall be the truth, the whole truth, and nothing but the truth. *So help you God.*"

Art. 74. On the trials of cases not capital, before courts martial, the deposition of witnesses, not in the line or staff of the army, may be taken before some justice of the peace, and read in evidence; provided the prosecutor and person accused are present at the taking the same, or are duly notified thereof.

Art. 75. No officer shall be tried but by a general court martial, the deposition of witnesses, not in the line or staff of the army, may be taken before some justice of the peace, and read in evidence; provided the prosecutor and person accused are present at the taking the same, or are duly notified thereof.

Art. 76. No person whatsoever shall use any menacing words, signs, or gestures, in presence of a court martial, or shall cause any disorder or riot, or disturb their proceedings, on the penalty of being punished, at the discretion of the said court martial.

Art. 77. Whenever any officer shall be charged with a crime, he shall be arrested and confined in his barracks, quarters, or tent, and deprived of his sword, by the commanding officer. And any officer who shall leave his confinement before he shall be set at liberty by his commanding officer, or by a superior officer, shall be cashiered.

Art. 78. Non-commissioned officers and soldiers, charged with crimes shall be confined until tried by a court martial, or released by proper authority.

Art. 79. No officer or soldier, who shall be put in arrest, shall continue in confinement more than eight days, or until such time as a court martial can be assembled.

Art. 80. No officer commanding a guard, or provost marshal, shall refuse to receive or keep any prisoner committed to his charge by an officer belonging to the forces of the United States; provided the officer committing shall, at the same time, deliver an account in writing, signed by himself, of the crime with which the said prisoner is charged.

Art. 81. No officer commanding a guard, or provost marshal, shall presume to release any person committed to his charge without proper authority for so doing, nor shall he suffer any person to escape on the penalty of being punished for it, by a sentence of a court martial.

Art. 82. Every officer or provost marshal, to whose charge prisoners shall be committed, shall, within twenty-four hours after such commitment, or as soon as he shall be relieved from his guard, make report in writing, to the commanding officer, of their names, their crimes, and the names of the officers who committed them, on the penalty of being punished for disobedience or neglect, at the discretion of a court martial.

Art. 83. Any commissioned officer convicted before a general court martial of conduct unbecoming an officer and a gentleman, shall be dismissed [from] the service.

Art. 84. In cases where a court martial may think it proper to sentence a commissioned officer to be suspended from command, they shall have power also to suspend his pay and emoluments for the same time, according to the nature and heinousness of the offence.

Art. 85. In cases where a commissioned officer is cashiered for cowardice or fraud, it shall be added in the sentence, that the crime, name, and place of abode, and punishment of the delinquent, be published in the newspapers, in and about the camp, and of the particular State from which the offender came, or where he usually resides, after which it shall be deemed scandalous for an officer to associate with him.

Art. 86. The commanding officer of any post or detachment, in which there shall not be a number of officers adequate to form a general court martial, shall, in cases which require the cognizance of such a court, report to the commanding officer of the deportment, who shall order a court to be assembled at the nearest post or detachment, and the party accused with necessary witnesses, to be transported to the place where the said court shall be assembled.

Art. 87. No person shall be sentenced to suffer death but by the concurrence of two thirds of the members of a general court martial, nor except in cases herein expressly mentioned; nor shall more than fifty lashes be inflicted on any offender, at the discretion of a court martial;[1] and no officer, non-commissioned officer or soldier, or follower of the army, shall be tried a second time for the same offence.

Art. 88. No person shall be liable to be tried and punished by a general court martial for any offence which shall appear to have been committed more than two years before the issuing of the order for such trial, unless the person, by reason of having absented himself, or some other manifest impediment, shall not have been amenable to justice within that period.

Art. 89. Every officer authorized to order a general court martial, shall have power to pardon or mitigate any punishment ordered by such court, except the sentence of death, or of cashiering an officer; which in the cases where he has authority (by article 65) to carry them into execution, he may suspend until the pleasure of the President of the United States can be known; which suspension, together with copies of the proceedings of the court martial, the said officer shall immediately transmit to the President for his determination. And the colonel or commanding officer of the regiment or garrison, where any regimental or garrison court martial shall be held, may pardon or mitigate any punishment ordered by such court to be inflicted.

Art. 90. Every judge advocate, or persons officiating as such, at any general court martial, shall transmit, with as much expedition as opportunity of time and distance of place can admit, the original proceedings and sentence of such court martial, to the secretary of war, which said original proceedings and sentence shall be carefully kept and preserved in the office of said secretary, to the end that the persons entitled thereto may be enabled, upon application to the said office, to obtain copies thereof. The party tried by any general court martial, shall, upon demand thereof made by himself, or by any person or persons in his behalf, be entitled to a copy of the sentence and proceedings of such court material.

Art. 91. In cases where the general or commanding officer may order a court of inquiry to examine into the nature of any transaction, accusation or imputation, against any officer or soldier, the said court shall consist of one or more officers, not exceeding three, and a judge advocate, or other suitable person as a recorder, to reduce the proceedings and evidence the writing, all of whom shall be sworn to the faithful performance of their duty. This court shall have the

[1] Punishment by stripes or lashes abolished. See Act of May 16, 1812, Section 7.

same power to summon witnesses at a court martial, and to examine them on oath. But they shall not give their opinion of the merits of the case, excepting they shall be thereto specially required. The parties accused shall also be permitted to cross-examine, and interrogate the witnesses, so as to investigate fully the circumstances in question.

Art. 92. The proceedings of a court of inquiry must be authenticated by the signature of the recorder and the president, and delivered to the commanding officer; and the said proceedings may be admitted as evidence by a court martial, in cases not capital or extending to the dismissal of an officer, provided that the circumstances are such, that oral testimony cannot be obtained. But as courts of inquiry may be perverted to dishonorable purposes and may be considered as engines of destruction to military merit, in the hands of weak and envious commandants, they are hereby prohibited, unless directed by the President of the United States, or demanded by the accused.

Art. 93. The judge advocate, or recorder, shall administer to the members the following oath:

"You shall well and truly examine and inquire according to your evidence into the matter now before you, without partiality, favor, affection, prejudice, or hope of reward. *So help you God.*"

After which the president shall administer to the judge advocate, or recorder, the following oath:

"You A. B. Do swear, that you will, according to your best abilities, accurately and impartially record the proceedings of the court, and the evidence to be given in the case in hearing. *So help you God.*"

The witnesses shall take the same oath as witnesses sworn before a court martial.

Art. 94. When any commissioned officer shall die or be killed in the service of the United States, the major of the regiment, or officer doing the major's duty in his absence, or in any post or garrison, the second officer in command, or the assistant military agent, shall immediately secure all his effects or equipage then in camp or quarters, and shall make an inventory thereof, and forthwith transmit the same to the office of the department of war, to the end, that his executors or administrators may receive the same.

Art. 95. When any non-commissioned officer or soldier, shall die or be killed in the service of the United States, the then commanding officer of the troop, or company, shall, in the presence of two other commissioned officers, take an account of what effects the died possessed of, above his arms and accoutrements, and transmit the same to the office of the department of war; which said effects are to be accounted for, and paid to the representatives of such deceased officers and soldiers, should, before they have accounted to their representatives for the same, have occasion to leave the regiment or post, by preferment, or otherwise, they shall, before they be permitted to quit the same, deposit in the hands of the commanding officer, or of the assistant military agent, all the effects of such deceased non-commissioned officers and soldiers, in order that the same may be secured for, and paid to their respective representatives.

Art. 96. All officers, conductors, gunners, matrosses, drivers, or other persons whatsoever, receiving pay or hire, in the service of the artillery or corps of engineers of the United States, shall be governed by the aforesaid rules and articles, and shall be subject to be tried by courts martial, in like manner with the officers and soldiers of the other troops in the service of the United States.

Art. 97. The officers and soldiers of any troops, whether militia or others, being mustered and in pay of the United States, shall, at all times, and in all places, when joined, or acting in conjunction, with the regular forces of the United States, be governed by these rules and articles of war, and shall be subject to be tried by courts martial, in like manner with the officers and soldiers in the regular forces, save only, that such courts martial shall be composed entirely of militia officers.

Art. 98. All officers serving by commission from authority of any particular State, shall, on all detachments, court martial, or other duty, wherein they may be employed in conjunction with the regular forces of the United States, take rank, next after all officers of the like grade in said regular forces, notwithstanding the commissions of such militia or state officers may be elder than the commissions of the officers of the regular forces of the United States.

Art. 99. All crimes not capital, and all disorders and neglects, which officers and soldiers may be guilty of, to the prejudice of good order and military discipline, though not mentioned in the foregoing articles of war, are to be taken cognizance of by a general or regimental court martial, according to the nature and degree of the offence, and be punished at their discretion.

Art. 100. The President of the United States shall have power to prescribe the uniform of the army.

Art. 101. The foregoing articles are to be read and published once in every six months, to every garrison, regiment, troop or company, mustered or to be mustered in the service of the United States, and are to be duly observed and obeyed, by all officers and soldiers who are or shall be in said service.

Sec. 2. *And be it further enacted,* That in time of war, all persons not citizens of, or owing allegiance to the United States of America, who shall be found lurking as spies, in or about the fortifications or encampments of the armies of the United States, or any of them, shall suffer death, according to the law and usage of nations, by sentence of a general court martial.

Sec. 3. *And be it further enacted,* That the rules and regulations, by which the armies of the United States have heretofore been governed, are the resolves of Congress there unto annexed, and respecting the same, should henceforth be void and of no effect, except so far as may relate to any transaction under them, prior to the promulgation of this act, at the several posts and garrisons respectively, occupied by any part of the army of the United States.

Approved, April 10, 1806

Extract of an Act Passed 16th May, 1812

Sec. 7. *And be it further enacted,* That so much of the "Act for establishing rules and articles for the government of the armies of the United States," as authorizes the infliction of corporeal punishments, by stripes or lashes, be, and the same is hereby, repealed.

Militia

Extract from the Act of Congress

Organization and Discipline of the Militia

Each and every free able bodied white male citizen of the respective States, resident therein, who is or shall be of the age of eighteen years, and under the age of forty-five years, (except as is hereinafter excepted,) shall severally and respectively be enrolled in the militia by the captain or commanding officer of the company within whose bounds such citizen shall reside, and that within twelve months after the passing of this act. And it shall, at all times hereafter, be the duty of every such captain or commanding officer of a company, to enrol every such citizen as aforesaid, and also those who shall from time to time, arrive at the age of eighteen years, or being of the age of eighteen years and under the age of forty-five years, (except as before excepted,) shall come to reside within his bounds; and shall without delay, notify such citizen of the said enrolment, by a proper non-commissioned officer of the company, by whom such notice may be thereafter, provide himself with a good musket or fire lock, a sufficient bayonet and belt, two spare flints, and a knapsack, shot pouch, and powder horn, twenty balls suited to the bore of his rifle, and a quarter of a pound of powder; and shall appear, so armed, accoutred, and provided, when called out to exercise, or into service; except, that when called out on company days to exercise only, he may appear without a knapsack. The commissioned officers shall, severally, be armed with a sword or hanger, and espontoon: and that, from and after five years from the passing of this act, all muskets for arming the militia, as herein required, shall be of bores sufficient for balls of the eighteenth part of a pound. And every citizen so enrolled, and providing himself with the arms, ammunition, and accoutrements required as aforesaid, shall hold the same exempted from all suits distresses, executions, or sales, for debt, or for the payment of taxes.

Every citizen duly enrolled in the militia, shall be constantly provided with arms, accoutrements, and ammunition, agreeably to the preceding article, from and after he shall be duly notified of his enrolment; and any notice or warning to the citizens so enrolled, to attend a company, battalion, or regimental muster, or training, which shall be according to the laws of the State in which it is given for that purpose, shall be deemed a legal notice of his enrollment.

Appendix C

Chronology of the Nauvoo Legion in Illinois

Compiled by Hosea Stout (and revised by the authors)

1840

Fall	City charter approved by state legislature.
December 16	Governor Carlin signed charter.

1841

January 14	First Presidency issued proclamation detailing Nauvoo Charter and the Nauvoo Legion.
January 19	Joseph Smith received revelation in which the Lord said, "I am the Lord your God, and will save all those of your brethren, who have been pure in heart, and have been slain in the land of Missouri, saith the Lord your God."
January 31	William Smith recorded the court-martial of Stephen Kittle. Kittle had been charged for stating that Joseph Smith was not a prophet of the Lord, and that self-defense was not righteous, among other things.
February 1	City council elected.
February 3	Passage of city charter; Joseph Smith recorded events in Nauvoo and presented a bill for an ordinance organizing the legion. The bill described the general officers of the legion, from lieutenant general to drill officers. It also depicted which officers

	would belong to which staff and named the place and time of the first court-martial.
February 4	First court-martial held at the office of Joseph Smith. An election of the first general officers of the Nauvoo Legion took place.
February 16	Joseph received a Missouri resolution, passed in both the state senate and house, stating that 2,000 copies of a pamphlet concerning the "Mormon difficulties" would be published. Joseph wrote, "[I]s this Missouri's last struggle to retrieve her lost character, to publish to the world a one-sided statement of her robberies, murders, and extermination which she had committed without provocation, at a time when not one Saint was left in Missouri to tell the truth about them?"
February 20	Court-martial: legion fines, resolutions, days of parade, etc. Resolved that men aged of eighteen to forty-five will not be exempt from military duty, unless they are exempted by the United States. It also resolved that officers and legionaries will be fined for missing the general parade and that "Edward P. Duzette organize a band of music, not exceeding twenty men."
March 2	Court-martial.
March 9	Court-martial.
March 10	Governor Carlin issued a commission, declaring Joseph Smith the lieutenant general of the Nauvoo Legion.
March 15	Court-martial.
April 6	The first grand parade of the Nauvoo Legion took place and ended with the laying of the temple cornerstone. Sidney Rigdon spoke, followed by the laying of the first (southeast) cornerstone, prayer, a one-hour adjournment, and the remainder of the meeting. Later that day, Hosea Stout gave his poem the "Legion of Nauvoo."
April 7	Church general conference.
April 25	Alexander Neibaur recorded in his journal that Sunday meeting began with talks by John C. Bennett

and William Law concerning the falsities and misconduct of former members, to Joseph Smith's determination to "put down all iniquity," to an address by "Elder Green on the principles of the gospel." The meeting adjourned with a call upon the Nauvoo Legion to "furnish volunteers for secret service, in detecting thieves, etc."

May 1	Court-martial: First Cohort, First Regiment organized.
May 1	Robert B. Thompson recorded in the *Times and Seasons* the organization of the First Regiments of the First and Second Cohorts, and the Second Regiment of the Second Cohort of the Nauvoo Legion.
May 4	Joseph Smith issued general orders from the Nauvoo Legion's headquarters. In these orders he referred to Stephen Douglas's advice, the fact that the Nauvoo Legion wasn't exclusively for Latter-day Saints, and some general items of business (e.g., officers were ordered to treat their troops with marked respect).
May 25	Joseph issued an order for an escort, depicting the various duties of the legion's cohorts.
July 3	Court-martial, parade; organization of the Second Regiment, First Cohort, Third Regiment, Second Cohort, etc. On this day, Joseph gave a patriotic speech in which he declared, "I would ask for no greater boon, than to lay down my life for my country."
July 4	Independence Day parade.
August 10	Joseph Smith issued a letter to the Nauvoo Legion in which he touched upon the death of his brother Don Carlos (August 7).
August 28	Special court-martial.
September 2	Court-martial.
September 4	Court-martial; Charles C. Rich elected brigadier general, replacing Don Carlos Smith.
September 11	General parade.
September 13	Joseph Smith received an invitation from Brigadier General Ezekiel Swazey and Colonel Amos B.

	Fuller, of the militia of Lee County, Iowa, to attend the military parade at Montrose on the 14th.
September 14	Joseph recorded, "Went over to Montrose, accompanied by brothers Edward Hunter and William A. Gheen. I was very courteously received by General Swazey, the officers and Militia. Mr. D. W. Kilbourn attempted to get up an ill feeling by reading the following proclamation . . . which I insert verbatim: 'Citizens of Iowa—The laws of Iowa do not require you to muster under, or be reviewed by Joe Smith, or General Bennett, and should they have the impudence to attempt it, it is hoped that every person having a proper respect for himself, will at once leave the ranks.' This, however, had no effect whatever on the people."
October 30	Destruction of grog shop by Legion; Joseph Smith recorded, "In obedience to an order from the Mayor, I called out two companies of the Nauvoo Legion, and removed a grog shop kept by Pulaski S. Cahoon, which had been declared a nuisance by the City Council."
November 30	Court-martial regarding thieves.
December 20	Under the office of lieutenant general, Joseph Smith wrote in the *Times and Seasons* that Adam Snyder and John Moore, nominated for governor and lieutenant governor of the state of Illinois, respectively, were "friends" of the Mormons. Joseph also wrote that he cared "not a fig for a Whig or a Democrat."

1842

January 25	Joseph Smith issued an order to muster the legion. The public arms were to be inspected in preparation for the general parade that was to take place on May 9. Governor Ford is notable among Smith's many distinguished guests.
March 11	Parade; the Nauvoo Legion minutes reported the following: "The Nauvoo Legion was on parade and commanded by Lieutenant-General Joseph Smith in person. Several of the Twelve apostles rode in

the general staff as Chaplains. The line was formed at 10 o'clock, A.M. and soon the Legion marched from their usual place of parade below the temple, to Water Street, in front of General Smith's house, where the troops were inspected, and, after a recess marched west on the bank of the river, and taking a circuitous route, resumed their usual post on the parade ground, and closed the day in good order and with good feelings, and to the full satisfaction of the Commander-in-Chief."

March 12 — Joseph held a court-martial at his own home to discuss the "rank and station of several officers, and the more perfect organization of the Legion."

March 19 — Court-martial.

April 2 — The fourth regiment of the second cohort of the Nauvoo Legion was organized. Jonathan Dunham was elected Colonel.

April 6 — At a special conference of the Church of Jesus Christ of Latter-day Saints, "President William Law, General Bennett, President pro tem, and President Hyrum Smith all spoke upon the subject of military affairs, showing the necessity of a well organized and efficient force; that as we were bound to serve our country, if required, in common with all good citizens, we ought not to be behind any of our neighbors in point of good order, neat uniforms and equipments, and a well organized and thoroughly disciplined Legion."

April 12 — "Military appointment—James Arlington Bennett, of Arlington House, Long Island, is hereby appointed inspector general of the Nauvoo Legion, with the rank and title of major-general; his place to be supplied when absent, by the major general of the Legion, Joseph Smith."

April 28 — "Two issues from Joseph and General Bennett. Both concern the planning of the *programme militaire*."

May 5–6 — Officer drill. Attempted assassination of Lilburn W. Boggs (May 6).

May 7 — General parade. In one year, the Legion had grown from six to twenty-six companies. In the late afternoon, the legion divided and participated in a sham battle, about which Joseph Smith wrote, "I was solicited by General Bennett to take command of the first cohort during the sham battle . . . and if General Bennett's true feelings towards me are not made manifest to the world in a very short time, then it may be possible, that the gentle breathings of that Spirit, which whispered [to] me on parade, that there was 'mischief concealed in that sham battle,' were false; a short time will determine the point."

May 15 — "Joseph the Prophet attended meeting at the Stand at Nauvoo. . . . News of the attempted assassination of Gov. Boggs was confirmed by general report, as was mentioned on the stand."

May 17 — John C. Bennett resigned his office as mayor of Nauvoo.

May 19 — Joseph Smith wrote in his journal about his ascendancy to the mayor's seat of Nauvoo and reported on John C. Bennett's questioning of Joseph's character.

May 22 — News reports name Joseph Smith as a suspect in the Boggs assassination attempt.

June 3 — Court-martial, Ordinance number 2.

June 6 — Joseph Smith approved resolutions passed by a court-martial of the Nauvoo Legion.

June 11 — The [city] council resolved to publish the city charter, ordinances of the city council, and the Nauvoo Legion, before the first day of [the following] July.

June 23 — Joseph Smith published an editorial in the *Times and Seasons* detailing the treachery and promiscuity of John Cook Bennett.

July 4 — "The Nauvoo Legion appeared on parade under command of Brigadier General Wilson Law, ranking officers of the line. Lieutenant General Joseph Smith reviewed the Legion at 11 A.M., and continued in command through the day. . . . [A]t the close of the day General Smith expressed his entire satisfaction in an animated speech, in which he illustrated the design of the organization of the Legion, viz., to yield obedience to the institutions of our country, *and protect the Saints from mobs*, after which leave was given for strangers to address the Legion, when General Swazey, of Iowa, expressed his friendly feelings towards Nauvoo, and his gratification at the good discipline of the Legion."

July 5 — Court-martial; city council passes a resolution that "no citizen of this city shall be taken out of the city by any writs without the privilege of investigation before the municipal court."

July 12 — City ordinance modified Legion.

July 27 — Joseph Smith received a letter from Thomas Carlin that stated the following: "In reply to your expressed apprehensions of 'the possibility of an attack upon the peaceable inhabitants of the city of Nauvoo and vicinity, through the intrigues and false representations of John C. Bennett and others,' and your request that I would issue official orders to you to have the Nauvoo Legion in readiness, to be called out at a moment's warning in defence of the peaceable citizens &c. I must say that I cannot conceive of the least probability, or scarcely possibility, of an attack of violence upon the citizens of Nauvoo from any quarter whatever." Carlin went on to say that he had no power to suppress any mobocratic activity as long as he suspected none.

August 3 — Wilson Law elected major general of the Nauvoo Legion.

August 4 — Joseph the Prophet in company with fifteen others spend the day learning sword exercise with Colonel Brewer and attended a variety of business in Nauvoo.

August 13 — Court-martial, Ordinance number 3, vacancy of John C. Bennett.

August 15 — The *Times and Seasons* reported the following: "On Monday the 8th instant General Smith was arrested upon a warrant under the signature of Governor Carlin, in accordance as stated with a call from Governor Reynolds of Missouri, upon the affidavit of Ex-Governor Boggs."

September 2 — A report reached the city of Nauvoo this afternoon

	that the Sheriff was on his way to the city with an armed force.
September 3	Joseph Smith's house was illegally searched by the deputy sheriff, who had no warrant.
September 10	Joseph Smith recorded that, among other things, "this was the day for the training of the companies of the Nauvoo Legion." He spent the day in hiding.
September 23	Legion on parade; Colonel George Miller elected brigadier general of the First Cohort to fill the vacancy left by General Wilson Law.
September 24	Legion on parade; various officers elected.
October 15	Court-martial, Ordinance number 4.
October 16	In a letter to John C. Bennett, James Arlington Bennett defended the Mormons: "Gen. John C. Bennett has stated that to conquer the Mormon Legion it would require five to one against them, all things taken into consideration, and that they will die to a man sooner than give up their Prophet. Now is the arrest of this man worth such a sacrifice of life as must necessarily follow an open war with his people? The loss of, from one to three thousand lives, will no doubt follow in an attempt to accomplish an object not in the end worth a button."
December 9	Joseph Smith recorded in his journal the following: "Mr. Davis of Bond County introduced a resolution to the House of Representatives at Springfield concerning the charter of Nauvoo and urged its repeal. . . . Mr. Hicks was in favor of having the State arms taken from the Mormons. . . . The arms referred to consisted of 3 cannons or 6-pounders and a few score of muskets, swords, and pistols, which were furnished by the United States to Illinois, for the supply of her militia, for common defence, of which the Nauvoo Legion had received but a small portion to which it was entitled."
December 13	Joseph's delegation arrived at Springfield "this afternoon and found the repeal of the Nauvoo Charter in a high state of agitation in the legislature."[1]

[1] Smith, *History of the Church*, 5:204.

December 15	Court-martial.
December 31	Joseph Smith appeared in court.

1843

January 1	Joseph Smith in Springfield, Illinois, awaiting trial.
January 4–6	Court proceedings. Many witnesses testified that they saw Joseph Smith reviewing the Nauvoo Legion on May 7, 1842, which would mean that he could not have been in Illinois on May 6 (when Boggs was shot), and was thus not an accessory before the fact of the intended murder.
January 6	Joseph Smith acquitted.
January 30	The city council passed a bill organizing a city watch.
March 8	Joseph Smith signed "some documents in relation to the Nauvoo Legion."
March 10	Joseph Smith dreamed about the "old man" who sought protection from the legion.
March 25	Joseph Smith recorded to the church the following: "Know ye therefore that I, Joseph Smith, Mayor of the City of Nauvoo, will grant and insure protection against all personal mob violence to each and every citizen of this city who will freely and voluntarily come before me and truly make known the names of all such abominable characters as are engaged in said secret combination for stealing, or are accessory thereto, in any manner."
April 18	Joseph Smith appointed John F. Cowan as an aide-de-camp to the lieutenant general.
April 21	Officer drill.
April 22	The cohorts of the Nauvoo Legion were in exercise this day. Joseph's staff came out with him, and spent the day in riding, exercising and organizing, and sitting in court martial, to ascertain to what staff Robert D. Foster, surgeon general, Hugh McFall, adjuntant General, and Daniel H. Wells, commissary general, belonged.
May 3	The first issue of the *Nauvoo Neighbor* contained the following: "We have had, and may have to defend ourselves against the oppressions, persecutions, and

innovations of men. . . . [I]t has been our study to avoid contention, and we have never interfered with others until they have thrown down the gauntlet: and as we have not been to the present, so we are determined for the future not to be the aggressors."

May 4 "Joseph the Prophet" read a letter from James Arlington Bennett, showing that he was sick and could not attend the inspection of the Nauvoo Legion, according to his appointment.

May 6 Parade; Joseph Smith inspected the legion, of his remarks on this occasion, the following render the most significant information: "The Legion looked well, better than on any former occasion, and they performed their evolutions in admirable style. The officers did honor to the Legion; many of them were equipped and armed *cap-a-pie*. The men were in good spirits: they had made great improvements both in uniform and discipline, and we felt proud to be associated with a body of men which in point of discipline, uniform, appearance and a knowledge of military tactics, are the pride of Illinois, one of its strongest defences, and a great bulwark of the western country. In the course of my remarks on the prairie, I told the Legion that when we have petitioned those in power for assistance, they have always told us they had no power to help us, *damn such traitors*. When they give me the power to protect the innocent, I will never say I can do nothing for their good; I will exercise that power, so help me God."

May 14 Joseph Smith gave a lecture and, touching upon "good order and moderation," said, "In going to battle move slowly, dress up into line, and though your enemy rush upon you with fury, meet them slowly but firmly; let not confusion or terror seize upon you, but meet them firmly, and strike a heavy blow and conquer."

May 20 Court-martial.

June 10 Court-martial: "The court martial ordered an arsenal to be built in the city of Nauvoo, for the security of the public arms; and also ordered Brigadier General C. C. Rich to organize the second battalion, 1st regiment, 2nd cohort, into a regiment of light infantry, to be the 5th regiment, 2nd cohort."[2]

June 12 — The arsenal resolution passed. Also passed were resolutions naming Jonathan Dunham as the agent to build the arsenal, and Charles C. Rich as the organizer of the Second Battalion, First Regiment, Second Cohort.

June 23 — Sheriff Reynolds and company arrived in Nauvoo. Joseph Smith arrested.

June 25 — Joseph Smith recorded the following: "I sent Markham with a letter to Gen. Wilson Law directing him to meet me at Monmouth on Wednesday evening with sufficient force to prevent my being kidnapped into Missouri as I well knew that the whole country was swarming with men anxious to carry me there and kill me without any shadow of law or justice."

June 30 — Joseph Smith returned triumphantly to Nauvoo with Sheriff Reynolds as a guest at his home. Smith issued a resolution putting himself in custody of the municipal court of Nauvoo. At 4:00 P.M., he addressed a large congregation in the grove, to which he said the following: "I have dragged these men here by my hand, and will do it again; but I swear I will not deal so mildly with them again; for the time has come when forbearance is no longer a virtue: and if you or I are again taken unlawfully, you are at liberty to give loose to blood and thunder. But be cool, be deliberate, be wise, act with almighty power, and when you pull, do it effectually—make a sweepstakes for once! . . . But before I will be dragged away again, among my enemies, for trial, I will spill the last drop of blood in my veins, and will see all my enemies IN HELL! To bear it any longer would be a sin, and I will not bear it any longer. Shall we

[2] Smith, *History of the Church*, 5:422.

bear it any longer? (One universal NO! ran through all the vast assembly, like a loud peal of thunder.)"

July 1 — Hyrum Smith testified in court, "I being also a resident in said state during the same period of time; and I do know that Joseph Smith, Sen., never was subject to military duty in any state, neither was he in the state of Missouri, he being exempt by the amputation or extraction of a bone from his leg, and by having a license to preach the Gospel. . . . I do know that said Smith never bore arms, as a military man, in any capacity whatever." Joseph Smith was exonerated by the court.

July 3 — "About noon, Gen. C. C. Rich, with 25 men, returned, formed a square in front of my house, and sung a new song."[3]

July 6 — Governor Thomas Ford sent Sheriff Backenstos a copy of a letter originally sent to Governor Thomas Reynolds. On it, the governor wrote. "I have also to inform you that I had heard, before your arrival in this city of the escape of Smith, and rumors that he had been rescued by a military force." The letter was written to inform Reynolds that he was doing what he could to ascertain the facts of Smith's rescue and acquittal.

July 8 — Court-martial revised laws of Legion.

July 13 — Joseph Smith approved the revised laws of the Legion; Legion authorized the issue of Legion scrip in amounts up to $500.

July 25 — Joseph Smith introduced Nauvoo Legion scrip.

August 14 — Governor Thomas Ford wrote to Thomas Reynolds of Missouri to explain why he chose to decline Missouri's call for a militia-led expedition to return Joseph Smith to the state's custody. Among Ford's synopsis of the events was the following: "On the road, during their progress, they [Smith in Reynolds's custody and Reynolds in the sheriff's of Lee County] were met by parties of the citizens of Nauvoo; some or most of whom are said to have

[3] Smith, *History of the Church,* 5:486.

been members of the Nauvoo Legion, though there is no evidence that they appeared in a military capacity. There was no exhibition of arms of any description, nor was there any actual force used, though Mr. Reynolds testifies that he felt constraint, and that Smith, soon after meeting the first parties of Mormons, enlarged himself from his custody."

August 30 General James Arlington Bennett was baptized.

September 4 The *New York Sun* reported the following: "A great military despotism is growing up in the fertile west, increasing faster, in proportion, than the surrounding population, spreading its influence around, and marshalling multitudes under its banners, causing serious alarm to every patriot."

September 6 A public meeting in Carthage stated the following: "He has caused large bodies of his ragamuffin soldiery to arm themselves, and turn out in pursuit of officers, legally authorized to arrest himself; he being charged with high crimes and misdemeanors committed in the State of Missouri, and those officers arrested by the vilest hypocrisy, and placed in duress, that he might enable himself, to march triumphantly into Nauvoo, and bid defiance to the laws of the land."

September 8 General parade.

September 15 Officer drill.

September 16 General parade; from the journal: "General parade of the Nauvoo Legion near my farm—went in company with my staff to the muster, was met by an escort, and arrived before the Legion about noon. I was received and saluted with military honors. The Legion was dismissed about 1 P.M. for two hours, and I rode home to dinner . . . after the inspection I made a speech to the Legion on their increasing prosperity, and requested the officers to increase the Legion in numbers. I was highly gratified with the officers and soldiers, and I felt extremely well myself. About sun-down the Legion was dismissed. I rode home with my staff, highly delighted with the day's performance, and well paid for my services."

October 3	The day of the great feast. After more than a hundred people had dined at Joseph Smith's house, a committee was appointed to "draft resolutions suitable to the occasion." Among the resolutions was the following: "Resolved 2nd General Joseph Smith, whether we view him as a Prophet at the head of the Church; a General at the head of the Legion; a Mayor at the head of the City Council; or as a landlord at the head of his table, if he had equals he has no superior."
October 21	Court-martial.
October 24	W. W. Phelps and Jonathan Dunham went to Springfield to obtain a quota of state arms, "which belong[ed] to the Legion."
November 4	Court-martial.
November 30	Certain letters were written by W. L. D. Ewing and J. N. McDougall concerning the independence of the Nauvoo Legion. McDougall's inspection of the laws and regulations surrounding the Legion forced him to conclude that it was a separate entity, organized for the sole purpose of protecting the rights and ordinances of the municipalities of the city. And, inasmuch as it did not acquiesce with the state militia, it was subject to provide for its own. Thus, the state refused to make payment for the services of the officers. At this, Joseph Smith lamented, "[W]ere it not for the prejudice against us on account of our religion—his claim would have been paid without a word of complaint." The claim referred to was John Bills's appeal for payment under Section 53 of militia law.
December 6	Joseph Smith sent an affidavit to Governor Thomas Ford concerning Daniel Avery and his son's kidnapping. Interestingly, Smith wrote that he should "act according to the best of my judgment constitutionally, till I receive your instructions." He also added the following postscript: "Shall any portion of the Legion be called out?"
December 8	Joseph Smith wrote a letter to the marshal of Nauvoo, in which he ordered him to call out a portion of the legion to enforce obedience to the ordinances

and laws of the city. He also expressed his fear that other individuals would be kidnapped. Upon receiving the letter, H. G. Sherwood replied that "to have the ordinances of this city fully carried into effect . . . it will be necessary for you as mayor the city to issue orders to Major General Wilson Law, for a suitable portion of the Nauvoo Legion to be in readiness to compel obedience to said ordinances if necessary." Smith quickly complied.

December 8 Joseph Smith and the city council passed resolutions legalizing the arrest of individuals entering the city of Nauvoo with the intent to remove Smith on impudent and vituperative charges—both morally and politically illegal. The sentence for any such offender, if found guilty, was life in prison, without pardon, save by the consent of the state governor and mayor of Nauvoo.

December 9 At a large meeting, Joseph Smith spoke about the opinion of the attorney general, disagreeing that the Legion was a separate and aberrant military organization. With brevity, Smith declared that, as recorded, "[H]is commission declared that he (General Smith) was the Lieutenant General of the Nauvoo Legion, and of the militia of the State of Illinois, and as such it was not only his duty to enforce the city ordinances, but the laws of the State when called on by the Governor." Smith also received a letter from Major General Wilson Law requesting pecuniary aid and supplies.

December 12 Resolved that Joseph Smith select and command forty policemen for the peace of the city.

December 14 Joseph Smith received a letter from Governor Thomas Ford in which he refused Smith's request to "call out" the Legion. Ford solemnly denounced any use of the legion, save for purposes of extreme emergency.

December 15 Court-martial.

December 18 Aaron Johnson, a justice of the peace, requested a hundred men of the Nauvoo Legion to an imminent

	resistance by Levi Williams. Johnson had heard that Williams was gathering a mob to keep himself from being arrested.
December 19	Hosea Stout and his men, having come within two miles of Levi Williams's residence, returned home for weapons and ammunition. The Legion also paraded in Nauvoo and was instructed to be ready at a moment's notice.
December 29	Joseph Smith sent a letter to Governor Thomas Ford in which he related the events surrounding Levi Williams and his mob. Smith noted Aaron Johnson's request for a hundred armed men and his order to fulfill said request but pointed out that no portion of the legion "were ordered to march." Thus, they had only remained in readiness.

1844

January 3	A special city council was held. Several witnesses testified that William Law was the traitor of whom Joseph Smith had warned. Law felt denigrated, and he protested to such vilifications. Smith assured the court that there was no secret oath administered to the police outside the knowledge of the major general and instructed the police to put up their arms until further notice.
January 13	Court-martial.
February 10	Court-martial.
February 17	Joseph Smith wrote an article titled "Pacific Innuendo," in which he lauded Governor Thomas Ford as a peacemaker.
March 7	Joseph Smith met with an assembly of Latter-day Saints and presided over a conference. Among his several remarks was the following: "I will wage an eternal warfare with those that oppose me while I am laboring in behalf of the city." He also said, "As to politics, I care but little about the presidential chair, I would not give half as much for the office of President of the United States, as I would for the one I now hold as Lieut. General of the Nauvoo Legion."

March 26 — Joseph Smith drafted and sent to the U.S. Senate and House of Representatives an "Ordinance" proposing that Congress endow him with the rights and abilities to raise up to one hundred thousand volunteers "for the protection of the citizens of the United States emigrating to the adjoining Territories, and for the extension of the principles of universal liberty."

March 27 — Affidavits were sworn before Daniel H. Wells, justice of the peace, against the Law brothers, R. D. Foster, Chauncey L. Higbee, and Joseph H. Jackson, regarding their conspiracy to murder Joseph, Emma, Hyrum, and any other Smith directly related to the three.

March 31 — Alexander Mills informed Joseph Smith "that Chauncey L. Higbee drew a pistol on him the night before and threatened to shoot him. Joseph instructed Bro. Mills to make a complaint to Esquire Wells and have him apprehended."

April 6 — Sidney Rigdon and John Taylor spoke at a conference of the Church. Taylor's vivacious speech was categorized by the phrase "Hear it, ye great men, we are here in exile! Here are thousands of men in bondage in a land of liberty—of freedom!"

April 29 — "Lieut. Williams filed his affidavit versus Major General Wilson Law, and he was suspended from office to await his trial before a court martial of the Nauvoo Legion, for ungentlemanly conduct, &c. and he was notified of his command in the Legion being suspended, and Charles C. Rich was notified to take command, and also notified seven officers to sit as a court-martial."[4]

May 2 — Aaron Johnson of the legion made an affidavit concerning the ungentlemanly conduct of R. D. Foster and Wilson Law.

May 4 — Court-martial.

May 9 — Court-martial; Wilson Law was convicted of ungentlemanly conduct.

---

[4] Smith, *History of the Church*, 6:347–48.

May 10	Court-martial.
May 11	Legion muster.
May 18	Regimental training took place.
May 20	Court-martial.
May 21	Several affidavits were sworn and cases made for and against Joseph Smith and Chauncey Higbee, respectively.
[May]	Revised laws published.
June 10	Joseph Smith ordered the city marshal to destroy the *Nauvoo Expositor.* General Dunham was ordered to assist in any capacity necessary. Soon afterward, Joseph Smith was arrested for destruction of the *Expositor.*
June 16	Joseph Smith wrote to Governor Thomas Ford that a Carthage mob was gathering: "the Nauvoo Legion is at your service to quell all insurrections and support the dignity of the common wealth." Also on this day Smith wrote to Isaac Morley the following: "cause all the troops of said Legion in your vicinity to be in readiness to act at a moment's warning, and if the mob shall fall upon the Saints by force of arms defend them at every hazard, unless prudence dictate the retreat of the troops to Nauvoo, in which case the mob will not disturb your women and children; and if the mob move towards Nauvoo, either come before them or in their rear, and be ready to co-operate with the main body of the Legion. Instruct the companies to keep cool, and let all things be done decently and in order."
June 17	Joseph Smith wrote to Major General Dunham that he is obligated to do whatever is in his power to keep the peace and safety of the city. Smith then ordered a Legion parade for the next day, asked his staff and guard to meet at his headquarters—armed—and noted that the mobs were gathering. Smith wrote to Brigham Young, "Large bodies of armed men, cannon and munitions of war are coming on from Missouri in steam boats. . . . [Y]ou will readily see that we have to prepare from the onset."

June 18 — Legion parade; Joseph Smith delivered his last address in uniform. The city was placed under martial law.

June 19 — Legion parade; Chester Loveland was compelled by a mob led by James Charles to arrest Joseph Smith and the city council members. Loveland refused. Smith "gave orders to Gen. Dunham to have a picket guard under Col. Markham posted on all the roads leading out of the city; also an inner guard under Major Jesse P. Harmon posted in all the streets and alleys in the city, and also on the river bank. [He] also gave orders to have all the powder and lead in the city secured, and to see that all the arms were in use, and that all vacant arms be put in the hands of those who could use them."

June 20 — Obadiah Bowen reported hearing John Clark—a member of the mob—say, "it is no disgrace to shoot a Mormon, anyhow." Willard Richards wrote to J. A. Bennett, "We are already being surrounded by an armed mob, and if we can believe a hundredth part of their statements, we have no alternative but to fight or die."

June 22 — Last personal journal dictations of Joseph Smith: "I instructed Gen. Dunham to cause the regiments of the 2nd cohort to turn out to-morrow, and work by turns three or four hours each with intrenching tools, and to take the best measures in case of attack. I also gave orders that a standard be prepared for the nations."

June 22 — Governor Thomas Ford wrote a letter in which he declared, "I am anxious to preserve the peace. A small indiscretion may bring on a war. The whole country is now up in arms, and a vast number of people are ready to take the matter into their own hands. Such a state of things might force me to call out the militia to prevent a civil war." In this letter Ford also stated that he could do nothing for Smith or the people if Smith refused to acquiesce with the law.

June 22	Joseph Smith prophesied, "I told Stephen Markham that if I and Hyrum were ever taken again, we should be massacred, or I was not a prophet of God."
June 23	Joseph and Hyrum Smith decided to give themselves to the governor at Carthage.
June 24	Prior to leaving for Carthage, Joseph countersigned a state order from Governor Thomas Ford requiring the Legion to surrender its arms.
June 27	Joseph and Hyrum Smith were murdered in Carthage. In Nauvoo, the Legion paraded, well armed, even though the state arms had been confiscated. Governor Thomas Ford then arrived in Nauvoo with fifty soldiers, stood in front of the Mansion House and addressed the people.
June 29	The Nauvoo Legion, expecting a mob attack, was out all night between June 28 and 29. However, the city council resolved to do all it could to preserve peace within the city.
July 1	Governor Thomas Ford sent Colonel Fellows and Captain Jonas to Nauvoo to "ascertain whether any of them propose in any manner to revenge themselves, whether any threats have been used, and what is proposed generally, to be done by them. They are also requested to return to Warsaw and make similar inquiries there; ascertain how far false rumors have been put afloat for the purpose of raising forces; what is the purpose of the militia assembled, whether any attack is intended on Nauvoo."
July 2	General Dunham wrote a letter to Governor Thomas Ford, asking him to send "one hundred or two hundred men who you can depend upon as loyal, to quarter in the woods between here and Golden's Point, so that they can be between us and the mob to protect us. Our troops are worn out, and I shall soon expect an order from you to discharge my men from the duty they are obliged to perform, to fulfill your order."
July 31	Governor Thomas Ford wrote to the people of Warsaw, "Since the assassination of their two prin-

	cipal leaders, under circumstances well calculated to inflame their passions, and drive them to excesses for the purposes of revenge, they have been entirely peaceful and submissive; and have patiently awaited the slow operation of the laws to redress the wrongs of which they complained. There has been no retaliation, no revenge, and, for anything I can ascertain, there will be none."
August 31	Brigham Young elected lieutenant general of the Nauvoo Legion.
September 10	Brigham Young attended a meeting of the Nauvoo Legion officers, who passed a resolution to build an arsenal and gunsmith's shop.
September 16	Ground for the arsenal was broken. Brigham Young "dedicated the ground, by prayer, to the God of the armies of Israel."[5]
September 27	Brigham Young received his commission as lieutenant general. Charles C. Rich was commissioned as major general. Governor Thomas Ford arrived in Nauvoo with four hundred and seventy men, vowing to bring Thomas Sharp, Levi Williams and Jackson to justice.
September 28	The Nauvoo Legion was reviewed.
October	Governor Thomas Ford disbanded his troops. Thomas Sharp and Levi Williams had given themselves up and gone to Quincy under a contract with the governor.
October 9	Brigham Young received a letter from Governor Thomas Ford that addressed him as "Lieutenant General." The letter warned Young of a possible uprising and ordered him to hold in "readiness a sufficient force under your command of the Nauvoo Legion to act under the direction of the said Sheriff [of Hancock County] for the purposes aforesaid; and to suppress mobs which may be collected in said county to injure the persons or property to any of the citizens." Ford ended with this: "[T]he enclosed order is more intended as permission to use

[5] Smith, *History of the Church*, 7:271.

	the Legion in the manner indicated if upon the whole matter it is thought advisable than a compulsory command."
October 15	Levi Williams evaded the sheriff and escaped into Missouri.
October 24	The Nauvoo police force took most of the responsibility for guarding the city and Brigham Young through November.

1845

January 1	The repeal of the Nauvoo Charter was discussed in the Illinois senate.
February 10	Latter-day Saints mourned the repeal of the Nauvoo Charter.
March 31	Brigham Young wrote to Governor Thomas Ford "asking his counsel in relation to the reorganization of the Militia of the city of Nauvoo, as the legion was dissolved by a repeal of the Charter."
May 7	Hosea Stout recorded that he met with various officers of the legion "to regulate matters in case we should be attacked by our enemies. I was appointed to act as Brigadier-General second cohort."
June 25	James Arlington Bennett "applies to be consecrated a General of the Nauvoo Legion that he may fight Napoleon's battles over again, either in Nauvoo or elsewhere."[6]
September 15	First and Second Cohorts of the Legion met to place themselves in readiness to act at the Sheriff's call.
September 16	Sheriff Backenstos's house in Carthage is burned. He retreated to Warsaw but was pursued by a mob to Nauvoo. He met Rockwell and John Redding on the path and begged for their protection. Rockwell fired, on Backenstos's order, and killed Frank Worrell, and the "rest turned back and soon brought up a wagon to put his body into it."[7]
September 19	As the whole city gathered to defend it, Brigham Young told the Latter-day Saints that the temple

[6] Smith, *History of the Church*, 7:429.

[7] Smith, *History of the Church*, 7:447.

should be finished even "if they had to hold the sword in one hand and the trowel in the other."

October 25 — Major Warren entered Nauvoo, disgusted at seeing fifteen or so legionnaires on patrol. John Taylor then stated the following: "We lack confidence in the governor's troops under your command while hundreds of murderers, robbers, and house-burners roam at large unwhipped of justice. We shall take measures to protect ourselves. I, sir, have been shot all to pieces under the 'protection' of the governor's troops. Our leading men have been murdered in Carthage and we shall not trust ourselves unprotected again until the state gives some evidence more than it has done of its justice and humane intentions to enforce its laws."[8]

November 15 — Part of the mob set fire to a stack of straw near Solomon Hancock's barn. When Hancock and others went to extinguish the fire, they were fired upon by the concealed mobbers. Edmund Durfee was killed on the spot, and Joseph B. Brackenbury died of poisoning at Pomfret. Afterward they boasted that Mormon elders didn't have enough faith to stand poison.

November 18 — James Arlington Bennett asked to be appointed military commander in chief in the Church.

1846

January 29 — A number of the governor's troops were seen around Nauvoo and were suspected of seeking to arrest some of the leading men of the Church.

February 9 — Troops entered the city and apprehended a man named Samuel Smith.

February–April — Camps of Israel in Iowa Territory. Men of the Legion keeping watch as guards.

September — Battle of Nauvoo. Remnants of the Nauvoo Legion surrendered to Illinois troops.

---

[8] Smith, *History of the Church*, 7:487–88.

Appendix D

Commissioned and Noncommissioned Officers of the Nauvoo Legion (1841–1845)

Name	Birth Date	Death Date	Rank	Company
Abbot, Jacob Farnum	Sept 13, 1808	about 1872	3rd Lt.	2nd Co.
Abner, William M.			Capt.	
Aldridge, William	June 27, 1787	Aug 13, 1863	1st Lt.	1st Co.
Alexander, Horace M.	Feb 15, 1812	Sept 18, 1881	3rd Lt.	2nd Co.
Alexander, Horace M.	Feb 15, 1812	Sept 18, 1881	1st Lt.	1st Co.
Alexander, Horace M.	Feb 15, 1812	Sept 18, 1881	1st Lt.	
Allen, C.			1st Lt.	1st Co.
Allen, Charles	Dec 26, 1806	before 1880	Qm. Sgt.	
Allen, Orvil Morgan	June 9, 1805	Nov 12, 1893	Capt.	
Allen, Orvil Morgan	June 9, 1805	Nov 12, 1893	Capt.	3rd Co.
Allen, Philo	Jan 3, 1818	July 17, 1909	1st Sgt.	4th Co.
Allred, Isaac	June 28, 1813	May 12, 1859	Capt.	
Allred, Isaac	June 28, 1813	May 12, 1859	Capt.	
Allred, James Tillman S.	March 28, 1825	March 29, 1905	Capt.	
Allred, James Tillman S.	March 28, 1825	March 29, 1905	3rd Lt.	
Allred, Reuben Warren	Nov 18, 1815	Oct 4, 1896	3rd Lt.	1st Co.
Allred, Wiley Payne	May 31, 1818	March 28, 1912	3rd Lt.	
Allred, William Moore	Dec 24, 1819	Jan 8, 1901	3rd Lt.	1st Co.
Allred, William Moore	Dec 24, 1819	Jan 8, 1901	1st Lt.	1st Co.
Allred, William Moore	Dec 24, 1819	Jan 8, 1901	Capt.	
Ames, Ira V.	Sept 22, 1804	Jan 16, 1869	2nd Lt.	3rd Co.
Anderson, John	March 9, 1796	about 1870	3rd Lt.	
Anderson, Miles	Oct 30, 1795	July 23, 1876	1st Lt.	4th Co.
Anderson, Thomas			Capt.	
Andrews, Joseph Albert W.	Sept 19, 1810	Oct 8, 1843	Capt.	
Andrews, Joseph Albert W.	Sept 19, 1810	Oct 8, 1843	Capt.	2nd Co.
Andrews, Solomon	Sept 2, 1822		4th Sgt.	4th Co.
Angel, Truman Osborn	June 5, 1810	Oct 16, 1887	3rd Lt.	2nd Co.
Angel, Truman Osborn	June 5, 1810	Oct 16, 1887	2nd Lt.	
Angel, Truman Osborn	June 5, 1810	Oct 16, 1887	Capt.	2nd Co.
Annis, John Closson	Nov 17, 1784	June 1849	3rd Lt.	1st Co.
Ashton, Isaac	July 4, 1811	May 26, 1898	2nd Sgt.	3rd Co.
Austin, William	March 10, 1800	July 3, 1887	Capt.	8th Co.
Austin, William	March 10, 1800	July 3, 1887	2nd Lt.	3rd Co.
Backenstos, Jacob B.	Oct 8, 1811	Sept 25, 1857	Adjutant	
Backenstos, Jacob B.	Oct 8, 1811	Sept 25, 1857	Aide-de-Camp to Maj. Gen.	
Bacon, Chauncey	Nov 22, 1808	Aug 31, 1888	1st Lt.	7th Co.
Badlam, Alexander	Nov 28, 1808	Dec 4, 1894	2nd Lt.	2nd Co.

Battalion	Regiment	Cohort	Date of Rank	Commission
	4th	2nd	April 9, 1842	
	2nd	2nd	Nov 5, 1842	
2nd	3rd	2nd	July 3, 1841	Oct 16, 1841
2nd	3rd	2nd	Sept 4, 1841	Dec 14, 1841
	4th	2nd	April 9, 1842	
		2nd	April 16, 1842	
2nd	3rd	2nd	July 3, 1841	Oct 16, 1841
	1st	1st	May 1842	
		2nd	April 2, 1842	
2nd	5th	2nd	Aug 19, 1843	Oct 28, 1843
	4th	2nd		
	5th	2nd	July 1, 1842	Sept 19, 1842
	5th	2nd	April 8, 1843	
		2nd	March 9, 1841	Dec 16, 1843
		2nd	Sept 28, 1844	Dec 14, 1844
1st	3rd	2nd	Sept 10, 1842	Oct 28, 1843
	2nd	2nd	April 2, 1842	
2nd	1st	2nd	March 9, 1841	
2nd	1st	2nd	May 1, 1841	June 5, 1841
		2nd	March 5, 1842	
2nd	5th	2nd	Aug 19, 1843	Oct 28, 1843
		2nd	May 6, 1842	
2nd	5th	2nd	Oct 9, 1843	Oct 28, 1843
				Feb 19, 1840
	5th	2nd	Aug 19, 1843	
	5th	2nd	July 4, 1843	Oct 28, 1843
	5th	2nd		
1st	3rd	2nd	May 1, 1841	June 5, 1841
		2nd	June 28, 1842	
	1st	2nd	March 25, 1843	June 8, 1843
1st	1st	2nd	March 9, 1841	
	4th	2nd		
2nd	4th	2nd	Oct 14, 1843	Oct 28, 1843
1st	3rd	2nd	Aug 26, 1843	Oct 28, 1843
	1st	1st	May 1, 1841	June 5, 1841
	1st	1st	May 1, 1841	
2nd	4th	2nd	May 6, 1843	Dec 14, 1843
1st	1st	2nd	March 9, 1841	

Name	Birth Date	Death Date	Rank	Company
Badlam, Alexander	Nov 28, 1808	Dec 4, 1894	1st Lt.	2nd Co.
Bair, John	Nov 26, 1810	Oct 11, 1884	1st Lt.	8th Co.
Bair, John	Nov 26, 1810	Oct 11, 1884	1st Lt.	2nd Co.
Bair, John	Nov 26, 1810	Oct 11, 1884	2nd Lt.	2nd Co.
Baird, Robert E.	May 15, 1817	Aug 24, 1875	4th Cpl.	4th Co.
Banon, A. L.			1st Lt.	1st Co.
Barlow, Truman Root	Aug 9, 1818	Feb 1858	3rd Lt.	1st Co.
Barlow, Truman Root	Aug 9, 1818	Feb 1858	2nd Lt.	
Barlow, Truman Root	Aug 9, 1818	Feb 1858	1st Lt.	
Barnes, David Patten	Jan 15, 1809	after 1880	3rd Lt.	
Barnett, John Tipton	Oct 20, 1809	Sept 2, 1905	1st Lt.	1st Co.
Barnett, John Tipton	Oct 20, 1809	Sept 2, 1905	Bvt. Capt.	1st Co.
Barnett, John Tipton	Oct 20, 1809	Sept 2, 1905	Capt.	1st Co.
Barney, Edson	June 30, 1806	Feb 2, 1905	2nd Lt.	
Barney, Royale, Jr.	Dec 15, 1808	June 9, 1890	2nd Lt.	2nd Co.
Barnum, Charles A.	Aug 11, 1809	Sept 6, 1846	3rd Lt.	1st Co.
Barnum, Charles Days	May 9, 1800	Sept 9, 1894	3rd Lt.	1st Co.
Barnum, Charles Days	May 9, 1800	Sept 9, 1894	Capt.	2nd Co.
Barnum, Charles Days	May 9, 1800	Sept 9, 1894	Capt.	
Barton, John	June 22, 1808	May 16, 1887	1st Sgt.	3rd Co.
Bell, William			2nd Sgt.	6th Co.
Bennett, James Arlington	1788	Dec 25, 1863	Inspector Gen.	
Bennett, James Arlington	1788	Dec 25, 1863	Inspector Gen. with the rank of Maj. Gen.	
Bennett, John Cook	Aug 4, 1804	Aug 5, 1867	Aide-de-Camp to Maj. Gen. with rank of Brig. Gen.	
Bennett, John Cook	Aug 4, 1804	Aug 5, 1867	Maj. Gen.	
Bennett, John Cook	Aug 4, 1804	Aug 5, 1867	Inspector Gen.	Nauvoo Leg
Bennett, Samuel	1809	after 1880	Surgeon	
Bennett, Samuel	1809	after 1880	Maj.	
Bennett, Samuel	1809	after 1880	Surgeon	
Bent, Samuel	July 19, 1778	Aug 16, 1846	Col.	
Bentley, Richard	Oct 1, 1820	March 24, 1906	1st Lt.	1st Co.
Billings, Samuel	March 3, 1791	June 9, 1869	Maj.	
Billings, Titus	March 24, 1793	Feb 6, 1866	Capt.	1st Co.
Billings, Titus	March 24, 1793	Feb 6, 1866	Bvt. Maj.	
Billings, Titus	March 24, 1793	Feb 6, 1866	Lt. Col.	1st Co.
Billings, Titus	March 24, 1793	Feb 6, 1866	Col.	

Battalion	Regiment	Cohort	Date of Rank	Commission
1st	1st	2nd	Sept 9, 1841	Dec 14, 1841
	4th	2nd	Oct 3, 1843	Oct 28, 1843
	4th	2nd	Sept 9, 1843	
	4th	2nd	April 9, 1842	
	4th	2nd		
1st	3rd	2nd	May 1, 1841	June 5, 1841
1st		1st	April 6, 1841	Oct 16, 1841
			May 1, 1841	
		1st	Sept 24, 1842	April 27, 1843
		1st	June 17, 1842	Sept 19, 1842
2nd	1st	2nd	March 9, 1841	
2nd	1st	2nd	March 9, 1841	
2nd	1st	2nd	May 1, 1841	June 5, 1841
		2nd	March 11, 1842	
1st	2nd	2nd	March 11, 1842	
2nd	1st	2nd		
2nd	1st	2nd	May 1, 1841	June 5, 1841
	4th	2nd	April 2, 1842	
			April 2, 1842	
	4th	2nd		
	4th	2nd		
			April 12, 1841	
			April 12, 1842	May 2, 1842
			May 28, 1842	June 2, 1842
			Feb 5, 1841	
			July 5, 1841	Oct 16, 1841
		2nd	Nov 30, 1841	
			July 25, 1842	
			Nov 13, 1841	
	3rd	2nd	April 6, 1841	Oct 16, 1841
1st	5th	2nd	July 4, 1843	Oct 28, 1843
	4th	2nd	July 1, 1844	
1st	1st	2nd	March 9, 1841	
1st	1st	2nd	March 9, 1841	
1st	1st	2nd	May 1, 1841	June 5, 1841
	1st	2nd	Sept 4, 1841	Dec 14, 1841

Name	Birth Date	Death Date	Rank	Company
Bills, John	Sept 17, 1819	Feb 19, 1850	Sgt. Maj.	
Bills, John	Sept 17, 1819	Feb 19, 1850	Asst. Inspector Gen.	
Bills, John	Sept 17, 1819	Feb 19, 1850	Bvt. Brig. Gen.	
Bills, John	Sept 17, 1819	Feb 19, 1850	Maj.	
Bills, John	Sept 17, 1819	Feb 19, 1850	Brig. Maj.	
Binley, John Wesley	April 18, 1816	Feb 1893	Lt. Maj. Sgt.	
Bird, Charles	Sept 19, 1803	Sept 29, 1884	1st Lt.	
Bitter, William			4th Sgt.	1st Co.
Black, George	Oct 17, 1817	Aug 24, 1845	Capt.	
Bliss, Robert Stanton	Aug 1, 1805	1851	3rd Lt.	2nd Co.
Bliss, Robert Stanton	Aug 1, 1805	1851	1st Lt.	
Bonney, Amasa	1804	Dec 15, 1864	1st Lt.	2nd Co.
Bonney, Amasa	1804	Dec 15, 1864	Sgt. Maj.	
Bonney, Edward William	Aug 26, 1807	Feb 4, 1864	2nd Lt.	
Boren, Beverly Collins	1819		1st Lt.	4th Co.
Bowman, Isaac	June 29, 1826	May 1, 1892	2nd Lt.	1st Co.
Boyce, Josiah	March 10, 1802	about 1877	2nd Lt.	1st Co.
Boyce, Josiah	March 10, 1802	about 1877	1st Lt.	1st Co.
Bracken, Levi	May 14, 1792	Aug 1, 1852	Capt.	2nd Co.
Bracken, Levi	May 14, 1792	Aug 1, 1852	2nd Lt.	2nd Co.
Brandon, George Washington	Oct 20, 1809	June 3, 1849	Capt.	3rd Co.
Brooks, Alfred J. L.			1st Lt.	
Brown, Ebenezer S.	Dec 6, 1801	Jan 26, 1878	Adjutant	
Brown, James	Sept 30, 1801	Sept 30, 1863	Lt. Col.	
Brown, James	Sept 30, 1801	Sept 30, 1863	3rd Lt.	
Brown, James	Sept 30, 1801	Sept 30, 1863	3rd Lt.	Nauvoo Leg
Brown, James	Sept 30, 1801	Sept 30, 1863	3rd Lt.	2nd Co.
Brown, William	Jan 3, 1816	Sept 28, 1899	3rd Sgt.	1st Co.
Brownman, P. G.			2nd Lt.	1st Co.
Burbank, Daniel Marcus	Dec 3, 1814	Jan 15, 1894	3rd Lt.	2nd Co.
Burbank, Daniel Marcus	Dec 3, 1814	Jan 15, 1894	2nd Lt.	2nd Co.
Burbank, Daniel Marcus	Dec 3, 1814	Jan 15, 1894	3rd Lt.	2nd Co.
Burgess, James	Feb 25, 1818	June 18, 1904	2nd Cpl.	6th Co.
Burgess, Samuel J.	June 8, 1825	Oct 11, 1875	5th Sgt.	6th Co.
Burgess, William	May 20, 1794	Nov 20, 1880	Capt.	3rd Co.
Burghardt, John H.	1822	Dec 25, 1865	3rd Cpl.	2nd Co.
Burglow, Luther V.	Aug 27, 1810		4th Sgt.	1st Co.
Burglow, Luther V.	Aug 27, 1810		2nd Sgt.	1st Co.
Burns, David			3rd Lt.	

Battalion	Regiment	Cohort	Date of Rank	Commission
	2nd	1st	July 3, 1841	Oct 16, 1841
		2nd	Nov 30, 1841	Dec 14, 1841
			June 2, 1842	
			July 23, 1842	
	2nd	2nd	July 23, 1842	April 27, 1843
	4th	2nd	July 1, 1844	
		1st	July 4, 1842	Sept 19, 1842
	4th	2nd		
			May 18, 1844	Dec 14, 1844
1st	2nd	1st	July 3, 1841	Oct 16, 1841
			July 3, 1841	
1st	2nd	1st	July 3, 1841	Oct 16, 1841
	2nd	1st	June 6, 1842	
	2nd	2nd	Aug 5, 1843	
2nd	3rd	2nd	Sept 7, 1843	Oct 28, 1843
1st	3rd	2nd	May 1, 1841	
	4th	2nd	April 16, 1842	
	4th	2nd	Sept 9, 1843	
2nd	2nd	2nd	April 6, 1841	Oct 16, 1841
2nd	2nd	2nd	May 1, 1841	June 5, 1841
2nd	2nd	2nd	Aug 20, 1843	Oct 28, 1843
			Sept 25, 1842	June 8, 1843
	4th	2nd	April 2, 1842	
	4th	2nd	April 2, 1842	
		2nd	April 4, 1842	
		2nd	April 8, 1843	June 8, 1843
			April 8, 1843	June 8, 1843
	4th	2nd		
1st	3rd	2nd	May 1, 1841	June 5, 1841
	4th	2nd	Sept 5, 1843	
	4th	2nd	June 18, 1844	
	4th	2nd	July 18, 1844	
	4th	2nd	Sept 5, 1843	
	4th	2nd	Sept 5, 1843	
1st	5th	2nd	Sept 2, 1843	Oct 28, 1843
	4th	2nd	Sept 5, 1843	
	4th	2nd		
	4th	2nd	Sept 5, 1843	
		2nd	June 17, 1842	

Name	Birth Date	Death Date	Rank	Company
Butler, John Lowe	April 8, 1808	April 10, 1861	Aide-de-Camp	
Butterfield, Abel	Dec 1, 1811	Feb 26, 1886	3rd Sgt.	1st Co.
Cahoon, Pulaski Stephens	Sept 18, 1820	Feb 15, 1892	Qm. Sgt.	
Cahoon, Reynolds	April 30, 1790	April 29, 1861	Guard (Aide-de-Camp)	
Calkins, Luman Hopkins	Jan 15, 1816	Oct 21, 1892	Capt.	
Calkins, Sylvanus	Dec 30, 1823	July 10, 1901	Capt.	
Call, Anson	May 13, 1810	Aug 31, 1890	2nd Lt.	1st Co.
Call, Anson	May 13, 1810	Aug 31, 1890	1st Lt.	1st Co.
Call, Josiah Howe	Aug 12, 1822	Oct 7, 1858	3rd Lt.	
Carn, Daniel	Dec 13, 1802	April 22, 1872	2nd Lt.	
Carrico, Thomas	Sept 20, 1801	Feb 22, 1882	Adjutant	
Carrico, Thomas	Sept 20, 1801	Feb 22, 1882	2nd Lt.	2nd Co.
Case, Nathaniel			Capt.	7th Co.
Casteel, Jacob Israel	1797	May 1860	3rd Lt.	3rd Co.
Cathcart, Daniel R.	Aug 10, 1803		3rd Lt.	2nd Co.
Champlin, William	April 16, 1794	Jan 29, 1861	3rd Lt.	
Chapman, Welcome	July 24, 1805	Dec 9, 1893	3rd Lt.	
Chase, Charles Alvin	Nov 23, 1818		3rd Lt.	3rd Co.
Chase, Darwin J.	Feb 25, 1816	Feb 4, 1863	1st Lt.	1st Co.
Chase, Darwin J.	Feb 25, 1816	Feb 4, 1863	Capt.	1st Co.
Chase, Darwin J.	Feb 25, 1816	Feb 4, 1863	2nd Lt.	1st Co.
Chase, Darwin J.	Feb 25, 1816	Feb 4, 1863	Capt.	
Chase, Darwin J.	Feb 25, 1816	Feb 4, 1863	Capt.	1st Co.
Chase, Hyrum Barry	March 14, 1823		2nd Sgt.	2nd Co.
Chase, Stephen	April 11, 1799	Feb 11, 1847	1st Lt.	2nd Co.
Cheese, John			1st Lt.	2nd Co.
Cheese, John			1st Lt.	1st Co.
Chidester, John Maddison	Jan 22, 1809	Aug 29, 1893	1st Lt.	
Chidester, John Maddison	Jan 22, 1809	Aug 29, 1893	2nd Lt.	
Chidester, John Maddison	Jan 22, 1809	Aug 29, 1893	2nd Lt.	2nd Co.
Chidester, John Maddison	Jan 22, 1809	Aug 29, 1893	1st Lt.	
Chidester, John Maddison	Jan 22, 1809	Aug 29, 1893	1st Lt.	
Chomolan, William I.			2nd Cpl.	
Chrisman, Charles	Dec 25, 1807	March 23, 1893	1st Lt.	

Battalion	Regiment	Cohort	Date of Rank	Commission
			March 9, 1841	
	4th	2nd	Sept 5, 1843	
	2nd	2nd	July 3, 1841	Oct 16, 1841
			March 9, 1841	
		2nd	March 26, 1842	
			April 16, 1841	
2nd	1st	1st	March 9, 1841	
2nd	1st	1st	April 6, 1841	Oct 16, 1841
		1st	Oct 8, 1842	
		2nd	May 5, 1842	
	1st	2nd	March 25, 1843	
		2nd	March 25, 1843	June 8, 1843
2nd	4th	2nd		Dec 14, 1843
2nd	2nd	2nd	Aug 20, 1843	Oct 28, 1843
1st	1st	2nd	Sept 9, 1841	Dec 14, 1841
	5th	2nd	June 20, 1842	
	1st	2nd	June 30, 1842	
2nd	2nd	2nd	May 1, 1841	June 5, 1841
1st	5th	2nd	Sept 2, 1843	Oct 28, 1843
1st	2nd	2nd	April 6, 1841	Oct 16, 1841
1st	2nd	2nd	Sept 6, 1841	Dec 14, 1841
1st	2nd	2nd	March 9, 1841	
		2nd	May 1, 1841	
1st	2nd	2nd	Nov 6, 1841	
	4th	2nd		
3rd	3rd	2nd	July 22, 1843	Oct 28, 1843
2nd	3rd	2nd	Aug 18, 1843	Oct 28, 1843
		1st	April 18, 1843	
		2nd	April 8, 1843	June 8, 1843
			April 8, 1843	June 8, 1843
	5th	2nd	April 8, 1843	
		1st	April 8, 1843	Dec 14, 1844
	2nd	2nd	Oct 6, 1843	
		1st	June 18, 1842	Sept 19, 1842

Name	Birth Date	Death Date	Rank	Company
Clark, Hiram W.	Sept 22, 1795	Dec 28, 1853	1st Lt.	2nd Co.
Clark, Hiram W.	Sept 22, 1795	Dec 28, 1853	2nd Lt.	4th Co.
Clark, Isaac	May 7, 1806	Jan 24, 1854	2nd Lt.	
Clawson, Moses	Oct 8, 1801	June 14, 1877	Capt.	
Clawson, Moses	Oct 8, 1801	June 14, 1877	Capt.	5th Co.
Clawson, William Henry	Nov 6, 1825	Aug 1852	1st Sgt.	5th Co.
Clyde, George Washington	Aug 9, 1798	Sept 7, 1844	Capt.	
Cochran, John	July 23, 1804	Oct 29, 1887	3rd Lt.	3rd Co.
Colton, Philander	Jan 11, 1811	Aug 15, 1891	Lt. Col.	1st Co.
Colton, Philander	Jan 11, 1811	Aug 15, 1891	Lt. Col.	
Colton, Philander	Jan 11, 1811	Aug 15, 1891	2nd Lt.	1st Co.
Colton, Philander	Jan 11, 1811	Aug 15, 1891	1st Lt.	1st Co.
Colton, Philander	Jan 11, 1811	Aug 15, 1891	1st Lt.	1st Co.
Coltrin, Graham	Dec 11, 1796	May 16, 1851	3rd Lt.	
Conner, William James	Nov 2, 1819		1st Lt.	
Conover, Peter Wilson	Sept 19, 1807	Sept 20, 1892	Capt.	1st Co.
Conover, Peter Wilson	Sept 19, 1807	Sept 20, 1892	Maj.	
Conrad, Vincent Matthew	Sept 12, 1812	Dec 8, 1892	2nd Lt.	
Cooke, George			Bvt. Maj. Gen.	
Coolidge, Joseph Wellington	May 31, 1814	Jan 15, 1871	Sgt. Maj.	
Coolidge, Joseph Wellington	May 31, 1814	Jan 15, 1871	Adjutant	
Coray, George W.	May 11, 1819	1848	2nd Lt.	
Coray, George W.	May 11, 1819	1848	1st Lt.	
Corden, Alfred	Feb 28, 1817	March 13, 1871	1st Sgt.	
Coulson, George	Sept 22, 1801	Oct 8, 1851	Col.	
Crouse, George W.	about 1802	1892	Adjutant	
Curtis, Uriah	May 5, 1805	Oct 18, 1863	4th Cpl.	
Cutler, Alpheus	Feb 29, 1784	Aug 10, 1864	Guard	
Cutler, Alpheus	Feb 29, 1784	Aug 10, 1864	Capt. (Aide-de-Camp)	
Dame, William Horne	July 15, 1819	Aug 15, 1884	2nd Lt.	2nd Co.
Dana, Charles Root	Nov 8, 1802	Aug 7, 1868	Capt.	4th Co.
Darkey, Edward			Capt.	
Davis, Amos	May 28, 1811	1872	1st Lt.	2nd Co.
Davis, Amos	May 28, 1811	1872	Bvt. Capt.	2nd Co.
Davis, Amos	May 28, 1811	1872	Capt.	2nd Co.

Battalion	Regiment	Cohort	Date of Rank	Commission
2nd	1st	2nd	May 1, 1841	June 5, 1841
2nd	3rd	2nd	Sept 7, 1843	Oct 28, 1843
		1st	June 18, 1842	Sept 19, 1842
			March 26, 1842	
	4th	2nd	April 16, 1842	
	4th	2nd	Sept 5, 1843	
		2nd	June 4, 1842	Sept 19, 1842
	4th	2nd	July 4, 1843	Oct 28, 1843
1st	2nd	2nd	July 21, 1843	
	2nd	2nd	July 30, 1842	
1st	2nd	2nd	April 6, 1841	
1st	2nd	2nd	Sept 6, 1841	Dec 14, 1841
1st	2nd	2nd	Nov 6, 1841	
		1st	Sept 24, 1842	April 27, 1843
			June 4, 1842	Oct 15, 1842
2nd	2nd	2nd	May 1, 1841	June 5, 1841
2nd	2nd	2nd	Sept 9, 1843	Oct 28, 1843
		1st	July 4, 1842	Sept 19, 1842
			June 7, 1842	June 28, 1842
	2nd	2nd	July 3, 1841	Oct 16, 1841
	2nd	2nd	Sept 24, 1842	
		2nd	June 25, 1842	Sept 19, 1842
		2nd	Sept 17, 1842	
			Sept 17, 1842	
	2nd	1st	July 3, 1841	Oct 16, 1841
	5th	2nd	July 28, 1843	Oct 28, 1843
	2nd	2nd	Aug 6, 1843	
			March 9, 1841	
			March 9, 1841	
2nd	2nd	2nd	July 3, 1841	Oct 16, 1841
	4th	2nd	April 2, 1842	
		1st	July 18, 1842	Sept 19, 1842
1st	1st	1st	March 9, 1841	
1st	1st	1st		
1st	1st	1st	May 1, 1841	June 5, 1841

Name	Birth Date	Death Date	Rank	Company
Davis, Salisbury Baxter	1816	1843	Ensign	
Dean, Amos			Bvt. Brig. Gen. (Aide-de-Camp)	
Dean, John			Bvt. Brig. Gen. (Aide-de-Camp)	
Dean, John			Pioneer	5th Co.
Degraw, John Jerome	about 1810	July 22, 1843	Capt.	
Degraw, John Jerome	about 1810	July 22, 1843	1st Lt.	
Derby, Erastus Herman	Sept 14, 1801	Dec 3, 1890	Aide-de-Camp to Brig. Gen.	
Devott, David	Nov 27, 1805		Ensign	4th Co.
Dewley, Jacob	March 20, 1822	June 26, 1853	5th Sgt.	5th Co.
Dibble, Philo	June 6, 1806	June 11, 1895	Maj. (Herald and Armor Bearer)	
Dille, David Buel	April 5, 1812	Jan 1, 1887	3rd Lt.	8th Co.
Dille, David Buel	April 5, 1812	Jan 1, 1887	1st Lt.	8th Co.
Dilworth, A.			2nd Sgt.	4th Co.
Dixon, Nathan			Capt.	
Driggs, Lorenzo Dow	March 14, 1822	Jan 14, 1880	2nd Lt.	
Driggs, Lorenzo Dow	March 14, 1822	Jan 14, 1880	Lt.	
Driggs, Lorenzo Dow	March 14, 1822	Jan 14, 1880	3rd Lt.	
Driggs, Samuel	Feb 15, 1820	Jan 16, 1854	2nd Lt.	
Duel, Amos C.	March 4, 1797	Aug 1878	2nd Lt.	
Duel, Osman Merrit	Jan 1, 1802	Jan 11, 1889	2nd Lt.	2nd Co.
Duke, Jonathan Oldham	Aug 31, 1807	Dec 31, 1868	2nd Lt.	2nd Co.
Dunham, Jonathan R.	Jan 14, 1800	July 28, 1845	Col.	4th Co.
Dunham, Jonathan R.	Jan 14, 1800	July 28, 1845	Brig. Gen.	
Duzette, Edward Peas	Jan 24, 1812	Dec 9, 1874	Chief Musician	
Dykes, George Parker	Dec 24, 1814	Feb 25, 1888	1st Lt.	
Eagle, John	1800	before 1860	Adjutant	
Eagle, John	1800	before 1860	Aide-de-Camp to Maj. Gen.	
Earl, John	Sept 8, 1827	July 13, 1908	4th Cpl.	2nd Co.
Eggleston, Samuel	March 30, 1804	May 26, 1884	1st Lt.	
Ellis, John	Jan 4, 1814	April 3, 1871	3rd Lt.	
Ellis, John	Jan 4, 1814	April 3, 1871	3rd Lt.	3rd Co.
Ells, Josiah	March 4, 1806	Oct 15, 1885	Lt. Col.	
Evans, Horace	Sept 5, 1810		2nd Lt.	2nd Co.
Evans, Horace	Sept 5, 1810		3rd Lt.	2nd Co.
Evans, Horace	Sept 5, 1810		2nd Lt.	2nd Co.

Battalion	Regiment	Cohort	Date of Rank	Commission
		2nd	May 11, 1843	Dec 14, 1843
			June 2, 1842	June 28, 1842
			June 7, 1842	
	4th	2nd	Sept 5, 1843	
		1st	July 16, 1842	Sept 19, 1842
		2nd	April 30, 1842	
		1st	Nov 30, 1841	Dec 14, 1841
	4th	2nd	June 20, 1844	
	4th	2nd	Sept 5, 1843	
			March 1, 1842	
2nd	4th	2nd	Oct 14, 1843	Oct 28, 1843
	4th	2nd	Sept 14, 1844	
	4th	2nd		
	5th		Oct 16, 1841	
	5th		Aug 6, 1842	April 27, 1843
		2nd	May 6, 1842	
		2nd	Aug 6, 1842	
		1st	Sept 28, 1844	Dec 14, 1844
	5th	2nd	May 1, 1841	
2nd	1st	2nd	May 1, 1841	June 5, 1841
1st	3rd	2nd	May 6, 1843	Oct 28, 1843
	4th	2nd	April 2, 1842	
				Dec 14, 1843
			March 9, 1841	
		2nd	June 25, 1842	Sept 19, 1842
	2nd	1st	July 3, 1841	Oct 16, 1841
			March 12, 1842	
	4th	2nd		
		2nd	Sept 28, 1844	Dec 14, 1844
		2nd	April 23, 1842	
	4th	2nd	July 4, 1842	
1st	2nd	1st	July 3, 1841	Oct 16, 1841
2nd	3rd	2nd	Sept 4, 1841	Dec 14, 1841
2nd	3rd	2nd	July 3, 1841	Oct 16, 1841
2nd	3rd	2nd	Sept 4, 1842	Oct 28, 1843

Name	Birth Date	Death Date	Rank	Company
Ewell, John Martin	Aug 5, 1823	Oct 1, 1893	Capt.	1st Co.
Ewell, John Martin	Aug 5, 1823	Oct 1, 1893	3rd Lt.	
Ewell, Martin F.	May 5, 1819	Jan 10, 1900	2nd Lt.	
Farnham, Augus Alvin	May 20, 1815	May 2, 1865	1st Lt.	3rd Co.
Felshaw, Thomas			1st Lt.	
Filcher, Thomas Joseph	March 18, 1812	Dec 6, 1888	1st Lt.	2nd Co.
Filcher, Thomas Joseph	March 18, 1812	Dec 6, 1888	Capt.	1st Co.
Flack, James Madison	June 22, 1815	June 15, 1850	Capt.	4th Co.
Follett, King	July 26, 1788	March 9, 1844	Capt.	1st Co.
Foote, Timothy Bradley	Dec 29, 1799	April 18, 1866	Adjutant	
Forney, Frederick	Oct 9, 1813	May 11, 1880	5th Sgt.	
Foster, Robert D.	1811	about 1878	Surgeon Gen.	
Foster, Robert D.	1811	about 1878	Bvt. Brig. Gen.	
Foster, Solon	Jan 8, 1811	March 17, 1896	Aide-de-Camp to Brig. Gen.	
Foutz, Jacob	Jan 25, 1800	Feb 14, 1848	1st Lt.	
Foutz, Jacob	Jan 25, 1800	Feb 14, 1848	1st Lt.	
Fowler, George William	June 27, 1821	Aug 21, 1853	3rd Lt.	2nd Co.
Fowler, George William	June 27, 1821	Aug 21, 1853	3rd Lt.	4th Co.
Franklin, Thomas			1st Cpl.	1st Co.
Fry, William A.			2nd Lt.	1st Co.
Fullmer, Almon Linus	Sept 7, 1816	Oct 2, 1890	Adjutant	
Fullmer, David	July 7, 1803	Oct 21, 1879	Qm.	
Fullmer, John Solomon	July 21, 1807	Oct 8, 1883	Paymaster Gen.	
Fullmer, John Solomon	July 21, 1807	Oct 8, 1883	Bvt. Brig. Gen.	
Gardner, R.			3rd Lt.	2nd Co.
Gardner, William			3rd Lt.	
Gates, Hiram	Aug 11, 1802	Sept 5, 1850	Qm.	
Gee, Lysander	Sept 1, 1818	June 27, 1894	Capt.	1st Co.
Gleason, John Streator	Jan 13, 1819	Dec 21, 1904	Capt.	
Glover, Henry			Capt.	2nd Co.
Goddard, Stephen Hezekiah	Aug 23, 1810	Sept 10, 1898	2nd Lt.	1st Co.
Goddard, Stephen Hezekiah	Aug 23, 1810	Sept 10, 1898	2nd Lt.	1st Co.
Goddard, Stephen Hezekiah	Aug 23, 1810	Sept 10, 1898	Capt.	1st Co.
Goddard, Stephen Hezekiah	Aug 23, 1810	Sept 10, 1898	Capt.	
Golden, Aaron Houghton	Jan 3, 1807	1862	Maj.	

Battalion	Regiment	Cohort	Date of Rank	Commission
2nd	2nd	2nd	Sept 9, 1843	Oct 28, 1843
		2nd	April 2, 1842	
		2nd	May 5, 1842	
1st	1st	2nd	July 19, 1843	Oct 28, 1843
		2nd	June 25, 1842	Sept 19, 1842
		2nd	June 26, 1843	
	5th	2nd	July 4, 1843	Oct 28, 1843
1st	5th	2nd	Oct 9, 1843	Oct 28, 1843
2nd	2nd	1st	July 3, 1841	Oct 16, 1841
	3rd	2nd	July 3, 1841	Oct 16, 1841
	2nd	2nd	Oct 6, 1843	
			March 9, 1841	
			June 3, 1842	
		1st	March 9, 1841	
		2nd	June 14, 1842	
		2nd	July 4, 1842	Sept 19, 1842
2nd	3rd	2nd	Oct 6, 1842	
2nd	3rd	2nd	Oct 7, 1843	Oct 28, 1843
	4th	2nd	Sept 5, 1843	
2nd	2nd	2nd	July 3, 1841	Oct 16, 1841
	1st	1st	May 7, 1842	
			March 9, 1841	
			June 3, 1842	
	5th	2nd	Oct 2, 1843	Oct 28, 1843
2nd	2nd	2nd	May 1, 1841	June 5, 1841
	5th	2nd	May 5, 1842	
			Sept 14, 1844	
1st	3rd	2nd	May 1, 1841	June 5, 1841
		1st	July 4, 1842	Sept 19, 1842
2nd	3rd	2nd	July 3, 1841	Oct 16, 1841
1st	1st	2nd	March 4, 1841	
1st	1st	2nd	April 6, 1841	Oct 16, 1841
1st	1st	2nd	Aug 6, 1843	Oct 28, 1843
	5th	2nd	Aug 5, 1845	
2nd	5th	2nd	May 1, 1841	

Name	Birth Date	Death Date	Rank	Company
Goldsmith, Gilbert Davis	Nov 27, 1811	March 1, 1847	1st Lt.	
Gove, Carlos			Asst. Inspector Gen.	
Grant, Ezra Foote	Dec 1816	Oct 27, 1842	3rd Lt.	
Gray, Levi	April 15, 1803	Nov 19, 1875	2nd Lt.	7th Co.
Greene, John Portineus	Sept 3, 1793	Sept 10, 1844	Maj.	
Greene, John Portineus	Sept 3, 1793	Sept 10, 1844	Asst. Qm. Gen.	
Grover, Thomas	July 22, 1807	Feb 20, 1886	Guard (Aide-de-Camp)	
Grover, Thomas	July 22, 1807	Feb 20, 1886	Capt.	
Groves, Elisha Hurd	Nov 5, 1797	Dec 29, 1867	3rd Lt.	2nd Co.
Gully, Samuel	May 27, 1809	July 4, 1849	1st Lt.	
Gurley, Zenos Hovey	April 29, 1801	Aug 28, 1871	Aide-de-Camp to Lt. Gen.	
Gurley, Zenos Hovey	April 29, 1801	Aug 28, 1871	Aide-de-Camp to Lt. Gen.	
Guyman, Noah Thomas	June 30, 1819	Jan 7, 1911	1st Lt.	2nd Co.
Hale, Jonathan Harriman	Feb 1, 1800	Sept 4, 1846	Lt. Col.	
Hale, Jonathan Harriman	Feb 1, 1800	Sept 4, 1846	Qm. Sgt.	
Hales, James	Sept 18, 1825	Dec 25, 1886	4th Cpl.	2nd Co.
Haley, Eldred			3rd Lt.	4th Co.
Hall, Thomas	Sept 1, 1816	June 8, 1894	1st Sgt.	6th Co.
Hall, William B.			Aide-de-Camp to Lt. Gen.	
Hall, William B.			Aide-de-Camp to Lt. Gen.	
Hamilton, Andrew Marten	April 28, 1809	Aug 17, 1894	Capt.	
Hamilton, Andrew Marten	April 28, 1809	Aug 17, 1894	Capt.	
Hamilton, James B.			1st Lt.	3rd Co.
Hammond, Joseph	June 14, 1822	Aug 4, 1899	Col.	
Hammos, Elias			4th Sgt.	4th Co.
Hancock, Levi Ward	April 7, 1803	June 10, 1882	Musician	
Hancock, Solomon	Aug 15, 1794	Dec 2, 1847	Capt.	1st Co.
Hancock, Solomon	Aug 15, 1794	Dec 2, 1847	Maj.	
Hansen, John C.			Adjutant	
Harmon, Appleton Milo	May 29, 1820	Feb 26, 1877	Lt.	
Harmon, Appleton Milo	May 29, 1820	Feb 26, 1877	3rd Lt.	
Harmon, Jesse Pierce	Aug 11, 1795	Dec 24, 1877	Maj.	

Battalion	Regiment	Cohort	Date of Rank	Commission
		2nd	July 1, 1842	Sept 19, 1842
			March 4, 1841	Oct 16, 1841
		1st	April 23, 1842	
2nd	4th	2nd	May 6, 1844	
			March 1, 1842	
			March 1, 1842	
			March 9, 1841	
			March 9, 1841	
2nd	1st	1st	Dec 22, 1841	
		2nd	May 11, 1843	Dec 14, 1843
			March 4, 1841	
			April 6, 1841	Oct 16, 1841
1st	5th	2nd	Sept 2, 1843	Oct 28, 1843
	3rd	2nd	May 6, 1843	Oct 28, 1843
	3rd	2nd	July 3, 1841	Oct 16, 1841
2nd	3rd	2nd	Sept 7, 1843	Oct 28, 1843
			April 15, 1842	
			April 15, 1843	June 8, 1843
		2nd	April 30, 1842	
		1st	Oct 18, 1842	
2nd	2nd	2nd	Aug 20, 1843	Oct 28, 1843
			Sept 9, 1843	
			March 9, 1841	
1st	2nd	1st	July 3, 1841	Oct 16, 1841
	2nd	1st	Sept 17, 1842	April 27, 1843
			July 3, 1841	Oct 16, 1841
		2nd	May 6, 1842	
		2nd	May 6, 1842	
	4th	2nd	April 2, 1842	

Name	Birth Date	Death Date	Rank	Company
Harmon, Jesse Pierce	Aug 11, 1795	Dec 24, 1877	Col.	
Harper, Samuel			Lt.	
Harper, Samuel			1st Lt.	
Hart, James S.	June 9, 1914		Aide-de-Camp to Lt. Gen.	
Hatch, Josephus	July 2, 1802	March 25, 1874	Paymaster	
Haven, John	March 9, 1774	March 16, 1853	Adjutant	
Heap, William			3rd Lt.	
Herriman, Henry	June 9, 1804	May 17, 1891	1st Lt.	2nd Co.
Herriman, Henry	June 9, 1804	May 17, 1891	3rd Lt.	2nd Co.
Herriman, Henry	June 9, 1804	May 17, 1891	Capt.	
Herriman, Henry	June 9, 1804	May 17, 1891	Capt.	
Herriman, Thomas			1st Lt.	
Hibbard, Davison	1788	1856	Brig. Gen.	
Hibbard, Davison	1788	1856	Asst. Inspector Gen.	1st Co.
Hibbard, Roger Bixby	March 1817	after 1880	3rd Lt.	1st Co.
Hickerson, George W.	Dec 13, 1813	Aug 17, 1884	1st Lt.	
Hicks, Samuel	March 23, 1808	Oct 25, 1895	Herald and Armor Bearer	
Higbee, Chauncey Lawson	Sept 7, 1821	Dec 7, 1884	Aide-de-Camp to Maj. Gen.	
Higbee, Chauncey Lawson	Sept 7, 1821	Dec 7, 1884	1st Lt.	1st Co.
Higbee, Chauncey Lawson	Sept 7, 1821	Dec 7, 1884	Capt.	1st Co.
Higbee, Elias	Oct 23, 1795	June 8, 1843	Guard	
Higbee, Francis Marion	1820		Bvt. Maj.	
Higbee, Francis Marion	1820		Capt.	1st Co.
Higbee, Francis Marion	1820		Col.	
Higbee, John Somers	March 7, 1804	Oct 27, 1877	3rd Lt.	2nd Co.
Higbee, John Somers	March 7, 1804	Oct 27, 1877	2nd Lt.	2nd Co.
Higgins, Nelson D.	Sept 1, 1806	Nov 20, 1890	2nd Lt.	1st Co.
Higgins, Nelson D.	Sept 1, 1806	Nov 20, 1890	Lt. Col.	
Higgins, Nelson D.	Sept 1, 1806	Nov 20, 1890	Col.	
Hill, William Elisha	1802	1856	3rd Lt.	
Hill, William Elisha	1802	1856	3rd Lt.	
Hills, Gustavus	Jan 19, 1804	Oct 18, 1846	Musician	
Hoffheins, Peter	Oct 4, 1809	April 20, 1892	Pioneer	1st Co.
Holbrook, Joseph	Jan 16, 1806	Nov 14, 1885	Capt.	
Holbrook, Joseph	Jan 16, 1806	Nov 14, 1885	Capt.	1st Co.

Battalion	Regiment	Cohort	Date of Rank	Commission
	4th	2nd	Sept 14, 1844	
		1st	Dec 2, 1841	
		1st	Dec 22, 1841	
			May 1, 1841	
	4th	2nd	July 1, 1844	
		2nd	April 30, 1841	
		2nd	March 11, 1842	
1st	2nd	2nd	April 6, 1841	Oct 16, 1841
			Nov 6, 1841	
	2nd	2nd	Sept 9, 1843	
		2nd	July 30, 1842	April 27, 1843
			June 2, 1842	
		1st	March 12, 1842	
2nd	2nd	2nd	May 1, 1841	June 5, 1841
		3rd	Nov 18, 1843	Dec 14, 1843
			April 6, 1841	Oct 16, 1841
			Nov 30, 1841	Dec 14, 1841
1st	2nd	2nd	March 9, 1841	
2nd	2nd	2nd	April 6, 1841	Oct 16, 1841
			March 9, 1841	
1st	2nd	2nd	March 9, 1841	
1st	2nd	2nd	March 9, 1841	
	2nd	2nd	May 1, 1841	
1st	1st	2nd	March 9, 1841	
1st	1st	2nd	Sept 9, 1841	Dec 14, 1841
2nd	1st	2nd	March 9, 1841	
1st	2nd	2nd	May 1, 1841	June 5, 1841
	2nd	2nd	July 30, 1842	April 27, 1843
		2nd	June 30, 1842	
		1st	July 16, 1842	Sept 19, 1842
			March 19, 1842	
	4th	2nd	Sept 5, 1843	
			March 4, 1841	
2nd	1st	1st	April 6, 1841	Oct 16, 1841

Name	Birth Date	Death Date	Rank	Company
Holden, A. H.			Maj.	1st Co.
Holden, Wiley Hines	June 23, 1820	May 17, 1852	1st Lt.	
Holman, James Sawyer	Sept 17, 1805	June 21, 1873	2nd Lt.	
Holman, James Sawyer	Sept 17, 1805	June 21, 1873	2nd Lt.	
Holman, James Sawyer	Sept 17, 1805	June 21, 1873	2nd Lt.	2nd Co.
Holt, James	Feb 10, 1804	Jan 25, 1894	3rd Lt.	
Holt, Thomas			3rd Cpl.	1st Co.
Homer, James			1st Sgt.	1st Co.
Horr, Alvin	Sept 5, 1799		2nd Lt.	
Horr, Alvin	Sept 5, 1799		3rd Lt.	
Horr, Alvin	Sept 5, 1799		2nd Lt.	
Hovey, Joseph Grafton	Nov 17, 1812	May 6, 1868	3rd Lt.	
Hunt, Jefferson	Jan 22, 1804	May 11, 1879	Aide-de-Camp to Lt. Gen.	
Hunter, Edward	March 29, 1821	April 11, 1892	Herald and Armor Bearer	
Hunter, Jesse Divined	July 5, 1806	Aug 27, 1877	1st Lt.	2nd Co.
Hunter, Jesse Divined	July 5, 1806	Aug 27, 1877	Capt.	2nd Co.
Hunter, Jesse Divined	July 5, 1806	Aug 27, 1877	Maj.	
Hunter, Jesse Divined	July 5, 1806	Aug 27, 1877	Maj.	
Huntington, Dimick Baker	May 26, 1808	Feb 1, 1879	Musician	
Huntington, William Dresser	Feb 28, 1818	March 20, 1881	Capt.	1st Co.
Huntington, William Dresser	Feb 28, 1818	March 20, 1881	2nd Lt.	3rd Co.
Huntsman, James William	June 6, 1801	Nov 10, 1872	2nd Lt.	1st Co.
Huntsman, William	April 1803	Dec 2, 1887	2nd Lt.	3rd Co.
Hutchinson, John			Qm. Sgt.	
Hyde, Orson	Jan 8, 1805	Nov 28, 1878	Asst. Chaplain	
Ivins, E. King			Fife Maj.	
Ivins, Garrett	Sept 11, 1820	Jan 7, 1892	Cornet	
Ivins, Robert			Aide-de-camp to Maj. Gen.	
Ivins, Robert			Aide-de-camp to Maj. Gen.	
Jemison, John S.	Aug 25, 1805	June 28, 1882	3rd Lt.	1st Co.
Johnson, Aaron	June 22, 1806	May 10, 1877	3rd Lt.	1st Co.
Johnson, Aaron	June 22, 1806	May 10, 1877	1st Lt.	1st Co.
Johnson, James			3rd Lt.	

Battalion	Regiment	Cohort	Date of Rank	Commission
2nd	2nd	1st	May 1, 1841	June 5, 1841
	5th	2nd	April 8, 1843	
	2nd	2nd	July 1, 1842	
		2nd	Sept 17, 1842	April 27, 1843
2nd	3rd	2nd	June 6, 1842	
	5th	2nd	July 1, 1842	Sept 19, 1842
	4th	2nd	Sept 5, 1843	
		2nd	Sept 10, 1842	April 27, 1843
		2nd	May 5, 1842	
	2nd	2nd	Aug 5, 1843	
		2nd	June 30, 1842	
			May 1, 1841	June 15, 1841
			Sept 9, 1841	Dec 14, 1841
1st	1st	2nd	March 9, 1841	
1st	1st	2nd	Sept 9, 1841	Dec 14, 1841
	5th	2nd	June 23, 1843	
2nd	5th	2nd	July 4, 1843	Oct 28, 1843
			March 9, 1841	
2nd	3rd	2nd	July 3, 1841	Oct 16, 1841
1st	5th	2nd	Sept 16, 1843	Oct 28, 1843
1st	3rd	2nd	April 1, 1843	Oct 28, 1843
1st	5th	2nd	Sept 16, 1843	Oct 28, 1843
	3rd	2nd	Aug 19, 1843	
		1st	July 3, 1841	Oct 16, 1841
			July 1, 1844	
			April 15, 1843	June 8, 1843
		1st	Feb 1, 1842	
			April 20, 1843	June 8, 1843
2nd	2nd	2nd	Sept 9, 1843	Oct 28, 1843
1st	1st	2nd	April 6, 1841	Oct 16, 1841
1st	1st	2nd	Aug 6, 1843	Oct 28, 1843
		1st	June 18, 1842	Sept 19, 1842

Name	Birth Date	Death Date	Rank	Company
Johnson, Joseph Watkins	Dec 15, 1815	Sept 10, 1883	Qm. Sgt.	
Johnson, Robert Lewis	Aug 17, 1819	June 1901	1st Lt.	3rd Co.
Jones, William	Feb 12, 1799	Sept 30, 1879	2nd Lt.	
Kayle, Hiram	Aug 4, 1808	June 6, 1842	1st Lt.	2nd Co.
Kelsey, Easton R.	March 9, 1813	March 10, 1899	3rd Lt.	2nd Co.
Kelsey, Easton R.	March 9, 1813	March 10, 1899	2nd Lt.	2nd Co.
Kelsey, Easton R.	March 9, 1813	March 10, 1899	1st Lt.	2nd Co.
Keown, John			2nd Lt.	8th Co.
Kerr, Archibald	Feb 2, 1813	Sept 13, 1891	3rd Lt.	1st Co.
Kimball, Heber C.	June 14, 1801	June 22, 1868	Asst. Chaplain	
Kimball, Hiram	May 31, 1806	April 27, 1863	Asst. Adjutant Gen.	
Kimball, Hiram	May 31, 1806	April 27, 1863	Maj.	
King, John Morris	Sept 23, 1809	Nov 13, 1855	2nd Lt.	8th Co.
Knight, Vinson	March 14, 1804	July 31, 1842	Guard	
Knight, Wesley	1815	1871	2nd Lt.	
Knight, Wesley	1815	1871	Lt.	
Kreymeyer, Constans M.	1817	1876	Guard (Aide-de-Camp)	
Larkey, Edward	June 17, 1811	Feb 1884	3rd Lt.	2nd Co.
Larkey, Edward	June 17, 1811	Feb 1884	Lt.	
Larkey, Edward	June 17, 1811	Feb 1884	3rd Lt.	2nd Co.
Larkey, Edward	June 17, 1811	Feb 1884	2nd Lt.	2nd Co.
Larkey, Edward	June 17, 1811	Feb 1884	Capt.	
Law, William	Sept 8, 1809	Jan 19, 1892	Col. (Aide-de-Camp)	
Law, William	Sept 8, 1809	Jan 19, 1892	Bvt. Maj. Gen.	
Law, Wilson	1807	1877	Brig. Gen.	
Law, Wilson	1807	1877	Bvt. Maj. Gen.	
Law, Wilson	1807	1877	Maj. Gen.	
Law, Wilson	1807	1877	Qm.	
LeBaron, Alonzo Harrington	Nov 18, 1818	Feb 6, 1891	Capt.	
LeBaron, Alonzo Harrington	Nov 18, 1818	Feb 6, 1891	1st Lt.	1st Co.
Lee, Francis	June 26, 1811	July 17, 1866	2nd Sgt.	1st Co.
Lee, John Doyle	Sept 6, 1812	March 23, 1877	Capt.	4th Co.
Lee, John Doyle	Sept 6, 1812	March 23, 1877	Maj.	
Lemon, Peter	Sept 14, 1805		1st Lt.	2nd Co.
Lemon, Peter	Sept 14, 1805		2nd Lt.	2nd Co.
Lewis, Tarlton	May 18, 1805	Nov 22, 1890	2nd Lt.	

Battalion	Regiment	Cohort	Date of Rank	Commission
	2nd	1st	July 3, 1841	Oct 16, 1841
1st	5th	2nd	Sept 2, 1843	Oct 28, 1843
		2nd	July 1, 1842	Sept 19, 1842
1st	2nd	2nd	April 6, 1841	Oct 16, 1841
1st	1st	1st	March 9, 1841	
1st		1st	April 6, 1841	Oct 16, 1841
1st	1st	1st	Nov 6, 1841	Dec 14, 1841
2nd	4th	2nd	Oct 14, 1843	Oct 28, 1843
2nd	5th	2nd	Sept 9, 1843	Oct 28, 1843
		1st	July 3, 1841	Oct 16, 1841
		1st	June 3, 1842	
2nd	1st	1st	June 3, 1841	Oct 16, 1841
	4th	2nd	Oct 3, 1843	Oct 28, 1843
			March 9, 1841	
	2nd	2nd	April 2, 1842	
		2nd	April 16, 1842	
			March 9, 1841	
2nd	1st	1st	April 6, 1841	Oct 16, 1841
			Dec 28, 1841	
1st	1st	1st	March 4, 1841	
2nd	1st	1st	Dec 22, 1841	
		1st	June 18, 1842	
			March 9, 1841	
			Sept 2, 1841	Dec 14, 1841
		1st	Feb 5, 1841	
			Sept 2, 1841	Dec 14, 1841
			Aug 13, 1842	Sept 19, 1842
		2nd	June 25, 1842	Sept 19, 1842
1st	3rd	2nd	May 1, 1841	
		1st		
2nd	5th	2nd	Oct 9, 1843	Oct 28, 1843
		2nd	May 18, 1844	Dec 14, 1844
1st	3rd	2nd	May 1, 1841	June 5, 1841
2nd	1st	2nd	March 9, 1841	
	1st	2nd	July 19, 1843	

Name	Birth Date	Death Date	Rank	Company
Lewis, Tarlton	May 18, 1805	Nov 22, 1890	2nd Lt.	2nd Co.
Lincoln, Ira Elisha	March 28, 1821	Oct 26, 1845	Capt.	
Lincoln, Ira Elisha	March 28, 1821	Oct 26, 1845	1st Lt.	4th Co.
Littlefield, Lyman Omer	Nov 21, 1819	Sept 1, 1893	2nd Lt.	1st Co.
Littlefield, Lyman Omer	Nov 21, 1819	Sept 1, 1893	1st Lt.	
Loveless, John	June 24, 1807	Dec 6, 1880	Capt.	2nd Co.
Luce, Elias			Ensign	
Luce, John Grant	Sept 30, 1817		Capt.	1st Co.
Luce, John Grant	Sept 30, 1817		2nd Lt.	
Lyman, Amasa	March 30, 1813	Feb 4, 1877	Aide-de-Camp to Brig. Gen.	
Lyon, Windsor P.	Feb 8, 1809	Jan 1849	Asst. Adjutant Gen.	
Lyon, Windsor P.	Feb 8, 1809	Jan 1849	Asst. Qm. Gen.	
Lytle, Andrew	Dec 25, 1812	Dec 27, 1870	1st Lt.	1st Co.
Lytle, Andrew	Dec 25, 1812	Dec 27, 1870	1st Lt.	
Lytle, John	Aug 18, 1803	Oct 12, 1892	2nd Lt.	1st Co.
Mace, Wandle	Feb 19, 1809	Aug 10, 1890	2nd Lt.	1st Co.
Markham, Stephen	Feb 9, 1800	March 10, 1878	Capt.	2nd Co.
Markham, Stephen	Feb 9, 1800	March 10, 1878	Bvt. Maj.	
Markham, Stephen	Feb 9, 1800	March 10, 1878	Lt. Col.	
Markham, Stephen	Feb 9, 1800	March 10, 1878	Col.	
Markham, Stephen	Feb 9, 1800	March 10, 1878	Bvt. Col.	
Marks, William	Nov 15, 1792	May 22, 1892	Asst. Chaplain	
Marsh, Eliphaz	Sept 6, 1790	Feb 19, 1844	3rd Lt.	2nd Co.
Martin, John Dickey	Aug 12, 1816	Aug 12, 1846	1st Lt.	
Martin, John Dickey	Aug 12, 1816	Aug 12, 1846	Paymaster	
McArthur, Orange			2nd Cpl.	2nd Co.
McClure, John I.			2nd Lt.	3rd Co.
McEwan, John P.	Feb 24, 1824	Feb 27, 1878	Ensign	
McFall, Hugh			Adjutant Gen.	
McFall, Hugh			Bvt. Brig. Gen.	
McIntosh, John A.	April 14, 1806	Aug 8, 1897	3rd Lt.	3rd Co.
McRae, Alexander	Sept 7, 1807	June 20, 1891	Aide-de-Camp to Brig. Gen.	
Mecham, Ephraim	March 7, 1808	July 7, 1891	1st Cpl.	4th Co.
Mecham, Moses Worthen	Feb 19, 1804	July 22, 1878	3rd Sgt.	4th Co.
Mendenhall, William	April 8, 1815	June 3, 1906	2nd Sgt.	4th Co.
Merchants, Lucius	Feb 26, 1817	Aug 11, 1895	2nd Lt.	4th Co.
Merick, W.			2nd Lt.	1st Co.

Battalion	Regiment	Cohort	Date of Rank	Commission
1st	3rd	2nd	May 1, 1841	
			April 16, 1844	
	4th	2nd	May 6, 1842	
1st	2nd	2nd	Nov 6, 1841	Dec 14, 1841
	2nd	2nd	Sept 10, 1842	April 27, 1843
2nd	3rd	2nd	Sept 7, 1843	Oct 28, 1843
			June 20, 1844	
1st	3rd	2nd	April 1, 1843	Oct 28, 1843
		2nd	March 26, 1842	
	1st	1st	May 1, 1841	June 5, 1841
		2nd	June 3, 1842	
		1st	Feb 1, 1842	
1st	3rd	2nd	May 1, 1842	
		2nd	March 26, 1842	
1st	1st	2nd	Aug 6, 1843	Oct 28, 1843
1st	5th	2nd	Sept 9, 1843	Oct 28, 1843
1st	1st	1st	March 9, 1841	
1st	1st	1st	March 9, 1841	
1st	1st	1st	May 1, 1841	June 5, 1841
	1st	1st	Sept 24, 1842	April 27, 1843
		1st	June 3, 1842	
		2nd	July 3, 1841	Oct 16, 1841
2nd	2nd	2nd	April 6, 1841	Oct 16, 1841
		2nd	May 7, 1842	
	3rd	2nd	Aug 19, 1843	Oct 28, 1843
	4th	2nd		
2nd	3rd	2nd	April 1, 1843	Oct 28, 1843
		2nd	Sept 28, 1844	
			March 9, 1841	
			June 3, 1842	
2nd	5th	2nd	Aug 19, 1843	Oct 28, 1843
			March 9, 1841	
	4th	2nd	Sept 14, 1844	
2nd	2nd	2nd	May 1, 1841	

Name	Birth Date	Death Date	Rank	Company
Merriam, Edwin Parker	May 12, 1803		2nd Lt.	
Merrill, Justin Jared	Feb 18, 1806	Jan 14, 1889	3rd Lt.	2nd Co.
Merrill, Philemon Christopher	Oct 12, 1820	Sept 16, 1904	3rd Lt.	2nd Co.
Merrill, Philemon Christopher	Oct 12, 1820	Sept 16, 1904	2nd Lt.	2nd Co.
Merrill, T.			3rd Lt.	2nd Co.
Miles, Ira Simonds	Dec 25, 1809	July 31, 1878	Adjutant	
Miles, Joel Simonds			Qm. Sgt.	
Miles, Joel Simonds			Sgt. Maj.	
Miles, William	May 2, 1828		3rd Cpl.	3rd Co.
Mikesell, John Harrison	March 29, 1815	Aug 31, 1904	1st Lt.	
Mikesell, John Harrison	May 29, 1815	Aug 31, 1904	1st Lt.	3rd Co.
Miller, B.			3rd Sgt.	3rd Co.
Miller, George	Nov 25, 1794	Aug 27, 1855	Capt.	1st Co.
Miller, George	Nov 25, 1794	Aug 27, 1855	Bvt. Col.	
Miller, George	Nov 25, 1794	Aug 27, 1855	Col.	
Miller, George	Nov 25, 1794	Aug 27, 1855	Bvt. Maj. Gen.	
Miller, George	Nov 25, 1794	Aug 27, 1855	Capt.	
Miller, George	Nov 25, 1794	Aug 27, 1855	Brig. Gen.	
Miller, Henry William	May 1, 1807	Oct 9, 1885	Maj.	
Miller, Henry William	May 1, 1807	Oct 9, 1885	Aide-de-Camp to Brig. Gen.	
Miller, William	Feb 8, 1814	Aug 7, 1875	3rd Lt.	
Miller, William	Feb 8, 1814	Aug 7, 1875	Postmaster	
Milliken, Arthur	May 9, 1817	April 23, 1882	3rd Lt.	1st Co.
Milliken, Arthur	May 9, 1817	April 23, 1882	2nd Lt.	1st Co.
Milliken, Arthur	May 9, 1817	April 23, 1882	Capt.	
Mills, John	Jan 14, 1816	Nov 1, 1857	Sgt.	2nd Co.
Monenee, F. H.			1st Cpl.	3rd Co.
Moore, John Harvey	April 19, 1816	Nov 15, 1899	3rd Lt.	
Moorhouse, George W.			1st Lt.	
Morey, George	Nov 15, 1803	Dec 15, 1875	Lt. Col.	1st Co.
Morley, Isaac	March 11, 1786	July 21, 1864	Aide-de-Camp	
Morley, Isaac	March 11, 1786	July 21, 1864	Aide-de-Camp to Lt. Gen.	
Morse, Justus	March 27, 1809	Oct 30, 1887	1st Lt.	2nd Co.
Morse, Justus	March 27, 1809	Oct 30, 1887	Capt.	2nd Co.
Morse, Justus	March 27, 1809	Oct 30, 1887	1st Lt.	1st Co.
Mott, Lyman	1804	after 1860	2nd Lt.	1st Co.
Mott, Lyman	1804	after 1860	1st Sgt.	1st Co.

Battalion	Regiment	Cohort	Date of Rank	Commission
		2nd	July 4, 1842	April 27, 1843
1st	1st	1st	Sept 6, 1841	Dec 14, 1841
1st	1st	1st	April 6, 1841	Dec 14, 1841
1st	1st	1st	Nov 6, 1841	
1st	1st	1st	June 25, 1842	
	1st	2nd	July 3, 1841	Oct 16, 1841
	4th	2nd	April 2, 1842	
	4th	2nd	June 1, 1842	
	4th	2nd		
		2nd	June 25, 1842	Sept 19, 1842
2nd	3rd	2nd	June 18, 1842	
1st	1st	1st	March 9, 1841	
	1st	1st	March 9, 1841	
	1st	1st	May 1, 1841	June 5, 1841
			Sept 2, 1841	Dec 14, 1841
		1st	Sept 23, 1842	
			Sept 23, 1842	April 27, 1843
			March 1, 1842	
		2nd	May 7, 1842	Oct 28, 1843
	1st	2nd	April 9, 1842	
			Sept 8, 1843	
1st	1st	1st	March 9, 1841	
1st	1st	1st	April 6, 1841	Oct 16, 1841
		1st	Sept 24, 1842	April 27, 1843
	4th	2nd		
		2nd	April 16, 1842	
		1st	Oct 8, 1842	
1st	3rd	2nd	May 1, 1841	June 5, 1841
			March 4, 1841	
			April 6, 1841	Oct 16, 1841
2nd	1st	1st	March 4, 1841	
		1st	July 3, 1841	
2nd	1st	1st	April 6, 1841	Oct 16, 1841
	4th	2nd	Sept 9, 1843	
	4th	2nd		

Name	Birth Date	Death Date	Rank	Company
Mumford, Charles			2nd Lt.	2nd Co.
Munjar, William	Nov 25, 1792	Aug 16, 1884	3rd Lt.	1st Co.
Murphy, Joseph Harris	Jan 25, 1814	June 19, 1861	3rd Lt.	
Murphy, Joseph Harris	Jan 25, 1814	June 19, 1861	3rd Lt.	3rd Co.
Musick, Samuel	March 23, 1804		Capt.	3rd Co.
Muting, Edwin			1st Lt.	1st Co.
Nichols, Jesse Kinney	Sept 15, 1812		Capt.	3rd Co.
Nickerson, Moses Chapman	March 9, 1804	March 4, 1871	Qm. Sgt.	
Nickerson, Moses Chapman	March 9, 1804	March 4, 1871	2nd Maj. Sgt.	
Niswanger, William	May 11, 1796	Dec 18, 1882	Maj.	
Niswanger, William	May 11, 1796	Dec 18, 1882	Capt.	2nd Co.
Noble, Joseph Bates	Jan 14, 1810	Aug 17, 1900	Maj.	
Noble, Joseph Bates	Jan 14, 1810	Aug 17, 1900	Qm. Sgt.	
Norris, George W.			2nd Lt.	
Olmstead, Harvey	Feb 10, 1794	March 1, 1879	3rd Lt.	
Olney, John F.	Dec 10, 1815	Jan 19, 1890	Capt.	2nd Co.
Pace, James	June 15, 1811	April 6, 1888	3rd Lt.	2nd Co.
Pace, James	June 15, 1811	April 6, 1888	Capt.	
Pack, John	May 20, 1809	April 4, 1885	Capt.	
Pack, John	May 20, 1809	April 4, 1885	Maj.	
Packer, Nathan William	Jan 2, 1811	Oct 27, 1875	1st Sgt.	
Page, John Edward	Feb 25, 1799	Oct 14, 1867	Asst. Chaplain	
Paine, Samuel Langdon, Jr.	Sept 1, 1808	Nov 1, 1861	1st Lt.	
Palmer, Abraham	Dec 4, 1807	May 25, 1875	1st Lt.	3rd Co.
Palmer, Andrew			2nd Lt.	5th Co.
Palmer, Joseph Farel	Oct 7, 1802	Nov 7, 1885	3rd Lt.	
Parker, John Davis	Nov 22, 1799	Feb 27, 1891	Maj.	
Parker, John Davis	Nov 22, 1799	Feb 27, 1891	Bvt. Capt.	1st Co.
Parker, John Davis	Nov 22, 1799	Feb 27, 1891	1st Lt.	1st Co.
Parker, John Davis	Nov 22, 1799	Feb 27, 1891	Capt.	1st Co.
Parker, John Davis	Nov 22, 1799	Feb 27, 1891	Lt. Col.	
Parker, William Knowlton	Aug 11, 1809	Dec 16, 1885	Capt.	2nd Co.
Payne, Richard Babcock	Dec 23, 1806		2nd Lt.	
Pendleton, Calvin Crane	Aug 25, 1811	April 21, 1873	Paymaster	
Perkins, Ute	March 5, 1816	May 23, 1901	2nd Lt.	1st Co.
Perkins, Ute	March 5, 1816	May 23, 1901	3rd Lt.	1st Co.
Perkins, Ute	March 5, 1816	May 23, 1901	2nd Lt.	1st Co.

Battalion	Regiment	Cohort	Date of Rank	Commission
1st	2nd	2nd	July 3, 1841	Oct 16, 1841
2nd	3rd	2nd	July 3, 1841	Oct 16, 1841
		2nd	June 25, 1842	Sept 19, 1842
2nd	3rd	2nd	June 18, 1842	
	4th	2nd	April 2, 1842	
1st	2nd	1st		
1st	1st	2nd	July 19, 1843	Oct 28, 1843
	1st	1st	May 1, 1841	
			May 1, 1841	
2nd	3rd	2nd	April 6, 1841	Oct 16, 1841
2nd	2nd	2nd	May 1, 1841	June 5, 1841
			March 1, 1842	
	2nd	1st	June 3, 1842	April 27, 1843
		2nd	April 30, 1842	
		1st	April 30, 1842	
2nd	2nd	1st	July 3, 1841	Oct 16, 1841
1st	5th	2nd	Sept 9, 1843	
		2nd	Nov 18, 1843	Dec 14, 1844
		2nd	April 9, 1842	
	1st	2nd	July 21, 1843	Oct 28, 1843
			May 11, 1842	
		1st	July 3, 1841	Oct 16, 1841
		1st	May 7, 1842	Sept 19, 1842
1st	3rd	2nd	Aug 26, 1843	Oct 28, 1843
	4th	2nd	April 16, 1842	
	2nd	2nd	April 22, 1843	
	1st	2nd	July 21, 1843	
1st	1st	1st	March 9, 1841	
1st	1st	1st	March 9, 1841	
1st	1st	1st	May 1, 1841	June 5, 1841
	1st	1st	Sept 25, 1842	April 27, 1843
3rd	3rd	2nd	July 22, 1843	Oct 28, 1843
		1st	Oct 28, 1841	
		1st	Sept 28, 1844	Dec 14, 1844
2nd	2nd	1st	March 4, 1841	
2nd	1st	1st	March 9, 1841	
2nd	1st	1st	April 6, 1841	Oct 16, 1841

NAME	BIRTH DATE	DEATH DATE	RANK	COMPANY
Perry, Ashael	Feb 26, 1784	Feb 16, 1869	2nd Lt.	2nd Co.
Perry, Stephen Chadwick	Dec 22, 1818	Nov 16, 1888	2nd Lt.	
Perry, Stephen Chadwick	Dec 22, 1818	Nov 16, 1888	3rd Lt.	
Perry, William Chadwick	Jan 26, 1812	May 9, 1893	2nd Lt.	
Perry, William Chadwick	Jan 26, 1812	May 9, 1893	3rd Lt.	5th Co.
Phelps, Morris Charles	Dec 20, 1805	May 22, 1876	Capt.	1st Co.
Phelps, Morris Charles	Dec 20, 1805	May 22, 1876	1st Lt.	1st Co.
Phelps, Morris Charles	Dec 20, 1805	May 22, 1876	Capt.	1st Co.
Phelps, William Waterman	Jan 23, 1823	June 6, 1886	Adjutant	
Pierce, Joseph White	June 5, 1805	April 2, 1888	3rd Lt.	
Pierce, Joseph White	June 5, 1805	April 2, 1888	3rd Lt.	1st Co.
Pitt, William	Aug 16, 1813	Feb 21, 1873	Musician	1st Co.
Potter, Ephraim	Jan 16, 1817	March 16, 1876	Sgt. Maj.	
Powers, Solon	April 28, 1811	1854	4th Sgt.	
Pratt, Addison	Feb 21, 1802	Oct 14, 1872	3rd Lt.	1st Co.
Pratt, Orson	Sept 19, 1811	Oct 3, 1881	Asst. Chaplain	
Pratt, Parley Parker	April 12, 1807	May 13, 1857	Asst. Chaplain	
Pratt, William Dickinson	Sept 3, 1802	Sept 15, 1870	Qm. Sgt.	
Pratt, William Dickinson	Sept 3, 1802	Sept 15, 1870	Qm. Sgt.	
Ray, John			1st Lt.	
Redfield, David Harvy	Aug 31, 1807	Sept 11, 1863	1st Lt.	1st Co.
Redfield, David Harvy	Aug 31, 1807	Sept 11, 1863	2nd Lt.	1st Co.
Redfield, David Harvy	Aug 31, 1807	Sept 11, 1863	1st Lt.	1st Co.
Redfield, David Harvy	Aug 31, 1807	Sept 11, 1863	Bvt. Capt.	
Redfield, David Harvy	Aug 31, 1807	Sept 11, 1863	Brig. Inspector	
Reed, Luther	Aug 11, 1797	April 23, 1871	2nd Lt.	3rd Co.
Reed, Robert			3rd Sgt.	6th Co.
Reeves, John			2nd Lt.	6th Co.
Reighley, A. H.			3rd Lt.	3rd Co.
Rheinbolt, Hiram			Bvt. Maj.	
Rich, Charles Coulson	Aug 21, 1809	Nov 17, 1883	Capt.	2nd Co.
Rich, Charles Coulson	Aug 21, 1809	Nov 17, 1883	Bvt. Col.	
Rich, Charles Coulson	Aug 21, 1809	Nov 17, 1883	Bvt. Brig. Gen.	
Rich, Charles Coulson	Aug 21, 1809	Nov 17, 1883	Bvt. Maj. Gen.	
Rich, Thomas	Nov 29, 1817	Jan 26, 1884	1st Lt.	2nd Co.
Rich, Thomas	Nov 29, 1817	Jan 26, 1884	1st Lt.	2nd Co.
Rich, Thomas	Nov 29, 1817	Jan 26, 1884	2nd Lt.	2nd Co.
Rich, Thomas	Nov 29, 1817	Jan 26, 1884	Maj.	
Rich, Thomas	Nov 29, 1817	Jan 26, 1884	Capt.	2nd Co.

Battalion	Regiment	Cohort	Date of Rank	Commission
2nd	2nd	2nd	April 6, 1841	Oct 16, 1841
		2nd	May 11, 1843	Dec 14, 1844
		2nd	May 18, 1843	Dec 14, 1843
	4th	2nd	Sept 14, 1844	
	4th	2nd	April 16, 1842	
2nd	1st	1st	March 1, 1841	
2nd	1st	1st	March 9, 1841	
2nd	1st	1st	March 9, 1841	Oct 16, 1841
		1st	Sept 20, 1844	Dec 14, 1844
	4th	2nd	April 9, 1843	
1st	1st	2nd	Aug 6, 1843	Oct 28, 1843
	1st		April 2, 1842	
	3rd	2nd	July 3, 1841	Oct 16, 1841
	4th	2nd	Sept 17, 1842	June 8, 1843
		1st	July 3, 1841	Oct 16, 1841
		1st	July 3, 1841	Oct 16, 1841
	1st	2nd	May 1, 1841	June 5, 1841
			June 3, 1841	
		1st	Sept 28, 1844	
1st	1st	1st	March 4, 1841	
1st	1st	1st	March 9, 1841	
1st		1st	April 6, 1841	Oct 16, 1841
	1st	1st	June 3, 1842	
		1st	Aug 10, 1842	
1st	1st	2nd	July 19, 1843	Oct 28, 1843
	4th	2nd	May 6, 1844	
1st	1st	2nd	July 19, 1843	Oct 28, 1843
		1st	June 2, 1842	
1st	1st	1st	Nov 6, 1841	
	1st	1st	March 9, 1841	June 5, 1841
			Sept 4, 1841	
			June 3, 1842	
1st		1st	April 6, 1841	Oct 16, 1841
1st	1st	1st	March 4, 1841	
1st	1st	1st	March 9, 1841	
	1st	1st	Oct 8, 1842	
1st	1st	1st	Nov 6, 1841	Dec 14, 1841

Name	Birth Date	Death Date	Rank	Company
Richards, Levi	April 14, 1799	June 18, 1876	1st Lt.	6th Co.
Richards, Samuel Whitney	Aug 9, 1824	Nov 26, 1909	1st Sgt.	2nd Co.
Richards, Willard	June 24, 1804	March 11, 1854	Asst. Chaplain	
Richards, Willard	June 24, 1804	March 11, 1854	Maj.	
Rigdon, Sidney	Feb 19, 1793	July 14, 1876	Judge Advocate	
Rigdon, Sidney	Feb 19, 1793	July 14, 1876	Judge Advocate	
Riley, William Wommack	Feb 8, 1813	June 14, 1899	Capt.	3rd Co.
Ripley, Alanson	Jan 8, 1798		Sgt. Maj.	2nd Co.
Ripley, Alanson	Jan 8, 1798		Maj.	
Ritchey, W. J.			Capt.	
Robbins, Lewis	Sept 8, 1811	Feb 8, 1864	Lt.	
Robbins, Lewis	Sept 8, 1811	Feb 8, 1864	Capt.	2nd Co.
Roberts, John Wesley	April 9, 1803	July 23, 1850	2nd Lt.	2nd Co.
Robinson, Edward	Oct 16, 1807	April 18, 1896	2nd Cpl.	6th Co.
Robinson, George W.	May 14, 1814	1878	Bvt. Maj. Gen.	
Robinson, George W.	May 14, 1814	1878	Cornet	
Robinson, James	Aug 29, 1826		Qm. Sgt.	
Robinson, Joseph Lee	Feb 18, 1811	Jan 1, 1893	2nd Lt.	4th Co.
Robinson, Lewis	Oct 28, 1816	Nov 1, 1883	Sgt. Maj.	
Rockwood, Albert Perry	June 9, 1805	Nov 25, 1879	Bvt. Maj. Gen.	
Rockwood, Albert Perry	June 9, 1805	Nov 25, 1879	Col. (Drill Officer)	
Rodeback, James	May 22, 1807	May 25, 1875	3rd Lt.	1st Co.
Rolfe, Samuel Jones	Aug 26, 1794	July 1867	3rd Lt.	
Rolfe, Samuel Jones	Aug 26, 1794	July 1867	3rd Lt.	
Rotton, Anthony			1st Cpl.	
Roundy, Shadrach	Jan 1, 1789	July 2, 1872	Aide-de-Camp to Lt. Gen.	
Roundy, Shadrach	Jan 1, 1789	July 2, 1872	Aide-de-Camp to Lt. Gen.	
Rowen, Jon			2nd Lt.	
Rudd, Erastus Harper	Sept 22, 1816	May 23, 1863		5th Co.
Rushton, Edwin	June 1, 1824	Dec 28, 1904	2nd Lt.	
Rushton, Richard	June 5, 1814	Feb 4, 1884	Capt.	
Rust, William Walker	Aug 14, 1807	Sept 18, 1894	2nd Lt.	
Sanford, Elijah Monroe	1814		3rd Lt.	2nd Co.
Schinder, John			Aide-de-Camp	
Schindle, George			3rd Lt.	1st Co.
Schindle, George			Asst. to Inspector Gen.	

Battalion	Regiment	Cohort	Date of Rank	Commission
	4th	2nd	May 6, 1843	
	4th	2nd		
		2nd	June 3, 1841	Oct 16, 1841
			July 3, 1842	
			March 4, 1841	
			July 3, 1841	Oct 16, 1841
1st	3rd	2nd	Aug 26, 1843	Oct 28, 1843
			March 1, 1842	
	2nd	2nd	June 3, 1842	April 27, 1843
			June 4, 1842	Oct 15, 1842
		2nd	April 9, 1842	
1st	1st	2nd	Aug 5, 1843	Oct 28, 1843
1st	1st	2nd	Aug 5, 1843	Oct 28, 1843
			Sept 2, 1841	Dec 14, 1841
2nd	5th	2nd	Oct 9, 1843	Oct 28, 1843
	1st	2nd	March 1, 1841	June 5, 1841
			Sept 2, 1841	Dec 14, 1841
2nd	2nd	1st	July 3, 1841	Oct 16, 1841
		2nd	Sept 10, 1842	April 27, 1843
	2nd	2nd	Aug 5, 1843	
			Sept 2, 1843	
			March 4, 1841	
			April 6, 1841	Oct 16, 1841
	4th	2nd	May 6, 1844	
		1st	Sept 28, 1844	Dec 14, 1844
		1st	Sept 28, 1844	Dec 14, 1844
		1st	July 4, 1842	Sept 19, 1842
2nd	2nd	2nd	July 5, 1841	Oct 16, 1841
			March 9, 1841	
1st	2nd	2nd	March 9, 1841	
		1st	July 3, 1841	Oct 16, 1841

Name	Birth Date	Death Date	Rank	Company
Scott, Burton			4th Cpl.	5th Co.
Scott, James	1818		3rd Cpl.	5th Co.
Scott, John	May 6, 1811	Dec 16, 1876	Capt.	2nd Co.
Scott, John	May 6, 1811	Dec 16, 1876	Bvt. Maj.	
Scott, John	May 6, 1811	Dec 16, 1876	Maj.	2nd Co.
Scott, John	May 6, 1811	Dec 16, 1876	Lt. Col.	
Scott, John	May 6, 1811	Dec 16, 1876	Col.	
Scovil, Lucius Nelson	March 18, 1806	March 14, 1889	Lt.	
Scovil, Lucius Nelson	March 18, 1806	March 14, 1889	Qm. Sgt.	
Scovil, Lucius Nelson	March 18, 1806	March 14, 1889	Adjutant	
Shearer, T. K.			Capt.	2nd Co.
Sheffield, George			2nd Sgt.	6th Co.
Sheffield, George			3rd Cpl.	6th Co.
Sheffield, John	1808		3rd Cpl.	6th Co.
Sheffield, John	1808		2nd Sgt.	6th Co.
Sherwood, Henry Garlie	April 20, 1785	Nov 24, 1862	Guard	
Shoemaker, Jacob	Oct 17, 1798		1st Sgt.	3rd Co.
Shurtliff, Luman Andrus	March 13, 1807	Aug 25, 1844	Capt.	8th Co.
Shurtliff, Luman Andrus	March 13, 1807	Aug 25, 1844	1st Lt.	2nd Co.
Shurtliff, Luman Andrus	March 13, 1807	Aug 25, 1844	Capt.	
Singson, Samuel			2nd Lt.	2nd Co.
Sloan, James	Oct 28, 1792	Oct 1886	War Secretary to Maj. Gen.	
Smith, Alfred Alex	Dec 6, 1816		4th Cpl.	6th Co.
Smith, Christopher			3rd Sgt.	
Smith, D. T.			3rd Lt.	1st Co.
Smith, David	July 20, 1820	March 23, 1847	Adjutant	
Smith, David	July 20, 1820	March 23, 1847	Asst. to Inspector Gen.	
Smith, Don Carlos	March 25, 1816	Aug 7, 1841	Brig. Gen.	
Smith, Eden	1806	Dec 7, 1851	1st Lt.	
Smith, Eden	1806	Dec 7, 1851	1st Lt.	
Smith, George Albert	June 26, 1817	Sept 1, 1875	Asst. Chaplain	
Smith, George Albert	June 26, 1817	Sept 1, 1875	Maj.	
Smith, Hyrum	Feb 9, 1800	June 27, 1844	Chaplain	
Smith, Hyrum	Feb 9, 1800	June 27, 1844	Bvt. Maj. Gen.	
Smith, John P.			2nd Lt.	
Smith, Joseph, Jr.	Dec 23, 1805	June 27, 1844	Lt. Gen.	
Smith, Samuel	May 22, 1818	Oct 2, 1896	3rd Lt.	6th Co.
Smith, Samuel Harrison	March 13, 1808	July 30, 1844	Guard	
Smith, Warren	Oct 7, 1808	May 12, 1885	2nd Lt.	

Battalion	Regiment	Cohort	Date of Rank	Commission
	2nd	2nd		
	4th	2nd		
2nd	1st	2nd	March 9, 1841	
2nd	1st	2nd	March 9, 1841	
2nd	1st	2nd	May 1, 1841	June 5, 1841
1st	1st	2nd	Sept 4, 1841	Dec 14, 1841
	1st	2nd	July 21, 1843	Oct 28, 1843
		2nd	April 9, 1842	
	4th	2nd	June 1, 1842	
1st	2nd	2nd	May 1, 1841	June 5, 1841
	4th	2nd		
	4th	2nd	Sept 5, 1843	
	4th	2nd		
	4th	2nd	Sept 5, 1843	
			March 9, 1841	
	4th	2nd		
	4th	2nd	Oct 3, 1843	Oct 28, 1843
	1st	2nd	June 11, 1842	Sept 19, 1842
		2nd	Sept 9, 1843	
2nd	1st	1st	March 4, 1841	
			March 12, 1842	
	4th	2nd		
			Oct 6, 1843	
1st	1st	2nd	April 6, 1841	Oct 16, 1841
	1st	2nd	May 1, 1841	June 5, 1841
		2nd	July 3, 1841	Oct 16, 1841
		2nd	Feb 5, 1841	
		1st	May 7, 1842	
		1st	July 16, 1842	Sept 19, 1842
		2nd	July 3, 1841	Oct 16, 1841
			July 5, 1842	
			Sept 21, 1843	Dec 14, 1841
		2nd	April 23, 1842	
			Feb 5, 1841	
	4th	2nd	May 11, 1843	
			March 9, 1841	
		1st	Sept 24, 1842	April 27, 1843

Name	Birth Date	Death Date	Rank	Company
Smith, William	March 13, 1811	Nov 13, 1894	Asst. Chaplain	
Smith, William			Maj.	
Snow, James Chauncey	Jan 11, 1817	April 30, 1884	3rd Lt.	1st Co.
Snow, James Chauncey	Jan 11, 1817	April 30, 1884	2nd Lt.	
Snow, Lorenzo	April 3, 1814	Oct 10, 1901	Capt.	6th Co.
Snow, Warren Stone	June 15, 1818	Sept 19, 1896	1st Lt.	
Snyder, Jesse	April 12, 1825	May 20, 1853	4th Sgt.	1st Co.
Snyder, John	Feb 11, 1800	Dec 19, 1875	Guard	
Soby, Leonard	1801		Qm. Gen.	
Soby, Leonard	1801		Bvt. Brig. Gen.	
Spencer, William W.	March 29, 1808	Oct 11, 1892	1st Lt.	2nd Co.
Sprague, Gad	Nov 9, 1809	April 13, 1879	Pioneer	
St. John, Stephen Merritt	April 10, 1810	April 20, 1893	3rd Lt.	
Stafford, Augus	June 24, 1805		Capt.	8th Co.
Stafford, Augus	June 24, 1805		1st Lt.	8th Co.
Stanford, E. M.			3rd Lt.	2nd Co.
Stapp, Wyatt Berry	April 23, 1813	July 11, 1851	Brig. Gen.	
Stoddard, Sylvester B.	Feb 7, 1801	Aug 18, 1867	Capt.	
Stoker, Eller	July 28, 1816	July 18, 1855	2nd Lt.	
Stout, Allen Joseph	Dec 5, 1815	Dec 18, 1889	3rd Lt.	
Stout, Allen Joseph	Dec 5, 1815	Dec 18, 1889	Capt.	2nd Co.
Stout, Hosea	Sept 18, 1810	March 2, 1889	Maj.	
Stout, Hosea	Sept 18, 1810	March 2, 1889	Col.	
Taylor, Allen	Jan 17, 1814	Dec 5, 1891	2nd Lt.	1st Co.
Taylor, Allen	Jan 17, 1814	Dec 5, 1891	2nd Lt.	
Taylor, John	Nov 1, 1808	July 25, 1887	Asst. Chaplain	
Taylor, John	Nov 1, 1808	July 25, 1887	Judge Advocate	
Terry, Asahel	1782		2nd Lt.	2nd Co.
Terry, Joel	May 23, 1812	Sept 4, 1891	Qm.	
Thatcher, George W.			Asst. Brig. Gen.	
Thatcher, George W.			Adjutant	
Thompson, Charles Blanchard	Jan 27, 1814	Feb 25, 1895	1st Lt.	4th Co.
Thompson, Charles Blanchard	Jan 27, 1814	Feb 25, 1895	1st Lt.	2nd Co.
Thompson, Henry			4th Cpl.	1st Co.
Thompson, Robert Blashel	Oct 1, 1811	Aug 27, 1841	Aide-de-Camp	
Thompson, Samuel	March 30, 1813	April 22, 1892	2nd Lt.	2nd Co.
Thompson, Samuel	March 30, 1813	April 22, 1892	Lt.	
Thornton, Thomas	Jan 12, 1810	Aug 1846	Capt.	

Battalion	Regiment	Cohort	Date of Rank	Commission
		2nd	July 3, 1841	Oct 16, 1841
			July 3, 1841	
1st	2nd	1st	July 3, 1841	Oct 16, 1841
		1st	Sept 17, 1842	April 27, 1843
	4th	2nd	May 6, 1843	
		2nd	April 16, 1842	
	4th	2nd		
			March 9, 1841	
			May 1, 1841	June 15, 1841
			June 3, 1842	
1st	1st	2nd	Aug 5, 1842	Oct 28, 1843
			Oct 6, 1843	
		1st	Sept 17, 1842	
			Sept 14, 1844	
2nd	4th	2nd	Oct 14, 1843	Oct 28, 1843
2nd	2nd	1st	July 3, 1841	
			May 28, 1842	
		2nd	July 30, 1842	April 27, 1843
		1st	July 16, 1842	Sept 19, 1842
		2nd	June 4, 1842	Sept 19, 1842
			April 8, 1843	June 8, 1843
2nd	1st	2nd	Sept 2 (4), 1841	Dec 14, 1841
	5th	2nd	June 23, 1843	Oct 28, 1843
2nd	1st	2nd	May 1, 1841	June 5, 1841
			June 4, 1842	Oct 15, 1842
		2nd	July 3, 1841	Oct 16, 1841
			Nov 6, 1841	Dec 14, 1841
2nd	2nd	2nd		
	3rd	2nd	Aug 19, 1843	Oct 28, 1843
		1st	May 7, 1842	
	1st	1st	May 4, 1842	
2nd	3rd	2nd	Sept 7, 1843	Oct 28, 1843
2nd	3rd	2nd	Oct 6, 1843	
	4th	2nd		
			March 9, 1841	
2nd	1st	1st	April 6, 1841	Oct 16, 1841
		1st	May 6, 1842	
	2nd	1st	July 3, 1841	June 2, 1842

Name	Birth Date	Death Date	Rank	Company
Tippetts, Alva Lewis	March 12, 1809	Oct 24, 1847	1st Lt.	2nd Co.
Tippetts, Alva Lewis	March 12, 1809	Oct 24, 1847	Capt.	2nd Co.
Tippetts, John Harvey	Sept 5, 1810	Feb 14, 1890	2nd Lt.	2nd Co.
Tippetts, John Harvey	Sept 5, 1810	Feb 14, 1890	Capt.	
Tippetts, John Harvey	Sept 5, 1810	Feb 14, 1890	Qm. Sgt.	
Tippetts, John Harvey	Sept 5, 1810	Feb 14, 1890	Capt.	
Turley, Theodore	April 10, 1801	Aug 12, 1871	Capt.	2nd Co.
Turley, Theodore	April 10, 1801	Aug 12, 1871	Lt. Col.	
Undernite, Abel			Aide-de-Camp	
Verily, Thomas			2nd Lt.	
Vincent, Ezra	April 23, 1808	April 5, 1881	4th Sgt.	2nd Co.
Voorhess, George Washington	June 4, 1816		2nd Lt.	
Wakefield, John	Nov 15, 1812	Jan 13, 1854	3rd Lt.	1st Co.
Walker, George			4th Lt.	6th Co.
Warner, William	Jan 27, 1804	Oct 2, 1854	2nd Lt.	1st Co.
Warrington, Benjamin			Qm. Sgt. (Surgeon)	
Warrington, Benjamin			Qm. Gen.	
Wasson, Lorenzo D.	1818	July 1857	Sgt. Maj.	
Wasson, Lorenzo D.	1818	July 1857	Maj.	
Watson, S. W.			Sgt. Maj.	
Webb, Chauncey Griswold	Oct 24, 1812	March 7, 1903	1st Lt.	
Webb, Edward Milo	Aug 17, 1815	July 31, 1852	Capt.	
Webb, Pardon Knapp	Dec 26, 1818	July 29, 1892	2nd Lt.	
Weiler, Jacob	March 14, 1808	March 24, 1896	3rd Lt.	1st Co.
Weld, John F.	Dec 11, 1808	July 28, 1892	Surgeon	
Wellen, David			3rd Lt.	
Wells, Daniel Hammer	Oct 27, 1814	March 24, 1891	Gen.	
Wells, Daniel Hammer	Oct 27, 1814	March 24, 1891	Bvt. Brig. Gen.	
Wells, Daniel Hammer	Oct 27, 1814	March 24, 1891	Commissary	
Wells, Phares	Jan 7, 1814	March 17, 1906	1st Lt.	
Wescott, Benjamin Rose	Dec 27, 1811		Ensign	
Wescott, Benjamin Rose	Dec 27, 1811		1st Cpl.	5th Co.
West, Nathan Ayres	April 10, 1801	May 8, 1888	1st Lt.	3rd Co.
Whitesides, Isaiah	March 28, 1816		3rd Lt.	2nd Co.
Whiting, Edwin	Sept 9, 1809	Dec 8, 1890	Capt.	
Whiting, Edwin	Sept 9, 1809	Dec 8, 1890	1st Lt.	1st Co.
Whiting, George W.			3rd Lt.	
Whitmarsh, William			Herald and Armor Bearer	

Battalion	Regiment	Cohort	Date of Rank	Commission
2nd	1st	2nd	March 9, 1841	
1st	3rd	2nd	May 1, 1841	June 5, 1841
1st	1st	1st	April 6, 1841	Oct 16, 1841
		2nd	March 5, 1842	
			Sept 9, 1843	
	2nd	2nd	Sept 9, 1843	
2nd	1st	2nd	May 1, 1841	June 5, 1841
1st	5th	2nd	June 23, 1843	Oct 28, 1843
			June 2, 1842	
		2nd	June 4, 1842	Sept 19, 1842
	4th	2nd	Sept 4, 1843	
		2nd	April 30, 1842	
1st	3rd	2nd	May 1, 1841	June 5, 1841
	4th	2nd		
2nd	3rd	2nd	July 3, 1841	
			May 1, 1841	June 15, 1841
			May 5, 1841	
	1st	1st	May 1, 1841	June 5, 1841
		1st	May 1, 1841	
	1st	1st	May 1, 1841	
		2nd	June 28, 1842	April 27, 1843
		2nd	June 28, 1842	April 27, 1843
		2nd	June 30, 1842	April 27, 1843
	4th	2nd	Sept 2, 1844	
			March 9, 1841	
		2nd	May 7, 1842	
			March 9, 1841	
			June 3, 1842	
	4th	2nd	March 5, 1842	
			Sept 14, 1844	
	4th	2nd		
2nd	5th	2nd	Aug 19, 1843	Oct 28, 1843
1st	2nd	2nd	March 11, 1842	
		1st	Sept 17, 1842	April 27, 1843
1st	2nd	1st	July 3, 1841	Oct 16, 1841
		2nd	July 4, 1842	Sept 19, 1842
			Feb 1, 1842	

Name	Birth Date	Death Date	Rank	Company
Wight, Lyman	May 9, 1796	March 31, 1858	Aide-de-Camp	
Wight, Lyman	May 9, 1796	March 31, 1858	Bvt. Maj. Gen.	
Wightman, William	Dec 12, 1807	Dec 22, 1842	Capt.	1st Co.
Wightman, William	Dec 12, 1807	Dec 22, 1842	Maj.	
Wightman, William	Dec 12, 1807	Dec 22, 1842	Bvt. Lt. Col.	
Wilber, Benjamin S.	1810		1st Lt.	1st Co.
Wilber, Benjamin S.	1810		Lt. Col.	
Wilber, Benjamin S.	1810		Capt.	2nd Co.
Wilber, Melvin	Aug 10, 1802	Nov 15, 1885	3rd Lt.	
Wilcox, Henry	Jan 13, 1813	1850	3rd Lt.	7th Co.
Wilding, David	Nov 24, 1804	Oct 8, 1890	3rd Lt.	4th Co.
Wilkey, John	Aug 12, 1828	Oct 4, 1894	3rd Lt.	1st Co.
Wilkinson, Stephen			1st Lt.	3rd Co.
Williams, Alexander	Oct 10, 1803	Oct 5, 1876	1st Lt.	1st Co.
Williams, A. W.			4th Sgt.	3rd Co.
Williams, Robert	Sept 17, 1815	Jan 1, 1882	3rd Lt.	8th Co.
Williams, Robert	Sept 17, 1815	Jan 1, 1882	2nd Lt.	2nd Co.
Williams, Stephen	May 31, 1816	June 8, 1897	1st Lt.	1st Co.
Williams, Thomas Stephen	Jan 2, 1826	March 18, 1860	2nd Sgt.	
Wilson, Jasper			1st Lt.	2nd Co.
Wilson, T. W.			Capt.	
Wilson, Zachariah Davis	June 12, 1811	Aug 23, 1894	Capt.	3rd Co.
Winchester, Stephen	May 8, 1795	Jan 1, 1873	2nd Lt.	1st Co.
Winchester, Stephen	May 8, 1795	Jan 1, 1873	1st Lt.	1st Co.
Winn, James	July 26, 1822	Sept 8, 1847	2nd Lt.	3rd Co.
Wither, B. B.			Capt.	
Withnell, Richard H.	April 28, 1805		3rd Lt.	
Withnell, Richard H.	April 28, 1805		3rd Lt.	2nd Co.
Woodburn, William M.	July 1813	Sept 1873	5th Sgt.	3rd Co.
Woodruff, Wilford	March 1, 1807	Sept 2, 1898	Asst. Chaplain	
Woodward, George	Sept 9, 1817	Dec 17, 1903	2nd Lt.	
Woodward, George	Sept 9, 1817	Dec 17, 1903	Adjutant	
Woodworth, Lucien	April 3, 1799	1867	Aide-de-Camp to Maj. Gen.	
Wooley, Edwin Dilworth	June 28, 1807	Oct 14, 1881	Sgt. Maj.	
Worthington, James	Jan 9, 1803	July 29, 1885	Capt.	2nd Co.
Worthington, James	Jan 9, 1803	July 29, 1885	Maj.	
Wyrick, George	1820		Sgt. Maj.	
Wyrick, William	May 13, 1818		2nd Lt.	1st Co.
Yager, H.			3rd Lt.	1st Co.

Battalion	Regiment	Cohort	Date of Rank	Commission
			May 1, 1841	June 15, 1841
			Sept 2, 1841	Dec 14, 1841
2nd	1st	1st	March 9, 1841	
2nd	1st	1st	May 1, 1841	June 5, 1841
		1st	June 3, 1842	
1st	1st	2nd	March 9, 1841	
	1st	2nd	July 21, 1843	
1st	1st	2nd	May 1, 1841	June 5, 1841
		2nd	June 28, 1842	April 27, 1843
2nd	4th	2nd	May 6, 1843	Dec 14, 1843
2nd	3rd	2nd	Sept 7, 1842	Oct 28, 1843
	4th	2nd	Sept 5, 1843	
	4th	2nd	April 23, 1842	
2nd	2nd	2nd	May 1, 1841	June 5, 1841
	4th	2nd	Sept 5, 1843	
	4th	2nd	Oct 3, 1843	Oct 28, 1843
	4th	2nd		
2nd	2nd	2nd	May 1, 1841	
			April 2, 1842	
	4th	2nd	Sept 5, 1843	
		2nd	June 25, 1842	Sept 19, 1842
2nd	3rd	2nd	June 18, 1842	
1st	1st	2nd	March 9, 1841	
1st	1st	2nd	April 6, 1841	Oct 16, 1841
2nd	2nd	2nd	Aug 20, 1843	Oct 28, 1843
			May 1, 1841	
		2nd	June 25, 1842	April 27, 1843
1st	3rd	2nd	May 6, 1843	
	4th	2nd		
		2nd	July 3, 1841	Oct 16, 1841
		2nd	April 9, 1842	
			May 6, 1843	
			May 1, 1841	June 15, 1841
	4th	2nd	April 2, 1842	
2nd	3rd	2nd	July 3, 1841	Oct 16, 1841
	3rd	2nd	July 4, 1843	Oct 28, 1843
			March 9, 1841	
2nd	2nd	2nd	May 1, 1841	June 5, 1841
2nd	1st	1st	April 6, 1841	Oct 16, 1841

Name	Birth Date	Death Date	Rank	Company
Yale, Gad	Aug 21, 1790		3rd Lt.	2nd Co.
Yale, Gad	Aug 21, 1790		1st Lt.	1st Co.
York, Aaron Mereom	Aug 27, 1807	Nov 13, 1881	1st Lt.	
York, Aaron Mereom	Aug 27, 1807	Nov 13, 1881	2nd Lt.	1st Co.
Young, Alphonso	Sept 23, 1805		Surgeon	
Young, Brigham	June 1, 1801	Aug 29, 1877	Asst. Chaplain	
Young, Brigham	June 1, 1801	Aug 29, 1877	Lt. Gen.	
Young, Henry Icabod	Nov 13, 1798	Nov 7, 1885	2nd Lt.	
Young, Henry Icabod	Nov 13, 1798	Nov 7, 1885	Col.	4th Co.
Young, John			4th Cpl.	2nd Co.
Young, Joseph	April 7, 1797	July 16, 1881	Aide-de-Camp to Gen.	

Battalion	Regiment	Cohort	Date of Rank	Commission
2nd	2nd	2nd	May 1, 1841	June 5, 1841
3rd	2nd	2nd	July 3, 1841	Oct 16, 1841
		1st	Sept 17, 1842	April 27, 1843
1st	2nd	1st	July 3, 1841	Oct 16, 1841
			Aug 19, 1843	
		1st	July 3, 1841	Oct 16, 1841
			Aug 31, 1844	
		2nd	June 25, 1842	Sept 19, 1842
2nd	3rd	2nd	April 15, 1843	Oct 28, 1843
	4th	2nd		
		2nd	March 1, 1842	

Appendix E

Privates in the Nauvoo Legion (1841–1845)

Name	Birth Date	Death Date
Abbot, Rufus, Jr.	1824	Oct 21, 1901
Abel, Elijah	July 25, 1810	Dec 25, 1884
Adams, Arza	Jan 22, 1804	15 April 1889
Alexander, Randolph	March 22, 1802	March 12, 1879
Alleman, John	June 28, 1808	Oct 28, 1883
Allen, Daniel, Jr.	Dec 9, 1804	Jan 15, 1892
Allen, Rufus	March 22, 1814	Dec 4, 1887
Allred, Ezra Heeley		
Allred, Levi		Dec 16, 1800
Allred, Paulinus Harvey	June 26, 1829	Nov 19, 1900
Allred, Reddick Newton	Feb 21, 1822	Oct 10, 1905
Allred, Reddin Alexander	Feb 21, 1822	Aug 3, 1889
Allred, Reuben Warren	Nov 18, 1815	Oct 4, 1896
Ames, Daniel C.	1823	
Ames, Ira V.	Sept 22, 1804	Jan 16, 1869
Anderson, Buckley Burnham	June 14, 1819	July 1895
Averett, Elijah	Dec 12, 1810	Sept 12, 1886
Babcock, George	April 27, 1798	Oct 28, 1874
Baldwin, Caleb Clark	June 3, 1817	Jan 2, 1905
Baldwin, Wheeler	March 7, 1793	May 11, 1887
Ballard, Phillip	July 18, 1802	May 13, 1868
Barlow, Johnathan Watson	Jan 6, 1808	July 20, 1851
Barney, Amasa		
Benner, George W.	Dec 27, 1797	May 5, 1859
Benson, Jerome Messenger	Nov 5, 1810	April 17, 1873
Bentley, Benjamin R.	July 10, 1816	
Bentley, Johnson G.	June 1811	March 1882
Bigler, Jacob G.	April 4, 1813	Feb 23, 1907
Billings		
Billings, Ebenezer	1819	
Bills, John	Sept 17, 1819	Feb 19, 1850
Bingham, James R.		
Bird, George W.	Oct 13, 1823	July 1, 1917
Bird, N. R.		
Bird, Phineas Reeves	Jan 29, 1802	July 25, 1850
Bird, Richard	Oct 13, 1820	Feb 27, 1895
Bittlecomb, Nathan	Dec 18, 1823	April 27, 1907
Blodget, Newman Greenleaf	Sept 18, 1800	Aug 24, 1882
Bowman, P. G.		
Bowman, P. S.		
Boyce, Benjamin	Dec 28, 1812	1846
Boydston, Benjamin		

Rank	Company	Battalion	Regiment	Cohort
	2nd Co.	1st	2nd	2nd
Cavalry	1st Co.			1st
	2nd Co.			1st
Artillery	1st Co.	1st		2nd
	4th Co.			2nd
Cavalry	1st Co.			1st
Lancer	4th Co.			2nd
	2nd Co.			2nd
	4th Co.			2nd
	2nd Co.			2nd
	3rd Co.			2nd
	3rd Co.			1st
	3rd Co.	1st		1st
	2nd Co.	1st	2nd	2nd
Cavalry			5th	2nd
Rifle Ranger	2nd Co.			2nd
Fifer				
Lancer	2nd Co.			2nd
	Rifle Co.			2nd
Field Artillery				
Rifle Ranger				
Cavalry				
Cavalry				
Rifle Ranger				
	3rd Co.			1st
	3rd Co.			1st
	Rifle Co.			2nd
	2nd Co.			2nd
Fifer				
	2nd Co.			2nd
Cavalry				
Cavalry				
	2nd Co.			2nd
Artillery				
Field Artillery				
Cavalry				
	2nd Co.	1st	2nd	2nd
Artillery				
	4th Co.			2nd
Lancer				2nd
	2nd Co.			2nd
Field Artillery				

Name	Birth Date	Death Date
Bracken, James Bennett	Jan 14, 1816	March 31, 1900
Brady, Lindsey Anderson	June 11, 1811	June 26, 1885
Brown, Alanson		
Brown, Alfred	Jan 17, 1806	June 28, 1850
Brown, Lorenzo	Feb 2, 1823	Jan 28, 1902
Burkett, John	March 21, 1822	Dec 12, 1885
Butler, Nathan	1823	
Butterfield		
Carnes (Cairns), John	Oct 21, 1808	Sept 1885
Cathcart, Daniel R.	1803	
Champlin, William Sisson	April 16, 1794	Jan 29, 1861
Cheney, Nathan Calhoon	Feb 11, 1811	Feb 10, 1852
Chidester, John Maddison	Jan 22, 1809	Aug 29, 1893
Clapp, Benjamin Lynn	Aug 19, 1814	Oct 31, 1865
Clapper, J. Christian	July 4, 1807	June 26, 1891
Clark, Daniel Porter	Sept 27, 1824	April 17, 1885
Clark, John Milton	Jan 4, 1823	
Clements, Albert	March 19, 1801	April 9, 1882
Clements, Alvin	Nov 23, 1822	Sept 12, 1855
Clothier, Andrew Jackson	Jan 15, 1823	May 3, 1914
Cluff, David, Jr.	July 26, 1826	Oct 3, 1883
Colby, Alanson	May 9, 1813	Oct 19, 1880
Coltrin, Graham	Dec 11, 1796	May 16, 1851
Crosby, Jesse Wentworth	Nov 25, 1820	June 11, 1893
Crosby, John Knowles	Aug 19, 1812	July 15, 1898
Crosby, Jonathan	July 20, 1807	June 12, 1892
Curtis, George	Oct 27, 1823	Feb 5, 1911
Curtis, Joseph	Dec 24, 1818	Aug 1, 1882
Curtis, Lyman	Jan 21, 1812	Aug 3, 1897
Cutler, Harmon	July 16, 1799	Jan 28, 1869
Cutler, Thaddeus	June 18, 1809	May 2, 1896
Cutler, William Lathrop	Feb 6, 1821	Nov 1, 1851
Daily (Dayley), James Ray	March 26, 1815	July 23, 1905
Dibble, Philo	June 6, 1806	June 11, 1895
Dort, David D.	Jan 6, 1793	March 10, 1841
Dort, Stephen		
Dow, Eli Lorenzo		
Dudley, Joseph	July 8, 1817	Aug 24, 1903
Dudley, William	Oct 3, 1809	Dec 23, 1842
Durfee, Edmond	Sept 4, 1814	Jan 19, 1861
Durfee, George Washington	March 15, 1823	Nov 5, 1896
Durfee, Jabez	May 10, 1828	Dec 27, 1884

Rank	Company	Battalion	Regiment	Cohort
	2nd Co.			2nd
Field Artillery				
Cavalry				
	2nd Co.			2nd
Field Artillery				
	2nd Co.			2nd
	2nd Co.	1st	2nd	2nd
Lancer				2nd
Cavalry				
	2nd Co.	1st	1st	2nd
Rifle Ranger				
Artillery				
Artillery				
Field Artillery				
Rifle Ranger				
	4th Co.			1st
Fifer				
	4th Co.			2nd
Lancer	4th Co.			2nd
Fifer				
Field Artillery				
	2nd Co.			2nd
Cavalry				
	3rd Co.			1st
	4th Co.			1st
	3rd Co.			1st
	2nd Co.			2nd
	2nd Co.			2nd
	2nd Co.			2nd
	3rd Co.			1st
Cavalry				
Rifle Ranger				
	2nd Co.	1st	2nd	2nd
Cavalry				
Field Artillery				
Artillery				
Fifer				
	2nd Co.			2nd
	2nd Co.			2nd
	4th Co.			1st
Cavalry				
Cavalry				

Name	Birth Date	Death Date
Duzett, Alfred	Dec 3, 1819	Jan 20, 1842
Dykes, George Parker	Dec 24, 1814	Feb 25, 1888
Earl, Asa Colton	May 2, 1810	Dec 1, 1891
Earl, Jacob Sypher	Dec 28, 1822	Sept 9, 1910
Earl, William Henry		
Edmonds, Thomas Jefferson	Jan 21, 1820	Jan 1891
Edwards, Elisha Franklin	Dec 13, 1806	March 6, 1878
Edwards, Esias	April 10, 1812	June 8, 1897
Edwards, Walter M.	April 21, 1816	
Edwards, William Holliday	June 13, 1821	
Egbert, Joseph Teasdale	March 10, 1818	May 24, 1898
Eldridge, B.		
Evans, John	May 29, 1822	
Ewell, Thomas Maxey	May 6, 1819	Jan 10, 1900
Farr, Aaron Freeman	Oct 31, 1818	Nov 8, 1903
Farr, Lorin Freeman	July 27, 1820	Jan 12, 1908
Field, William	June 8, 1799	Sept 1845
Fish, Horace	Jan 6, 1799	July 6, 1870
Fish, William		
Fisher, Edmond	July 7, 1803	Sept 5, 1872
Flake, James Madison	June 22, 1815	June 15, 1850
Ford, William, Jr.	Oct 17, 1820	Aug 4, 1860
Forney, Frederick	Oct 9, 1813	May 11, 1880
Forney, George	Sept 25, 1820	April 16, 1880
Forney, Jacob	April 17, 1816	Aug 30, 1910
Foster, Solon	Jan 8, 1811	March 17, 1896
Frampton, Nathaniel	March 5, 1798	Sept 1883
Frampton, Samuel	Oct 26, 1826	Feb 9, 1904
Freeman, Elijah Norman	April 17, 1822	Nov 28, 1846
Fullmer, David	July 7, 1803	Oct 21, 1879
Gamet, David Mallory	Dec 4, 1812	Dec 1882
Gaylord, Elijah Baker	Sept 6, 1804	Aug 18, 1873
Gaylord, Lyman	March 21, 1819	
Gibson, Levi		
Gifford, Ichabod	April 14, 1822	
Gillett, Truman	May 21, 1811	
Goff, James	April 27, 1808	Aug 4, 1887
Golden, Aaron Houghton	Jan 3, 1807	1862
Goldsmith, Gilbert D.	Nov 27, 1811	
Gov, Curtis		
Grant, George Davis	Sept 10, 1812	Sept 20, 1876
Groves, Elisha Hurd	Nov 5, 1797	Dec 29, 1867

Rank	Company	Battalion	Regiment	Cohort
	3rd Co.			1st
Lancer				2nd
	3rd Co.			1st
	2nd Co.			2nd
	2nd Co.			2nd
Cavalry				
Field Artillery				
	2nd Co.			2nd
	3rd Co.			1st
Field Artillery	3rd Co.			1st
	3rd Co.			2nd
Lancer				2nd
Rifle Co.				2nd
Rifle Ranger				
	2nd Co.			2nd
	2nd Co.			2nd
Field Artillery				
	2nd Co.	1st	2nd	2nd
Artillery				
Rifle Ranger				
	2nd Co.			2nd
Lancer	4th Co.			2nd
Rifle Ranger				
Rifle Ranger				
Rifle Ranger				
Cavalry				
	3rd Co.			1st
	3rd Co.			1st
	2nd Co.			2nd
Artillery	3rd Co.			1st
Artillery	1st Co.	1st		2nd
	3rd Co.			1st
	4th Co.			2nd
Cymbals				
	4th Co.			2nd
Field Artillery				
Cavalry	2nd Co.			2nd
Rifle Ranger				
Cavalry				
	1st Co.			1st
Field Artillery				
	3rd Co.			1st

Name	Birth Date	Death Date
Hale, Aroet Lucius		
Hall, Samuel	Aug 25, 1813	Dec 9, 1878
Hardy, John W.		
Harrison, Isaac	Nov 2, 1815	March 2, 1894
Helm, William Riley		
Henderson, John	Nov 20, 1810	Dec 2, 1851
Henderson, Martin		
Henderson, Samuel, Jr.	Oct 19, 1820	Oct 29, 1904
Hendrickson, Jordan Paddocks	Jan 8, 1809	
Hewitt, Wilkinson	March 20, 1812	
Hewitt, William		
Hicks, Amon	1803	
Hicks, George Barton	Dec 15, 1803	Jan 13, 1885
Hicks, John A.	1810	May 16, 1887
Hicks, Robert F.	Aug 9, 1818	
Hicks, Samuel Burton	March 23, 1808	Oct 25, 1895
Hicks, William Armstrong		
Higbee, Chauncey Lawson	Dec 7, 1821	Dec 9, 1884
Higbee, Isaac	Dec 23, 1797	Feb 16, 1874
Higbee, William W.	1826	
Higgins, Nelson D.	Sept 1, 1806	Nov 20, 1890
Holbrook, Chandler	Sept 16, 1807	Sept 3, 1889
Holman, David	July 15, 1808	
Holmes, Francis	July 5, 1815	
Horr, Alvin	Sept 5, 1799	
Houghton, James William	Sept 3, 1814	May 15, 1884
Houghton, Newell	Dec 14, 1822	Aug 23, 1862
Houghton, Ornan (Omon)	Oct 1, 1806	Aug 18, 1847
Hubbard, Charles Wesley	Feb 7, 1810	Dec 19, 1903
Hulet, Francis	March 3, 1802	March 17, 1882
Hunt, William		
Huntington, Dimick Baker	May 26, 1808	Feb 1, 1879
Huntington, John Dickinson	Feb 11, 1827	Feb 15, 1900
Huntington, Oliver Boardman	Oct 14, 1823	Feb 7, 1907
Huntsman, Jacob	Feb 18, 1807	March 1, 1893
Huntsman, John	1809	
Huntsman, James William	Oct 8, 1806	Feb 26, 1867
Isham, Cyrus Orvis	about 1824	1868
Jackman, Ammi Rumsey	Feb 6, 1825	Dec 3, 1898
Jackman, Albert Brady	Aug 12, 1812	March 1, 1891
Jackman, William Ruel	Oct 6, 1818	Aug 8, 1851
Jackson, William		

Rank	Company	Battalion	Regiment	Cohort
Rifle Ranger				
	3rd Co.			1st
	2nd Co.			2nd
	2nd Co.			2nd
	4th Co.			2nd
	1st Co.			1st
	Rifle Co.			2nd
	2nd Co.			2nd
	1st Co.	1st		2nd
Field Artillery				
	2nd Co.			2nd
Cavalry				
	2nd Co.			2nd
	Rifle Co.			2nd
Cavalry				
	Rifle Co.			2nd
	Rifle Co.			
Artillery				
	Rifle Co.			2nd
	3rd Co.			2nd
	3rd Co.			1st
Cavalry				
	4th Co.			2nd
	Rifle Co.			2nd
Rifle Ranger				
Rifle Ranger				
Rifle Ranger				
Cavalry				
	3rd Co.			1st
	2nd Co.			2nd
Drums				
Triangles				
Tambourine				
	4th Co.			2nd
Cavalry	2nd Co.	1st	2nd	2nd
Cavalry				
	2nd Co.			2nd
	2nd Co.			1st
	2nd Co.			2nd
Fifer	2nd Co.			2nd
	2nd Co.	1st	2nd	2nd

Name	Birth Date	Death Date
Jacobs, Henry Bailey	May 5, 1817	Aug 1, 1886
James, Alonzo True	Aug 7, 1810	
Johnson, Artemas	April 18, 1809	
Johnson, George Washington	Feb 19, 1823	Jan 22, 1900
Johnson, Huntington	Feb 15, 1796	Nov 21, 1863
Johnson, Joel Hills	March 23, 1802	Sept 24, 1882
Jolley, Alan		
Jones, Abram		
Jones, Benjamin	Feb 24, 1797	April 4, 1875
Jones, David	Aug 20, 1799	
Jones, Moses Ayres	March 18, 1825	
Kelly, James		
Kelsey, Easton	March 9, 1813	March 10, 1899
Kempton, Benjamin	Dec 8, 1814	March 4, 1844
King, Culbert	1822	
King, Eleazer	Dec 11, 1811	March 23, 1897
King, John Morris	Sept 23, 1809	Nov 13, 1855
Lake, Leander		
Lambert, John	Jan 31, 1820	Nov 25, 1893
Lane, Johnson F.	Feb 22, 1803	
Lane, William West	Aug 29, 1797	July 8, 1852
Larkey, Edward	June 17, 1809	Feb 1884
Lawson, John	June 20, 1805	Jan 16, 1884
Leavitt, Jeremiah	May 30, 1796	Aug 4, 1846
Leavitt, Nathaniel	Nov 17, 1823	April 7, 1896
Lisenbee (Lazenbee), John	1820	
Livermore, William B.		
Loveland, Chester	Dec 30, 1817	March 5, 1886
Loveland, Levi	Feb 20, 1816	June 31, 1846
Luce, John Grant	Sept 30, 1817	
Luce, Stephen Thomas	July 10, 1801	April 28, 1872
Lyons, David	1817	
Mackley, John	March 20, 1796	
Markham, Stephen	Feb 9, 1800	March 10, 1878
Markham, William	about 1798	1894
Marks, Ephraim Robinson	Feb 12, 1818	April 7, 1842
Mason, Nathan		
Maston, Henry		
McBride, James	May 9, 1818	Jan 6, 1881
McCall, J. S.		
McCall, John		
McCall, Joseph A.		

Rank	Company	Battalion	Regiment	Cohort
Fifer				
	2nd Co.	1st	2nd	2nd
Cavalry				
	3rd Co.			1st
Cavalry	1st Co.			1st
Cavalry	3rd Co.			1st
	2nd Co.			2nd
Field Artillery				
	2nd Co.			2nd
Cavalry				
	2nd Co.			2nd
Surgeon				2nd
Cavalry				
	3rd Co.			1st
	1st Co.			1st
Fifer	2nd Co.			2nd
Cymbals				
	2nd Co.			2nd
	2nd Co.			1st
	2nd Co.			2nd
	4th Co.			2nd
	4th Co.			2nd
	3rd Co.			1st
	2nd Co.	1st	2nd	2nd
Field Artillery	2nd Co.	1st	2nd	2nd
	2nd Co.			2nd
Rifle Ranger				
	3rd Co.			1st
	3rd Co.			1st
Lancer				2nd
	4th Co.			2nd
	2nd Co.			2nd
Artillery				
Cavalry				
	2nd Co.			2nd
Color Bearer				
	4th Co.			1st
	Rifle Co.			2nd
	2nd Co.	1st	2nd	2nd
Cavalry				
	4th Co.			2nd
Cavalry				

Name	Birth Date	Death Date
McIntire, William Patterson	May 29, 1813	Jan 7, 1882
McMeans, Rufus		
McMillan, James		
McOlney, Davis	Feb 24, 1796	
McRae, Alexander	Sept 7, 1807	June 20, 1891
Melton, Stephen		
Merkley, Christopher	Dec 18, 1808	May 2, 1893
Meservy, William		
Milam, William	March 18, 1799	Feb 24, 1853
Miller, John	Aug 15, 1801	
Milliken, Arthur	May 9, 1817	April 23, 1882
Moffett, Armstead	Feb 7, 1814	March 27, 1891
Moffit, James		
Moon, Francis	1797	
Morrill, Laban	Dec 8, 1814	Dec 8, 1900
Morton, Samuel R.	1829	
Moses, James	Feb 28, 1806	March 30, 1891
Moss, Thomas	Feb 12, 1808	Oct 9, 1872
Mouth, W.		
Munjar, Thomas	1825	May 21, 1898
Napier, R.		
Nelson, C. G.		
Newell		
Norris, Patrick	about 1806	June 27, 1850
Olney, Milton Johnson	Dec 29, 1822	Jan 13, 1904
Olney, Newton	1821	1841
Olney, Oliver	Aug 11, 1796	
Omstead, Asa		
Ondercark, Isaac	April 1, 1809	Dec 16, 1884
Outhouse, John Miles	Sept 20, 1823	April 17, 1889
Outhouse, Joseph	March 20, 1820	Oct 13, 1873
Outhouse, William		
Pace, Elisha	Oct 1804	Oct 1, 1844
Pack, John	May 20, 1809	April 4, 1885
Packard, Loren	Sept 30, 1825	
Packard, Noah	May 7, 1796	Feb 17, 1859
Packard, Noah	April 24, 1821	Jan 26, 1900
Packer, Jonathan Taylor	July 26, 1817	Jan 29, 1889
Page, Ebenezer	Oct 7, 1807	1870
Parkman, John A.		
Peck, Hezekiah	March 12, 1820	Oct 20, 1859
Peck, Matthew Long	Nov 21, 1822	

Rank	Company	Battalion	Regiment	Cohort
Field Artillery				
	4th Co.			2nd
	2nd Co.	1st	2nd	2nd
	2nd Co.			2nd
Aide-de-Camp				
	4th Co.			2nd
	2nd Co.			1st
	4th Co.			2nd
Cavalry				
	2nd Co.			2nd
Cavalry				
	2nd Co.			2nd
	3rd Co.			1st
	4th Co.			2nd
	2nd Co.	1st	2nd	2nd
	2nd Co.			2nd
Field Artillery				
	4th Co.			2nd
Cavalry				
	2nd Co.			2nd
	3rd Co.			1st
	2nd Co.			1st
Drums				
	4th Co.			2nd
Cavalry				
	2nd Co.			2nd
Cavalry				
	2nd Co.			2nd
	2nd Co.			2nd
	2nd Co.			2nd
	2nd Co.			2nd
	2nd Co.			2nd
	4th Co.			2nd
Clarinet				
	Rifle Co.			2nd
	2nd Co.			2nd
Artillery	1st Co.	1st		2nd
Rifle Ranger				
	3rd Co.			1st
	1st Co.			1st
	3rd Co.			1st
	3rd Co.			1st

Name	Birth Date	Death Date
Perkins, Andrew Houston	Dec 5, 1808	March 18, 1851
Perkins, David Martin	Aug 23, 1823	April 4, 1874
Perkins, William Lewis	June 18, 1819	Jan 7, 1899
Perry, Philander Jackson	Sept 29, 1821	Sept 27, 1902
Phelps, William Waterman	Jan 23, 1823	June 6, 1886
Phippin, James Worthington	Oct 12, 1819	Dec 13, 1908
Pierce, Joseph White	June 4, 1805	April 2, 1888
Plumb, J.		
Price, Charles	Sept 1, 1800	Jan 1873
Randall, Horace		
Rawson, Horace Strong	July 15, 1799	Oct 10, 1882
Read, William Smith	Dec 1, 1816	Dec 1, 1891
Reed, Calvin	Oct 18, 1821	Oct 25, 1895
Rockwell, Horace	April 30, 1825	Oct 1893
Rockwell, Merit	July 26, 1821	1848
Rockwell, Orrin Porter	Jan 25, 1815	June 9, 1878
Rockwell, Orrin Porter	Jan 25, 1815	June 9, 1878
Rogers, Amos Philemon	Sept 27, 1820	June 25, 1846
Rogers, Chandler	Jan 27, 1795	Oct 1, 1846
Rogers, Isaac	Nov 3, 1793	April 1849
Rogers, Noble	Aug 10, 1799	
Rogers, Russell	May 18, 1820	Dec 21, 1890
Rogers, S. C.		
Rogers, Samuel Holister	March 1, 1819	Sept 20, 1891
Rogers, Z.		
Rolfe, Benjamin Williams	Oct 7, 1822	May 31, 1890
Rolfe, Samuel Jones	Aug 26, 1794	July 1867
Roundy, Lorenzo Wesley	June 18, 1819	May 24, 1876
Russell, Robert Anderson	March 12, 1812	Dec 16, 1879
Sagers, William Henry Harrison	May 3, 1815	June 19, 1886
Savage, Rufus, Jr.		
Shever, Thomas, Jr.		
Shirts, Peter	Aug 23, 1808	1880
Shumway, Alanson Burt	Aug 8, 1821	Aug 29, 1847
Skinner, Levi Lewis	Oct 27, 1819	1864
Smith		
Smith, D.		
Smith, Jackson Osbourne	April 2, 1815	June 19, 1880
Smith, Warren	Oct 7, 1808	May 12, 1885
Speirs, Thomas	July 14, 1804	July 8, 1877
Sprague, Ithamer	Sept 18, 1807	April 13, 1879
Standly, Alexander Schoby	May 12, 1800	Dec 29, 1854

Rank	Company	Battalion	Regiment	Cohort
	3rd Co.			1st
	3rd Co.			1st
	3rd Co.			1st
	2nd Co.			2nd
	4th Co.			2nd
Field Artillery				
Field Artillery				
Cavalry				
	4th Co.			2nd
Field Artillery				
Artillery				
	2nd Co.			2nd
	2nd Co.			2nd
	2nd Co.			2nd
	2nd Co.			2nd
	2nd Co.			2nd
Cavalry	1st Co.			1st
Cavalry	1st Co.			1st
	2nd Co.			1st
	3rd Co.			1st
Cavalry	1st Co.			2nd
Cavalry				
	3rd Co.			1st
Lancer				2nd
	1st Co.			1st
Cavalry	1st Co.			1st
				2nd
	1st Co.			1st
	2nd Co.			1st
Cavalry	2nd Co.	1st	2nd	2nd
	2nd Co.	1st	2nd	2nd
Cavalry				
	2nd Co.			1st
	3rd Co.			1st
	2nd Co.			2nd
Drums				
Rifle Co.	2nd Co.			2nd
	2nd Co.			2nd
Cavalry				
Field Artillery				
Rifle Ranger				
Cavalry				

Name	Birth Date	Death Date
Stephens, Huite W.		
Stevens, Lyman	Feb 7, 1812	April 18, 1886
Stevens, Roswell	Nov 17, 1808	May 14, 1880
Stewart, Levi	April 28, 1812	June 14, 1878
Stiles, George Philander	July 18, 1816	
Strong, Jacob	Oct 9, 1799	Feb 18, 1872
Teeples, George Bentley	March 17, 1803	Sept 18, 1884
Thompson, Samuel S.	Feb 13, 1812	March 14, 1901
Thornhill, Leonard	1815	July 26, 1844
Tidwell, John	Jan 14, 1807	Jan 24, 1887
Tippets, John Harvey	Sept 5, 1810	Feb 14, 1890
Tracy, Moses	April 11, 1810	Aug 25, 1858
Turpin, John	Dec 24, 1808	
Tyler, Ira (Ezra)	Aug 22, 1797	
Ure, William	June 7, 1822	Oct 11, 1860
Wakefield, G.		
Wakefield, John Flemming	Nov 15, 1812	Jan 13, 1854
Weeks, William	April 11, 1813	March 8, 1890
White, Samuel Stephen	April 8, 1821	Oct 15, 1900
Whitesides		
Whitlock, Andrew Hiram	Jan 15, 1805	April 13, 1865
Whitlock, Perry		
Whitman, Rockwood		
Whitmark, William P.		
Whitney, Horace Kimball	July 25, 1823	Nov 22, 1884
Wicks, Allen		
Wiggins, Ebenezer Fairchild	Feb 4, 1806	Dec 5, 1873
Williams, Alexander	Oct 10, 1803	Oct 5, 1876
Williams, Samuel	March 22, 1789	Nov 10, 1855
Wilson, Bradley Barlow	Oct 11, 1806	Jan 12, 1874
Wilson, George Clinton	Aug 22, 1800	May 9, 1874
Wilson, George Deliverance	Dec 28, 1807	Oct 18, 1887
Wilson, Henry Hardy	May 16, 1803	Dec 30, 1878
Wilson, Irwin Riley	Jan 22, 1822	Jan 7, 1907
Wilson, Wellington Paul	Feb 1, 1814	May 29, 1896
Wilson, Whitford Gill	June 4, 1789	Nov 26, 1862
Winegar, Alvin	May 13, 1816	June 12, 1874
Woolsey, James Hopkins	March 2, 1822	Oct 14, 1903
Wyrick, James	1823	1886
Young, Ahira	Aug 5, 1809	
Younger, Joseph	Dec 10, 1803	
Zemmer, Samuel		

Rank	Company	Battalion	Regiment	Cohort
Artillery				
Field Artillery				
Field Artillery	2nd Co.			2nd
Rifle Co.				2nd
	3rd Co.			1st
	4th Co.			2nd
Cavalry (Rifle Ranger)				
Field Artillery				
Cavalry				
	4th Co.			2nd
Artillery				
	2nd Co.			2nd
	2nd Co.			2nd
	2nd Co.			2nd
	2nd Co.			2nd
Lancer				2nd
	4th Co.			2nd
				2nd
	3rd Co.			1st
	2nd Co.	1st	2nd	2nd
	4th Co.			2nd
	2nd Co.	1st	2nd	2nd
	3rd Co.			1st
Cavalry				
Fifer				
Field Artillery				
	2nd Co.	1st	2nd	2nd
Rifle Ranger				
Field Artillery				
Field Artillery				
Field Artillery	2nd Co.			2nd
	3rd Co.			1st
Field Artillery	1st Co.	1st		2nd
	3rd Co.			1st
Field Artillery				
Artillery (Cavalry)				
Rifle Co.				2nd
Rifle Co.				2nd
Rifle Ranger				
	2nd Co.			2nd
	3rd Co.			2nd
	4th Co.			2nd

Bibliography

Manuscript and Archival Sources

Adams, Arza. "Diary of Arza Adams, 1830–1844." L. Tom Perry Special Collections, Harold B. Lee Library, Brigham Young University, Provo, Utah.

"Affidavit of Justus Morse, March 23, 1887, Pleasanton, Iowa," Church History Library. The Church of Jesus Christ of Latter-day Saints. Salt Lake City, Utah.

Alvord, D. S. "'Mormon Collection', 1832–1886, from the Chicago Historical Society," n.p., n.d. L. Tom Perry Special Collections, Harold B. Lee Library, Brigham Young University, Provo, Utah.

Bullock, Thomas. "Manuscript Copy of Thomas Bullock Journal." Church History Library. The Church of Jesus Christ of Latter-day Saints, Salt Lake City, Utah.

Bushman, Richard Lyman. "The Mormon War and Mormon Violence." Smith Institute Seminar, June 13, 2002, Brigham Young University, Provo, Utah.

Butler, John Lowe. "Autobiography of John Lowe Butler." L. Tom Perry Special Collections, Harold B. Lee Library, Brigham Young University, Provo, Utah.

———. "A Short History of the Biography of John L. Butler Partly from his Own Writing." L. Tom Perry Special Collections, Harold B. Lee Library, Brigham Young University, Provo, Utah.

Cahoon, William F. "William F. Cahoon Autobiography." Church History Library. The Church of Jesus Christ of Latter-day Saints, Salt Lake City, Utah.

Campbell, Robert Lang. "Robert Lang Campbell Collection." L. Tom Perry Special Collections, Harold B. Lee Library. Brigham Young University, Provo, Utah.

Carlin, Thomas [Governor]. "Know Ye, That Joseph Holbrook Having Been Duly Elected to the Office of Captain of the 2nd Company 2nd Battalion 1st Regiment 1st Cohort of the Nauvoo Legion of the Militia of the State of Illinois." n.p., n.d. Church History Library. The Church of Jesus Christ of Latter-day Saints, Salt Lake City, Utah.

Carter, Catherine Vigdus Bearnson. "The Nauvoo Legion." Salt Lake City, Utah: n.d. In the authors' possession.

"Collected Accounts of Addresses of Joseph Smith to the Nauvoo Legion 1844 June," Church History Library. The Church of Jesus Christ of Latter-day Saints, Salt Lake City, Utah.

"Commission Record of Hyrum Smith to the office of Brevet Major General of the Nauvoo Legion by Thomas Carlin, Governor of the State of Illinois, December 14, 1841." Church History Library. The Church of Jesus Christ of Latter-day Saints, Salt Lake City, Utah.

Crow, Julina Markham. "History of the Life of Stephen Markham, ca. 1950." L. Tom Perry Special Collections, Harold B. Lee Library. Brigham Young University, Provo, Utah.

Duke, Jonathan Oldham. "Journal of Jonathan Oldham Duke." L. Tom Perry Special Collections, Harold B. Lee Library. Brigham Young University, Provo, Utah.

Fleek, Sherman. Letter to Donald Cannon, November 26, 2005. In the authors' possession.

Fullmer, John S. "John S. Fullmer Diary." Church History Library. The Church of Jesus Christ of Latter-day Saints, Salt Lake City, Utah.

———. Letters of John Solomon Fullmer, 1836–1901. Church History Library. The Church of Jesus Christ of Latter-day Saints, Salt Lake City, Utah.

Haight, Isaac Chauncy. "Biographical Sketch and Diary of Isaac Chauncy Haight." L. Tom Perry Special Collections, Harold B. Lee Library. Brigham Young University, Provo, Utah.

Hale, Aroet Lucius. "Aroet Lucius Hale Papers." MS 17081, Church History Library. The Church of Jesus Christ of Latter-day Saints, Salt Lake City, Utah.

Hale, Jonathan H. "Jonathan H. Hale Papers." Church History Library. The Church of Jesus Christ of Latter-day Saints, Salt Lake City, Utah.

Hess, Margaret Steed. "Biographies, 1900–1940," n.p., n.d. L. Tom Perry Special Collections, Harold B. Lee Library. Brigham Young University, Provo, Utah.

———. "Life Sketch of Caroline Holland Steed." L. Tom Perry Special Collections, Harold B. Lee Library. Brigham Young University, Provo, Utah.

Higbee. "Higbee Papers." Church History Library. The Church of Jesus Christ of Latter-day Saints, Salt Lake City, Utah.

Holbrook, Joseph. "Autobiography of Joseph Holbrook." Church History Library. The Church of Jesus Christ of Latter-day Saints, Salt Lake City, Utah.

———. "The Life of Joseph Holbrook, 1806–1871." L. Tom Perry Special Collections, Harold B. Lee Library. Brigham Young University, Provo, Utah.

———. "Papers of Joseph Holbrook." Church History Library. The Church of Jesus Christ of Latter-day Saints, Salt Lake City, Utah.

Hovey, M. R., comp. "Biography of Joseph Grafton Hovey," L. Tom Perry Special Collections, Harold B. Lee Library. Brigham Young University, Provo, Utah.

Huntington, Oliver B. "Diary of Oliver B. Huntington." L. Tom Perry Special Collections, Harold B. Lee Library. Brigham Young University, Provo, Utah.

Huntington, William. "Diary and Autobiography of William Huntington, 1784–1846." L. Tom Perry Special Collections, Harold B. Lee Library. Brigham Young University, Provo, Utah.

———. "Papers of William Huntington." Church History Library. The Church of Jesus Christ of Latter-day Saints, Salt Lake City, Utah.

Hyde, William. "The Private Journal of William Hyde, 1968." L. Tom Perry Special Collections, Harold B. Lee Library. Brigham Young University, Provo, Utah.

Jacob, Norton. "Record of Norton Jacob." L. Tom Perry Special Collections, Harold B. Lee Library. Brigham Young University, Provo, Utah.

Johnson, Philo. "Journal of Philo Johnson." L. Tom Perry Special Collections, Harold B. Lee Library. Brigham Young University, Provo, Utah.

"Journal History of the Church." Church History Library. The Church of Jesus Christ of Latter-day Saints, Salt Lake City, Utah.

Laub, George. "Diary of George Laub." L. Tom Perry Special Collections, Harold B. Lee Library. Brigham Young University, Provo, Utah.

Law, William. "Diary of William Law." L. Tom Perry Special Collections, Harold B. Lee Library. Brigham Young University, Provo, Utah.

Law of the Lord. Church History Library. The Church of Jesus Christ of Latter-day Saints, Salt Lake City, Utah.

Lee, John D. "Papers of John D. Lee." Church History Library. The Church of Jesus Christ of Latter-day Saints.

Lillywhite, Eva J. "Biographical Sketch of the Life of Luman Andros Shurtliff, 1807–1864." L. Tom Perry Special Collections, Harold B. Lee Library. Brigham Young University, Provo, Utah.

Mace, Wandle. "Autobiography of Wandle Mace." L. Tom Perry Special Collections, Harold B. Lee Library. Brigham Young University, Provo, Utah.

Magnus, Estella Rebecca Draper. "William and Lydia Draper Biographical Sketch," Church History Library. The Church of Jesus Christ of Latter-day Saints, Salt Lake City, Utah.

"Manuscript Document File, 1842." Church History Library. The Church of Jesus Christ of Latter-day Saints, Salt Lake City, Utah.

"Manuscript History of the Church." Church History Library. The Church of Jesus Christ of Latter-day Saints, Salt Lake City, Utah.

"Manuscript Subject File of the Nauvoo Legion. Original documents of orders, rank rolls, and minutes." Church History Library. The Church of Jesus Christ of Latter-day Saints, Salt Lake City, Utah.

Markham, Stephen. "History of the Life of Stephen Markham." L. Tom Perry Special Collections. Harold B. Lee Library, Brigham Young University, Provo, Utah.

" 'Militia Regiments' Ledger, 1819–1835." Illinois State Archives, Springfield.

"Minutes and Ordinances of Organization of the Nauvoo Legion, February 3, 1841, to October 20, 1844." Church History Library. The Church of Jesus Christ of Latter-day Saints, Salt Lake City, Utah.

Moore, Andrew. "Reminiscences of Andrew Moore, 1846." Church History Library. The Church of Jesus Christ of Latter-day Saints, Salt Lake City, Utah.

Morgan, Dale Lowell, comp. "The Mormons and the Far West: Transcripts from American Newspapers, 1811–1855." L. Tom Perry Special Collections, Harold B. Lee Library. Brigham Young University, Provo, Utah.

"Morning Report of 2nd Cohort for Brig. June 27, 1844," Joseph Smith Papers. Church History Library. The Church of Jesus Christ of Latter-day Saints, Salt Lake City, Utah.

Morse, Justus. "Affidavit of Justus Morse." Pleasanton, Iowa.

Mott, John. Letters of John Mott, 1839 and 1842. Church History Library. The Church of Jesus Christ of Latter-day Saints, Salt Lake City, Utah.

Nauvoo City Council Minutes. Church History Library. The Church of Jesus Christ of Latter-day Saints, Salt Lake City, Utah.

Nauvoo LDS Census, February 1842. Church History Library. The Church of Jesus Christ of Latter-day Saints, Salt Lake City, Utah.

Nauvoo Legion. "A Bill for an Act to Incorporate the City of Nauvoo." Illinois State Archives, Springfield.

———. "Commission, 1854 June 3 Nauvoo Legion." L. Tom Perry Special Collections, Harold B. Lee Library. Brigham Young University, Provo, Utah.

———. "Meeting of Police." Church History Library. The Church of Jesus Christ of Latter-day Saints, Salt Lake City, Utah.

———. "Papers." Church History Library. The Church of Jesus Christ of Latter-day Saints, Salt Lake City, Utah.

———. "Nauvoo Legion Redeemable Script, 1843." L. Tom Perry Special Collections, Harold B. Lee Library, Brigham Young University, Provo, Utah.

———. "Rank Roll of the Nauvoo Legion, 1842." L. Tom Perry Special Collections, Harold B. Lee Library. Brigham Young University, Provo, Utah.

Noble, Joseph Bates. "Reminiscences of Joseph Bates Noble, 1810–1900." Church History Library. The Church of Jesus Christ of Latter-day Saints, Salt Lake City, Utah.

Noble, Joseph P. "Collection." Church History Library. The Church of Jesus Christ of Latter-day Saints, Salt Lake City, Utah.

Pace, James. "Papers of James Pace." Church History Library. The Church of Jesus Christ of Latter-day Saints, Salt Lake City, Utah.

Pace, William Byram. "Diary of William Byram Pace." L. Tom Perry Special Collections, Harold B. Lee Library. Brigham Young University, Provo, Utah.

Perry, Stephen Chadwick. "Stephen Chadwick Perry Statement, Ca., 188[?]." Church History Library. The Church of Jesus Christ of Latter-day Saints, Salt Lake City, Utah.

Platt, Lyman D. "Commission Records, Illinois State Militia, 1834–1855." In the authors' possession.

"Rank Roll of the Nauvoo Legion." Church History Library. The Church of Jesus Christ of Latter-day Saints, Salt Lake City, Utah.

"Reply of Joseph Smith, to the Letter of J. A. B[——]. [James Arlington Bennet] of A[rlingto]n house, New York," Liverpool, R. Hedlock and T. Ward [1843?]. Church History Library. The Church of Jesus Christ of Latter-day Saints, Salt Lake City, Utah.

"Return of Hosea Stout, Brig. Gen. 2nd Cohort, Nauvoo Legion, June 27, 1844, Hosea Stout." Church History Library. The Church of Jesus Christ of Latter-day Saints, Salt Lake City, Utah.

"Return of J. W. Coolidge, Adjt. 2nd Regiment, 2nd Cohort, Nauvoo Legion, June 27, 1844." Church History Library. The Church of Jesus Christ of Latter-day Saints, Salt Lake City, Utah.

Rich, Charles Coulson. "Autobiography of Charles Coulson Rich." L. Tom Perry Special Collections, Harold B. Lee Library. Brigham Young University, Provo, Utah.

Rich, Mary. "Autobiography of Mary Rich." L. Tom Perry Special Collections, Harold B. Lee Library. Brigham Young University, Provo, Utah.

Rich, Sarah. "Autobiography of Sarah Rich." L. Tom Perry Special Collections, Harold B. Lee Library. Brigham Young University, Provo, Utah.

Richards, Levi. "Levi Richards Papers." Church History Library. The Church of Jesus Christ of Latter-day Saints, Salt Lake City, Utah.

Richards, S. W. "Journal of S. W. Richards." L. Tom Perry Special Collections, Harold B. Lee Library. Brigham Young University, Provo, Utah.

———. "S. W. Richards Collection." Church History Library. The Church of Jesus Christ of Latter-day Saints, Salt Lake City, Utah.

Rockwood, Albert Perry. "Papers of Albert Perry Rockwood, 1840–1845."

Church History Library. The Church of Jesus Christ of Latter-day Saints, Salt Lake City, Utah.

———. "Papers of Albert Perry Rockwood, 1838–1839." Church History Library. The Church of Jesus Christ of Latter-day Saints, Salt Lake City, Utah.

"Roll of the Lieut. Gen. Staffs of the Nauvoo Legion, September 15, 1843." Church History Library. The Church of Jesus Christ of Latter-day Saints, Salt Lake City, Utah.

"Roll of the Lieutenant General's Staff (Guards) of the Nauvoo Legion." Church History Library. The Church of Jesus Christ of Latter-day Saints, Salt Lake City, Utah.

Rollins, James Henry. "Autobiography of James Henry Rollins." L. Tom Perry Special Collections, Harold B. Lee Library. Brigham Young University, Provo, Utah.

Sharp, Thomas. "The Thomas C. Sharp and Allied Anti-Mormon Papers, 1844–1846." Church History Library. The Church of Jesus Christ of Latter-day Saints, Salt Lake City, Utah.

Shurtliff, Luman A. "Biographical Sketch of Luman A. Shurtliff." L. Tom Perry Special Collections, Harold B. Lee Library. Brigham Young University, Provo, Utah.

Smith, Joseph. "Journal of Joseph Smith." Church History Library. The Church of Jesus Christ of Latter-day Saints, Salt Lake City, Utah.

———. "Letterbooks." Church History Library. The Church of Jesus Christ of Latter-day Saints, Salt Lake City, Utah.

———. "Papers of Joseph Smith." Church History Library. The Church of Jesus Christ of Latter-day Saints, Salt Lake City, Utah.

Smith, Lela. "Community and Civic Affairs 1839–46." L. Tom Perry Special Collections, Harold B. Lee Library. Brigham Young University, Provo, Utah.

Snow, Eliza R. "Eliza R. Snow Diaries." Church History Library. The Church of Jesus Christ of Latter-day Saints, Salt Lake City, Utah.

Steed, Caroline Holland. "Life Sketches of Caroline Holland Steed." L. Tom Perry Special Collections, Harold B. Lee Library. Brigham Young University, Provo, Utah.

Stevenson, Edward. "Journal of Edward Stevenson." Church History Library. The Church of Jesus Christ of Latter-day Saints, Salt Lake City, Utah.

Stout, Allen Joseph. "Journal of Allen Joseph Stout." L. Tom Perry Special Collections, Harold B. Lee Library. Brigham Young University, Provo, Utah.

Stout, Hosea. "Papers, 1840–1872." Church History Library. The Church of Jesus Christ of Latter-day Saints, Salt Lake City, Utah.

———. "Legion of Nauvoo for Journal History of the Church of Jesus

Christ of Latter-day Saints, April 6, 1841." Church History Library. The Church of Jesus Christ of Latter-day Saints, Salt Lake City, Utah.

Terry, Joshua. "Biography of Joshua Terry." L. Tom Perry Special Collections, Harold B. Lee Library. Brigham Young University, Provo, Utah.

Whitney, Newel Kimball. "Papers, 1825–1846." L. Tom Perry Special Collections, Harold B. Lee Library. Brigham Young University, Provo, Utah.

———. "Papers, 1825–1846." MS 17390, Reel 3, Fd 2, Church History Library. The Church of Jesus Christ of Latter-day Saints, Salt Lake City, Utah.

Woodruff, Wilford. "Journal of Wilford Woodruff." Church History Library. The Church of Jesus Christ of Latter-day Saints, Salt Lake City, Utah.

———. "Wilford Woodruff Journal, 1833." Church History Library. The Church of Jesus Christ of Latter-day Saints, Salt Lake City, Utah.

Young, Richard W. "The Nauvoo Legion." Church History Library. The Church of Jesus Christ of Latter-day Saints, Salt Lake City, Utah.

Newspapers

Alton Telegraph and Democratic Review. J. Bailhache & Co., 1841–50, Alton, Illinois.

Bloomington Herald, H. D. La. Cossitt, 1848–62, Bloomington, Iowa.

Daily Evening Gazette, 1836–46, St. Louis, Missouri.

Daily National Intelligencer, 1844.

Davenport Gazette, 1839, Davenport, Iowa.

Franklin Times, Franklin, Illinois.

Hawkeye and Iowa Patriot, 1841. Burlington, Iowa.

Illinois Herald, 1841–1842, Quincy, Illinois.

Iowa City Standard, Iowa City, Iowa.

Lee County Democrat, R. Wilson Albright and William E. Mason, 1841–47, Fort Madison, Iowa.

Logansport Telegraph, 1837–49, Logansport, Indiana.

Millennial Star, 1840–1848, Manchester, England.

Monmouth Atlas, 1846–present, Monmouth, Illinois.

National Intelligencer, 1810–69, Washington, D.C.

The Nauvoo Expositor, 1844, Nauvoo, Illinois.

The Nauvoo Neighbor, 1843–45, Nauvoo, Illinois.

The New York Herald, 1842.

The Niles' National Register. 1842–43.

The Peoples Miscellany, Alton, Illinois.

The Peoria Register and North Western Gazetteer, 1841. Peoria, Illinois.

Saint's Herald, Reorganized Church of Jesus Christ of Latter Day Saints, Independence, Missouri.

Sangamo Journal, S & J Francis, 1831–47, Springfield, Illinois.
St. Louis Reporter, Saint Louis, Missouri.
Times and Seasons, 1839–46, Nauvoo, Illinois.
Warsaw Message. Warsaw, Illinois.
Warsaw Signal, Sharp & Galloway, 1841–50, Warsaw, Illinois.
Wasp (Nauvoo Wasp), William Smith, 1842–43, Nauvoo, Illinois.

Government Documents

"An Act to Incorporate the Invincible Dragoons of the Second Division of Illinois Militia" In *Laws of Incorporation of the State of Illinois Passed by the Eleventh General Assembly.* Vandalia: Wm. Walters, 1839.

Carlin, Thomas [Governor]. "Know ye, That Joseph Holbrook having been duly elected to the office of Captain of the 2nd Comp. 2nd Batt. 1st Regiment 1st Cohort of the Nauvoo Legion of the Militia of the State of Illinois." Illinois State Archives, Springfield.

Commission Records of the Illinois State Militia: Ledger Book, 1835–1846. Illinois State Archives, Springfield.

Constitution of the United States. Retrieved February 11, 2009, from http://www.archives.gov/exhibits/charters/constitution.html.

Document Containing the Correspondence, Orders, etc. in Relation to the Disturbances with the Mormons; and the Evidence Given Before the Hon. Austin A. King, Judge of the Fifth Judicial District . . . in a Criminal Court of Inquiry, begun Nov. 12, 1838. Fayette, Mo.: Boon's Lick Democrat, 1841.

"Governor's Correspondence, 1837–1839." Illinois State Archives, Springfield.

"Governor's Correspondence, 1840–1849: Military Affairs." Illinois State Archives, Springfield.

"Governor's Correspondence: Military—Hancock County and Nauvoo Legion, 1840–1849." Illinois State Archives, Springfield.

"Governor's Military Correspondence to the Nauvoo Legion, 1840–1844." Illinois State Historical Society, Springfield.

Governors' Letter-Books, 1820–1848. Illinois State Archives, Springfield.

Illinois State Register. Illinois State Archives, Springfield, Illinois.

Illinois Statutes, March 4, 1837. Illinois State Archives, Springfield.

Journal of the House of Representatives of the Eighth General Assembly of the State of Illinois. Vandalia: Greiner and Sherman, 1833.

Journal of the House of Representatives of the Eleventh General Assembly, 1838. Vandalia: Wm. Walters, 1838.

Journal of the House of Representatives of the Ninth General Assembly of the State of Illinois, 1834–5. Vandalia: J. Y. Sawyer, 1835.

Journal of the House of Representatives of the Tenth General Assembly of the State of Illinois. Vandalia: William Walters, 1836.

Journal of the House of Representatives of the Twelfth General Assembly of the State of Illinois, 1840. Vandalia: William Walters, 1840.

The Journal of the Senate, 1839, January 6 and 9, 1839. Vandalia, Ill.: Greiner and Sherman, 1839.

Journal of the Senate of the Eleventh General Assembly of the State of Illinois, 1838–1839. Vandalia, Ill.: William Walters, 1838.

Journal of the Senate of the Fourteenth General Assembly of the State of Illinois, 1844. Springfield: Walters and Weber, 1844.

Journal of the Senate of the Twelfth General Assembly of the State of Illinois, 1840. Springfield: William Walters, 1840.

Journal of the Tenth Assembly of the State of Illinois, 1836. Illinois State Archives, Springfield.

Laws of the State of Illinois Passed by the Tenth General Assembly. Vandalia: William Walters, 1837.

Laws Passed by the First General Assembly of the State of Illinois at their Second Session. Kaskaskia: Blackwell and Berry, 1819.

Laws Passed by the Fourth General Assembly of the State of Illinois at their First Session, 1824–1825. Vandalia: Robert Blackwell and Co., 1825.

Laws Passed by the Second General Assembly of the State of Illinois at their First Session. Vandalia: Brown and Berry, 1821.

Laws Passed by the Third General Assembly of the State of Illinois. Vandalia: Blackwell and Berry, 1823.

Message of the Governor of the State of Illinois, in Relation to the Disturbances in Hancock County, December 23, 1844. Springfield, Ill.: Walters and Weber, 1844. Illinois State Archives, Springfield.

Militia Regiments Ledger. Illinois State Archives, Springfield.

Poinsett, J. R. "A System of Reorganization of the Militia of the United States," March 20, 1840. In Senate Documents, 26th Congress, 1st Session, 1839. #531, 7:29.

Report from the Secretary of War, Transmitting Aspects of the Returns of the Militia of the Militia Act of the State of Illinois.

The Revised Code of Laws, Illinois. Vandalia: Robert Blackwell, 1827.

Revised Statutes of the State of Illinois. Springfield, Ill.: Walters and Weber, 1845.

Senate Documents, 26th Congress, 1st Session, 1839. Submitted February 4, 1840.

Books

Anderson, Fred. *Crucible of War: The Seven Years War and the Fate of Empire in British North America, 1754–1766*. New York: Alfred Knopf, 2000.

Anderson, Mary Audentia, ed. *Joseph Smith III and the Restoration*. Independence, Mo.: Herald House, 1952.

Anderson, Richard Lloyd. *Joseph Smith's New England Heritage: Influences of Grandfathers Solomon Mack and Asael Smith.* Salt Lake City: Deseret Book, 2003.

Andreas, A. T. *History of Cook County, Illinois: From the Earliest Period to the Present Time.* Chicago: A. T. Andreas, 1884.

Andrus, Hyrum L., and Helen Mae Andrus, comp. *They Knew the Prophet.* Salt Lake City: Deseret Book, 1999.

Arrington, Leonard J. *Brigham Young: American Moses.* New York: Alfred A. Knopf, 1985.

———. *Charles C. Rich: Mormon General and Western Frontiersman.* Provo, Utah: Brigham Young University Press, 1974.

Averett, George Washington Gill. *Biographical Sketch of George Washington Gill Averett.* Provo, Utah: Brigham Young University, 1956.

Backman, Milton V., Jr. *The Heavens Resound: A History of the Latter-day Saints in Ohio, 1830–1838.* Salt Lake City: Deseret Book, 1983.

Basler, Roy P., ed. *The Collected Works of Abraham Lincoln.* New Brunswick, N.J.: Rutgers University Press, 1953.

Bateman, Newton, and Paul Selby, eds. *Historical Encyclopedia of Illinois.* Chicago: Munsell, 1900.

Bennett, John C. *A History of the Saints: An Exposé of Joe Smith and the Mormons.* Boston: LeLand and Whiting, 1842.

Bennett, Richard Edmond. *Mormons at the Missouri: Winter Quarters, 1846–52.* Norman: University of Oklahoma Press, 2004.

———. *We'll Find the Place: The Mormon Exodus, 1846–1848.* Salt Lake City: Deseret Book, 1997.

Benton, Thomas Hart. *Thirty Years' War; or, A History of the Working of the American Government for Thirty Years, from 1820 to 1850.* 2 vols. New York: Thomas Hart Benton, 1859.

Black, Susan Easton. *Membership of the Church of Jesus Christ of Latter-day Saints, 1830–1848.* 50 vols. Salt Lake City: Corporation of the President of The Church of Jesus Christ of Latter-day Saints, 1990.

Black, Susan Easton, and Richard E. Bennett, eds. *A City of Refuge: Quincy, Illinois.* Salt Lake City: Millennial Press, 2000.

Black, Susan Easton, and William G. Hartley, eds. *The Iowa Mormon Trail.* Orem, Utah: Helix, 1997.

Black, Susan Easton, and Andrew C. Skinner, eds. *Joseph: Exploring the Life and Ministry of the Prophet.* Salt Lake City: Deseret Book, 2005.

Book of Mormon. Translated by Joseph Smith, Jr. Palmyra, N.Y.: E. B. Grandin, 1830. Reprint, Salt Lake City: The Church of Jesus Christ of Latter-day Saints, 1981.

Borneman, Walter R. *1812: The War that Forged a Nation.* New York: HarperCollins, 2004.

Brodie, Fawn Mckay. *No Man Knows My History: The Life of Joseph Smith, the Mormon Prophet.* New York: Alfred A. Knopf, 1971.

Bruce, Dickson D., Jr. *Violence and Culture in the Antebellum South.* Austin: University of Texas Press, 1979.
Bushman, Richard. *Joseph Smith and the Beginnings of Mormonism.* Urbana: University of Illinois Press, 1984.
Bushman, Richard Lyman. *Joseph Smith: Rough Stone Rolling.* New York: Alfred A. Knopf, 2005.
Campbell, J. Duncan, and Edgar M. Howell. *American Military Insignia, 1800–1851.* Washington, D.C.: Smithsonian Institution, 1963.
Cannon, Donald Q., and Larry E. Dahl. *The Prophet Joseph Smith's King Follett Discourse.* Provo, Utah: Brigham Young University Religious Studies Center, 2001.
Cannon, George Q. *Life of Joseph Smith, the Prophet.* Salt Lake City: Deseret Book, 1986.
Cash, W. T. *The Mind of the South.* New York: Alfred A. Knopf, 1957.
Chadwick, Bruce. *The First American Army: The Untold Story of George Washington and the Men behind America's First Fight for Freedom.* Naperville, Ill.: Sourcebooks, 2005.
Clark, James R. *Messages of the First Presidency of the Church of Jesus Christ of Latter-day Saints, 1833–1964.* 6 vols. Salt Lake City: Bookcraft, 1965.
Clark, J. Reuben. *On the Way to Immortality and Eternal Life.* Salt Lake City: Deseret Book, 1953.
The Combined History of Edwards, Lawrence and Wabash Counties, Illinois. Philadelphia: J. L. McDonough, 1883.
Corrill, John. *A Brief History of the Church of Jesus Christ of Latter-day Saints.* Saint Louis: self-published, 1839.
Crackel, Theodore J. *Jefferson's Army: Political and Social Reform of the Military Establishment, 1801–1809.* New York: New York University Press, 1987.
Cross, Trueman. *Military Laws of the United States.* Washington, D.C.: Edward Dekrofft, 1825.
Cunliffe, Marcus. *Soldiers and Civilians: The Martial Spirit in America, 1775–1865.* Boston: Little, Brown and Company, 1968.
Current, Richard N., T. Harry Williams, and Frank Freidel. *American History: A Survey.* New York: Alfred A Knopf, 1963.
Davis, George T. M. *An Authentic Account of the Massacre of Joseph Smith the Mormon Prophet and Hyrum Smith, His Brother, Together with a Brief History of the Rise and Progress of Mormonism and All the Circumstances Which Led to Their Death.* Saint Louis: Chambers and Knapp, 1844.
Dickerson, Theodore Earl. *Conflicts between the Mormons and Non-Mormons, Nauvoo, Illinois, 1839–1846.* Urbana: University of Illinois Library, 1957.
The Doctrine and Covenants of the Church of Jesus Christ of Latter-day Saints. Salt Lake City: The Church of Jesus Christ of Latter-day Saints, 1981.
Duane, William. *A Military Dictionary or Explanation of the Several Systems of Discipline of Different Kinds of Troops, Infantry, Artillery, and Cavalry.* Philadelphia: n.p., 1810.

Eby, Cecil D. *"That Disgraceful Affair": The Black Hawk War.* New York: W. W. Norton, 1973.

Ehat, Andrew F., and Lyndon Cook. *The Words of Joseph Smith: The Contemporary Accounts of the Nauvoo Discourses of the Prophet Joseph Smith.* Provo, Utah: Religious Studies Center, Brigham Young University, 1980.

Feldberg, Michael. *The Turbulent Era: Riot and Disorder in Jacksonian America.* New York: Oxford University Press, 1980.

Flanders, Robert Bruce. *Nauvoo: Kingdom on the Mississippi.* Urbana: University of Illinois Press, 1965.

Ford, Thomas. *A History of Illinois: From its Commencement as a State in 1818 to 1847.* Chicago: S. C. Griffs, 1854. Reprint, Urbana and Chicago: University of Illinois Press, 1995.

Franklin, John Hope. *The Militant South, 1800–1861.* Cambridge, Mass.: Harvard University Press, 1956.

Ganoe, William Addleman. *The History of the United States Army.* Ashton, Md.: Eric Lundberg, 1964.

Garr, Arnold K., Donald Q. Cannon, and Richard O. Cowan, eds. *Encyclopedia of Latter-day Saint History.* Salt Lake City: Deseret Book, 2000.

Garr, Arnold K., and Clark V. Johnson, eds. *Regional Studies in Latter-day Saint Church History: Missouri.* Provo, Utah: Department of Church History and Doctrine, Brigham Young University, 1994.

Garrett, H. Dean, ed. *Regional Studies in Latter-day Saint Church History: Illinois.* Provo, Utah: Department of Church History and Doctrine, Brigham Young University, 1995.

Gilje, Paul A. *Rioting in America.* Bloomington: Indiana University Press, 1996.

Goodspeed, A., and Daniel D. Healy, eds. *History of Cook County, Illinois.* Chicago: Hammond, 1909.

Greene, Evarts Boutell, and Clarence Walworth Alvord, eds. *The Governors' Letter-Books, 1818–1834.* Collections of the Illinois State Historical Library, vol. 4. Springfield: Illinois State Historical Library, 1909.

Greene, Evarts Boutell, and Charles Manfred Thompson, eds. *Governors' Letter-Books, 1840–1853.* Collections of the Illinois State Historical Library, vol. 7. Springfield: Illinois State Historical Library, 1911.

Grimsted, David. *American Mobbing, 1828–1861: Toward Civil War.* New York: Oxford University Press, 1998.

Hafen, John. *Lieutenant-General Joseph Smith: First Commander of the Nauvoo Legion.* Salt Lake City: Contributor, 1888.

Hajicek, John J. *Newsclippings from Iowa and Illinois, 1841–1849.* Burlington, Wisc.: J. Hajicek, 1992.Hale, Heber O. *Bishop Jonathan H. Hale of Nauvoo: His Life and Ministry.* Salt Lake City: n.p., 1938.

Hale, Heber O. *Bishop Jonathon H. Hale of Nauvoo: His Life and Ministry.* Salt Lake City: n.p., 1938.

Hallwas, John E., and Roger D. Launius, eds. *Cultures in Conflict: A Doc-*

umentary History of the Mormon War in Illinois. Logan: Utah State University Press, 1995.

Hamersly, Thomas H. S. *Regular Army Register of the United States, 1779–1879.* Washington, D.C.: Thomas H. S. Hamersly, 1880.

Hampshire, Annette P. *Mormonism in Conflict: The Nauvoo Years.* New York: Edwin Mellen, 1985.

Hansen, Klaus J. *Mormonism and the American Experience.* Chicago: University of Chicago Press, 1981.

———. *Quest for Empire: the Political Kingdom of God and the Council of Fifty in Mormon History.* Lansing: Michigan State University Press, 1967.

Harris, William. *Mormonism Portrayed.* Warsaw, Ill.: Sharp and Gamble, 1841.

Heitman, Francis B. *Historical Register and Dictionary of the United States Army from its Organization, September 29, 1789 to March 2, 1903.* 2 vols. Washington, D.C.: Government Printing Office, 1903. Reprint, Urbana: University of Illinois Press, 1965.

Hill, Donna. *Joseph Smith, the First Mormon.* Salt Lake City: Signature Books, 1999.

Hill, Jim Dan. *The Minute Man in Peace and War: A History of the National Guard.* Harrisburg, Pa.: Stackpole, 1964.

Hill, Marvin S. *Quest for Refuge: The Mormon Flight from American Pluralism.* Salt Lake City: Signature Books, 1989.

History of the Church of Jesus Christ of Latter-day Saints. Ed. Joseph Smith, Jr. 7 vols. Salt Lake City: Deseret Book, 1980.

Hofstadter, Richard, and Michael Wallace, eds. *American Violence: A Documentary History.* New York: Alfred A. Knopf, 1970.

Howard, Simeon. "A Sermon Preached to the Ancient and Honorable Artillery Company in Boston." In *American Political Writing during the Founding Era, 1760–1805,* ed. Charles S. Hyneman and Donald S. Lutz. Indianapolis: Liberty Fund, 1983.

Huntington, Oliver Boardman. *Diary of Oliver Boardman Huntington.* Provo, Utah: Brigham Young University, 1942.

Hyneman, Charles, and Donald S. Lutz. *Illinois Volunteers in the Mormon War: The Disturbances in Hancock County, 1844–1846.* Taylorville, Ill.: Genie Logic Enterprises, 1997.

———. *American Political Writing During the Founding Era: 1760–1805.* Indianapolis: Liberty Fund, 1983.

Jacob, C. Edward, and Ruth S. Jacob, eds. *The Record of Norton Jacob.* Provo, Utah: Norton Jacob Family Association, 1953.

Jacobs, James Ripley. *The Beginning of the U.S. Army, 1783–1812.* Princeton, N.J.: Princeton University Press, 1947.

Johnson, Melvin C. *Polygamy on the Pedernales: Lyman Wight's Mormon Villages in Antebellum Texas, 1845–1851.* Logan: Utah State University Press, 2006.

Joseph: Exploring the Life and Ministry of the Prophet. Ed. Susan Easton Black and Andrew C. Skinner. Salt Lake City: Deseret Book, 2005.

Journal of Discourses. 26 vols. Salt Lake City: The Church of Jesus Christ of Latter-day Saints, 1967.

Jung, Patrick J. *The Black Hawk War of 1832.* Norman: University of Oklahoma Press, 2007.

Kingdom on the Mississippi Revisited: Nauvoo in Mormon History. Ed. Roger D. Launius and John E. Hallwas. Urbana: University of Illinois Press, 1996.

Knopf, Richard C., ed. *Anthony Wayne, a Name in Arms: Soldier, Diplomat, Defender of Expansion Westward of a Nation: The Wayne-Knox-Pickering-McHenry Correspondence.* Pittsburgh, Pa.: University of Pittsburgh Press, 1959.

Launius, Roger D. *Alexander William Doniphan: Portrait of a Missouri Moderate.* Columbia: University of Missouri Press, 1997.

———. *Zion's Camp: Expedition to Missouri, 1834.* Independence, Mo.: Herald House, 1984.

Launius, Roger D., and John E. Hallwas, eds. *Kingdom on the Mississippi Revisited: Nauvoo in Mormon History.* Urbana: University of Illinois Press, 1996.

Leonard, Glen M. *Nauvoo: A Place of Peace, a People of Promise.* Salt Lake City: Deseret Book, 2002.

LeSueur, Stephen C. *The 1838 Mormon War in Missouri.* Columbia: University of Missouri Press, 1987.

Linn, William Alexander. *The Story of the Mormons: From the Date of Their Origin to the Year 1901.* New York: Macmillan, 1923.

Ludlow, Daniel H., ed. *Encyclopedia of Mormonism.* 4 vols. New York: Macmillan, 1992.

Macomb, Alexander. *A Treatise on Martial Law and Courts-Martial, as Practiced in the United States of America.* Charleston, S.C.: J. Hoff, 1809.

A Manual for Courts-martial, Courts of Inquiry, and Retiring Boards, and of Other Procedure under Military Law. Washington, D.C.: Government Printing Office, 1910.

March, David D. *The History of Missouri.* New York: Lewis Historical Publishing Company, 1967.

Martin, James Kirby, and Mark Edward Lender. *A Respectable Army: The Military Origins of the Republic, 1763–1789.* Arlington Heights, Ill.: Harlan, Davidson, 1982.

McCandless, Perry. *A History of Missouri, 1820 to 1860.* 2 vols. Columbia: University of Missouri Press, 1971 and 2000.

McConkie, Joseph Fielding, and Craig J. Ostler. *Revelations of the Restoration: A Commentary on the Doctrine and Covenants and Other Modern Revelations.* Salt Lake City: Deseret Book, 2000.

McPherson, James M. *Battle Cry of Freedom: The Civil War Era.* New York: Oxford University Press, 1988.

Meinig, D.W. *The Shaping of America: A Geographical Perspective on 500 Years of History in Continental America, 1800–1867.* 2 vols. New Haven, Conn.: Yale University Press, 1993.

Meyer, Eduard. *Ursprung und Geschichte der Mormonen, mit Exkursen über die Anfänge des Islâms und des Christentums.* Halle, Germany: Max Niemeyer, 1912.

Miller, David E., and Della S. Miller. *Nauvoo: The City of Joseph.* Salt Lake City: Peregrine Smith, 1974.

Millett, Albert R., and Peter Maslowski. *For the Common Defense: A Military History of the United States of America.* New York: The Free Press, 1984.

Millis, Walter. *Arms and Men: A Study in American Military History.* New York: B. P. Putnam's Sons, 1956.

Millis, Walter, ed. *American Military Thought.* Indianapolis: Bobbs-Merrill, 1966.

Nauvoo [Ill.] Charters. *The City Charter: Laws, Ordinances and Acts of the City Council of the City of Nauvoo. And Also, the Ordinances of the Nauvoo Legion: From the Commencement of the City to This Date.* Nauvoo, Ill.: David C. Martin, 1970.

Nauvoo Legion. *Revised Laws of the Nauvoo Legion, from the Constitution of the United States. By Authority.* Nauvoo, Ill.: J. Taylor, 1844.

Newell, Linda King, and Valeen Tippetts Avery. *Mormon Enigma: Emma Hale Smith.* Urbana: University of Illinois Press, 1994.

O'Brien, John. *A Treatise on American Military Laws, and the Practice of Courts Martial; with Suggestions for Their Improvement.* Philadelphia: Lea and Blanchard, 1846.

Osgood, Herbert L. *The American Colonies in the Seventeenth Century.* 3 vols. New York: Macmillan, 1904. Reprint, New York: Columbia University Press, 1930.

Palmer, Dave Richard, and James W. Strykes. *Early American Wars and Military Institutions.* West Point: Department of History, United States Military Academy, 1973.

Parkman, Francis. *Montcalm and Wolfe: The French and Indian War.* First printing, 1884. Reprint, New York: Da Capo Press, 2001.

Prucha, Francis Paul. *The Sword of the Republic: The United States Army of the Frontier 1783–1846.* London: Collier-Macmillan, 1969.

Quincy, Josiah. *Figures of the Past.* Boston: Roberts Brothers, 1888.

Quinn, D. Michael. *The Mormon Hierarchy: Origins of Power.* Salt Lake City: Signature Books, in association with Smith Research Associates, 1994.

Rafferty, Milton D. *Historical Atlas of Missouri.* Norman: University of Oklahoma Press, 1982.

Regional Studies in Latter-day Saint Church History: Illinois. Ed. H. Dean Garrett. Provo, Utah: Department of Church History and Doctrine, Brigham Young University, 1995.

Regional Studies in Latter-day Saint Church History: Missouri. Ed. Arnold H. Garr. Provo, Utah: Department of Church History and Doctrine, Brigham Young University, 1994.

Remini, Robert Vincent. *Joseph Smith.* New York: Viking, 2002.

Revised Laws of the Nauvoo Legion. Nauvoo, Ill.: John Taylor, 1844.

Roberts, B. H. *The Rise and Fall of Nauvoo.* Salt Lake City: Bookcraft, 1965.

Roberts, B. H. *A Comprehensive History of the Church of Jesus Christ of Latter-day Saints.* 6 vols. Salt Lake City: Deseret New Press, 1930. Reprint, Provo, Utah: Brigham Young University Press, 1965.

Robinson, Stephen E. and H. Dean Garrett. *A Commentary on the Doctrine and Covenants* 3 vols. Salt Lake City: Deseret Book, 2004.

Ropp, Theodore. *War in the Modern World.* New York: Collier Books, 1962.

Schindler, Harold. *Orrin Porter Rockwell: Man of God, Son of Thunder.* Salt Lake City: University of Utah Press, 1983.

Sherman, Michael, Gene Sessions, and P. Jeffrey Potash. *Freedom and Unity: A History of Vermont.* Barre: Vermont Historical Society, 2004.

Shoemaker, Floyd C., et al. *Messages and Proclamations of the Governors of the State of Missouri.* 13 vols. Columbia: The State Historical Society of Missouri, 1922–1947.

Smith, Adam. *An Inquiry into the Nature and Causes of the Wealth of Nations.* London: W. Strahan and T. Cadell, 1776.

Smith, Andrew F. *The Saintly Scoundrel: The Life and Times of Dr. John Cook Bennett.* Urbana: University of Illinois Press, 1997.

Smith, Carlton B. *Military Affairs.* 30 vols. Carlisle, Pa.: U.S. Army Military History Institute, 1976.

Smith, Joseph. *The Papers of Joseph Smith: Autobiographical and Historical Writings.* Ed. Dean C. Jessee. 2 vols. Salt Lake City: Deseret Book Company, 1989.

———. *The Personal Writings of Joseph Smith.* Comp. and ed. Dean C. Jessee. Salt Lake City: Deseret Book Company, 1984.

———. *Last Public Address of the Prophet Joseph Smith, Delivered Before the Nauvoo Legion, June 18, 1844.* Salt Lake City: J. H. Parry and Company, 1880.

———. *The Voice of Truth, Containing the Public Writings, Portrait, and Last Sermon of President Joseph Smith.* Nauvoo, Ill.: John Taylor, 1845. Online Collections at Brigham Young University.

———. *General Joseph Smith's Appeal to the Green Mountain Boys, December 1843.* Nauvoo, Ill.: Taylor and Woodruff, 1843. Reprint, Nauvoo, Ill.: David C. Martin, 1974.

Smith, Joseph Fielding, comp. *Teachings of the Prophet Joseph Smith.* Salt Lake City: Deseret Book, 1976.

Smith, Lucy Mack. *Lucy's Book: A Critical Edition of Lucy Mack Smith's Family Memoir.* Ed. Lavina Fielding Anderson. Salt Lake City: Signature Books, 2001.

———. *The Revised and Enhanced History of Joseph Smith by His Mother.* Ed. Scot Facer Proctor and Maurine Jensen Proctor. Salt Lake City: Bookcraft, 1996.

Spicer, Edward H. *A Short History of the Indians of the United States.* New York: Van Norstrand Reinhold, 1969.

Stagg, J. C. A. *Mr. Madison's War: Politics, Diplomacy, and Warfare in the Early American Republic, 1783–1830.* Princeton, N.J.: Princeton University Press, 1983.

Stevens, Walter B. *Centennial History of Missouri (The Center State): One Hundred Years in the Union, 1820–1921* 2 vols. Saint Louis: S. J. Clarke, 1921.

Taylor, Samuel W. *Nightfall at Nauvoo.* New York: Avon Books, 1971.

Temple, Wayne C. *Lincoln's Arms, Dress and Military Duty during and after the Black Hawk War.* Springfield: State of Illinois Military and Naval Department, February 1981.

Urwin, Gregory J. W. *The United States Infantry: An Illustrated History 1775–1918.* New York: Sterling Press, 1991.

Van Wagoner, Richard S. *Sidney Rigdon: A Portrait of Religious Excess.* Salt Lake City: Signature Books, 1994.

Walworth, Ellen Hardin. *The Mormon Theocracy in Illinois, 1840–1845.* N.p., n.d.

Weigley, Russell F *History of the United States Army.* Bloomington: Indiana University Press, 1984.

———. *The American Way of War: A History of the United States Military Strategy and Policy.* New York: Macmillan, 1973.

Werner, John M. *Reaping the Bloody Harvest: Race Riots in the United States during the Age of Jackson, 1824–1849.* New York: Garland, 1986.

Whipple, George M. *History of the Salem Light Infantry from 1805 to 1890.* Salem, Mass.: Salem Press, 1890.

White, Leonard D. *The Jeffersonians: A Study in Administrative History, 1801–1829.* New York: Macmillan, 1959.

Whitman, Omer (Greg) W., and James L. Varner. *Neither Saint nor Scoundrel: Almon Whiting Babbitt, Territorial Secretary of Utah.* Baltimore: PublishAmerica, 2009.

Wicks, Robert Sigfrid. *Junius and Joseph: Presidential Politics and the Assassination of the First Mormon Prophet.* Logan: Utah State University Press, 2005.

Williams, Harry, ed. *Abraham Lincoln: Selected Speeches, Messages and Letters.* New York: Hold, Rinehart, and Winston, 1957.

Winders, Richard Bruce. *Mr. Polk's Army: The American Military Experience in the Mexican War.* College Station: Texas A&M University Press, 1997.

Window of Faith: Latter-day Saint Perspectives on World History. Ed. Roy Prete. Provo, Utah: Religious Studies Center, Brigham Young University, 2005.

Winn, Kenneth H. *Exiles in a Land of Liberty: Mormons in America, 1830–1846.* Chapel Hill: The University of North Carolina Press, 1989.

Winthrop, William. *Military Laws and Precedents.* Washington, D.C.: Government Printing Office, 1920.

Woodruff, Wilford. *Wilford Woodruff's Journal, 1833–1898 typescript.* 9 vols. Ed. Scott G. Kenney. Midvale, Utah: Signature Books, 1983–1984.

Woods, Fred E. *Gathering to Nauvoo.* American Fork, Utah: Covenant Communications, 2002.

Wright, Robert K., Jr. *The Continental Army.* Army Lineage Series. Washington, D.C.: Center of Military History, United States Army, 1983.

Articles

Allaman, John Lee. "Uniforms and Equipment of the Black Hawk War and the Mormon War." *Western Illinois Regional Studies* 13, no. 1 (Spring 1990): 5–18.

———. "Joseph Smith's Visits to Henderson County." *Western Illinois Regional Studies* 8, no. 1 (Spring 1985): 46–55.

Ansell, S. T. "Legal and Historical Aspects of the Militia." *Yale Law Journal* 26 (1917): 471–80.

Arrington, Leonard J. "Church Leaders in Liberty Jail." *BYU Studies* 13, no. 1 (Fall 1972): 20–26.

Barron, Charles M., Jr., and Detmar A. Finke. "United States Army Bandsmen 1832–37." *Military Collector and Historian* 23, no. 4 (Winter 1971): 124–26.

Beecher, Maureen Ursenbach. "'All Things Move in Order in the City': The Nauvoo Diary of Zina Diantha Huntington." *BYU Studies* 19, no. 3 (Spring 1979): 285–320.

Bennett, Richard E., and Rachel Cope. "'A City on a Hill': Chartering the City of Nauvoo." *The John Whitmer Historical Association: 2002 Nauvoo Conference Special Edition.* Ed. Joni Wilson. (Kansas City: John Whitmer Historical Association, 2002), 17–40.

Bergera, Gary James. "Joseph Smith and the Hazards of Charismatic Leadership." *The John Whitmer Historical Association Journal* 6 (1986): 33–42.

Blair, Alma. "The Haun's Mill Massacre." *BYU Studies* 13, no. 1 (Fall 1972): 62–67.

Burgess, Donald A. and Carroll H. Walker. "Norfolk Light Artillery Blues." *Military Collector and Historian* 14, no. 4 (Winter 1962): 128–29.

Bushman, Richard Lyman. "The Character of Joseph Smith." *BYU Studies* 42, no. 2 (2003): 23–34.

———. "Mormon Persecutions in Missouri, 1833." *BYU Studies* 3, no. 1 (1963): 11–20.

Cannon, Donald Q. "Reverend George Moore's Comments on Nauvoo, the Mormons, and Joseph Smith." *Western Illinois Regional Studies* 5, no. 1 (Spring 1982): 5–16.

Cannon, Donald Q., and Zachary L. Largey."The Martyrdom." In *Joseph: Exploring the Life and Ministry of the Prophets,* ed. Susan Easton Black and Andrew C. Skinner, 400–409. Salt Lake City. Deseret Book, 2005.

Carmack, John. "Missouri Era: Residue of Wisdom." In *Regional Studies in Latter-day Saint Church History: Missouri,* 1–12.

Chin, Brian, and J. Phillip Langellier. "General Stephen Watts Kearney and Officers of the 1st U.S. Dragoons, 1847." *Military Collector and Historian: Journal of the Company of Military Collectors and Historians* 31, no. 2 (Summer 1979): 82–83.

Cook, Lyndon W. "William Law, Nauvoo Dissenter." *BYU Studies* 22, no. 1 (Winter 1982): 47–72.

———. "'Brother Joseph is Truly a Wonderful Man, He Is All We Could Wish a Prophet to Be': Pre-1844 Letters of William Law." *BYU Studies* 20, no. 2 (Winter 1980): 207–18.

Craighead, Major Alexander McC. "Military Art in America, 1750–1914, Part II." *Military Collector and Historian: Journal of the Company of Military Collectors and Historians* 15, no. 2 (Summer 1963): 73–79.

Crawley, Peter. "Two Rare Missouri Documents." *BYU Studies* 14, no. 4 (Summer 1974): 520–27.

Curtis, John Obed. "Some Contemporary Views of the New England Militia." *Military Collector and Historian: Journal of the Company of Military Collectors and Historians* 30, no. 3 (Fall 1978): 101–108.

Dorsett, Lyle Wesley. "Slaveholding in Jackson County, Missouri." *Bulletin.* Missouri Historical Society 20 (October 1963): 25–37.

Draper, Maurice L. "Prophets Are Human Too." *The John Whitmer Historical Association Journal,* 11 (1991): 3–16.

Durham, Reed C., Jr. "The Election Day Battle at Gallatin." *BYU Studies* 13, no. 1 (Fall 1972): 36–61.

Ehrman, Keith A., and Dennis A. Henigan. "The Second Amendments in the Twentieth Century." *University of Dayton Law Review* 15 (February 1989): 1–51.

Esplin, Ronald K. "The Significance of Nauvoo for Latter-day Saints." *Kingdom on the Mississippi Revisited: Nauvoo in Mormon History,* ed. Roger D. Launius and John E. Hallwas, 19–38. Urbana: University of Illinois Press, 1996.

———. "Life in Nauvoo, June 1844: Vilate Kimball's Martyrdom." *BYU Studies* 19 no. 2 (Winter 1979): 231–240.

Faragher, John Mack, "From Ethnic Mixing to Ethnic Cleansing on the Frontier." In *Contact Points: American Frontiers from the Mohawk Valley to the Mississippi, 1750–1830*, ed. Andrew R. L. Clayton and Frederika J. Teutt, 304–26. Chapel Hill: University of North Carolina Press, 1998.

Fluhman, J. Spencer. "An 'American Mahomet': Joseph Smith, Muhammad, and the Problem of Prophets in Antebellum America." *Journal of Mormon History* 35, no. 3 (Summer 2008): 23–45.

Forde, Frank. "The 64th Regiment of New York." *The Irish Sword: The Journal of the Military History Society of Ireland* 17 (1989): 141–58.

Gardner, Hamilton. "The Nauvoo Legion, 1840–1845: A Unique Military Organization." *Journal of the Illinois State Historical Society* 54, no. 1 (Summer 1961): 181–97.

Garland, John F. "The Montgomery Guard of New York." *The Irish Sword: The Journal of the Military History Society of Ireland* 15 (Winter 1982): 132–35.

Garr, Arnold K. "Joseph Smith: Candidate for President of the United States." In *Regional Studies in Latter-day Saint Church History: Illinois*, ed. Dean H. Garrett, 151–168. Provo, Utah: Department of Church History and Doctrine, Brigham Young University, 1995.

Garrett, H. Dean. "Obtaining and Protecting the Plates." In *Joseph: Exploring the Life and Ministry of the Prophet*, eds. Susan Easton Black and Andrew C. Skinner, 67–75. Salt Lake City: Deseret Book, 2005.

———. "Seven Letters from Liberty." In *Regional Studies in Latter-day Saint Church History: Missouri*. Ed. Dean H. Garrett, 189–200. Provo, Utah: Department of Church History and Doctrine, Brigham Young University, 1994.

Gayler, George R. "Governor Ford and the Smiths." *Journal of the Illinois State Historical Society* 50, no. 4 (Winter 1957): 391–411.

Godfrey, Kenneth W. "Non-Mormon Views of the Martyrdom: A Look at Some Early Published Accounts." *The John Whitmer Association Journal* 7 (1987): 12–20.

Gregg, Thomas L. "Historical Sketches of the Mormon Era in Hancock County, Illinois." *Dollar Monthly and Old Settler's Memorial* 1 (1873): 75.

Hackney, Sheldon. "Southern Violence." *American Historical Review* 74 (1969): 906–25.

Hallwas, John E. "Mormon Nauvoo from a Non-Mormon Perspective." *Journal of Mormon History* 16 (1990): 53–70.

Hamilton, Marshall. "From Assassination to Expulsion: Two Years of Distrust, Hostility, and Violence." *BYU Studies* 32, 1–2 (1992): 229–48.

———. "Thomas Sharp's Turning Point: Birth of an Anti-Mormon." *Sunstone* 13 (October 1989): 16–22.

Harper, Steven C. "'Overwhelmingly Democratic': Cultural Identity in Jackson County, Missouri, 1827–1833." *Mormon Historical Studies* 9, no. 2 (Fall 2008): 1–18.

Hill, Marvin S. "Carthage Conspiracy Reconsidered: A Second Look at the Murder of Joseph and Hyrum Smith." *Journal of the Illinois State Historical Society* 97, no. 2 (Summer 2004): 107–134.

———. "Religion in Nauvoo: Some Reflections." In *Kingdom on the Mississippi Revisited,* ed. Roger D. Lanius and John E. Hallwas, 119–29. Urbana: University of Illinois Press, 1996.

———. "Counter-Revolution: The Mormon Reaction to the Coming of an American Democracy," *Sunstone* 13, no. 3 (June 1989): 24–33.

Huntress, Keith. "Governor Thomas Ford and the Murderers of Joseph Smith." *Dialogue: A Journal of Mormon Thought* 4, no. 2 (Summer 1969): 41–52.

Hurt, Douglas. "Planters and Slavery in Little Dixie," *Missouri Historical Review* 88 (July 1994): 397–415.

Jennings, Warren E. "Two Iowa Postmasters View Nauvoo: Anti-Mormon Letters to the Governor of Missouri." *BYU Studies* 11, no. 3 (Spring 1971): 275–92.

Jessee, Dean C. " 'Walls, Grates, and Screeking Iron Doors': The Prison Experience of Mormon Leaders in Missouri, 1838–1839." In *New Views of Mormon History,* ed. Davis Bitton and Maureen Ursenbach Beecher, 19–42. Salt Lake City: University of Utah Press, 1987.

Jessee, Dean C., ed. "The John Taylor Nauvoo Journal, January 1845–September 1845." *BYU Studies* 23, no. 3 (Summer 1983): 1–97.

Jessee, Dean C., and David J. Whittaker, eds. "The Last Months of Mormonism in Missouri: The Albert Perry Rockwood Journal." *BYU Studies* 28, no. 1 (Winter 1988): 5–41.

Jones, Dan. "The Martyrdom of Joseph Smith and His Brother Hyrum." *BYU Studies* 24, no. 1 (Winter 1984): 78–109.

Kimball, James L. "The Nauvoo Charter: A Reinterpretation." In Roger D. Launius and John E. Hallwas, eds., *Kingdom on the Mississippi Revisited: Nauvoo in Mormon History,* 39–47. Urbana: University of Illinois Press, 1996.

Kimball, James L., Jr. "A Wall to Defend Zion: The Nauvoo Charter." *BYU Studies* 15, no. 4 (Summer 1975): 491–97.

Launius, Roger D. "The Murders in Carthage: Non-Mormon Reports of the Assassination of the Smith Brothers." *The John Whitmer Association Journal,* 15 (1995): 17–34.

———. "Anti-Mormonism in Illinois: Thomas C. Sharp's Unfinished History of the Mormon War, 1845." *Journal of Mormon History* 15 (1989): 27–46.

———. "American Home Missionary Society Ministers and Mormon Nauvoo: Selected Letters." *Western Illinois Regional Studies* 8, no. 1 (Spring 1985): 16–45.

Lyon, Joseph, and David W. Lyon. "Physical Evidence at Carthage Jail and What It Reveals about the Assassination of Joseph and Hyrum Smith." *BYU Studies* 47, no. 4 (2008): 4–50.

Madsen, Gordon A. "Joseph Smith and the Missouri Court of Inquiry: Austin A. King's Quest for Hostages." *BYU Studies* 43, no. 4 (2004): 92–136.

McBarron, H. Charles, and Detmar H. Finke. "United States Army and Bandsmen, 1832–1937." *Military Collector and Historian: Journal of the Company of Military Collectors and Historians* 23, no. 4 (Winter 1971): 124–25.

McBarron, H. Charles, and Frederick P. Todd. "3rd Regiment, New York State Militia (Hussars) 1850–1860." *Military Collector and Historian: Journal of the Company of Military Collectors and Historians* 10, no. 4 (Winter 1958): 107–108.

McMaster, Fitzhugh. "Military Dress: The Uniform of the Militia of South Carolina, 1939–1849: Infantry." *Military Collector and Historian: Journal of the Company of Military Collectors and Historians* 30, no. 4 (Winter 1978): 173–76.

Moncure, Thomas M., Jr. "Who Is the Militia? The Virginia Ratification Convention and the Right to Bear Arms." *Lincoln Law Review* 19, no. 1 (1990): 1–25.

Moody, Thurmon Dean. "Nauvoo's Whistling and Whittling Brigade." *BYU Studies* 15, no. 4 (Summer 1975): 480–90.

"The Nauvoo Charter." *Journal of History* 7, no. 1 (January 1914): 439–52.

Nelson, Mark B., and Steven Harper. "The Imprisonment of Martin Harris in 1833," *BYU Studies* 45, no. 4 (2006): 113–19.

Nihart, Col. Brook. "A New York Regiment in California, 1846–1848." *Military Collector and Historian: Journal of the Company of Military Collectors and Historians* 21, no. 1 (Spring 1969): 4.

Oaks, Dallin H. "The Suppression of the *Nauvoo Expositor*." *Utah Law Review* 9, no. 4 (Winter 1965): 862–903.

Pratt, Fletcher. "Anthony Wayne, the Last of the Romans." In *Eleven Generals: Studies in American Command,* 37–58. New York: William Sloane, 1949.

Prince, Carl E. "The Great 'Riot Year': Jacksonian Democracy and Patterns of Violence in 1834." *Journal of the Early Republic* 5 (1985): 1–19.

Quinn, D. Michael. "The Council of Fifty and Its Members, 1844–1845." *BYU Studies* 20, no. 2 (Winter 1989): 163–98.

Reinders, Robert. "Militia and Public Order in Nineteenth-Century America." *Journal of American Studies* 11, no. 1 (1977): 81–101.

Riling, Joseph R. "The Wayne Artillery, 1842–1845." *Military Collector and Historian: Journal of the Company of Military Collectors and Historians* 19, no. 4 (Winter 1967): 118–24.

Riling, Ray. "Milwaukee Light Guards Music Cover, 1859." *Military Collector and Historian: Journal of the Company of Military Collectors and Historians* 12, no. 4 (Winter 1960): 117–18.

Robertson, R. J. "The Mormon Experience in Missouri, 1830–1839." *Missouri Historical Review* 68 (1974): 280–98, 393–415.

Saunders, Richard L. "Officers and Arms: The 1843 General Return of the Nauvoo Legion's Second Cohort." *BYU Studies* 35, no. 2 (1995): 138–51.

Skinner, Andrew C. "John C. Bennett: For Prophet or Profit?" In *Regional Studies in Latter-day Saint Church History: Illinois,* ed. Dean H. Garrett, 249–65. Provo, Utah: Department of Church History and Doctrine, Brigham Young University, 1995.

Smith, James E. "Frontier Nauvoo: Building a Picture from Statistics." *Ensign* 9 (September 1979): 17–19.

Smith, Paul Tincher. "Militia of the United States from 1846 to 1860." *Indiana Magazine of History* 15 (March 1919): 20–47.

Swartz, Willis G. "Mormonism in Illinois." *American Whig Review* (March 1852): 221–27.

Thurston, Morris A. "The Boggs Shooting and Attempted Extradition: Joseph Smith's Most Famous Case." *BYU Studies* 48, no. 1 (2009): 4–56.

Todd, Frederick P. "The State Forcibles of New York: A Study of Regimentation." *Military Collector and Historian* 23, no. 2 (Summer 1976): 65–72.

———. "Our National Guard: An Introduction to its History in Military Affairs." *Journal of the American Military Institute* 5 (1941): 73–86.

Van Wagoner, Richard, and Steven C. Walker. "The Joseph/Hyrum Smith Funeral Sermon." *BYU Studies* 23, no. 1 (Winter 1983): 3–18.

Wallace, Lee A., Jr., and Detmar A. Finke. "First Regimental Band and Drum Corps in V8 Military Forces, 1858–1860." *Military Collector and Historian* 10, no. 4 (Winter 1958): 61–70, 101.

Wells, Eugene T. "The Growth of Independence, Missouri, 1827–1850." *The Bulletin.* Missouri Historical Society. 16 (October 1959): 33–46.

Whisker, James B. "The Citizen Soldier under Federal and State Law." *West Virginia Law Review* 94 (1992): 947–88.

Whitman, Omer (Greg) W., and James L. Varner, "Sheriff Jacob B. Backenstos: Defender of the Saints." *Journal of Mormon History* 29, no. 2 (Spring 2003): 150–78.

Wiener, Frederick B. "The Militia Clause of the Constitution." *Harvard Law Review* 54, no. 2 (December 1940): 181–220.

Wirthlin, LeRoy S. "Joseph Smith's Boyhood Operation: An 1813 Surgical Success." *BYU Studies* 21, no. 2 (1981): 131–54.

Theses and Dissertations

Baugh, Alexander. "A Call to Arms: The 1838 Mormon Defense of Northern Missouri." Ph.D. Dissertation, Brigham Young University, 1996. Reprint, Provo, Utah: Joseph Fielding Smith Institute for Latter-day Saint History and BYU Studies, 2000.

Dickerson, Theodore Earl. "Conflicts between Mormons and Non-Mormons, Nauvoo, Illinois, 1839–1848." M.A. thesis, University of Illinois, 1956.

Godfrey, Kenneth W. "Causes of Mormon Non-Mormon Conflict in Hancock County, Illinois, 1839–1846." Ph.D. diss., Brigham Young University, 1967.

Guthrie, Gary Dean. "Joseph Smith as an Administrator." M.A. thesis, Brigham Young University, 1969.

Jennings, Warren A. "Zion Is Fled: The Expulsion of the Mormons from Jackson County, Missouri." Ph.D. diss., University of Florida, 1962.

Kimball, James. "A Study of the Nauvoo Charter." M.A. Thesis, University of Iowa, 1966.

Largey, Zachary. "The Rhetoric of Persecution: Mormon Crisis Rhetoric from 1838–1860." M.A. thesis, Brigham Young University, 2006.

Sweeney, John. "A History of the Nauvoo Legion in Illinois." M.A. thesis, Brigham Young University, 1974.

Westover, John Glendower. "The Evolution of the Missouri Militia, 1804–1919." Ph.D. diss., University of Missouri, 1948.

Index